CliffsTestPrep®

The NEW *SAT

includes the New *PSAT/NMSQT

3RD EDITION

by

Jerry Bobrow, Ph.D.

Contributing Authors/Consultants

Bernard V. Zandy, M.S.

William A. Covino, Ph.D.

Allan Casson, Ph.D.

Jean Eggenschwiler, M.A.

Don Gallaher, M.S.

WILEY

Wiley Publishing, Inc.

About the Author

Jerry Bobrow, Ph.D., is a national authority in the field of test preparation. As executive director of Bobrow Test Preparation Services, he has been administering the test preparation programs at more than 25 California institutions for the past 30 years. Dr. Bobrow has authored more than 40 national best-selling test preparation books, and his books and programs have assisted more than two million test-takers. Each year, Dr. Bobrow personally lectures to thousands of students on preparing for graduate, college, and teacher credentialing exams.

I would like to thank Michele Spence for her many hours of editing the original manuscript, and Christina Stambaugh, of Wiley, for her assistance and careful attention to the production process. I would also like to thank my office staff of Joy Mondragon, Cindy Hadash, and Deena Mondragon for their assistance. Finally, I would like to thank my wife, Susan; daughter, Jennifer; and sons, Adam and Jonathan, for their patience, moral support, and comic relief.

Publisher's Acknowledgments

Editorial

Project Editor: Christina Stambaugh

Acquisitions Editor: Greg Tubach

Copy Editor: Christina Stambaugh

Production

Proofreader: Debbye Butler

Wiley Publishing, Inc. Composition Services

CliffsTestPrep® The NEW *SAT, 3rd Edition

Published by:
Wiley Publishing, Inc.
111 River Street
Hoboken, NJ 07030-5774
www.wiley.com

Copyright © 2005 Jerry Bobrow, Ph.D.

Published by Wiley, Hoboken, NJ
Published simultaneously in Canada

Library of Congress Cataloging-in-Publication Data

Bobrow, Jerry.
   The NEW SAT / by Jerry Bobrow; contributing authors, Bernard V. Zandy ... [et al.].— 3rd ed.
      p. cm.— (CliffsTestPrep)
  Includes bibliographical references.
  ISBN 0-7645-5916-8 (pbk.)
1. Scholastic Assessment Test—Study guides. 2. Preliminary Scholastic Assessment Test—Study guides. 3. Universities and colleges—United States—Entrance Examinations—Study guides. I. Title. II. Series.
  LB2353.57.B635 2005
  378.1'662—dc22
                    2004023268

Printed in the United States of America

10 9 8 7 6 5 4 3 2 1

3B/RX/RS/QU/IN

For general information on our other products and services or to obtain technical support, please contact our Customer Care Department within the U.S. at 800-762-2974, outside the U.S. at 317-572-3993, or fax 317-572-4002.

Wiley also publishes its books in a variety of electronic formats. Some content that appears in print may not be available in electronic books. For more information about Wiley products, please visit our web site at www.wiley.com.

WILEY

Table of Contents

PART II: PRACTICE-REVIEW-ANALYZE-PRACTICE

PART III: ABOUT THE PSAT/NMSQT

Preface

The SAT and PSAT/NMSQT have changed, but good scores can still make the difference! And because of these facts, you can't afford to take a chance. Prepare with the best! Because better scores result from thorough preparation, your study time must be used most effectively. *CliffsTestPrep The NEW SAT,* 3rd Edition has been designed by leading experts in the field of test preparation to be the most comprehensive guide that you can realistically complete in a reasonable time. In keeping with the fine tradition of CliffsNotes, this guide is written for the student. It is direct, precise, compact, easy to use, and thorough. The testing strategies, techniques, and materials have been researched, tested, and evaluated and are presently used in SAT test preparation programs at many leading colleges and universities. This book emphasizes the Bobrow Test Preparation Services approach, developed during the past 30 years with thousands of students in preparation programs. The Bobrow approach focuses on the six major areas that should be considered when preparing for the new SAT:

1. Ability Tested
2. Basic Skills Necessary
3. Understanding Directions
4. Analysis of Directions
5. Suggested Approaches with Samples
6. Practice-Review-Analyze-Practice

This guide combines introductory analysis sections for each exam area with lots of practice—four full-length practice tests (three new SATs and one new PSAT/NMSQT). These practice tests have complete answers, in-depth explanations, analysis charts, and score range approximators to give you a thorough understanding of the *new* SAT and PSAT/NMSQT.

CliffsTestPrep The NEW SAT was written to give you the edge in doing your best by giving you maximum benefit in a reasonable amount of time and is meant to augment, not substitute for, formal or informal learning throughout junior high and high school.

Don't take a chance. Be prepared! Follow the Study Guide Checklist in this book and study regularly. You'll get the best test preparation possible.

SAT Study Guide Checklist

❏   1.   Read the new SAT information bulletin. Get information online at www.collegeboard.org.

❏   2.   Become familiar with the test format, page 1.

❏   3.   Familiarize yourself with the answers to Questions Commonly Asked about the new SAT, pages 4–6.

❏   4.   Learn the techniques of the Successful Overall Approaches, pages 6–8.

❏   5.   Carefully read Part I: Analysis of Exam Areas, beginning on page 9.

❏   6.   Strictly observing time allotments, take Practice Test 1, section by section (take Section 1 and then check your answers; take Section 2 and then check your answers, and so on), beginning on page 133.

❏   7.   Review the answers and explanations for each question on Practice Test 1, beginning on page 191.

❏   8.   Analyze your Practice Test 1 answers by filling out the analysis charts, pages 189–191. Have a teacher, tutor, or knowledgeable friend review your essay using the checklist included.

❏   9.   Review your math skills as necessary.

❏ 10.   Review or reread Part I: Analysis of Exam Areas, beginning on page 9, to see whether you applied some of the strategies.

❏ 11.   Strictly observing time allotments, take Practice Test 2, beginning on page 219. Take a very short break after each hour of testing.

❏ 12.   Check your answers and use the Score Range Approximator (pages 387–388) to get a very general score range.

❏ 13.   Analyze your Practice Test 2 answers by filling out the analysis charts on pages 273–275. Have a teacher, tutor, or knowledgeable friend review your essay using the checklist included.

❏ 14.   While referring to each item of Practice Test 2, study all of the answers and explanations that begin on page 276.

❏ 15.   Selectively review some basic skills as necessary.

❏ 16.   Strictly observing time allotments, take Practice Test 3, beginning on page 303. Take a very short break after each hour of testing.

❏ 17.   Check your answers and use the Score Range Approximator (pages 387–388) to get a very general score range.

❏ 18.   Analyze your Practice Test 3 answers by filling out the analysis charts on pages 363–365. Have a teacher, tutor, or knowledgeable friend review your essay using the checklist included.

❏ 19.   While referring to each item of Practice Test 3, study all of the answers and explanations that begin on page 365.

❏ 20.   Again, selectively review Part I: Analysis of Exam Areas, beginning on page 9, and any other basic skills or exam areas you feel are necessary.

❏ 21.   Carefully read "Final Preparation" on page 453.

PSAT/NMSQT Study Guide Checklist

❑ 1. Read the PSAT/NMSQT free Information Bulletin available from your high school counselor or the College Board.

❑ 2. Familiarize yourself with the new PSAT/NMSQT by reading the General Description on page 393.

❑ 3. Review the test format, page 393.

❑ 4. Learn the techniques of the Successful Overall Approaches, pages 6–8.

❑ 5. Carefully read Part I: Analysis of Exam Areas, beginning on page 9.

❑ 6. Review the SAT Critical Reading section, page 11.

❑ 7. Review the SAT Math section, page 39.

❑ 8. Review the Writing Skills Multiple Choice section, page 101.

❑ 9. Strictly observing time allotments, take the practice PSAT/NMSQT starting on page 397.

❑ 10. Review the answers and explanations for each question on page 435.

❑ 11. Analyze your practice test by filling out the analysis charts, pages 433–434.

❑ 12. Use the PSAT/NMSQT Score Range Approximator (pages 449–450) to get a very general score range.

❑ 13. Review your math skills as necessary.

❑ 14. Review the list of prefixes, suffixes, and roots starting on page 37.

❑ 15. If you have time for extra practice, work the problems on Practice Test 1 (page 133).

❑ 16. Review the answers and explanations for each question on page 191.

❑ 17. Analyze your Practice Test 1 answers by filling out the analysis charts, pages 189–191.

❑ 18. For additional practice, work as many of the additional practice tests as you want.

❑ 19. Be sure to review your answers and explanations for each test.

❑ 20. Carefully read "Final Preparation" on page 453.

Introduction

General Format of the New SAT		
Section 1	**Writing—Essay**	**1 Question**
25 Minutes	Writing—Essay	1 Essay Question
Section 2	**Critical Reading**	**24–28 Questions**
25 Minutes	Sentence Completions	8–10 Questions
	Short Reading Passages	4–6 Questions
	Long Reading Passages	12–14 Questions
Section 3	**Mathematics**	**20 Questions**
25 Minutes	Multiple Choice	20 Questions
Section 4	**Writing—Multiple Choice**	**33–37 Questions**
25 Minutes	Improving Sentences	7–13 Questions
	Identifying Sentence Errors	15–19 Questions
	Improving Paragraphs	6–10 Questions
Section 5	**Critical Reading**	**24–27 Questions**
25 Minutes	Sentence Completions	5–9 Questions
	Short Reading Passages	4–6 Questions
	Long Reading Passages	10–12 Questions
Section 6	**Mathematics**	**20 Questions**
25 Minutes	Multiple Choice	10 Questions
	Grid-ins	10 Questions
Section 7	**Critical Reading**	**15–20 Questions**
20 Minutes	Reading Passages (possible sentence completions)	13–15 Questions (4–6)
Section 8	**Mathematics**	**14–15 Questions**
20 Minutes	Multiple Choice	14–15 Questions
Section 9	**Critical Reading, Math, Writing**	**20–35 Questions**
25 Minutes		20–35 Questions
Section 10	**Writing—Multiple Choice**	**14–15 Questions**
10 Minutes	Improving Sentences	14–15 Questions
Total Testing Time: Approximately 225 Minutes = 3 Hours, 45 Minutes		**202–212 Questions**

Note: The **order** in which the sections appear, the **question types** within a section, and the **number of questions** may vary, and there may be many forms of the test. Only three of the critical reading sections (two 25-minute sections and one 20-minute section) and three of the math sections (two 25-minute sections and one 20-minute section) and the writing essay (25 minutes) and multiple-choice sections (one 25-minute section and one 10-minute section) actually count toward your new SAT score.

One 25-minute section is a *pretest,* or experimental, section that does not count toward your score. The pretest or experimental section can be a critical reading, math, or writing multiple-choice section and can appear anywhere on your exam. It does not have to be Section 9. You should work all of the sections as though they count toward your score.

General Description

The new SAT is used along with your high school record and other information to assess your competence for college work. The test lasts 3 hours and 45 minutes and consists of mostly multiple-choice type questions, with some grid-in questions, and an essay. The critical reading sections test your ability to read critically, to comprehend what you read, and to understand words in context. The math sections test your ability to solve problems using mathematical reasoning and your skills in arithmetic, algebra I and II, and geometry. The writing ability sections test your ability to write a clear, precise essay and to find grammar and usage errors, to correct sentence errors, and to improve paragraphs.

A Close Look at the New SAT	
Question Type	*Approximate Number of Questions*
Critical Reading	
Sentence Completions	19
Passage-Based Questions	48
Total Critical Reading Questions	67
Mathematics	
Multiple Choice	44
Grid-Ins	10
Total Mathematics Questions	54
Writing—Multiple Choice	
Improving Sentences	25
Identifying Sentence Errors	18
Improving Paragraphs	6
Total Writing Multiple Choice	49
Writing—Essay	One Question

The problems in the math sections (multiple-choice and grid-ins) and the sentence completions section of the new SAT are slightly graduated in difficulty. Many students make simple mistakes because they rush through the easy questions to get to the difficult ones. *Keep in mind that each question within a section is of equal value, so getting an easy question right is worth the same as getting a difficult question right.*

Comparing the "Older" SAT to the New SAT

	Older SAT	*New SAT*
	Verbal Reasoning	**Critical Reading**
Time:	75 minutes (two 30-minute sections and one 15-minute section)	70 minutes (two 25-minute sections and one 20-minute section)
Content:	Sentence completion	Sentence completion (Approx. 19 questions)
	Analogies	Short paragraph-length reading passages
	Long reading comprehension passages	Long reading passages (Approx. total passage-based reading, long and short, 48 questions)
Score:	200–800	200–800
	Mathematical Reasoning	**Mathematics**
Time:	75 minutes (two 30-minute sections and one 15-minute section)	70 minutes (two 25-minute sections and one 20-minute section)
Content:	Multiple-choice questions	Multiple-choice questions (Approx. 44 questions)
	Quantitative comparisons	Grid-in questions (Approx. 10 questions)
	Grid-in questions	(will include some algebra II content)
Score:	200–800	200–800
	Not on Test	*Writing*
Time:	N/A	25-minute essay
		35-minute multiple choice (a 25-minute section and a 10-minute section)
Content:	N/A	Essay: support a position, effectively communicate a viewpoint
		Multiple-Choice questions (Approx. 49) Improving sentences (Approx. 18 questions) Identifying sentence errors (Approx. 25 questions) Improving paragraphs (Approx. 6 questions)
Score:	N/A	200–800
Subscores:		Essay 2–12
		Multiple choice 20–80

Special Notes for the New SAT

- Verbal analogies are no longer on the exam.
- Quantitative comparison math questions are no longer on the exam.
- Critical reading sections now also include paragraph-length passages.
- Math sections have been enhanced, including some algebra II problems.
- The first part of the test will always be an essay.
- Writing multiple-choice sections have been added.

Questions Commonly Asked about the New SAT

Q: WHO ADMINISTERS THE NEW SAT?

A: The new SAT is part of the entire Admissions Testing Program (ATP), which is administered by the College Entrance Examination Board in conjunction with Educational Testing Service of Princeton, New Jersey.

Q: HOW IS THE NEW SAT DIFFERENT FROM THE "OLDER VERSION" SAT?

A: Starting in March 2005, the format and content areas of the SAT will be new. Basically, there will be three types of sections, Critical Reading, Mathematics, and Writing (multiple choice and essay). Verbal analogies and math quantitative comparisons will be eliminated. Some algebra II questions will be added to the math, while paragraph-length reading passages will be added to the Critical Reading. The new sections are the written essay and the multiple-choice writing skills. For a complete comparison of the tests see page 3, "Comparing the "Older" SAT to the New SAT."

Q: HOW IS THE NEW SAT SCORED?

A: The scoring will be as follows:

> Critical Reading: 200–800
>
> Mathematics: 200–800
>
> Writing: 200–800 (sub-scores essay 2–12, multiple choice 20–80)
>
> Total possible score: 600–2400

Q: WILL THE NEW SAT BE MORE DIFFICULT?

A: No. The new SAT has been designed so that a student who could score a 500 on the math section of the old SAT I could score a 500 on the math section of the new SAT. This is the same for the Critical Reading, formerly called Verbal Reasoning.

Q: IS THERE A DIFFERENCE BETWEEN THE NEW SAT AND THE SAT II?

A: Yes. The new SAT assesses general critical reading, mathematical reasoning, writing, and editing abilities that you have developed over your lifetime. The SAT II measures your proficiency in specific subject areas. The SAT II tests how well you have mastered a variety of high school subjects.

Q: CAN I TAKE THE NEW SAT MORE THAN ONCE?

A: Yes. On past score reports, scores up to five years old were also included on the report. It is not uncommon for students to take the test more than once.

Q: WHAT MATERIALS MAY I BRING TO THE NEW SAT?

A: Bring your registration form, positive identification, a watch, three or four sharpened no. 2 pencils, a good eraser, and an approved calculator. You may not bring scratch paper or books. You may do your figuring in the margins of the test booklet or in the space provided.

Q: **IF NECESSARY, MAY I CANCEL MY SCORE?**

A: Yes. You may cancel your score on the day of the test by telling the test center supervisor, or you may write, fax, or e-mail a cancellation to College Board ATP. See specific instructions for canceling your score in the *Student Bulletin*. Your score report will record your cancellation, along with any completed test scores.

Q: **SHOULD I GUESS ON THE NEW SAT?**

A: If you can eliminate one or more of the multiple-choice answers to a question, it is to your advantage to guess. Eliminating one or more answers increases your chance of choosing the right answer. To discourage wild guessing, a fraction of a point is subtracted for every wrong answer, but no points are subtracted if you leave the answer blank. On the grid-in questions, there is no penalty for filling in a wrong answer.

Q: **HOW SHOULD I PREPARE FOR THE NEW TEST?**

A: Understanding and practicing test-taking strategies helps a great deal, especially on the critical reading sections. Subject-matter review is particularly useful for the math section, and a review of basic grammar and usage will be helpful on the writing sections. Reviewing the writing process and practicing timed essay writing will also be helpful. The College Board offers additional practice online.

Q: **WHEN WILL THE FIRST NEW SAT BE ADMINISTERED AND HOW OFTEN ARE THE TESTS ADMINISTERED?**

A: The new SAT will be administered for the first time in March 2005. The test is usually scheduled to be administered nationwide seven times during the school year, in October, November, December, January, March, May, and June. Some special administrations are given in limited locations.

Q: **WHERE IS THE SAT ADMINISTERED?**

A: Your local college testing or placement office will have information about local administrations; ask for the *Student Bulletin*. The SAT is administered at hundreds of schools in and out of the United States.

Q: **HOW AND WHEN SHOULD I REGISTER?**

A: A registration packet, complete with return envelope, is attached to the ***Student Bulletin***. Mailing in these forms, plus the appropriate fees, completes the registration process. You can also register online at **www.collegeboard.org**. You should register about six weeks prior to the exam date.

Q: **IS WALK-IN REGISTRATION PROVIDED?**

A: Yes, on a limited basis. If you are unable to meet regular registration deadlines, you may attempt to register on the day of the test. (An additional fee is required.) You will be admitted only if space remains after preregistered students have been seated.

Q: **CAN I GET MORE INFORMATION?**

A: Yes. If you require information that is not available in this book, you can check online at **www.collegeboard.org**. You can also write or call one of these College Board regional offices.

Middle States: 3440 Market Street, Suite 410, Philadelphia, Pennsylvania 19104-3338. (215) 387-7600. Fax (215) 387-5805.
or
126 South Swan Street, Albany, New York 12210-1715. (518) 472-1515. Fax (518) 472-1544.

Midwest: 1560 Sherman Avenue, Suite 1001, Evanston, Illinois 60201-4805. (847) 866-1700. Fax (847) 866-9280.

New England: 470 Totten Pond Road, Waltham, Massachusetts 02451-1982. (781) 890-9150. Fax (781) 890-0693.

South: 100 Crescent Centre Parkway, Suite 340, Tucker, Georgia 30084-7039. (770) 908-9737. Fax (770) 934-4885.
or
HighPoint Center, Suite 900, 106 East College Avenue, Tallahassee, Florida 32301-7732. (850) 222-7999. Fax (850) 224-3077.

Southwest: 4330 South MoPac Expressway, Suite 200, Austin, Texas 78735. (512) 891-8400.
Fax (512) 891-8404.

West: 2099 Gateway Place, Suite 480, San Jose, California 95110-1017. (408) 452-1400.
Fax (408) 453-7396.
or
Capitol Place, 915 L Street, Suite 1200, Sacramento, California 95814. (916) 444-6262.
Fax (916) 444-2868.

Taking the New SAT: Successful Overall Approaches for Multiple-Choice Questions

I. The "Plus-Minus" System

Many who take the new SAT won't get their best possible score because they spend too much time on difficult questions, leaving insufficient time to answer the easy questions. Don't let this happen to you. Because every question within each section is worth the same amount, use the following system, marking on your answer sheet:

1. Answer easy questions immediately.
2. Place a "+" next to any problem that seems solvable but is too time-consuming.
3. Place a "–" next to any problem that seems impossible.

Act quickly; don't waste time deciding whether a problem is a "+" or a "–."

After working all the problems you can do immediately, go back and work your "+" problems. If you finish them, try your "–" problems (sometimes when you come back to a problem that seemed impossible, you suddenly realize how to solve it).

Your answer sheet should look something like this after you finish working your easy questions:

1. Ⓐ ● Ⓒ Ⓓ Ⓔ
+**2.** Ⓐ Ⓑ Ⓒ Ⓓ Ⓔ
3. Ⓐ Ⓑ ● Ⓓ Ⓔ
–**4.** Ⓐ Ⓑ Ⓒ Ⓓ Ⓔ
+**5.** Ⓐ Ⓑ Ⓒ Ⓓ Ⓔ

Make sure to erase your "+" and "–" marks before your time is up. The scoring machine may count extraneous marks as wrong answers.

II. The Elimination Strategy

Take advantage of being allowed to mark in your testing booklet. As you eliminate an answer choice from consideration, make sure to mark it out in your question booklet as follows:

(A̶)
? (B)
(C̶)
(D̶)
? (E)

Notice that some choices are marked with question marks, signifying that they may be possible answers. This technique helps you avoid reconsidering those choices you have already eliminated and helps you narrow down your possible answers. These marks in your testing booklet do not need to be erased.

III. The "Avoiding Misreads" Method

Sometimes a question may have different answers depending upon what is asked. For example,

If $6y + 3x = 14$, what is the value of y?

The question may instead have asked, "What is the value of x?"

Or   If $3x + x = 20$, what is the value of $x + 2$?

Notice that this question doesn't ask for the value of x, but rather the value of $x + 2$.

Or   All of the following statements are true EXCEPT . . .

Or   Which of the expressions used in the first paragraph does NOT help develop the main idea?

Notice that the words EXCEPT and NOT change these questions significantly.

To avoid "misreading" a question (and, therefore, answering it incorrectly), simply circle what you must answer in the question. For example, do you have to find x or $x + 2$? Are you looking for what is true or the exception to what is true? To help you avoid misreads, mark the questions in your test booklet in this way:

If $6y + 3x = 14$, what is the value of y?
If $3x + x = 20$, what is the value of $x + 2$?
All of the following statements are true EXCEPT . . .
Which of the expressions used in the first paragraph does NOT help develop the main idea?

And, once again, these circles in your question booklet do not have to be erased.

IV. The Multiple-Multiple-Choice Technique

Some math and verbal questions use a "multiple-multiple-choice" format. At first glance, these questions appear more confusing and more difficult than normal five-choice (A, B, C, D, E) multiple-choice problems. Actually, once you understand "multiple-multiple-choice" problem types and technique, they are often easier than a comparable standard multiple-choice question. For example,

If x is a positive integer, then which of the following must be true?

I. $x > 0$
II. $x = 0$
III. $x < 1$

A.   I only
B.   II only
C.   III only
D.   I and II only
E.   I and III only

Because x is a positive integer, it must be a counting number. Note that possible values of x could be 1, or 2, or 3, or 4, and so on. Therefore, statement I, $x > 0$, is always true. So next to I on your question booklet, place a T for *true*.

T   I. $x > 0$
     II. $x = 0$
     III. $x < 1$

Now realize that the correct final answer choice (A, B, C, D, or E) *must* contain *true statement I*. This eliminates B and C as possible correct answer choices, because they do not contain true statement I. You should cross out B and C on your question booklet.

Statement II is *incorrect*. If x is positive, x cannot equal zero. Thus, next to II, you should place an *F* for *false*.

T	I.	$x > 0$
F	II.	$x = 0$
	III.	$x < 1$

Knowing that II is false allows you to eliminate any answer choices that contain *false statement II*. Therefore, you should cross out D, because it contains false statement II. Only A and E are left as possible correct answers. Finally, you realize that statement III is also false, as x must be 1 or greater. So you place an *F* next to III, thus eliminating choice E and leaving A, I only. This technique often saves some precious time and allows you to take a better educated guess should you not be able to complete all parts (I, II, III) of a multiple-multiple-choice question.

A Summary of General Strategies

- *Set a goal.* Remember that an average score is about 50 percent right.
- *Know the directions.*
- Go into each section *looking for the questions you can do and should get right.*
- *Don't get stuck* on any one question.
- Be sure to *mark your answers in the right place.*
- Be careful. *Watch out for careless mistakes.*
- *Don't make simple mistakes by rushing through the easy questions in math* to get to the difficult ones.
- *Know when to skip a question.*
- *Guess only if you can eliminate* one or more answers.
- Don't be afraid to *fill in your answer or guess on grid-ins.*
- Practice using the *"Plus-Minus" System,* the *Elimination Strategy,* the *"Avoiding Misreads" Method,* and the *Multiple-Multiple-Choice Technique.*
- *Remember to erase* any extra marks on your answer sheet.

PART I

ANALYSIS OF EXAM AREAS

Introduction to the Critical Reading Section

The Critical Reading sections (formerly called "verbal reasoning" sections) of the new SAT consist of two basic types of questions: sentence completions and critical reading (short and long passages).

Two Critical Reading sections are 25 minutes in length and one is 20 minutes in length. Since one section of the test is experimental (although you won't know which one), you could have an additional Critical Reading section.

Although the order of the sections and the number of questions may change, at this time the three sections total about 65 to 70 questions that count toward your score. These three sections generate a scaled critical reading score that ranges from 200 to 800. About 50% right should generate an average score.

The sentence completion questions are generally arranged in a slight graduation of difficulty from easier to more difficult. Basically, the first few questions are the easiest; the middle few are of average difficulty; and the last few are difficult. There is no such pattern for the critical reading passages or questions.

Sentence Completion

You will have approximately 19 total sentence completions spread through the critical reading sections of the exam. In each section, the sentence completions will basically be arranged in order from easy to difficult.

Ability Tested

This question type tests your ability to complete sentences with a word or words that retain the meaning of the sentence and are structurally and stylistically correct.

Basic Skills Necessary

Good reading comprehension skills help in this section, as does a good twelfth-grade vocabulary. Some vocabulary building books can be helpful, although the best way to build a vocabulary is to read, read, read.

Directions

Each blank in the following sentences indicates that something has been omitted. Consider the lettered words beneath the sentence and choose the word or set of words that best fits the whole sentence.

Analysis of Directions

1. Note that you must choose the best word or words.
2. In cases where several choices might fit, select the one that fits the meaning of the sentence most precisely.
3. If the sentence contains two blanks, remember that both of the words corresponding to your choice must fit.

Suggested Approaches with Samples

Think of Words You Would Insert as the Answer

After reading the sentence and before looking at the answer choices, think of words you would insert and look for synonyms of them.

Samples

> **1.** Money _____ to a political campaign should be used for political purposes and nothing else.
>
> *How would you fill in the blank? Maybe with the word given or donated? Now look at the choices and find a synonym for given or donated.*
>
> **A.** attracted
> **B.** forwarded
> **C.** contributed
> **D.** ascribed
> **E.** channeled

Contributed is the nearest synonym of *given* or *donated* and makes good sense in the sentence. The best choice is C.

> **2.** Although it was not apparent at the time, in _____ we can see how Miles Davis's performances in the 1970s were _____ by what was happening then in popular music.
>
> **A.** retrospect . . . influenced
> **B.** effect . . . modified
> **C.** fact . . . unchanged
> **D.** foresight . . . endangered
> **E.** time . . . engendered

After reading the sentence, you may decide that the phrase *not apparent at the time* would suggest *looking back* for the first blank and that the second word needs to be *affected*. You could read the sentence "Although it was not apparent at the time, in *looking back* we can see how Miles Davis's performances in the 1970s were *affected* by what was happening then in popular music." Now, looking for synonyms for *looking back* and *affected* gives you choice A, *retrospect . . . influenced*. The best choice is A.

Look for Signal Words Connecting Contrasting Ideas

Some signal words, such as *however, although, on the other hand, but, instead, despite, regardless, rather than,* and *except,* connect contrasting ideas.

Samples

> **1.** Can public opinion be influenced so that it _____ rather than encourages the proliferation of the sale of firearms?
>
> **A.** redoubles
> **B.** advances
> **C.** inverts
> **D.** impedes
> **E.** amplifies

The clue here is *rather than encourages*. You need a verb whose object is *proliferation* and that means the opposite of *encourages*. The best choice is *impedes*, which means obstructs or retards. To *invert* is to turn upside down. The best choice is D.

2. Most candidates spend _____ they can raise on their campaigns, but others wind up on election day with a _____.

    A.   all . . . debt
    B.   whatever . . . liability
    C.   everything . . . surplus
    D.   every cent . . . deficit
    E.   nothing . . . war chest

But signals that the first half of the sentence *contrasts* with the second half. The fact that most candidates spend *everything* (and end up with nothing) contrasts with those who end up with a *surplus*. The best choice is C.

3. The critic praised the scenery of the film enthusiastically, but _____ her enthusiasm when she discussed its plot and characterizations.

    A.   expanded
    B.   established
    C.   augmented
    D.   declined
    E.   tempered

But signals that you need a verb denoting something different from the enthusiasm of the first part of the sentence. Choices A, B, and C contradict *but*. The verb *tempered* (moderated, reduced in intensity) is both more suitable in meaning and more idiomatic than D. The best choice is E.

Notice Signal Words Connecting Similar Ideas

Other signal words, such as *in other words, besides, and, in addition, also, therefore, furthermore,* and *as,* often connect similar ideas.

Samples

1. We need experiments to discover whether the systems that we have designed that work in theory also work in _____, in other words, in the real world.

    A.   hypotheses
    B.   fact
    C.   space
    D.   part
    E.   essence

The key words here are *in other word*s, which tell you that your choice must be similar to *the real world*. The terms *in fact* and *in the real world* both refer to similar ideas in this sentence. The best choice is B.

2. This treatise is concerned only with the process unique to the period in question; therefore, no attempt has been made to _____ phenomena _____ to that era.

- **A.** include . . . unrelated
- **B.** omit . . . irrelevant
- **C.** re-create . . . germane
- **D.** discuss . . . essential
- **E.** evaluate . . . pertinent

The words in the first half of the sentence that are especially related to those to be filled in in the second half are *is concerned only* and *unique to the period*. The verb in the first blank is parallel to *is concerned* and describes the contents. Choices A, *include*, D, *discuss*, and possibly E, *evaluate*, are possible. The second blank needs an adjective that will make the phrase *to that era* parallel to *unique to the period*. Choice B, *irrelevant*, would work, but only A has the correct first word. The best choice is A.

Focus on Signal Words that Help Define Other Words

Some words or phrases will actually give you a definition or point you to the definition of the word needed.

Samples

1. The tools found in the New Mexico excavation are _____, as a single implement might have several edges, each with a different use.

- **A.** ancient
- **B.** primitive
- **C.** ferrous
- **D.** versatile
- **E.** reliable

The tools the sentence describes have several edges and several uses, and the missing adjective should fit these conditions. *Versatile* means capable of many things. The best choice is D.

2. The unique world of the film is _____, both wholly recognizable and unfamiliar.

- **A.** contradictory
- **B.** realistic
- **C.** simplistic
- **D.** timeless
- **E.** unchanging

The second part of this sentence, *both wholly recognizable and unfamiliar*, is a perfect example of the word needed, *contradictory*. The words *recognizable* and *unfamiliar* contradict each other (are opposites). The best choice is A.

Watch for Contrasts between Positive and Negative

As you read the sentence, watch for contrasts between positive and negative words. Look for words like *not, never,* and *no.*

Samples

---

1. A virtuous person will not shout _____ in public; he or she will respect the _____ of other people.

The first blank is obviously a negative word, something that a good person would not shout; the second blank is a positive word, something that a good person would respect. Here are the choices:

   A. obscenities . . . feelings
   B. loudly . . . comfort
   C. anywhere . . . presence
   D. blessings . . . cynicism
   E. insults . . . threat

Choice B is neutral-positive; C is neutral-neutral; D is positive-negative; E is negative-negative. Only choice A offers a negative-positive pair of words. The best choice is A.

---

2. The chairperson was noted for not being obstinate; on the contrary, the members praised her _____.

   A. resistance
   B. experience
   C. coherence
   D. verbosity
   E. flexibility

The correct answer must describe a praiseworthy quality opposite to *obstinacy.* Although B and C are good qualities, only *flexibility,* E, means pliancy, the quality of being flexible. The best choice is E.

Be Aware of the Direction of the Sentence

Negative words can change the direction of the sentence, sometimes making the logic of the sentence more difficult to follow.

Samples

---

1. Tamino's choice of the quest to rescue Pamina is _____ not accidental, and he undertakes it with _____ and steadfastness.

   A. considered . . . trepidation
   B. circumstantial . . . valor
   C. intentional . . . reluctance
   D. deliberate . . . courage
   E. fortuitous . . . ardor

The adjective must be the opposite of *accidental*. The better choices are the synonyms of A, C, and D—*considered, intentional,* and *deliberate*. Choices B and E do not fit this context. The second blank requires a noun that is like *steadfastness* or describes a sterling quality. Choice A, *trepidation,* means fear or hesitancy, and choice C, *reluctance,* means unwillingness. Neither will do, but choice D, *courage,* is what is needed. The best choice is D.

---

2. The room was in an advanced state of disrepair; not only were the velvet draperies _____, but they were also mottled and _____.

    A. bright . . . torn
    B. old . . . clean
    C. faded . . . frayed
    D. new . . .mangled
    E. tattered . . . original

The logic of this sentence could be difficult to follow because of the negative wording. *State of disrepair* tips you off that both blanks must be filled with negative words. Choice C, *faded . . . frayed,* is the only negative pair. The words also fit the meaning of the sentence. The best choice is C.

Attempt Questions One Word at a Time

Questions with two words missing should be attempted one word at a time.

Samples

---

1. The _____ predictions of greatly decreased revenues next year have frightened lawmakers into _____ budget reductions.

    A. encouraging . . . sizeable
    B. convincing . . . minute
    C. alarming . . . negligible
    D. optimistic . . . huge
    E. dire . . . drastic

Notice that trying the first word will help you eliminate answer choices A, B, and D. If the predictions are of decreasing funds and frightening to lawmakers, the first adjective must be either *alarming,* C, or *dire,* E, (fearful, dreadful). Now try the second choice to get the correct answer. Since the lawmakers have been scared into action, you can infer that the reductions are *drastic,* E, rather than *negligible,* C. The best choice is E.

---

2. The government _____ that the new laws are necessary to prevent unscrupulous business owners from _____ off the profits while the workers are underpaid.

    A. implies . . .dilating
    B. anticipates . . . privatizing
    C. infers . . . acquiring
    D. requires . . . living
    E. contends . . . siphoning

The only first words that make sense in the sentence are choices A, *implies,* B, *anticipates,* and E, *contends*. But the second word in choice E, *siphoning,* is the only one that fits. "*Siphoning* off profits" is a common phrase and is something that unscrupulous business owners might try to do. The best choice is E.

Work from the Second Blank First

Sometimes it is more efficient to work from the second blank first.

Samples

---

1. Her parents were _____ when, despite losing the first three games, Sally _____ to win the set by a 6–3 score.

    A. surprised . . . failed
    B. relieved . . . came back
    C. puzzled . . . refused
    D. alarmed . . . attempted
    E. delighted . . . was unable

There are no clues here to tell you which of the first words describes the reaction of the parents. Any of the five might work. But if you deal with the second blank first, you can see that the word *despite* makes it clear that Sally must *win the set.* Choice B, *came back,* looks like the best choice, although D is possible. That B is better is confirmed by the first word, as *relieved* is better than *alarmed.* The best answer is B.

---

2. The merger will eliminate _____ and provide more _____ cross-training of staff.

    A. profit . . . and more
    B. paperwork . . . or less
    C. duplication . . . effective
    D. bosses . . . wasteful
    E. competitors . . . aggressive

The second blank is something that is provided. Chances are that the something provided is a positive word, and *effective* seems like a good choice. Reading choice C into the sentence, you will find that it makes good sense and is stylistically and structurally correct. The best choice is C.

Read in Each Choice

If you don't spot any signal words or you don't know the meaning of some of the choices (or if you're just stumped), quickly read each answer choice in and see which sounds best. Sometimes this last method will help you at least eliminate some of the choices so that you can take an educated guess.

Samples

---

1. The fertile and productive fields are located at the _____ of the Gila and the Arizona Rivers and are _____ by waters from both.

    A. junction . . . desiccated
    B. confluence . . . irrigated
    C. bank . . . drained
    D. source . . . submerged
    E. end . . . inundated

The first word probably refers to the place where the rivers are close, since the fields are watered by both. Except for C, any of the four nouns is possible. *Confluence* means a flowing together, the place where two waterways come together. The past participle must refer to the watering of these fertile lands. So *desiccated* (dried up) or *drained* can be eliminated. If the fields are productive, *irrigated* (supplied with water) makes better sense than *inundated* or *submerged*, which suggest destructive flooding. The best choice is B.

---

2. Many lawyers now believe that the _____ of the tobacco industry is so widely _____ by the public that juries will finally be willing to convict the corporations when the cases go to trial.

   A.   advertising . . . disseminated
   B.   propaganda . . . credited
   C.   repute . . . queried
   D.   mendacity . . . queried
   E.   guilt . . . acknowledged

If you quickly read each choice into the sentence, you'll notice that some of the choices just don't seem to make sense, sound right, or fit. Since the last part of the sentence says *willing to convict the corporations when the cases go to trial*, the idea that the guilt is *acknowledged* sounds good and fits perfectly. The best choice is E.

A special reminder: Always read your answer into the sentence to make sure that it makes sense. This will often help you avoid oversights or simple mistakes.

A Summary of Strategies for Sentence Completion Questions

■   After reading the sentence and before looking at the choices, think of words you would insert and look for synonyms of them.

■   Look for signal words like *however*, *although*, and *but* that connect contrasting ideas.

■   Look for signal words like *and*, *in other words*, and *therefore* that often connect similar ideas.

■   Focus on signal words or phrases that help define or lead to definitions of missing words.

■   Watch for contrasts between positive and negative words.

■   Negative words can change the direction of the sentence, sometimes making the logic of the sentence difficult to follow.

■   Questions with two words missing should be attempted one word at a time.

■   Sometimes it is more efficient to work from the second blank first.

■   If you're stumped, quickly read each answer choice into the sentence and see which sounds best.

■   Always read your answer into the sentence to make sure that it makes sense.

Critical Reading Passages (Short and Long)

Remember, there are three Critical Reading sections that count toward your score—two 25-minute sections and one 20-minute section. These sections will include short paragraph-length critical reading passages, longer reading comprehension passages, and/or paired passages or related passages. The short paragraph-length critical reading passages are new to the SAT. The reading passages and the questions following the reading passages are NOT in order of difficulty.

Ability Tested

This section tests your ability to understand, interpret, and analyze reading passages on a variety of topics. The passages on each exam will come from four content areas: humanities, social sciences, natural sciences, and narrative (fiction or nonfiction).

The common types of questions are those that ask you

- about the meaning of a word or phrase in the passage.
- about the main idea, main point, purpose, or even a possible title of the passage.
- about information that is directly stated in the passage.
- about information that is assumed, implied, suggested, or can be inferred.
- to recognize applications of the author's opinions or ideas.
- to evaluate how the author develops and presents the passage.
- to recognize the style or tone of the passage.

Basic Skills Necessary

Students who have read widely and know how to read and mark a passage actively and efficiently tend to do well on this section.

Directions

Questions follow each of the passages below. Using only the stated or implied information in each passage and in its introduction, if any, answer the questions.

Analysis of Directions

1. Answer all the questions for one passage before moving on to the next one. If you don't know the answer, take an educated guess or skip it.
2. If there is an introduction to the passage, read it carefully. It may be helpful in answering the questions.
3. Use only the information given or implied in a passage. Do not consider outside information, even if it seems more accurate than the given information.

Suggested Approaches with Sample Passages

General Strategies

- **Read Actively.** Read the passage actively, marking main points and other items you feel are important such as conclusions, names, definitions, places, and numbers. Make only a few such marks per paragraph. Remember, these marks are to help you understand the passage.

- **Preread a few questions.** You may want to skim a few questions first, marking words that give you a clue about what to look for when you read the passage. This method, called prereading questions, can be especially helpful on unfamiliar passages. Try it on a variety of passages to see how it works for you.

- **Pace yourself.** Don't get stuck on the passage or on any one question. If you have difficulty with one question, either take an educated guess by eliminating some choices or leave it blank and return to it briefly before you read the next passage (if there is more than one passage).

- **Answers are from information given or implied.** Base your answer on what you read in the passage, the introduction to the passage, or footnotes given following the passage. The passage must support your answer. All questions can and should be answered from information given or implied in the passage.

- **Be sure to answer the question.** Some good or true answers are not correct. Make sure that the answer you select is what the question is asking for according to the passage.

- **Read all choices.** Be sure to read all of the choices to make sure that you have the best of the ones given. Some other choices may be good, but you're looking for the best.

- **Avoid the attractive distractor.** Watch out for "attractive distractors," that is, answers that look good, but aren't the best answer. These attractive distractors are usually the most common wrong answers. They are answers that are carefully written to be close to the best answer. When you narrow your choice down to two answers, one is probably the attractive distractor. If you are down to two answers, reading the question again can help you find the best one.

- **Eliminate.** Use an elimination strategy. If you know an answer is incorrect, mark it out immediately in your question booklet.

- **You can skip passages.** When more than one reading passage is given, you may want to first read the passage that is of more interest or familiarity to you and answer those questions before reading the next passage. But be careful if you skip a passage to mark your answers in the proper place on your answer sheet.

Specific Strategies for Questions Based on Single Passages

- Read the passage looking for its main point and its structure.
- Make sure that your answer is supported by the passage.
- As you read, note the tone of the passage.
- Take advantage of the line numbers.
- Use the context to figure out the meaning of the words, even if you're unfamiliar with them.
- Read all the choices, since you're looking for the *best* answer given.

The Approaches

Read the passage actively, marking the main points and other items you feel are important.

Mark the Passage

You can mark a passage by underlining or circling important information. But be sure you don't overmark, or you'll defeat the purpose of the technique. The following passage shows one way a test taker might mark a passage to assist in understanding the information given and to quickly return to particular information in the passage when necessary. You may find that circling works better for you or using other marks that you personally find helpful.

Sample Long Reading Passage

Human beings have in recent years discovered that they may have succeeded in achieving a <u>momentous</u> but rather <u>unwanted accomplishment.</u> Because of our numbers and our technology, it now seems likely that we have begun <u>altering</u> the climate of our planet.

(5) Climatologists are confident that over the past century, the global <u>average</u> <u>temperature</u> has <u>increased</u> about half a degree Celsius. This warming is thought to be at least <u>partly</u> the <u>result</u> of <u>human activity</u>, such as the burning of fossil fuels in power plants and automobiles. Moreover, because populations, national economies, and the use of technology are all growing, the global average temperature is <u>expected to continue increasing</u>, by an additional 1.0 to 3.5 degrees C by the year 2100.

(10) Such warming is just one of the many consequences that climate change can have. Nevertheless, the ways that warming might affect the planet's environment—and, therefore, its life—are among the most <u>compelling issues</u> in earth science. Unfortunately, they are also among the most difficult to predict. The effects will be complex and vary considerably from place to place. <u>Of particular interest</u> are the changes in <u>regional climate</u> and local weather and especially <u>extreme events</u>—record temperatures, heat waves, very heavy rainfall, or drought, for example—which could very well have staggering effects on societies, agriculture, and ecosystems.

(15) Based on studies of how the earth's weather has changed over the past century as global temperatures edged up-ward as well as on sophisticated computer models of climate, it now seems probable that warming will accompany <u>changes</u> in <u>regional weather</u>. For example, longer and more intense heat waves—a likely consequence of an in-crease in either the mean temperature or in the variability of daily temperatures—would <u>result</u> in public <u>health threats</u> and even unprecedented levels of <u>mortality</u>, as well as in such costly <u>inconveniences</u> as road buckling and
(20) high cooling loads, the latter possibly leading to electrical brownouts or blackouts.

<u>Climate change</u> would also <u>affect</u> the <u>patterns</u> of <u>rainfall</u> and other precipitation, with some areas getting more and others less, changing global patterns and occurrences of droughts and floods. Similarly, increased variability and extremes in precipitation can <u>exacerbate existing problems</u> in water quality and sewage treatment and in erosion and urban storm-water routing, among others. Such possibilities underscore the <u>need to understand</u> the <u>consequences</u> of
(25) humankind's effect on global climate.

Researchers have <u>two main</u>—and complementary—<u>methods of investigating</u> these climate changes. Detailed <u>meteorological records</u> go back about a century, which coincides with the period during which the global average temperature increased by half a degree. By examining these measurements and records, climatologists are begin-ning to get a picture of how and where extremes of weather and climate have occurred.

(30) It is the <u>relation between these extremes</u> and the <u>overall</u> <u>temperature increase</u> that really interests scientists. This is where <u>another critical research tool</u>—global ocean-atmosphere <u>climate models</u>—comes in. These high-performance computer programs simulate the important processes of the atmosphere and oceans, giving researchers insights into the <u>links between human activities</u> and <u>major weather and climate events</u>.

The <u>combustion</u> of fossil fuels, for example, increases the concentration in the atmosphere of certain <u>green-</u>
(35) <u>house gases</u>, the fundamental agents of the global warming that may be attributable to humans. These gases, which include carbon dioxide, methane, ozone, halocarbons, and nitrous oxide, let in sunlight but tend to insulate the planet against the loss of heat, <u>not unlike the glass of a greenhouse</u>. Thus a <u>higher</u> <u>concentration</u> means a <u>warmer</u> <u>climate</u>.

Preread a Few Questions

Prereading can give you a clue about the passage and what to look for. Quickly reading a few of the questions before reading the passage may be very helpful, especially if the passage seems difficult or unfamiliar to you. *In prereading, read only the questions and NOT the answer choices* (which aren't included in the following examples). Notice that you should mark (underline or circle) what the question is asking. After you read the passage, you'll go on to read the ques-tions again and each of their answer choices. The following questions give examples of ways to mark as you preread.

1. Which of the following would be the <u>best title</u> for this passage?

Notice that *best title* is marked. This is a main-point question and tips you off that you should be sure to read for the main point in the passage.

2. Which of the following <u>inferences</u> is <u>NOT supported</u> by information in the passage?

Notice that *inferences. . . NOT supported* is marked. To answer this question, you'll need to draw information from the passage by "reading between the lines."

3. According to the passage, which of the following terms best <u>describes</u> the <u>effects</u> of <u>global warming</u>?

Notice that *best describes . . . effects of global warming* is marked. You now know that the passage involves the effects of global warming.

4. Which of the following best describes the <u>author's tone</u> in this passage?

The words *author's tone* are marked here. You now know to pay special attention to the tone of the passage.

After such prereading and marking of the questions, you should go back and read the passage actively. The passage is reprinted here without the marking. Try marking it yourself this time before you go on to the sample questions that follow.

Questions 1–8 are based on the following reading passage.

Human beings have in recent years discovered that they may have succeeded in achieving a momentous but rather unwanted accomplishment. Because of our numbers and our technology, it now seems likely that we have begun altering the climate of our planet.

Climatologists are confident that over the past century, the global average temperature has increased about half
(5)   a degree Celsius. This warming is thought to be at least partly the result of human activity, such as the burning of fossil fuels in power plants and automobiles. Moreover, because populations, national economies, and the use of technology are all growing, the global average temperature is expected to continue increasing, by an additional 1.0 to 3.5 degrees C by the year 2100.

Such warming is just one of the many consequences that climate change can have. Nevertheless, the ways that
(10) warming might affect the planet's environment—and, therefore, its life—are among the most compelling issues in earth science. Unfortunately, they are also among the most difficult to predict. The effects will be complex and vary considerably from place to place. Of particular interest are the changes in regional climate and local weather and especially extreme events—record temperatures, heat waves, very heavy rainfall, or drought, for example—which could very well have staggering effects on societies, agriculture, and ecosystems.

(15) Based on studies of how the earth's weather has changed over the past century as global temperatures edged upward as well as on sophisticated computer models of climate, it now seems probable that warming will accompany changes in regional weather. For example, longer and more intense heat waves—a likely consequence of an increase in either the mean temperature or in the variability of daily temperatures—would result in public health threats and even unprecedented levels of mortality, as well as in such costly inconveniences as road buckling and
(20) high cooling loads, the latter possibly leading to electrical brownouts or blackouts.

Climate change would also affect the patterns of rainfall and other precipitation, with some areas getting more and others less, changing global patterns and occurrences of droughts and floods. Similarly, increased variability and extremes in precipitation can exacerbate existing problems in water quality and sewage treatment and in erosion and urban storm-water routing, among others. Such possibilities underscore the need to understand the consequences of
(25) humankind's effect on global climate.

Researchers have two main—and complementary—methods of investigating these climate changes. Detailed meteorological records go back about a century, which coincides with the period during which the global average temperature increased by half a degree. By examining these measurements and records, climatologists are beginning to get a picture of how and where extremes of weather and climate have occurred.

(30) It is the relation between these extremes and the overall temperature increase that really interests scientists. This is where another critical research tool—global ocean-atmosphere climate models—comes in. These high-performance computer programs simulate the important processes of the atmosphere and oceans, giving researchers insights into the links between human activities and major weather and climate events.

The combustion of fossil fuels, for example, increases the concentration in the atmosphere of certain green-
(35) house gases, the fundamental agents of the global warming that may be attributable to humans. These gases, which include carbon dioxide, methane, ozone, halocarbons, and nitrous oxide, let in sunlight but tend to insulate the planet against the loss of heat, not unlike the glass of a greenhouse. Thus a higher concentration means a warmer climate.

Read the Passage Looking for Its Main Point and Structure

As you read the passage, try to focus on "what the author is really saying" or "what point the author is trying to make." There are many ways to ask about the main point of a passage.

> **1.** Which of the following would be the best title for this passage?
>
>   **A.** The History of Climate
>   **B.** Fossil Fuels and Greenhouse Gases
>   **C.** Extremes of Climate
>   **D.** Global Warming and the Changing Climate
>   **E.** Methods of Researching Global Climate

Asking for the *best title* is a main-point, or main-idea, type question. Now take a careful look at each answer choice. Choice A is too broad; also, the passage doesn't actually deal with the *history* of climate. Choices B, C, and E, on the other hand, are too narrow. While it's true that all of these topics are touched upon in the passage, a title should cover the passage as a whole. The best choice is D.

Make Sure that Your Answer Is Supported by the Passage

Every single correct answer is in the passage or can be directly inferred from the passage.

> **2.** Which of the following inferences is NOT supported by information in the passage?
>
>   **A.** Computer models of climate have proved superior to old meteorological records in helping climatologists pinpoint changes.
>   **B.** Changes in climate are affected by both natural and human activities.
>   **C.** Whatever the changes that occur in North America's climate over the next two hundred years, it is unlikely they will be accompanied by cooler average temperatures.
>   **D.** Dramatic changes in precipitation could have negative effects, producing both droughts and floods.
>   **E.** Increased industrialization in developing countries could lead to increases in the rate of global warming.

This is a tricky question, since it asks you which of the answer choices is NOT supported by the passage. The author mentions two ways of researching climate changes but describes them as *complementary*, not as superior or inferior. Therefore, choice A is not supported by the passage. You might be tempted by choice B, but notice that line 5 states that warming is thought to be at least *partly* the result of human activity, suggesting that natural forces are involved as well. Choice C is supported in lines 15–20, choice D in lines 21–22, and choice E in lines 6–8. The best choice is A.

Make Sure that the Answer You Select "Answers the Question"

Some good or true answers are not correct. Even though more than one choice may be true, you're looking for the best answer to the questions given.

3. According to the passage, which of the following terms best describes the effects of global warming?

    A. Complex
    B. Disastrous
    C. Predictable
    D. Inconvenient
    E. Inconsequential

Although it's true that some effects will cause inconvenience, making choice D a possible answer, the passage indicates that more far-reaching effects are probable as well. Another possible answer is choice B, but according to the passage, effects will vary from place to place; *disastrous* is too strong a word and not as accurate as choice A, *complex* (line 11). Choice C can be eliminated, since the passage states that the effects can't be predicted easily (lines 9–11). Choice E is also clearly incorrect; global warming will have significant effects (lines 13–14). The best choice is A.

As You Read, Note the Tone of the Passage

The words that the author uses to describe events, people, or places will help give you an understanding of what and how the author wants you to feel or think. Pay careful attention to the types of words—are they emotional, calm, positive, negative, subjective, or objective?

4. Which of the following best describes the author's tone in this passage?

    A. Alarmist
    B. Irate
    C. Concerned
    D. Accusatory
    E. Indifferent

Although the author does mention some possible *staggering* effects, the tone is calm and concerned, not emotional as in choice A. Nor is the tone *irate*, choice B, or *accusatory*, choice D; the author presents facts about fossil fuels' role in global warming but doesn't place blame. Choice E is also incorrect; see, for example, lines 34–38, which clearly indicate the author is not indifferent to the issue of humans' effect on global climate. The best choice is C.

Take Advantage of the Line Numbers

All passages have the lines numbered, which, in questions that mention specific line numbers, gives you the advantage of being able to quickly spot where the information is located. After you spot the location, be sure to read the line(s) before and after the lines mentioned. This nearby text can be very helpful in putting the information in the proper context and answering the question.

5. The name "greenhouse gases," first mentioned in lines 34–35, is appropriate because these gases

    A. are hot.
    B. are produced in controlled circumstances.
    C. filter the sun's harmful rays.
    D. are highly concentrated.
    E. prevent heat loss.

Although *greenhouse gases* are first mentioned in lines 34–35, the answer to the question is actually found in lines 36–38. You can eliminate choice B, even though it is true that a greenhouse is a controlled climate. Also, nothing in the passage suggests that these gases are hot, choice A, or that they filter out harmful rays, choice C. Although it is true that the gases can be highly concentrated, choice D, high concentration has nothing to do with the term *greenhouse.* The best choice is E.

Use the Context to Figure Out the Meaning of Words, Even if You're Unfamiliar with Them

Some of the questions deal with "vocabulary in context," that is, with understanding the meaning of a word as it is used in the passage. Even if you don't know the meaning of the word, the passage will give you good clues. You can also read the sentence from the passage, leaving the word space blank, and plug in each choice to see which answer choice makes sense in the sentence.

---

6. The best definition of "exacerbate" in line 23 is

    A. worsen.

    B. change.

    C. cause.

    D. complicate.

    E. affect.

As it is used in this sentence, *exacerbate* means to aggravate or irritate (make worse). The passage describes the problems as already existing; therefore, choice C could not be correct. From context, it is also clear that choices B, D, and E are too mild; none of them includes the concept of an existing problem (such as water quality) becoming *worse* because of variable and extreme precipitation. In this case, a common meaning is the correct answer, but remember that the common meaning of the word is not always the meaning used in the passage. The best choice is A.

Read All the Choices, Since You're Looking for the Best Answer Given

Best is a relative term; that is, determining what is best may mean choosing from degrees of good, better, or best. Although you may have more than one good choice, you're looking for the best of those given. Remember, the answer doesn't have to be perfect, just the best of those presented to you. So don't get stuck on one choice before you read the rest.

---

7. According to the passage, scientists are most interested in the link between global warming and extreme changes in regional climate because

    A. such a link has never been made and cannot be easily explained.

    B. establishing the link will prove their current theories about the causes of global warming.

    C. it could help explain the effects of natural forces, such as gravitational pull, on climate.

    D. finding it will solve the problem of global warming.

    E. it could help pinpoint which human activities are involved in climate extremes.

It is possible that choices A and B are peripheral reasons for their interest, but not their main reason and, therefore, not the *best* answer. Choice C is not the best answer because scientists are more interested in the effects of human activities than those of natural forces on global warming. Even though it is a step toward a solution, understanding the link wouldn't in itself *solve* the problem of global warming, thus eliminating choice D. Notice that some of the choices here are possible, but choice E is the *best* because it is clearly supported in lines 31–33. The correct answer is E.

Use an Elimination Strategy

Often you can arrive at the right answer by eliminating other answers. Watch for key words in the answer choices to help you find the main point given in each choice. Notice that some incorrect choices are too general, too specific, irrelevant, or off topic or that they contradict information given in the passage.

8. If true, which of the following would call into question current theories of global warming?

   A. A dramatic increase in world precipitation
   B. A dramatic decrease in world precipitation
   C. An increase in the rate of global warming following the elimination of the use of fossil fuels
   D. Below-normal temperature recordings in Canada for two years
   E. The discovery that average global temperatures were lower 500 years ago than they are today

Since experts believe that the use of fossil fuels is partly responsible, one would expect the elimination of that use to lead to a *decrease*, not an increase, in the rate of global warming. Both increases and decreases in precipitation are expected, and, therefore, choices A and B are incorrect and can be eliminated. Two years of decreased temperatures in a particular area wouldn't disprove global warming; its effects vary considerably from place to place, according to the passage; thus, choice D can be eliminated. Finally, you can eliminate choice E, since it would support the theory, not call it into question. The best choice is C.

Another Sample Reading Passage

Questions 1–5 are based on the following passage.

Woodrow Wilson is usually ranked among the country's great presidents in spite of his failures to win Senate approval of the League of Nations. Wilson had yearned for a political career all his life; he won his first office in 1910 when he was elected governor of New Jersey. Two years later he was elected president in one of the most rapid political rises in our history. For a while Wilson had practiced law but found it both boring and unprofitable;
(5)   then he became a political scientist of great renown and finally president of Princeton University. He did an outstanding job at Princeton but lost out in a battle with Dean Andrew West for control of the graduate school. When he was asked by the Democratic boss of New Jersey, Jim Smith, to run for governor, Wilson readily accepted because his position at Princeton was becoming untenable.

Until 1910 Wilson seemed to be a conservative Democrat in the Grover Cleveland tradition. He had denounced
(10) Bryan in 1896 and had voted for the National Democratic candidate who supported gold. In fact, when the Democratic machine first pushed Wilson's nomination in 1912, the young New Jersey progressives wanted no part of him. Wilson later assured them that he would champion the progressive cause, and so they decided to work for his election. It is easy to accuse Wilson of political expediency, but it is entirely possible that by 1912 he had changed his views as had countless other Americans. While governor of New Jersey, he carried out his election pledges by
(15) enacting an impressive list of reforms.

Wilson secured the Democratic nomination on the forty-sixth ballot after a fierce battle with Champ Clark of Missouri and Oscar W. Underwood of Alabama. Clark actually had a majority of votes but was unable to attract the necessary two-thirds. In the campaign, Wilson emerged as the middle-of-the-road candidate—between the conservative William H. Taft and the more radical Theodore Roosevelt. Wilson called his program the New Freedom, which
(20) he said was the restoration of free competition as it had existed before the growth of the trusts. In contrast, Theodore Roosevelt was advocating a New Nationalism, which seemed to call for massive federal intervention in the economic life of the nation. Wilson felt that the trusts should be destroyed, but he made a distinction between a trust and a legitimately successful big business. Theodore Roosevelt, on the other hand, accepted the trusts as inevitable but said that the government should regulate them by establishing a new regulatory agency. The former
(25) president also felt that a distinction should be made between the "good" trusts and the "bad" trusts.

Always look for the main point of the passage.

> **1.** The author's main purpose in writing this passage is to
>
>   **A.** argue that Wilson is one of the great U.S. presidents.
>   **B.** survey the differences between Wilson, Taft, and Roosevelt.
>   **C.** explain Wilson's concept of the New Freedom.
>   **D.** discuss some major events of Wilson's career.
>   **E.** suggest reasons that Wilson's presidency may have started World War I.

Remember that there are many ways to ask about the main point of a passage. What is the main idea? What is the best title? What is the author's purpose? Choices A and E are irrelevant to the information in the passage, and choices B and C mention secondary purposes rather than the primary one. The best choice is D.

Be aware of information not directly stated in the passage.

> **2.** The author implies which of the following about the New Jersey progressives?
>
>   **A.** They did not support Wilson after he was governor.
>   **B.** They were not conservative Democrats.
>   **C.** They were more interested in political expediency.
>   **D.** Along with Wilson, they were supporters of Bryan in 1896.
>   **E.** They particularly admired Wilson's experience as president of Princeton University.

Read between the lines. Implied information can be valuable in understanding the passage and in answering some questions. In the second paragraph, Wilson's decision to champion the progressive cause after 1912 is contrasted with his earlier career, when he seemed to be a conservative Democrat. Thus, it may be concluded that the progressives, whom Wilson finally joined, were not conservative Democrats, as was Wilson earlier in his career. Choices A and D contradict information in the paragraph, while choices C and E are not suggested by any information given in the passage. The best choice is B.

Watch for important conclusions or information that supports a conclusion.

> **3.** The passage supports which of the following conclusions about the progress of Wilson's political career?
>
>   **A.** Few politicians have progressed so rapidly toward the attainment of higher office.
>   **B.** Failures late in his career caused him to be regarded as a president who regressed instead of progressed.
>   **C.** Wilson encountered little opposition once he determined to seek the presidency.
>   **D.** The League of Nations marked the end of Wilson's reputation as a strong leader.
>   **E.** Wilson's political progress was aided by Champ Clark and Oscar Underwood.

This choice is explicitly supported by the third sentence in the first paragraph in which you are told that Wilson was *elected president in one of the most rapid political rises in our history.* The best choice is A.

Understand the meaning and possible reason for using certain words or phrases.

> **4.** At the end of the first paragraph in the phrase *his position at Princeton was becoming untenable* (line 8), the meaning of *untenable* is which of the following?
>
> **A.** Unlikely to last for ten years
> **B.** Filled with considerably less tension
> **C.** Difficult to maintain or continue
> **D.** Filled with achievements that would appeal to voters
> **E.** Something he did not have a tenacious desire to continue

Be alert to the positive and negative connotations of words and phrases in each passage, as well as in the questions themselves. In the case of *untenable*, the prefix *un-* suggests that the word has a negative connotation. The context in which the word occurs does as well. Wilson *left* his position at Princeton; therefore, you may conclude that the position was somehow unappealing or something else was more appealing. Only two of the answer choices, C and E, provide a negative definition. Although choice E may attract your attention because *tenacious* looks similar to *tenable*, the correct choice is C, which, in this case, is the conventional definition of *untenable*. The best choice is C.

Eliminate those choices that are not supported by the passage.

> **5.** According to the passage, which of the following was probably true about the presidential campaign of 1912?
>
> **A.** Woodrow Wilson won the election by an overwhelming majority.
> **B.** The inexperience of Theodore Roosevelt accounted for his radical position.
> **C.** Wilson was unable to attract two-thirds of the votes but won anyway.
> **D.** There were three nominated candidates for the presidency.
> **E.** Wilson's New Freedom did not represent Democratic interests.

Your answer choice must be supported by information either stated or implied in the passage. Choices A, B, and C contain information that is not addressed in the passage and can be eliminated as irrelevant. Choice E contradicts the fact that Wilson was a Democratic candidate. The discussion of Taft and Roosevelt as the candidates who finally ran against Wilson for the presidency supports choice D, which is the correct answer. The best choice is D.

Short Paragraph-Length Reading Passages

The new SAT now includes paragraph-length critical reading passages. These short passages, about 100 words in length, are usually followed by two questions. All of the strategies for the longer reading comprehension passages also apply here. As you attempt to answer the questions to the first passage, apply the strategies:

- Read the passage looking for its main point and its structure.
- Make sure that your answer is supported by the passage.
- As you read, note the tone of the passage.
- Take advantage of the line numbers.
- Use the context to figure out the meaning of the words, even if you're unfamiliar with them.
- Read all the choices, since you're looking for the *best* answer given.

Samples

Questions 1–2 are based on the following passage.

Potatoes changed history, or rather, the lack of potatoes changed history. The Great Famine in Ireland (1846–1849) was partly the result of a potato fungus that destroyed the major food source of the Irish and was particularly devastating to the poor. Food relief from the British was inadequate and came too late. Some estimates place the number of deaths at 750,000, with an equal number of the Irish poor emigrating to Britain, Canada,
(5) Australia, and the United States. British economic policy—including the policy of laissez faire, which argued against state intervention—was partly responsible for the disaster. Among the other culprits were the nature of Irish land-holdings, destructive farming methods, and a lack of agricultural diversity.

---

1. The first sentence of the paragraph can best be described as intended to

   A. create interest.
   B. mislead the reader.
   C. provide facts.
   D. promote a myth.
   E. provide a humorous perspective.

Note that this question is asking for the intent of the first sentence. You should have underlined the key words. *What is the first sentence trying to do?* Instead of beginning immediately with facts as in choice C, the author chooses to create interest by making a surprising statement ("Potatoes changed history. . . ."). The intent is not to mislead as in choice B or to "promote" a myth as in choice D. The most likely wrong answer is E, but nothing in this paragraph is seen from a "humorous perspective" as in choice E. The best choice is A.

---

2. From the passage, one can infer that during the famine, aid from the British came too late because of

   A. animosity between the English and the Irish.
   B. poor methods of food distribution.
   C. inadequate communication about the extent of the disaster.
   D. the British policy of laissez faire.
   E. the lack of agricultural diversity.

First, you should have underlined the words "infer" and "aid came too late because." Remember, inference questions are asking you to *read between the lines*. Focusing on lines 5–6 will give you the answer. The British government didn't intervene in the famine earlier because British economic policy was "hands off," that is, the less intervention by government, the better—the British policy of laissez faire, choice D. It is possible that A, B, and C are accurate, but none of these is covered in the passage. E doesn't make sense as an answer here. The best choice is D.

Did you read the passage actively, marking major points? Did you preread the two questions? Did you mark the key words in the questions?

Let's try one more short reading passage.

Questions 3–4 are based on the following passage.

Chipmunks recently challenged the scientific dogma that small mammals were forced south during the Ice Age 18,000 years ago. DNA samples from more than 200 chipmunks in Illinois and Wisconsin were used to construct a family tree showing that chipmunks migrated further south only after glaciers receded. Scientists determined the chipmunks' migration routes by analyzing mutations in their genes. The longer a group of animals remains in one (5) place, the more mutations they accumulate, increasing their genetic diversity. Animals leaving the refuge for a new area take only a few of the changes, and, therefore, the new group has less variety in its genes. The chipmunk populations found in the south had fewer mutations than those in northern Illinois and Wisconsin.

---

3. In the passage, the best definition of "dogma" (line 1) is

   A. truth.
   B. accepted opinion.
   C. faith.
   D. strict rules.
   E. myth.

What does the word "dogma" mean in the passage? From the context of the first sentence, you should understand that "dogma" refers to something held as an established or accepted opinion (choice B). The paragraph's content contradicts choice A. Since "dogma" is often used in a religious context, choice C might be tempting, but there is no connection between the definition of "dogma" and faith. Choice D doesn't make sense, and choice E is simply incorrect. The best choice is B.

---

4. According to the passage, less genetic diversity in a chipmunk population supports which of the following statements?

   A. Some chipmunk populations migrated south more recently than previously believed.
   B. Chipmunks are the most resilient of the small mammal groups.
   C. Northern and southern chipmunks are in fact two different species.
   D. Frigid temperatures change the genetic structure of mammals.
   E. DNA samples are an unreliable technique in establishing a sequence of events.

This question asks you to find *which statement is supported by the passage.* Less genetic diversity in the southern chipmunk population points to the chipmunks migrating after the Ice Age, choice A, not before (lines 2–3). No evidence supports choice D. Although choice B could be true, it is irrelevant, and choice C is simply inaccurate and not suggested anywhere in the passage. The scientists' conclusions about the later migration of chipmunks are based on genetic information, and any doubts there might be about DNA evidence as in choice E are outside the scope of the passage. The best answer is A.

Related, or Paired, Passages

You'll be given two passages (paired passages) that have a common theme or subject. Each passage in some way relates to the other passage—sometimes supporting, sometimes opposing the views given. In some instances, the two passages are about the same subject but were written at different times—years, decades, or centuries—or in different places. You can use all of the general strategies given on pages 19–20 for these paired passages. In addition, many of the strategies given for single passages are also effective here, but there are some new strategies you can use for paired passages.

Specific Strategies for Questions Based on Paired Passages

- Carefully read any introductory material describing or giving information about the two passages.
- Note that the first group of questions refers to the first passage; the second group of questions refers to the second passage; and the last group of questions refers to both passages as they relate to each other.
- Consider reading the first passage, then answering the first group of questions, and then reading the second passage, and answering the remaining questions.
- Be aware that the first question can (and sometimes does) ask for the primary purpose of both passages.
- Be aware of how the passages are alike and different.
- Watch out for choices that are true for one passage but not the other.
- Read the passages looking for the main point and the structure of each passage.
- Make sure that your answer is supported by the passages. Some good or true answers are not correct.
- As you read, note the tone of each passage.
- Take advantage of the line numbers.
- Use the context to figure out the meaning of words, even if you're unfamiliar with them.
- Read all the choices, since you're looking for the *best* answer given.
- Use an elimination strategy.

Following is a set of "paired passages" with questions and explanations. Try your hand at marking the passages and the questions and answering the questions before you read the explanation and analysis of each.

Samples

Questions 1–13 are based on the following passages.

The following two passages, written in 1960 and 1980, discuss some limitations of television programs.

Passage 1

Despite all this increase in commercialization some—but not all—advertising men have wanted still greater control of the total content of the shows they sponsor. One producer, John E. Hasty, who had made shows for both Hollywood and television, was quoted as arguing that television could reach its full potential as an advertising medium only when advertising men produced the shows. "TV viewers cannot be regarded as an audience to be en-
(5)   tertained," he said. "They are prospects . . . for what the sponsor has to sell. This fact constitutes the show's reason for being. . . . Thus in a TV production the selling motive stands as the dominant factor."

He granted that showmen from Broadway and Hollywood might possess certain important skills that affect scripts, talent, music, and choreography, and that they might be generously endowed with skill and imagination. But, he asked, "Does this overbalance a seasoned adman's experience in mass selling?"
(10)   Many sponsors tend to view their television vehicles as total advertisements. The Institute for Advertising Research has begun offering a new measuring technique called Television Program Analysis which weights the total value of a program as an ad for the company. And an advertising trade journal in 1960 observed, "From all indications, a better tailoring of program type to advertiser, and commercial to program, is in the making. Taken together, commercials and programs in many cases accentuate the values of a high-consumption economy."
(15)   Marketing consultant Victor Lebow summed up the powerful appeal television has as a selling medium when he pointed out: "It creates a new set of conditions, impelling toward a monopoly of the consumer's attention. For the first time, almost the entire American consuming public has become a captive audience. . . . Television actually sells the generalized idea of consumption." Cases in point to support this theory that television sells "the generalized idea of consumption" might be the squeals and ahs of television audiences on panel shows when prizes such
(20)   as stoves, refrigerators, rotisseries, and matched luggage are unveiled amid fanfare.

One might speculate also on what it does to a people's sense of values—especially to children's—when discussions of significant events are followed on television by announcers who in often louder and more solemn voices announce a great new discovery for a hair bleach. Or, to consider another kind of juxtaposition, a broadcast appeal to aid hungry children in mid-1960 was followed immediately by a dog-food commercial.

31

Passage 2

(25)   A story's "newsworthiness" is often determined by geography. Journalist Thomas Griffith describes how he and his colleagues used to argue over "how many people would have to be killed where to make news—three people in an auto wreck in your own town? Ten people drowning in a shipwreck in the English Channel; twenty-five in an avalanche in the Alps—and now the numbers increase sharply—one hundred in an earthquake in Turkey; three hundred in the collapse of a bridge in Bolivia; one thousand in a typhoon off Calcutta; fifteen hundred in a fire in

(30)   China?" News, it appears, is what happens in your own backyard.

This kind of reporting helps to magnify our provincialism. The average American, asked to draw a map of the world, would probably show the U.S.A. occupying half of the land surface, with Europe and Russia and China and Africa tucked off in some untidy, insignificant corner of the globe.

Television news dissolves meaning in a wash of flashy images. The takeover of Afghanistan is summed up with

(35)   a close-up view of a weeping widow, the problem of inflation with an image of the interior of a supermarket with a tight shot of the price of hamburger, the importance of gold price fluctuations with footage of gold traders frantically jostling each other to get their orders in. A typical half-hour news broadcast has fifteen to twenty stories. Allowing time for commercial interruptions, that leaves an average of one minute per story. Congressman Michael Synar says this makes for a simple-minded electorate: "When I go home I have to deal with people, and all they

(40)   know of a four-hundred-page bill is one paragraph in the Sunday paper or a thirty-second TV spot. Issues don't break that way, but people just don't grasp the complexity."

The criterion for how much time a story gets, or whether it appears at all, is not its relative importance in world affairs. "We like stories that have wiggle," one network executive says. "Sexy stories. Iran has wiggle. Defectors from the Bolshoi have wiggle. Stories about government agencies have no wiggle."

(45)   In the mind of many network news executives, the difference between a good news story and Marilyn Monroe's posterior is undetectable. Reporters are told to go after the human interest angle to a story—the "people factor"— rather than to explore the how or why of a particular event. Researcher David Altheide once accompanied a reporter assigned to do a story on proposed alternatives to achieve racial integration. As they left the studio, the reporter explained how he planned to do the story: "Just barely give a background as to what these alternatives are.

(50)   Explain the story over film of kids, bless their little hearts, who have no say in the matter whatsoever, caught in a game of politics between their parents and the school board." The dramatic peg for the story was thus determined before the reporter had even arrived at the scene!

Notice that the line numbers of the passages continue from the first to the second passage. The first group of questions is typically about Passage 1.

1. Which of the following best fulfills the ideal of the producer quoted in the first two paragraphs of Passage 1?

   A.   Music television
   B.   Educational television
   C.   Home-shopping television
   D.   Twenty-four hour television news
   E.   Situation comedy

Because the producer believes that selling is the real reason for television and sees the audience only as buyers, his ideal would be realized by home-shopping television in which there is no pretense about buying and selling. The best answer is C.

2. In line 9, *seasoned* means

   A.   improved in quality.
   B.   experienced.
   C.   softened.
   D.   flavored.
   E.   changed in ability.

Although a dictionary would list all five of these definitions of *seasoned*, here it means experienced or mature. The best choice is B.

---

3. According to Passage 1, television programs may be expected to become

    A. increasingly dependent on comedy and games.

    B. more carefully crafted to sell a product.

    C. more dependent on Broadway and Hollywood directors.

    D. less dependent on depicting sex and violence.

    E. more carefully edited to suit children's viewing.

The third paragraph speaks of *a better tailoring of program type to advertiser, and commercial to program.* The best choice is B.

---

4. The sentence *Television actually sells the generalized idea of consumption* (lines 17–18) is best understood to mean that

    A. the more people watch television, the more likely they are to buy an advertised product.

    B. television is by and large indifferent to the ecological needs of the modern world.

    C. television, more than any other medium, is suited to the selling of products to a mass audience.

    D. game and panel programs which feature costly prizes pander to the greed of the audience.

    E. by reflecting the consumer values of society, television encourages its viewer to consume more.

Although some of the statements here may be true or may express ideas that the passage is in sympathy with, only E specifically paraphrases or interprets the quotation of the question. By showing consumer products and luxury, television programs make the idea of owning more attractive to viewers. The best choice is E.

---

5. In line 23, the word *juxtaposition* means

    A. placing side by side.

    B. sequence of events.

    C. misunderstanding.

    D. unintentional joke.

    E. inappropriate comparison.

A *juxtaposition* is a placing side by side. The best choice is A.

The next group of questions is usually about Passage 2.

---

6. Which of the following best answers the question of the first paragraph of Passage 2, *how many people would have to be killed where to make news* (line 26)?

    A. A small number of deaths will not make news.

    B. The number killed in an earthquake must be at least four times greater than the number killed in an avalanche.

    C. Local accidents are not news.

    D. The smaller the number of deaths, the closer to home they must be.

    E. Ten deaths in an air crash in East Africa would be more likely to make news than ten deaths in an explosion in West Africa.

The question asks both *how many* and *where*. The passage makes clear that news, on television, is *what happens in your own backyard*, so a small number of local deaths would make news, but in distant areas, the size and spectacle would have to be much greater. The best choice is D.

---

7. In the second paragraph of Passage 2, the point of describing the world map an average American would draw is to show that

   A. Americans know less about geography than the citizens of other countries.
   B. the United States occupies half of the world's land surface.
   C. Americans have a false notion of the importance of the United States.
   D. Americans are usually unable to identify the capital cities of other nations.
   E. Americans' knowledge of geography has improved since television became popular.

The paragraph is about the provincialism, that is, the narrowness of outlook, of most Americans, and the map most Americans would draw reveals how little they know about the rest of the world and how much they overestimate their own importance. The passage does not tell us whether or not people elsewhere are more or less provincial. The best choice is C.

---

8. In Passage 2 (line 40), the word *bill* means

   A. a statement of charges for services or goods.
   B. any written document with a seal.
   C. a list of things offered.
   D. a draft of a law.
   E. a bank note.

As it is used here, bill means the draft of a law. The speaker is a Congressman speaking of his constituents' ignorance of legislation in Congress. The best choice is D.

---

9. The phrase to *have wiggle* used in the fourth paragraph of Passage 2 is best taken to mean to

   A. have popular appeal.
   B. have overt sexual interest.
   C. involve stars of film or theater.
   D. move sinuously.
   E. have serious implications.

As it is used here, *wiggle* is figurative, not literal, since *Iran has wiggle*. It stands for what has popular appeal. The best choice is A.

---

10. Of the following aspects of television mentioned in Passage 2, which does the author believe should be foremost in news broadcasting?

   A. flashy images (line 34)
   B. wiggle (line 43)
   C. the human interest angle (line 46)
   D. the "people factor" (line 46)
   E. the how or why of a particular event (line 47)

The author would favor television news that deals with the how or why of events, although television programmers have preferred the four other options. The best choice is E.

---

11. From Passage 2, it can be inferred that a news story on which of the following topics would be least likely to appear on television news broadcasts?

A. The computer systems of the Internal Revenue Service
B. A local woman's entry in the Miss America contest
C. The marriage of a rock star and a soap opera actress
D. The effect of flooding on the Mississippi
E. Espionage in New York City

The computers of the IRS have little drama, human interest, or local appeal, so they are less likely to be considered newsworthy. The best choice is A.

The last group of questions usually relies on both passages, comparing and contrasting general ideas and specific points.

---

12. Unlike Passage 2, Passage 1 is an attack upon television chiefly for its

A. parochialism.
B. materialism.
C. superficiality.
D. anti-intellectualism.
E. lack of objectivity.

The focus of Passage 1 is on materialism, television as a vehicle for selling. Passage 2 attacks the parochialism, superficiality, and anti-intellectualism of television news broadcasts. The best choice is B.

---

13. Which of the following best describes the primary difference between the two passages?

A. Passage 1 is serious in tone, while Passage 2 is comic and colloquial.
B. Passage 1, on the whole, approves of television programming, while Passage 2 is harshly critical.
C. Passage 1 is concerned with the way that television harms the moral values of all viewers, while Passage 2 is concerned with the failure to report world events accurately.
D. Passage 1 is chiefly concerned with the influence of advertisers on television, while Passage 2 is chiefly concerned with the superficiality of television news programs.
E. Passage 1 is concerned with the audience of television programs, while Passage 2 is concerned with the programs.

Passage 2, though colloquial, is very serious in tone. Neither passage approves of television as it is. Passage 1 mentions value in only one paragraph. Both passages are concerned with audience and programs. Choice D is a reasonable summary of the two passages. The best choice is D.

A Summary of Strategies for Critical Reading Questions

■ Read the passage actively, marking main points and other items you feel are important.

■ You may want to skim a few questions first, marking words that give you a clue about the passage before you read the passage.

■ Base your answer on what you read in the passage, the introduction to the passage, or footnotes given following the passage.

■ The passage must support your answer.

■ Some good or true answers are not correct. Make sure that the answer you select is "what the question is asking."

■ Be sure to read all of the choices to make sure that you have the best of the ones given.

■ Pace yourself. Don't get stuck on the passage or any one question.

■ When more than one reading passage is given, you may want to first read the passage that is of more interest or familiarity to you and answer those questions first. When skipping, be extra careful to mark your answers in the proper place on your answer sheet.

■ On paired passages, the first questions will refer to Passage 1, the next group of questions to Passage 2, and the final group to both passages as they relate to each other.

Three Final Strategies

If you're having real trouble with a passage or simply running out of time, try one of these three strategies.

■ **Skip a difficult passage.** You could skip a difficult passage entirely, along with the questions based on it, and come back to them later. Remember that you can return to those questions only while you're working in that section. Also, if you use this strategy, take care to mark your answers in the correct spaces on the answer sheet when you skip a group of questions.

■ **Skim the passage.** If you're running out of time, you might want to skim the passage and then answer the questions—referring back to the passage when necessary.

■ **Potshot questions and spots in the passage.** For this "last resort method," simply read the questions that refer to specific lines in the passage and read only those specific lines in the passage (potshot them) to try to answer the question. This final strategy may help you at least eliminate some answer choices and take some educated guesses.

Common Prefixes, Suffixes, and Roots

The following list should help you to arrive at definitions of unfamiliar words in the critical reading sections of the SAT and PSAT/NMSQT. These prefixes, suffixes, and roots apply to thousands of words.

Prefixes		
Prefix	*Meaning*	*Example*
ad-	to, toward	advance
anti-	against	antidote
bi-	two	bicycle
com-	together, with	composite
de-	away, from	deter
epi-	upon	epilogue
equi-	equal, equally	equivalent
ex-	out of	expel
homo-	same, equal, like	homogenized
hyper-	over, too much	hyperactive
hypo-	under, too little	hypodermic
in-	not	insufficient
in-	into	instruct
inter-	between	interstate
mal-	bad	malfunction
mis-	wrong	mistake
mono-	alone, one	monolith
non-	not	nonentity
ob-	against	objection
omni-	all, everywhere	omniscient
over-	above	overbearing
poly-	many	polymorphous
pre-	before	precede
pro-	forward	propel
re-	back, again	regress
retro-	backward	retrograde
semi-	half, partly	semicircle
sub-	under	submarine
trans-	across, beyond	transcend
un-	not	unneeded

Suffixes		
Suffix	*Meaning*	*Example*
-able, -ible	able to	usable
-er, -or	one who does	competitor
-ism	the practice of	rationalism
-ist	one who is occupied with	feminist
-less	without, lacking	meaningless
-ship	the art or skill of	statesmanship
-fy	to make	dignify
-ness	the quality of	aggressiveness
-tude	the state of	rectitude
-logue	a particular kind of speaking or writing	prologue

Roots		
Root	*Meaning*	*Example*
arch	to rule	monarch
belli	war, warlike	belligerent
bene	good	benevolent
chron	time	chronology
dic	to say	indicative
fac	to make, to do	artifact
graph	writing	telegraph
mort	to die	mortal
port	to carry	deport
vid, vis	to see	invisible

Introduction to the Mathematics Section

The Mathematical sections of the new SAT consist of two basic types of questions: regular multiple-choice questions and student-produced responses, also known as grid-ins.

Two Math sections are 25 minutes in length and one Math section is 20 minutes in length. Since one section of the test is experimental (although you don't know which one), you could have an additional 25-minute Math section.

Although the order of the sections and the number of questions may change, at this time, the three sections total about 52 to 56 math questions that count toward your score. These three sections generate a scaled math score that ranges from 200 to 800. About 50% right should generate an average score.

The math sections are slightly graduated in difficulty. That is, the easiest questions are basically at the beginning and the more difficult ones at the end. If a section has two types of questions, usually each type starts with easier problems. For example, a section starts with easy multiple-choice questions, and the last few multiple-choice questions are more difficult before you start the grid-ins; the grid-ins start with easy questions and move toward the more difficult ones at the end.

You will be given reference information preceding each Mathematics section. You should be familiar with this information.

You may use an approved calculator on the SAT. Bring a calculator with which you are familiar.

Using Your Calculator

The new SAT allows the use of approved calculators, and the College Board (the people who sponsor the exam) recommends that each test taker take a calculator to the test. Even though no question will require the use of a calculator—that is, each question can be answered without a calculator—in some instances, using a calculator will save you valuable time.

You should

- Bring your own calculator, because you can't borrow one during the exam.
- Bring a calculator even if you don't think you'll use it. Make sure that you are familiar with the use of your calculator.
- Make sure that your calculator has new, fresh batteries and is in good working order.
- Practice using your calculator on some of the problems to see when and where it will be helpful.
- Check for a shortcut to any problem that seems to involve much computation. But use your calculator if it will be time effective. If there appears to be too much computation or the problem seems impossible without the calculator, you're probably doing something wrong.
- Before doing an operation, check the number that you keyed on the display to make sure that you keyed in the right number. You may want to check each number as you key it in.

Be careful that you

- Don't rush out and buy a sophisticated calculator for the test.
- Don't bring a calculator that you're unfamiliar with.
- Don't bring a pocket organizer, handheld mini-computer, laptop computer, or calculator with a typewriter-type keypad or paper tape.
- Don't bring a calculator that requires an outlet or any other external power source.
- Don't bring a calculator that makes noise.

- Don't try to share a calculator.
- Don't try to use a calculator on every problem.
- Don't become dependent on your calculator.

Following is the Calculator Policy for new SAT as given by the College Board:

"The following are **not** permitted:

- Powerbooks and portable/handheld computers
- Electronic writing pads or pen-input/stylus-driven (e.g., Palm, PDAs, Casio ClassPad 300)
- Pocket organizers
- Models with QWERTY (i.e., typewriter) keyboards (e.g., TI-92 Plus, Voyage 200)
- Models with paper tapes
- Models that make noise or "talk"
- Models that require an electrical outlet
- Cell phone calculators"

Take advantage of using a calculator on the test. Learn to use a calculator efficiently by practicing. As you approach a problem, first focus on how to solve that problem and then decide whether the calculator will be helpful. Remember, a calculator can save you time on some problems, but also remember that each problem can be solved without a calculator. Also remember that a calculator will not solve a problem for you. You must understand the problem first.

Basic Skills and Concepts that You Should Know

Number and Operations

- Operations with fractions
- Applying addition, subtraction, multiplication, and division to problem solving
- Arithmetic mean (average), mode, and median
- Ratio and proportion
- Number properties: positive and negative integers, odd and even numbers, prime numbers, factors and multiples, divisibility
- Word problems, solving for: percents, averages, rate, time, distance, interest, price per item
- Number line: order, consecutive numbers, fractions, betweenness
- Sequences involving exponential growth
- Sets (union, intersection, elements)

Algebra and Functions

- Operations with signed numbers
- Substitution for variables
- Absolute value
- Working with algebraic expressions
- Manipulating integer and rational exponents
- Solving rational equations and inequalities
- Working with linear functions—graphs and equations
- Solving radical equations

- Basic factoring
- Direct and inverse variation
- Function notation and evaluation
- Concepts of range and domain
- Working with positive roots
- Solving quadratic equations
- Working with quadratic functions and graphs

Geometry and Measurement

- Vertical angles
- Angles in figures
- Perpendicular and parallel lines
- Perimeter, area, angle measure of polygons
- Circumference, area, radius, diameter
- Triangles: right, isosceles, equilateral, angle measure, similarity
- Special triangles: $30°$-$60°$-$90°$, $45°$-$45°$-$90°$
- Pythagorean theorem
- Volume and surface area of solids
- Coordinate geometry: coordinates, slope, distance formula, midpoint formula
- Geometric notation for length, segments, lines, rays, and congruence
- Properties of tangent lines
- Problems in which trigonometry could be used as an alternate solution method
- Qualitative behavior of graphs and functions
- Transformations and their effect on graphs and functions

Data Analysis, Statistics, and Probability

- Interpreting graphs, charts, and tables
- Scatter plots
- Matrices
- Probability
- Geometric probability
- Basic statistics (mean, mode, median, range)

Multiple-Choice Questions

You should have a total of about 42 to 46 multiple-choice questions spread throughout the three Math sections that count toward your score.

Ability Tested

The Mathematics multiple-choice questions test your ability to solve mathematical problems involving arithmetic, algebra I and II, geometry, data interpretation, basic statistics and probability, and word problems by using problem-solving insight, logic, and the application of basic skills.

Basic Skills Necessary

The basic skills necessary to do well on this section include high school algebra I and II, and intuitive or informal geometry. No calculus is necessary. Logical insight into problem-solving situations is also necessary.

Directions

Solve each problem in this section by using the information given and your own mathematical calculations, insights, and problem-solving skills. Then select the one correct answer of the five choices given and mark the corresponding circle on your answer sheet. Use the available space on the page for your scratch work.

Notes

- All numbers used are real numbers.
- Calculators may be used.
- Some problems may be accompanied by figures or diagrams. These figures are drawn as accurately as possible EXCEPT when it is stated in a specific problem that a figure is not drawn to scale. The figures and diagrams are meant to provide information useful in solving the problem or problems. Unless otherwise stated, all figures and diagrams lie in a plane.
- A list of data that may be used for reference is included.

Analysis of Directions

1. All scratch work is to be done in the test booklet; get used to doing this because no scratch paper is allowed into the testing area.
2. You are looking for the one correct answer; therefore, although other answers may be close, there is never more than one right answer.

Suggested Approaches with Samples

Circle or Underline

> Take advantage of being allowed to mark on the test booklet by always underlining or circling what you are looking for. This will ensure that you are answering the right question.

Samples

---

1. If $x + 6 = 9$, then $3x + 1 =$

    A.   3
    B.   9
    C.   10
    D.   34
    E.   46

You should first circle or underline $3x + 1$ because this is what you are solving for. Solving for x leaves $x = 3$, then substituting into $3x + 1$ gives $3(3) + 1$, or 10. The most common mistake is to solve for x, which is 3, and *mistakenly choose A* as your answer. But remember, you are solving for $3x + 1$, not just x. You should also notice that most of the other choices would all be possible answers if you made common or simple mistakes. *Make sure that you are answering the right question.* The correct answer is C.

2. Together, a hat and coat cost $125. The coat costs $25 more than the hat. What is the cost of the coat?

A. $25
B. $50
C. $75
D. $100
E. $125

The key words here are *cost of the coat,* so circle those words. To solve algebraically,

$$x = \text{hat}$$
$$x + \$25 = \text{coat (cost \$25 more than the hat)}$$

Together they cost $125.

$$(x + 25) + x = 125$$
$$2x + 25 = 125$$
$$2x = 100$$
$$x = 50$$

But this is the cost of the hat. Notice that $50 is one of the answer choices, B. Since $x = 50$, then $x + 25 = 75$. Therefore, the coat costs $75, which is choice C. *Always answer the question that is being asked.* Circling the key word or words will help you do that. The correct answer is C.

3. If $x^3 + y^3 = 11$ and $x^3 - y^3 = 5$, then what is the value of $x^6 - y^6$?

A.   6
B.   8
C.   16
D.   55
E.   Cannot be determined from the given information

First circle or underline $x^6 - y^6$.

Now factor this difference of two squares.

$$x^6 - y^6 = (x^3 + y^3)(x^3 - y^3)$$

Next substitute in 11 for $x^3 + y^3$ and 5 for $x^3 - y^3$

$$= (11)(5)$$
$$= 55$$

The correct answer is D.

Pull Out Information

"Pulling" information out of the word problem structure can often give you a better look at what you are working with; therefore, you gain additional insight into the problem.

Samples

---

1. If a mixture is $\frac{3}{7}$ alcohol by volume and $\frac{4}{7}$ water by volume, what is the ratio of the volume of alcohol to the volume of water in this mixture?

    A. $\frac{3}{7}$

    B. $\frac{4}{7}$

    C. $\frac{3}{4}$

    D. $\frac{4}{3}$

    E. $\frac{7}{4}$

The first bit of information that should be pulled out should be what you are looking for: ratio of the volume of alcohol to the volume of water. Rewrite it as $A:W$ and then into its working form: $\frac{A}{W}$. Next, you should pull out the volumes of each:

$$A = \frac{3}{7} \text{ and } W = \frac{4}{7}.$$

Now the answer can be easily figured by inspection or substitution. Using $\left(\frac{3}{7}\right) \div \left(\frac{4}{7}\right)$, invert the bottom fraction and multiply to get $\frac{3}{7} \times \frac{7}{4} = \frac{21}{28} = \frac{3}{4}$. The ratio of the volume of alcohol to the volume of water is 3 to 4. The correct answer is C.

When pulling out information, actually write out the numbers and/or letters to the side of the problem, putting them into some helpful form and eliminating some of the wording.

---

2. Bill is ten years older than his sister. If Bill was twenty-five years of age in 1983, in what year could he have been born?

    A. 1948

    B. 1953

    C. 1958

    D. 1963

    E. 1968

The key words here are *in what year* and *could he have been born*. Thus, the solution is simple: $1983 - 25 = 1958$, answer C. Notice that you pulled out the information *twenty-five years of age* and *in 1983*. The fact about Bill's age in comparison to his sister's age was not needed, however, and was not pulled out. The correct answer is C.

Work Forward

If you quickly see the method to solve the problem, then do the work.

Samples

---

1. Which of the following numbers is between $\frac{1}{3}$ and $\frac{1}{4}$?

    A. .45

    B. .35

    C. .29

    D. .22

    E. .20

You should first underline or circle *between $\frac{1}{3}$ and $\frac{1}{4}$*? If you know that $\frac{1}{3}$ is .333... and $\frac{1}{4}$ is .25, you might have insight into the problem and should simply work forward. .29 is the only number between .333... and .25, correct answer is C. By the way, a quick peek at the answer choices would tip you off that you should work in decimals.

---

2. $\left(64a^{10}b^{6}\right)^{\frac{1}{2}} =$

   A. $32a^{8}b^{4}$
   B. $8a^{8}b^{4}$
   C. $32a^{5}b^{3}$
   D. $8a^{5}b^{3}$
   E. $64a^{5}b^{3}$

Since this problem is very mechanical, if you know the method, work forward.

Place each item within the ( ) to the $\frac{1}{2}$ power.

$$\left(64a^{10}b^{6}\right)^{\frac{1}{2}} = \left(64\right)^{\frac{1}{2}} \cdot \left(a^{10}\right)^{\frac{1}{2}} \cdot \left(b^{6}\right)^{\frac{1}{2}}$$

Next, take the square root of each one. $= 8a^{5}b^{3}$

The correct answer is D.

---

3. If $2x - 5 > 3$, what are the possible values of x?

   A. $x < 4$
   B. $x < 2$
   C. $x > 0$
   D. $x > 2$
   E. $x > 4$

First circle or underline "possible values of x." Now solve the problem as follows:

$$2x - 5 > 3$$

Add 5 to each side, $+5 \quad +5$

This gives $2x \quad > 8$

Now divide by 2, $\frac{2x}{2} > \frac{8}{2}$

So $x > 4$

The correct answer is E.

---

4. If y varies inversely to x and $y = 8$ when $x = 3$, then what is the value of y when $x = 4$?

   A.   24
   B. $\frac{32}{3}$
   C.   9
   D.   7
   E.   6

First underline or circle "value of y." Next, work the problem forward.

Since y varies inversely to x,

$$y = \frac{k}{x}$$

Next plug in for x and y, $\quad 8 = \frac{k}{3}$

$$k = 24$$

Hence, $y = \frac{24}{x}$ and $y = \frac{24}{4} = 6$

The correct answer is E.

---

5. What are the x-intercepts of the ellipse $9x^2 + 4y^2 = 36$?

   A. $(\pm 36, 0)$
   B. $(\pm 9, 0)$
   C. $(\pm 4, 0)$
   D. $(\pm 3, 0)$
   E. $(\pm 2, 0)$

First, circle or underline "x-intercepts." Next, if you know how to solve the problem, work forward.

To find x-intercepts, set $y = 0$ and solve for x.

$$9x^2 + 4(0^2) = 36$$
$$9x^2 = 36$$
$$x^2 = 4$$
$$x = \pm 2$$

The correct answer is E.

If you didn't know how to work the problem forward, you could have worked backwards, from the answers by simply plugging in.

Work Backwards

In some instances, it will be easier to work from the answers. Do not disregard this method because it will at least eliminate some of the choices and could give you the correct answer.

Samples

---

1. What is the approximate value of $\sqrt{1596}$?

   A. 10
   B. 20
   C. 30
   D. 40
   E. 50

Without the answer choices, this could be a difficult problem. By working up from the answer choices, however, the problem is easily solvable. Since $\sqrt{1596}$ means what number times itself equals 1596, you can take any answer choice and multiply it by itself. As soon as you find the answer choice that when multiplied by itself approximates 1596, you've got the correct answer. You may want to start working from the middle choice, since the answers are usually in increasing or decreasing order. In the problem above, start with choice C, 30. Since $30 \times 30 = 900$, which is too small, you could now eliminate A, B, and C as too small. But $40 \times 40 = 1600$, approximately 1596. Choice D is correct. If your calculator computes square roots, you could have used it to compute the square root and then rounded off.

---

2. If $\frac{x}{4} + 2 = 22$, what is the value of x?

   A.   40
   B.   80
   C. 100
   D. 120
   E. 160

If you cannot solve this algebraically, you may use the *work up from your choices* strategy. But start with C, 100. What if $x = 100$?

$$\frac{x}{4} + 2 = 22$$
$$\frac{100}{4} + 2 \stackrel{?}{=} 22$$
$$25 + 2 \stackrel{?}{=} 22$$
$$27 \neq 22$$

Note that since 27 is too large, choices D and E will also be too large. Therefore, try A. If A is too small, then you know the answer is B. If A works, the answer is A.

$$\frac{x}{4} + 2 = 22$$
$$\frac{40}{4} + 2 \stackrel{?}{=} 22$$
$$10 + 2 \stackrel{?}{=} 22$$
$$12 \neq 22$$

Since A is too small, the correct answer must be B.

---

3. What is the greatest common factor of the numbers 18, 24, and 30?

   A.   2
   B.   3
   C.   4
   D.   6
   E. 12

The largest number which divides evenly into 18, 24, and 30 is 6. You could have worked from the answers. But here you should start with the largest answer choice, since you're looking for the *greatest* common factor. The correct answer is D.

---

4. If $8^{x+3} = 32^{x+3}$, then $x =$

   A. −4
   B. −3
   C.   0
   D.   3
   E.   4

First underline or circle "$x =$". If you don't know how to solve this problem, work backwards.

Start by plugging in the value in choice C, 0.

$$8^{0+3} \overset{?}{=} 32^{0+3}$$
$$8^3 \neq 32^3$$

Since you can quickly see that these two are not equal, try choice D, 3.

$$8^{3+3} \overset{?}{=} 32^{3+3}$$
$$8^6 \neq 32^6$$

Since these are not equal, and it is evident that no positive value for x will work, you should try choice B, –3.

$$8^{-3+3} \overset{?}{=} 32^{-3+3}$$
$$8^0 = 32^0$$

Since any number to the zero power equals one, these two are equal. **The correct answer is B.**

Solving this algebraically would look like this:

$$8^{x+3} = 32^{x+3}$$
$$\left(2^3\right)^{x+3} = \left(2^5\right)^{x+3}$$
$$2^{3x+9} = 2^{5x+15}$$
$$3x + 9 = 5x + 15$$
$$-6 = 2x$$
$$-3 = x$$

Use Your Calculator

Some questions will need to be completely worked out. If you don't see a fast method but do know that you could compute the answer, use your calculator.

Samples

1. What is the final cost of a watch that sells for $49.00 if the sales tax is 7%?

    A. $49.07
    B. $49.70
    C. $52.00
    D. $52.43
    E. $56.00

Since the sales tax is 7% of $49.00,

$$7\% \text{ of } \$49.00 = (.07)(\$49.00) = \$3.43$$

The total cost of the watch is therefore

$$\$49.00 + \$3.43 = \$52.43$$

The correct answer is D.

Your calculator would have helped with these calculations.

Price List	
Top sirloin	$2.99 per pound or 2 pounds for $5.00
Filet mignon	$4.00 per pound
London broil	$1.79 per pound or 3 pounds for $5.00

2. Randy owns and manages Randy's Steakhouse. He needs to buy the following meats in order to have enough for the weekend business: 9 pounds of top sirloin, 8 pounds of filet mignon, and 7 pounds of London broil. Using the price list given above, what is the least amount Randy can spend to buy the meat he needs for the weekend business?

    A. $97.00
    B. $71.44
    C. $66.78
    D. $54.99
    E. $34.78

top sirloin: 8 pounds + 1 pound
                    $= (4 \times \$5.00) + \$2.99$ (note: 2 pounds for $5.00)
                    $= \$20.00 + \$2.99$
                    $= \$22.99$

filet mignon: 8 pounds
                    $= 8 \times \$4.00$
                    $= \$32.00$

London broil: 6 pounds + 1 pound
                    $= (2 \times \$5.00) + \$1.79$ (note: 3 pounds for $5.00)
                    $= \$10.00 + \$1.79$
                    $= \$11.79$

Add to find the total: $\$22.99 + \$32.00 + \$11.79 = \$66.78$

The correct answer is C.

Your calculator would have helped with these calculations.

3. If the nth term of sequence 4, 12, 36, 108,... is $4 \cdot 3^{n-1}$, what is the 10th term of the sequence?

    A.   4,000
    B.   19,683
    C.   59,049
    D.   78,732
    E.   236,196

To find the 10th term of the sequence simply plug in 10 for n as follows:

$$4 \cdot 3^{10-1} = 4 \cdot 3^9$$
$$4 \cdot 19,683$$
$$= 78,732$$

This problem could have taken a very long time without your calculator. The correct answer is D.

Substitute Simple Numbers

Substituting numbers for variables can often be an aid to understanding a problem. Remember to substitute simple numbers, since you have to do the work.

Samples

---

1. If $x > 1$, then which of the following decreases as x decreases?

   I. $x + x^2$
   II. $2x^2 - x$
   III. $\dfrac{1}{x+1}$

   A. I only
   B. II only
   C. III only
   D. I and II only
   E. II and III only

This problem is most easily solved by taking each situation and substituting in simple numbers. However, in the first situation (I. $x + x^2$), you should recognize that this expression will decrease as x decreases. Trying $x = 2$ gives $2 + (2)^2 = 6$. Now, trying $x = 3$ gives $3 + (3)^2 = 12$. Notice that choices B, C, and E are already eliminated because they do not contain I. You should also realize that now you need to try only the values in II. Since III is not paired with I as a possible choice, III cannot be one of the answers.

Trying $x = 2$ in the expression $2x^2 - x$ gives $2(2)^2 - 2$, or $2(4) - 2 = 6$. Now, trying $x = 3$ gives $2 + 3^2 = 12$ or $2(9) - 3 = 15$. This expression also decreases as x decreases. Therefore, the correct answer is D. Once again, notice that III was not even attempted because it was not one of the possible choices. Be sure to make logical substitutions. Use a positive number, a negative number, or zero when applicable to get the full picture.

---

2. If x is a positive integer in the equation $12x = q$, then q must be

   A. a positive even integer.
   B. a negative even integer.
   C. zero.
   D. a positive odd integer.
   E. a negative odd integer.

At first glance, this problem appears quite complex. But let's plug in some numbers, and see what happens. For instance, first plug in 1 (the simplest positive integer) for x.

$$12x = q$$
$$12(1) = q$$
$$12 = q$$

Now try 2,

$$12x = q$$
$$12(2) = q$$
$$24 = q$$

Try it again. No matter what positive integer is plugged in for x, q will always be positive and even. Therefore, the correct answer is A.

---

3. If $f(x) = 3^x$, which of the following CANNOT be a value of $f(x)$?

A. -3
B. $\dfrac{1}{3}$
C. 1
D. 3
E. 9

Notice that you are looking for "CANNOT be a value of $f(x)$." Try some simple numbers $(0, 1, -1)$ and you will see that regardless of the values used for x, 3^x cannot be a negative number (or zero).

$$f(0) = 3^0 = 1$$
$$f(1) = 3^1 = 3$$
$$f(-1) = 3^{-1} = \frac{1}{3}$$

So $f(x) = 3^x > 0, f(x) \neq -3$

The correct answer is A.

Use 10 or 100

Some problems may deal with percent or percent change. If you don't see a simple method for working the problem, try using the values of 10 or 100 and see what you get.

---

1. A corporation triples its annual bonus to 50 of its employees. What percent of the employees' new bonus is the increase?

A. 50%
B. $66\frac{2}{3}$%
C. 100%
D. 200%
E. 300%

Let's use $100 for the normal bonus. If the annual bonus was normally $100, tripled it would now be $300. Therefore, the increase ($200) is $\frac{2}{3}$ of the new bonus ($300). Two-thirds is $66\frac{2}{3}$%. The correct answer is B.

2. Tom is building a square wooden framework to pour cement. His first frame is too small, so he increases each side by 20%. After careful measurement, he realizes this frame is too large, so he decreases each side by 10%. The area contained by his final wooden frame is what percent greater than the original wooden frame?

  A. 10%
  B. 10.8%
  C. 16.64%
  D. 20%
  E. 40.44%

First circle or underline what you are looking for, in this case—*area . . . percent greater . . . than original.*

Next, draw the diagram.

Now try some simple numbers. In this case 10":

```
           10″
      ┌──────────┐
      │          │
 10″  │ 100 sq. in. │
      │          │
      └──────────┘
```

Increasing this measurement by 20% gives a side of 12":

```
           12″
      ┌──────────┐
      │          │
 12″  │ 144 sq. in. │
      │          │
      └──────────┘
```

Decreasing this measurement by 10% gives 12 – 1.2 = 10.8. (10% × 12 = 1.2.)

```
           10.8″
      ┌──────────┐
      │          │
10.8″ │ 116.64 sq. in. │
      │          │
      └──────────┘
```

The area of the original was 100 sq. in. The area of the new figure is 116.64 sq. in. So the percent greater than the original would be 116.64 – 100 = 16.64 compared to the original 100 gives 16.64%. The correct answer is C. Your calculator could have been helpful in this problem.

Be Reasonable

Sometimes you will immediately recognize a simple method to solve a problem. If this is not the case, try a reasonable approach and then check the answers to see which one is most reasonable.

Samples

1. Barney can mow the lawn in 5 hours, and Fred can mow the lawn in 4 hours. How long will it take them to mow the lawn together?

   A. 5 hours

   B. $4\frac{1}{2}$ hours

   C. 4 hours

   D. $2\frac{2}{9}$ hours

   E. 1 hour

Suppose that you are unfamiliar with the type of equation for this problem. Try the "reasonable" method. Since Fred can mow the lawn in 4 hours by himself, it will take less than 4 hours if Barney helps him. Therefore, choices A, B, and C are ridiculous. Taking this method a little further, suppose that Barney could also mow the lawn in 4 hours. Then, together it would take Barney and Fred 2 hours. But since Barney is a little slower than this, the total time should be a little more than 2 hours. The correct answer is D, $2\frac{2}{9}$ hours.

Using the equation for this problem would give the following calculations:

$$\frac{1}{5} + \frac{1}{4} = \frac{1}{x}$$

In 1 hour, Barney could do $\frac{1}{5}$ of the job, and in 1 hour, Fred could do $\frac{1}{4}$ of the job. Unknown $1/x$ is that part of the job they could do together in one hour. Now solving, you calculate as follows:

$$\frac{4}{20} + \frac{5}{20} = \frac{1}{x}$$

$$\frac{9}{20} = \frac{1}{x}$$

Cross multiplying gives $$9x = 20$$

Therefore, $$x = \frac{20}{9} \text{ or } 2\frac{2}{9}$$

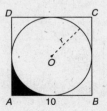

2. Circle O is inscribed in square $ABCD$ as shown above. The area of the shaded region is approximately

   A. 10

   B. 25

   C. 30

   D. 50

   E. 75

Using a reasonable approach, you would first find the area of the square: $10 \times 10 = 100$. Then divide the square into four equal sections as follows:

Since a quarter of the square is 25, then the shaded region must be much less than 25. The only possible answer is choice A, 10.

Another approach to this problem would be to first find the area of the square: $10 \times 10 = 100$. Then subtract the approximate area of the circle:

$$A = \pi(r^2) \cong 3(5^2) = 3(25) = 75.$$

Therefore, the total area inside the square but outside the circle is approximately 25. One quarter of that area is shaded. Therefore, $\frac{25}{4}$ is approximately the shaded area. The closest answer is A, 10.

Sketch a Diagram

Sketching diagrams or simple pictures can also be very helpful in problem solving because the diagram may tip off either a simple solution or a method for solving the problem.

Samples

1. If all sides of a square are halved, the area of that square is

   A. halved
   B. divided by 3
   C. divided by 4
   D. divided by 8
   E. divided by 16

One way to solve this problem is to draw a square and then halve all its sides. Then compare the two areas.

Your first diagram

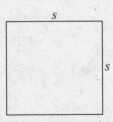

Halving every side

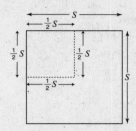

Notice that the total area of the new square will now be one-fourth of the original square. The correct answer is C.

---

2. If P lies on $\overarc{ON}$ such that $\overarc{OP} = 2\overarc{PN}$ and Q lies on $\overarc{OP}$ such that $\overarc{OQ} = \overarc{QP}$, what is the ratio of $\overarc{OQ}$ to $\overarc{PN}$?

   A. $\frac{1}{3}$

   B. $\frac{1}{2}$

   C. 1

   D. $\frac{2}{1}$

   E. $\frac{3}{1}$

A sketch would look like this:

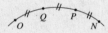

It is evident that $\overarc{OQ} = \overarc{PN}$, so the ratio is $\frac{1}{1}$, or 1. Or you could assign values on $\overarc{ON}$ such that $\overarc{OP} = 2\overarc{PN}$: $\overarc{OP}$ could equal 2, and $\overarc{PN}$ could equal 1. If Q lies on $\overarc{OP}$ such that $\overarc{OQ} = \overarc{QP}$, then $\overarc{OP}$ (2) is divided in half. So $\overarc{OQ} = 1$, and $\overarc{QP} = 1$. So the ratio of $\overarc{OQ}$ to $\overarc{PN}$ is 1 to 1. The correct answer is C.

---

3. What is the maximum number of milk cartons, each 2" wide by 3" long by 4" tall, that can be fit into a cardboard box with inside dimensions of 16" wide by 9" long by 8" tall?

   A. 12

   B. 18

   C. 20

   D. 24

   E. 48

Drawing a diagram, as shown below, may be helpful in envisioning the process of fitting the cartons into the box. Notice that 8 cartons will fit across the box, 3 cartons deep, and two "stacks" high:

$$8 \times 3 \times 2 = 48 \text{ cartons}$$

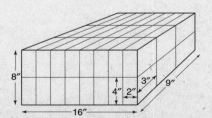

The correct answer is E.

4. If points $P(1, 1)$ and $Q(1, 0)$ lie on the same coordinate graph, which of the following must be true?

   I. P and Q are equidistant from the origin.
   II. P is farther from the origin than P is from Q.
   III. Q is farther from the origin than Q is from P.

   A. I only
   B. II only
   C. III only
   D. I and II only
   E. I and III only

First draw the coordinate graph and then plot the points as follows:

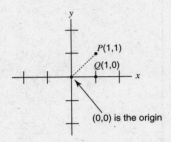

Only II is true. P is farther from the origin than P is from Q. The correct answer is B.

Mark in Diagrams

Marking in or labeling diagrams as you read the questions can save you valuable time. Marking can also give you insight into how to solve a problem because you will have the complete picture clearly in front of you.

Samples

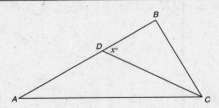

1. In the triangle above, CD is an angle bisector, angle ACD is 30°, and angle ABC is a right angle. What is the measurement of angle x in degrees?

   A. 30°
   B. 45°
   C. 60°
   D. 75°
   E. 80°

You should have read the problem and marked as follows: In the triangle above, *CD* is an angle bisector (*stop and mark in the drawing*), angle *ACD* is 30° (*stop and mark in the drawing*), and angle *ABC* is a right angle (*stop and mark in the drawing*). What is the measurement of angle *x* in degrees? (*Stop and mark in or circle what you are looking for in the drawing.*)

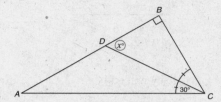

Now, with the drawing marked in, it is evident that, since angle *ACD* is 30°, then angle *BCD* is also 30° because they are formed by an angle bisector (divides an angle into two equal parts). Since angle *ABC* is 90° (right angle) and angle *BCD* is 30°, then angle *x* is 60° because there are 180° in a triangle.

$$180 - (90 + 30) = 60$$

The correct answer is C. *Always mark in diagrams as you read descriptions and information about them. This includes what you are looking for.*

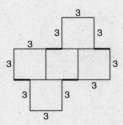

2. If each square in the figure above has a side of length 3, what is the perimeter?

   A. 12
   B. 14
   C. 21
   D. 30
   E. 36

Mark the known facts.

We now have a calculation for the perimeter: 30 *plus* the darkened parts. Now look carefully at the top two darkened parts. They will add up to 3. (Notice how the top square may slide over to illustrate that fact.)

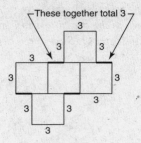

The same is true for the bottom darkened parts. They will add up to 3.

Thus, the total perimeter is 30 + 6 = 36, choice E.

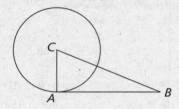

3. In the figure above, $\overline{AB}$ is tangent at A to the circle with center C at A with $\angle ACB = 60°$ and $AB = 12$. What is the radius of circle C?

A. 4
B. 6
C. $4\sqrt{3}$
D. $6\sqrt{3}$
E. Cannot be determined from the given information

As always, first circle or underline what you are looking for, in this case *radius of circle C*.

Next, mark in the diagram as follows.

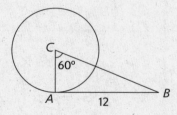

Since $\overline{AB}$ is tangent to the circle at A, $\angle A = 90°$ and $\angle B = 30°$.

So add the following information:

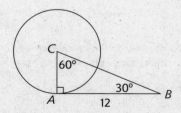

The radius of the circle is $\overline{AC}$ and since this is a 30-60-90 triangle the ratio of the sides are $1:2:\sqrt{3}$.

Therefore,
$$AB = \sqrt{3} \cdot AC$$

Now solve for AC algebraically as follows:

$$12 = \sqrt{3} \cdot AC$$
$$\frac{12}{\sqrt{3}} = AC$$
$$AC = \frac{12}{\sqrt{3}}$$

Multiplying by $\frac{\sqrt{3}}{\sqrt{3}}$:

$$AC = \frac{12}{\sqrt{3}} \cdot \frac{\sqrt{3}}{\sqrt{3}}$$
$$= \frac{12\sqrt{3}}{3}$$
$$= 4\sqrt{3}$$

The trigonometric solution is as follows:

$$\tan \angle ACB = \frac{AB}{AC}$$
$$\tan 60° = \frac{12}{AC}$$
$$\sqrt{3} = \frac{12}{AC}$$
$$\sqrt{3} \cdot AC = 12$$
$$AC = \frac{12}{\sqrt{3}} = 4\sqrt{3}$$

The correct answer is C. Marking the diagram can give you additional insight into the problem.

Even though the following information isn't given in the form of a diagram, take advantage of being allowed to write in the test booklet. Make whatever marks or notes that you feel will be helpful.

1, 3, 6, 10, 15 . . .

4. Which of the following is the next number in the series given above?

   A. 20
   B. 21
   C. 25
   D. 26
   E. 30

Some problems may ask you to identify a sequence of either numbers or figures. If numbers are given, look for an obvious pattern (odd numbers then even numbers, increasing, decreasing, etc.). You may wish to first check for a common difference between the numbers.

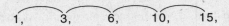

Notice that the pattern here is based on the difference between the numbers:

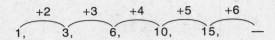

Therefore, the correct answer is B, 21.

Watch for Diagrams Not Drawn to Scale

Diagrams are drawn as accurately as possible, unless a diagram is labeled "not drawn to scale." That label is the tip-off that the diagram could be drawn differently or is out of proportion. In this case, mark the diagram and/or quickly redraw it differently. Marking and/or redrawing will give you insight into what information you really have about the diagram.

Sample

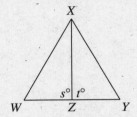

Note: Figure not drawn to scale.

1. In △WXY above, WX = XY. Which of the following must be true?

   A.   WZ = ZY
   B.   s = t
   C.   perimeter of △WXZ = perimeter of △ZXY
   D.   area of △WXZ = area of △ZXY
   E.   ∠XWZ = ∠XYZ

Before doing anything else, underline or circle *must be true*. Now mark the diagram as follows.

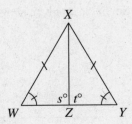

Next, since the figure is *not* drawn to scale, quickly redraw it another way that still conforms to the given information.

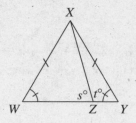

Notice that by looking at the way the figure is initially drawn, you might think that $WZ = ZY$ because they appear to be equal. But after you redraw the figure, you can see that WZ and ZY don't have to be equal, eliminating choice A.

The same can be noticed of s and t. They don't have to be equal, eliminating choice B.

A quick look at the redrawn figure will help you eliminate choice C as well, since it's evident that triangles WXZ and ZXY don't necessarily have equal perimeters.

You can also eliminate choice D because even though the heights of triangles WXZ and ZXY are equal, their bases could be different, so the areas could be different. This fact is also evident from your redrawing of the diagram.

Choice E is the correct answer because in any triangle, equal angles are across from equal sides. Your markings in the figure remind you that this is true.

Approximate

If it appears that extensive calculations are going to be necessary to solve a problem, check to see how far apart the choices are and then approximate. The reason for checking the answers first is to give you a guide to how freely you can approximate.

Sample

1. Which of the following is the best approximation of $\dfrac{(.899 \times 55)}{9.97}$ to the nearest tenth?

A. 49.1
B. 7.7
C. 4.9
D. 4.63
E. .5

Before starting any computations, take a glance at the answers to see how far apart they are. Notice that the only close answers are C and D. But D is not possible, since it is to the nearest hundredth, not tenth. Now, making some quick approximations, $.899 \cong 1$ and $9.97 \cong 10$, which leaves the problem in this form:

$$\frac{1 \times 55}{01} = \frac{55}{10} = 5.5$$

The closest answer is C. Therefore it is the correct answer. Notice that choices A and E are not reasonable. **You could also have used your calculator to obtain an exact answer and then rounded to the nearest tenth.**

Try Some Possibilities

Some questions will involve probability and possible combinations. If you don't know a formal method, try some possibilities. Set up what could happen. But set up only as much as you need to.

Samples

1. What is the probability of throwing two dice in one toss so that they total 11?

   A. $\frac{1}{6}$

   B. $\frac{1}{11}$

   C. $\frac{1}{18}$

   D. $\frac{1}{20}$

   E. $\frac{1}{36}$

You should simply list all the possible combinations resulting in 11, (5 + 6) and (6 + 5), and realize that the total possibilities are 36 (6 × 6). Thus the probability equals

$$\frac{\text{possibilities totaling } 11}{\text{total possibilities}} = \frac{2}{26} = \frac{1}{18}$$

The correct answer is C.

2. What is the probability of tossing a penny twice so that both times it lands heads up?

   A. $\frac{1}{8}$

   B. $\frac{1}{4}$

   C. $\frac{1}{3}$

   D. $\frac{1}{2}$

   E. $\frac{2}{3}$

The probability of throwing a head in one throw is

$$\frac{\text{chances of a head}}{\text{total chances}(1 \text{ head} + 1 \text{ tail})} = \frac{1}{2}$$

Since you are trying to throw a head twice, multiply the probability for the first toss $\left(\frac{1}{2}\right)$ times the probability for the second toss (again $\frac{1}{2}$). Thus, $\frac{1}{2} \times \frac{1}{2} = \frac{1}{4}$, and $\frac{1}{4}$ is the probability of throwing heads twice in two tosses. Another way of approaching this problem is to look at the total number of possible outcomes:

	First Toss	Second Toss
1.	H	H
2.	H	T
3.	T	H
4.	T	T

Thus, there are four different possible outcomes. There is only one way to throw two heads in two tosses. Thus, the probability of tossing two heads in two tosses is 1 out of 4 total outcomes, or $\frac{1}{4}$.

The correct answer is B.

---

3. How many combinations are possible if a person has 4 sports jackets, 5 shirts, and 3 pairs of slacks?

    A.   4
    B.   5
    C.   12
    D.   60
    E.   120

Since each of the 4 sports jackets may be worn with 5 different shirts, there are 20 possible combinations. These may be worn with each of the 3 pairs of slacks for a total of 60 possible combinations. Stated simply, $5 \times 4 \times 3 = 60$ possible combinations.

The correct answer is D.

Glance at the Choices

Some problems may not ask you to solve for a numerical answer or even an answer including variables. Rather, you may be asked to set up the equation or expression without doing any solving. A quick glance at the answer choices will help you know what is expected.

Samples

1. Which equation can be used to find the perimeter, P, of a rectangle that has a length of 18 feet and a width of 15 feet?

    A. $P = (18)(15)$
    B. $P = 18 + 15$
    C. $P = 2(15)(18)$
    D. $P = (2)15 + 18$
    E. $P = 2(15 + 18)$

The perimeter of a rectangle can be found by adding the length to the width and doubling this sum: $P = 2(15 + 18)$. The correct answer is E.

Harold's age is 3 years less than half Sue's age.

If Harold is 9 years old, how old is Sue?

2. Suppose S represents Sue's age. Which of the following equations can be used to find Sue's age?

   A. $9 = \frac{1}{2}(S) - 3$

   B. $9 - 3 = \frac{1}{2}(S)$

   C. $9 = 3 - \frac{1}{2}(S)$

   D. $3 - 9 = \frac{1}{2}(S)$

   E. $\frac{1}{2}(9) = S - 3$

Changing the word sentence into a number sentence (equation):

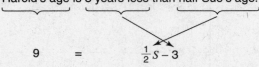

$$9 \qquad = \qquad \tfrac{1}{2}S - 3$$

The correct answer is A.

3. Rick is three times as old as Maria, and Maria is four years older than Leah. If Leah is z years old, what is Rick's age in terms of z?

   A. $3z + 4$
   B. $3z - 12$
   C. $3z + 12$
   D. $\dfrac{(z+4)}{3}$
   E. $\dfrac{(z-4)}{3}$

Since

$$z = \text{Leah's age}$$
$$z + 4 = \text{Maria's age}$$
$$3(z + 4) = \text{Rick's age}$$
$$3z + 12 = \text{Rick's age}$$

The correct answer is C.

Look for Definitions

In some problems, you may be given special symbols that you are unfamiliar with. Don't let these special symbols alarm you. They typically represent an operation or combination of operations that you are familiar with. Look for the definition of the special symbol or how it is used.

Sample

---

1. If $\odot$ is a binary operation such that $a \odot b$ is defined as $\dfrac{a^2 - b^2}{a^2 + b^2}$, then what is the value of $3 \odot 2$?

    A. $-\dfrac{5}{13}$

    B. $\dfrac{1}{13}$

    C. $\dfrac{1}{5}$

    D. $\dfrac{5}{13}$

    E. 1

The value of $a \odot b =$

$$\frac{a^2 - b^2}{a^2 + b^2}$$

Simply replacing a with 3 and b with 2 gives

$$\frac{3^2 - 2^2}{3^2 + 2^2} = \frac{9 - 4}{9 + 4} = \frac{5}{13}$$

The correct answer is D.

A Summary of Strategies for Multiple-Choice Math Questions

- Circle or underline.
- Pull out information.
- Work forward.
- Work backwards.
- Use your calculator.
- Substitute simple numbers.
- Use 10 or 100.
- Be reasonable.
- Draw or sketch diagrams and figures.
- Mark in or label diagrams.
- Watch for diagrams not drawn to scale.
- Approximate.
- Try some possible outcomes.
- Glance at the choices.
- Look for definitions.
- Finally, don't get stuck on any one problem!

Grid-In Questions

The new SAT grid-in question type is very similar to the familiar multiple-choice question except that you will now solve the problem and enter your answer by carefully marking the circles on a special grid. You will not be selecting from a group of possible answers.

Since you will not be selecting from a group of possible answers, you should be extra careful in checking and double-checking your answer. Your calculator can be useful in checking answers. Also, keep in mind that answers to grid-in questions are given either full credit or no credit. There is no partial credit. No points are deducted for incorrect answers in this section. That is, there is no penalty for guessing or attempting a grid-in, so at least take a guess.

Ability Tested

The grid-in questions test your ability to solve mathematical problems involving arithmetic, algebra I and II, geometry, data interpretation, basic statistics and probability and word problems by using problem-solving insight, logic, and application of basic skills.

Basic Skills Necessary

The basic skills necessary to do well on this question type include high school algebra I and II and intuitive or informal geometry. No calculus is necessary. Skills in arithmetic and basic algebra I and II, along with some logical insight into problem-solving situations, are also necessary to do well on this question type. Understanding the rules and procedures for gridding in answers is important.

Before you begin working grid-in questions, it is important that you become familiar with the grid-in rules and procedures and learn to grid accurately. Let's start explaining the rules and procedures by analyzing the directions.

Directions with Analysis

The following questions require you to solve the problem and enter your answer by carefully marking the circles on the special grid. Examples of the appropriate way to mark the grid follow. (Comments in parentheses have been added to help you understand how to grid properly.)

Answer: 3.7

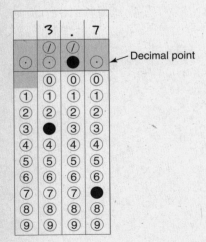

Decimal point

(Notice that the decimal point is located in the shaded row, just above the numbers. Also notice that the answer has been written in above the gridding. You should always write in your answer, but the filled-in circles are most important because they are the ones scored.)

Answer: $\frac{1}{2}$

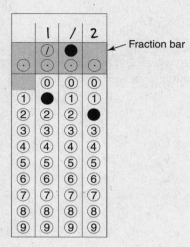

Fraction bar

(Notice that the slash mark (/) indicates a fraction bar. This fraction bar is located in the shaded row and just above the decimal point in the two middle columns. Obviously, a fraction bar cannot be in the first or last column.)

Answer: $1\frac{1}{2}$

Do not grid in mixed numbers in the form of mixed numbers. **Always** change mixed numbers to improper fractions or decimals.

Change to 1.5 or Change to $\frac{3}{2}$

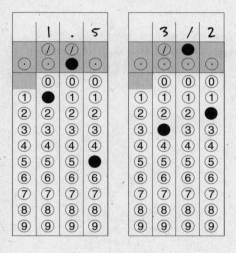

(Either an improper fraction or a decimal is acceptable. Never grid in a mixed number because it will always be misread. For example, $1\frac{1}{2}$ will be read by the computer doing the scoring as $\frac{11}{2}$.)

Answer: 123

Space permitting, answers may start in any column. Each grid-answer below is correct.

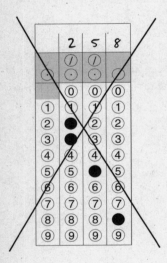

(You should try to grid your answers from right to left, learning to be consistent as you practice. But space permitting, you may start in any column.)

Note: Circles must be filled in correctly to receive credit. Mark only one circle in each column. No credit will be given if more than one circle in a column is marked. Example:

Answer: 258 (no credit)

(Filling in more than one circle in a column is equivalent to selecting more than one answer in a multiple-choice question. This type of answer fill-in will never receive any credit. Be careful to avoid this mistake.)

Answer: $\frac{8}{9}$

Accuracy of decimals: Always enter the most accurate decimal value that the grid will accommodate. For example: An answer such as .8888 . . . can be gridded as .888 or .889. Gridding this value as .8, .88, or .89 is considered inaccurate and therefore not acceptable. The acceptable grid-ins of $\frac{8}{9}$ are

$\frac{8}{9}$ .888   .889

(Review "accuracy of decimals" a second time. Notice that you must be as accurate as the grid allows.)

Be sure to write your answers in the boxes at the top of the circles before doing your gridding. Although writing out the answers above the columns is not required, it is very important to ensure accuracy. Even though some problems may have more than one correct answer, grid only one answer. Grid-in questions contain no negative answers.

(Fractions can be reduced to lowest terms, but it is not required as long as they will fit in the grid. You are not required to grid a zero before a fraction. For example, either .2 or 0.2 is acceptable. If your answer is zero, you are required only to grid a zero in one column. Important: If you decide to change an answer, be sure to erase the old gridded answer completely.)

Practice Grid-Ins

The following practice exercises will help you become familiar with the gridding process. Properly filled in grids are given following each exercise. Hand write and grid in the answers given.

Exercise 1

Answer: 4.5

Answer: .7

Answer: 22.7

Answer: $\frac{1}{3}$

Answer: $\frac{4}{7}$

Answer: $\frac{9}{2}$

Answer: $3\frac{1}{4}$

Answer: $4\frac{1}{2}$

Answer: $9\frac{1}{7}$

Answers to Exercise 1

Answer: 4.5

Answer: .7

Answer: 22.7

or $\frac{9}{2}$

or $\frac{7}{10}$

Answer: $\frac{1}{3}$

Answer: $\frac{4}{7}$

Answer: $\frac{9}{2}$

or .333

or .571

or 4.5

Answer: $3\frac{1}{4}$

Answer: $4\frac{1}{2}$

Answer: $9\frac{1}{7}$

$3\frac{1}{4}$ must be changed to $\frac{13}{4}$ or 3.25 $4\frac{1}{2}$ must be changed to $\frac{9}{2}$ or 4.5 $9\frac{1}{7}$ must be changed to $\frac{64}{7}$ or 9.14

Exercise 2

Answer: 0

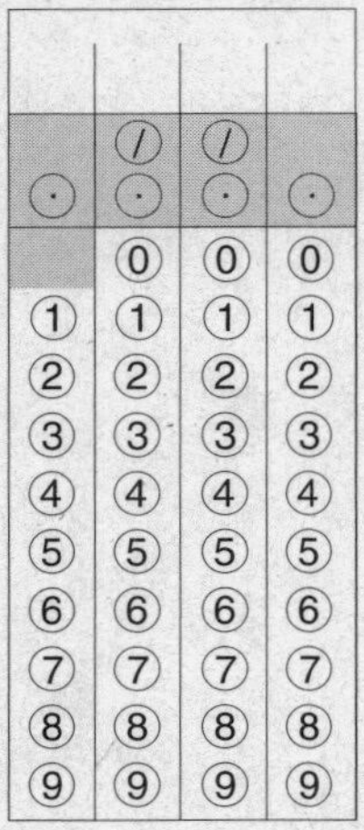

Answer: 39

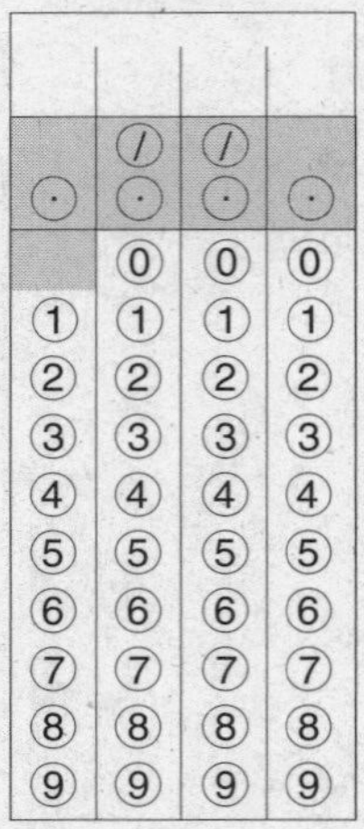

Answer: 1,542

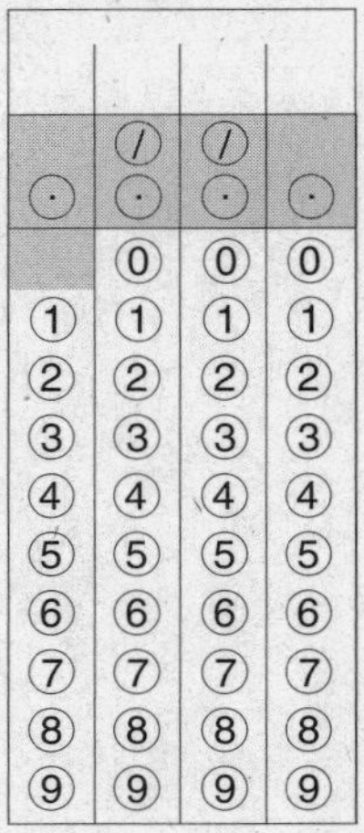

Answer: $7\frac{1}{3}$

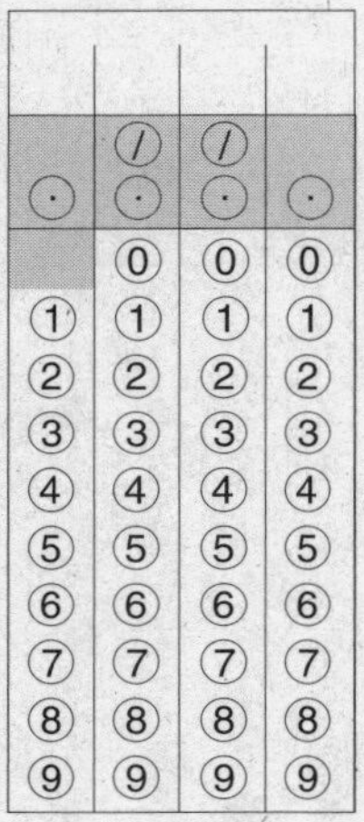

Answer: 1

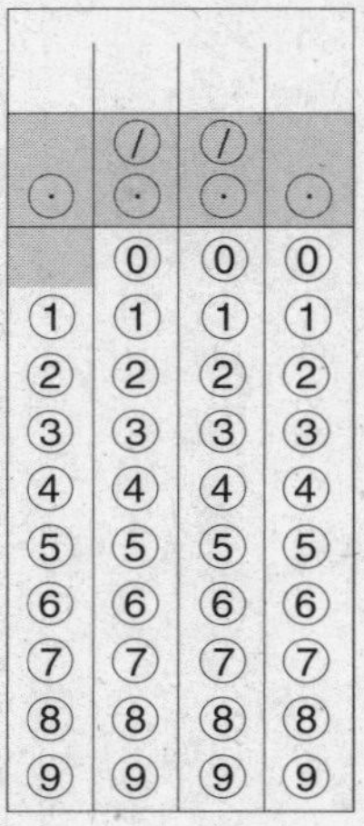

Answer: 685

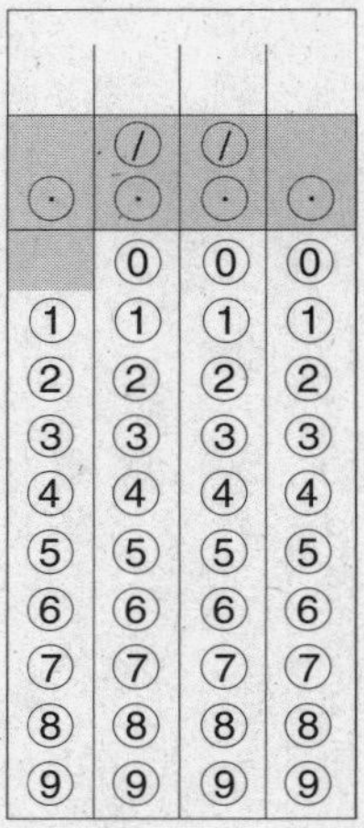

Answer: .7272

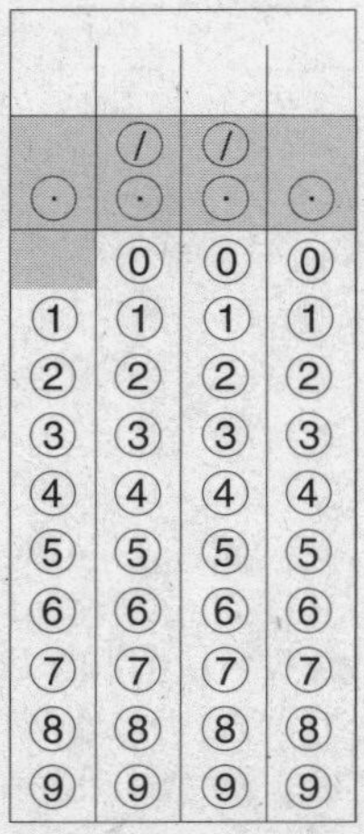

Answer: .666 . . .

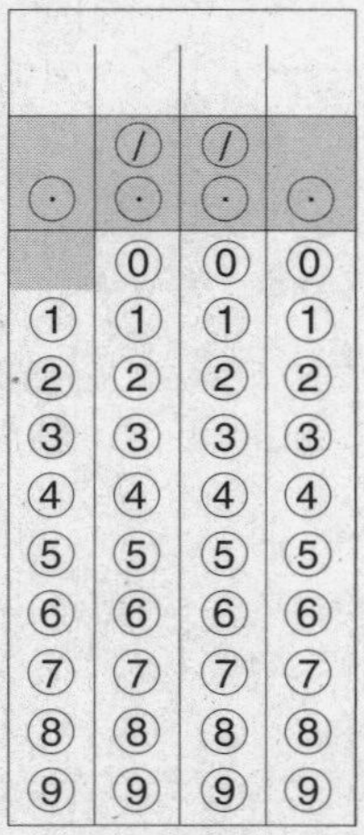

Answer: .222 . . .

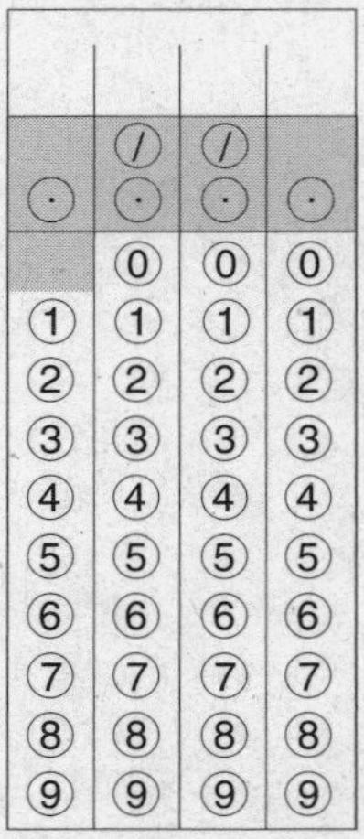

Answers to Exercise 2

Answer: 0

Answer: 39

Answer: 1,542

Disregard the comma (,)

Answer: $7\frac{1}{3}$

Answer: 1

Answer: 685

$7\frac{1}{3}$ must be changed to $\frac{22}{3}$ or 7.33

Answer: .7272

Answer: .666 . . .

Answer: .222 . . .

.72 or .73 will **not** be correct

.666 will also be correct or $\frac{2}{3}$ (.66, .67, .7, or .6 will **not** be correct)

$\frac{2}{9}$ will also be correct (.2 or .22 will **not** be correct)

Suggested Approaches with Samples

Most of the following strategies, described and suggested in the multiple-choice section, will also work on grid-in questions.

- Circle or underline what you are looking for.
- Substitute numbers for variables to understand a problem.
- Try simple numbers to solve a problem.
- Pull information out of word problems.
- Draw/sketch diagrams or simple figures.
- Mark in diagrams.
- Use your calculator when appropriate to solve a problem.

You should also

- Make sure that your answer is reasonable.
- Jot down your scratch work or calculations in the space provided in your test booklet.
- Approximate or use your calculator to check your answers if time permits.

There are some specific items and strategies that should be noted for grid-in questions:

- There is no penalty for guessing on grid-in questions. Although it may be difficult to get an answer correct by simply writing in a wild guess, you should not be afraid to fill in your answer—even if you think it's wrong.
- Make sure to answer what is being asked. If the question asks for percent and you get an answer of 57%, grid in <u>57</u>, not .57. Or if a question asks for dollars and you get an answer of 75 cents, remember that 75 cents is .75 dollar. Grid in <u>.75</u> *not* 75.
- In some questions, more than one answer is possible. Grid in only one answer. If you work out a question and get the answer $x > 5$, grid in 6, or 7, or 8 but *not more than one* of them.
- Some questions will have a note in parentheses ( ) that says, *Disregard the % sign when gridding your answer,* or *Disregard the $ sign when gridding your answer.* Follow the directions. If your answer is 68%, grid in <u>68</u>, or if it's $95, grid in <u>95</u>.

- Answers that are mixed numbers such as $3\frac{1}{2}$ or $7\frac{1}{4}$ must be changed to improper fractions ($3\frac{1}{2} = \frac{7}{2}$, $7\frac{1}{4} = \frac{29}{4}$) or decimals ($3\frac{1}{2} = 3.5$, $7\frac{1}{4} = 7.25$) before being gridded. Improper fractions or decimals can be gridded. Mixed numbers cannot. The scoring system cannot distinguish between $3\frac{1}{2}$ and $\frac{31}{2}$.

- Since you cannot work from answer choices that are given or eliminate given choices, you will have to actually work out each answer. The use of your calculator on some problems in this section could enhance the speed and accuracy of your work.

- Writing in your answer in the space provided at the top of the grid is for your benefit only. It's wise to always write in your answer, but remember, the grid-in answer is the only one scored. Be sure to grid accurately and properly.

Following are some sample grid-in questions. Consider for each how you would grid in the answer in the proper places on the answer sheet. Also consider when it would be appropriate to use a calculator to help you work out problems and to check the accuracy of your work.

Acceptable Answers

Fraction and decimal forms are acceptable.

Sample

1. If $\frac{1}{3}z - \frac{1}{4} = \frac{1}{2}$, then $z =$

To solve for z you could multiply both sides of the equation by the lowest common denominator of 12 to get rid of the fractions as follows:

$$12\left(\frac{1}{3}z - \frac{1}{4}\right) = 12\left(\frac{1}{2}\right)$$
$$4z - 3 = 6$$
$$4z = 9$$
$$z = \frac{9}{4} = 2.25$$

The correct answer is $\frac{9}{4}$ or 2.25. (Either answer will receive full credit.)

Grid Carefully

Your gridding is what counts. Your written-in answer is for your benefit. Be accurate.

Sample

1. Acme Taxi lists the following rates on its door:

$1.20 for the first $\frac{1}{4}$ mile

$0.90 for each additional $\frac{1}{4}$ mile

$6.00 per hour for waiting

At these rates, if there was a 15-minute wait at the bank, how much will a 1.5-mile taxi trip cost? (Disregard the $ sign when gridding your answer.)

You should solve the problem as follows:

At \$6.00 per hour, a 15-minute ($\frac{1}{4}$ hour) wait will cost \$1.50. The first $\frac{1}{4}$ mile will cost \$1.20. The remaining $1\frac{1}{4}$, or $\frac{5}{4}$ miles will cost 5(.90) = \$4.50. The total bill will be the sum.

$$\$1.50 + \$1.20 + \$4.50 = \$7.20$$

The correct answer is \$7.20, gridded as 7.20. (You would **not** get credit for gridding 7.00, 7, 72, or 720, even if you had written the right answer above the grid circles.)

Answer the Question

Make sure that you answer the question that is being asked. Your answer must be in the units asked for.

Sample

> **1.** If Gina completed $\frac{2}{3}$ of her project in 12 days, how many days are needed to do the entire project?

To solve, let n = number of days to complete the project. Then

$$\frac{2}{3} \cdot n = 12$$
$$n = 12 \div \frac{2}{3}$$
$$= \frac{12}{1} \cdot \frac{3}{2}$$
$$= \frac{36}{2}$$
$$= 18$$

The question asks for the number of days to complete the project. Therefore, 432 hours or $2\frac{4}{7}$ weeks would not be correct.

The correct answer is 18.

Grid Only One Answer

Even if more than one answer is possible, grid in only one answer.

Sample

> **1.** If $-4x + 12 > -16$ and $x > 0$, then what is one possible integer value for x?

You could solve the problem as follows:

$$-4x + 12 > -16$$

Add -12 to each side

$$-4x + 12 + (-12) > -16 + (-12)$$

leaving

$$-4x > -28$$

Dividing each side by (–4) gives

$$x < 7$$

(Note: The inequality sign is reversed.)

The correct answer is 1, 2, 3, 4, 5, or 6. (Any of these answers would give you full credit. Do not grid more than one of them, however.)

Reduced Fractions Not Necessary

Fractions do not have to be reduced as long as they fit into the grid. (You probably should be in the habit of reducing them anyway, although that's not required here.)

Sample

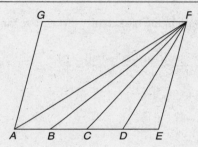

1. In the preceding parallelogram, if *AB* = *BC* = *CD* = *DE,* what is the ratio of the area of triangle *ABF* + triangle *BCF* to the area of triangle *CDF* + triangle *DEF?*

You could mark the diagram and solve the problem as follows:

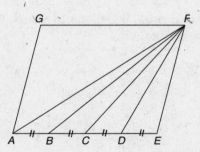

In parallelogram *AEFG,* if all the triangles marked have the same base and they all meet at *F* (giving them all the same height because the formula for the area of a triangle is $\frac{1}{2} \times$ base $\times$ height), then they all have equal areas. Therefore, the ratio of the area of triangle *ABF* + triangle *BCF* to the area of triangle *CDF* + triangle *DEF* is 2/2.

The correct answer is 1/1. (A 2/2 answer would also be acceptable because you don't have to reduce fractions.)

Follow Directions About Signs

Follow directions when you're told to disregard the sign.

Sample

> **1.** A basketball is fully inflated to 24 pounds per square inch. A football is fully inflated to 16 pounds per square inch. The air pressure in the basketball is what percentage of the air pressure in the football? (Disregard the % sign when gridding your answer.)

You could have worked the problem as follows:

To compute percentage, simply plug into the formula

$$\frac{\text{is number}}{\text{of number}} = \text{percentage}$$

Note that the question reads: The air pressure in the basketball is what percentage of the air pressure in the football? Therefore,

$$\frac{\text{air pressure in basketball}}{\text{air pressure in football}} = \frac{24}{16} = 1.5 = 150\%$$

The correct answer is 150%, which is gridded as <u>150</u>.

Answers Must Fit Grid

Change your answer into a form to fit the grid if necessary.

Sample

> **1.** A collection of coins consists of 19 quarters, 21 dimes, and 16 nickels. What percentage of the coins is dimes? (Disregard the % sign when gridding your answer.)

You could solve the problem as follows: There is a total of 56 coins, of which 21 are dimes. The percentage of dimes (d) is

Set up a ratio:

$$\frac{d}{100} = \frac{21}{56}$$

Reduce one side:

$$\frac{d}{100} = \frac{3}{8}$$

Cross multiply:

$$8d = (3)(100)$$
$$8d = 300$$

Divide by 8:

$$d = \frac{300}{8} = 37\frac{4}{8}$$

$$d = 37\frac{1}{2} = 37.5$$

The correct answer is 37.5. (Even though your answer could have been $37\frac{1}{2}$, this answer could not have been placed in the grid.)

Calculators Can Help

Use the calculator to your advantage. Work out calculations and check your answers.

Samples

> **1.** A speed of 75 miles per hour is approximately equivalent to how many feet per second?

You could solve this problem as follows:

$$75 \text{ miles per hour} = \frac{75 \text{ miles}}{1 \text{ hour}}$$

Since 1 mile = 5280 feet and 1 hour = 60 minutes = 3600 seconds,

$$\frac{75 \text{ miles}}{1 \text{ hour}} = \frac{75 \times 5280 \text{ feet}}{1 \times 3600 \text{ seconds}}$$
$$= 110 \text{ feet per second}$$

The correct answer is 110.

> **2.** What is $\frac{3}{4}\%$ of 540?

You could solve this question as follows:

$$\frac{3}{4}\% \text{ of } 540 = \left(\frac{3}{4}\%\right)(540)$$
$$= (0.75\%)(540)$$
$$= (0.0075)(540)$$
$$= 4.05$$

The correct answer is 4.05.

Bowler	Score
1	148
2	163
3	157
4	148
5	181
6	164
7	157
8	131
9	182

3. The preceding chart shows how each of nine bowlers scored in the first game of a bowling tournament. Their average score was how much greater than their median score?

To find the mean, simply total all scores and divide by 9. This step would give you $1431 \div 9 = 159$. To find the median, you must put the scores in order and count to the middle (the fifth spot).

131,148,148,157, <u>157</u>,163,164,181,182

The median is 157: $159 - 157 = 2$

The correct answer is 2.

A Summary of Strategies for Grid-In Questions

■ Realize that you receive no penalty for guessing.

■ Know the grid-in rules and procedures.

■ Change mixed numbers to improper fractions or decimals.

■ Understand that fractions and decimal forms are acceptable.

■ Write in your answer at the top, and remember that the grid-in part is scored.

■ Grid accurately and properly.

■ Be sure to answer the question being asked.

■ Grid in only one answer, even if more than one is possible.

■ Know that fractions do not have to be reduced if they fit.

■ Follow directions carefully.

■ Change your answer to fit the grid.

■ Use your calculator.

■ Draw figures.

■ Mark in diagrams.

■ Make sure that your answer is reasonable.

■ Jot down scratch work in the test booklet.

■ Check your answers.

■ Don't get stuck on any one problem!

Charts, Tables, and Graphs

The Mathematics sections of the new SAT also include some questions about charts, tables, and graphs. You should know how to (1) read and understand information that is given; (2) calculate, analyze, and apply the information given; and (3) spot trends and predict some future trends. When you encounter a chart, table, or graph, you should

- Focus on understanding the important information given.
- Not memorize the information, but rather refer to it when you need to.
- Review any additional information given with a graph (headings, scale factors, and legends, for example).
- Read the question and possible choices, noticing key words.
- Look for obvious large changes, high points, low points, and trends. Obvious information often leads to an answer.

Charts and Tables

Charts and tables are often used to give an organized picture of information, or data. Be sure that you understand what is given. Column headings and line items show important information. These titles give the numbers meaning.

Samples

Questions 1 and 2 are based on the following chart:

Burger Sales for the Week of August 8 to August 14		
Day	*Hamburgers*	*Cheeseburgers*
Sunday	120	92
Monday	85	80
Tuesday	77	70
Wednesday	74	71
Thursday	75	72
Friday	91	88
Saturday	111	112

1. On which day were the most burgers (hamburgers and cheeseburgers) sold?

    A. Saturday
    B. Monday
    C. Thursday
    D. Friday
    E. Sunday

Working from the answers is probably the easiest method of answering this question:

    A. Saturday   111 + 112 = <u>223</u>
    B. Monday   85 + 80 = 165
    C. Thursday   75 + 72 = 147
    D. Friday   91 + 88 = 179
    E. Sunday   120 + 92 = 212

The correct answer is A.

Another method is to *approximate* the answers.

2. On how many days were more hamburgers sold than cheeseburgers?

    A. 7
    B. 6
    C. 5
    D. 4
    E. 3

Hamburgers outsold cheeseburgers every day except Saturday. The correct answer is B.

Graphs

Information can be displayed in many ways. The three basic types of graphs you should know are bar graphs, line graphs, and pie graphs (or pie charts). You should also be familiar with a graph called the scatter plot.

Bar Graphs

Bar graphs convert the information in a chart into separate bars or columns. Some graphs list numbers along one edge and list places, dates, people, or things (individual categories) along another edge. Always try to determine the relationship between the columns in a graph or chart.

Sample

1. The preceding bar graph shows that Candidate 1 has how many more delegates committed than Candidate 2?

    A. 150
    B. 200
    C. 250
    D. 400
    E. 550

Notice that the graph shows the Number of Delegates Committed to Each Candidate, with the numbers given along the bottom of the graph in increases of 200. The names are listed along the left side. Candidate 1 has approximately 800 delegates (possibly a few more). The bar graph for Candidate 2 stops about three quarters of the way between 400 and 600. Consider that halfway between 400 and 600 is 500, so Candidate 2 is at about 550:

$$800 - 550 = 250.$$

The correct answer is C.

Line Graphs

Line graphs convert data into points on a grid. These points are then connected to show a relationship among the items, dates, and times, for example. Notice the slopes of the lines connecting the points. These lines show increases and decreases. The sharper the slope *upward*, the greater the *increase*. The sharper the slope *downward*, the greater the *decrease*. Line graphs can show trends, or changes, in data over a period of time.

Samples

Questions 1 and 2 are based on the following graph.

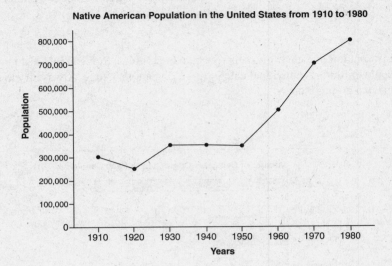

Native American Population in the United States from 1910 to 1980

1. In which of the following years were there about 500,000 Native Americans?

   A. 1930
   B. 1940
   C. 1950
   D. 1960
   E. 1970

The information along the left side of the graph shows the number of Native Americans in increases of 100,000. The bottom of the graph shows the years from 1910 to 1980. Notice that in 1960 about 500,000 Native Americans were in the United States. Using the edge of a sheet of paper as a straight edge or ruler helps you see that the dot in the 1960 column lines up with 500,000 on the left. The correct answer is D.

2. During which of the following time periods was there a decrease in the Native American population?

   A. 1910 to 1920
   B. 1920 to 1930
   C. 1930 to 1940
   D. 1960 to 1970
   E. 1970 to 1980

Because the slope of the line goes down from 1910 to 1920, there must have been a decrease. If you read the actual numbers, you will notice a decrease from 300,000 to 250,000. The correct answer is A.

Circle Graphs, or Pie Charts

A circle graph, or pie chart, shows the relationship between the whole circle (100%) and the various slices that represent portions of that 100%. The larger the slice, the higher the percentage.

Samples

Questions 1 and 2 are based on the following circle graph.

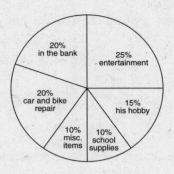

How John spends his monthly paycheck

---

1. If John receives $100 on this month's paycheck, how much will he put in the bank?

 A. $2
 B. $20
 C. $35
 D. $60
 E. $80

John puts 20% of his income in the bank, and 20% of $100 is $20, so he will put $20 in the bank. The correct answer is B.

---

2. What is the ratio of the amount of money John spends on his hobby to the amount he puts in the bank?

 A. $\frac{1}{6}$

 B. $\frac{1}{2}$

 C. $\frac{5}{8}$

 D. $\frac{5}{7}$

 E. $\frac{3}{4}$

To answer this question, you must use the information in the graph to make a ratio:

$$\frac{\text{his hobby}}{\text{in the bank}} = \frac{15\%}{20\%} = \frac{15}{20} = \frac{3}{4}$$

Notice that the ratio 15% / 20% reduces to $\frac{3}{4}$. The correct answer is E.

Scatter Plot

A *scatter plot* is a graph representing a set of data and showing a relationship or connection between the two quantities given. The graph is typically placed in one part of a coordinate plane (the upper right quarter, called Quadrant I). When the data is placed on the scatter plot, usually a relationship can be seen. If the points appear to form a line, a linear relationship is suggested.

If the line goes up to the right, that is, one quantity increases as another increases, then the relationship is called *a positive correlation*. For example:

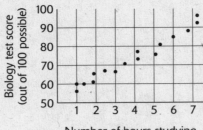

If the line goes down to the right, that is, one quantity decreases as another increases, then the relationship is called a *negative correlation*. For example:

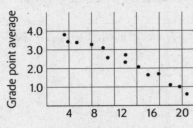

If the data does not appear to show any line or any relationship between the quantities, the scatter plot is said to show *no correlation*. For example:

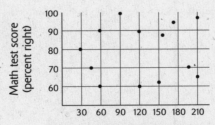

A Summary of Strategies
for Charts, Tables, and Graphs

■ Examine the entire graph, noticing labels and headings.

■ Focus on the information given.

■ Look for major changes—high points, low points, and trends.

■ Don't memorize the chart, table, or graph; refer to it.

■ Skimming questions can be helpful.

■ Circle or underline important words in the question.

■ Pay special attention to which part of the chart, table, or graph the question is referring to.

■ If you don't understand the graph, reread the labels and headings.

■ Don't get stuck on any one question!

Introduction to the Writing Section—Essay

The writing section of the new SAT requires every student to compose an essay on an assigned topic. This essay assignment will be the first section of the test. The prompt will contain a short paragraph featuring either a single quote or a pair of quotes about an issue that you are asked to discuss, supporting your ideas with an example or examples from your reading, personal experiences, or observations. The essay question generates a raw score that ranges from 2–12. (This raw score is the sum of the scores of two readers who each assign a score of 1–6.) You will have 25 minutes to complete the essay.

Ability Tested

The essay section of the exam tests your ability to read a topic carefully, to organize your ideas before you write, and to write a clear, well-written essay.

Basic Skills Necessary

This section requires good high school level writing, reading, and reasoning skills.

Directions

Writing—Essay

Time: 25 minutes

1 Essay Question

You have 25 minutes to plan and write an essay on the topic below. DO NOT WRITE ON ANOTHER TOPIC. AN ESSAY ON ANOTHER TOPIC WILL NOT BE SCORED.

The essay is intended to give you the chance to show your writing skills. Be sure to express your ideas on the topic clearly and effectively. The quality of your writing is much more important than the quantity, but to cover the topic adequately, you may want to write more than one paragraph. Be specific.

Your essay must be written on the two lined pages provided. You will not be given any additional paper. If you keep your handwriting to a reasonable size, write on every line, and avoid wide margins, you should have enough space to complete your essay.

Directions: Read the following paragraph and assignment carefully. Then prepare and write a persuasive essay. Be sure to support your reasons with specific examples that will make your essay more effective.

> "Work experience is the best teacher," say many sociologists. With this in mind, some parents encourage their high school students to get an after-school or weekend job. Other parents cite the importance of getting good grades to discourage their high school students from getting an after-school or weekend job.

Assignment: Which parents do you agree with? Using an example or examples from your reading, personal experiences, or observations, write an essay to support your position.

THE PROCTOR WILL ANNOUNCE WHEN 25 MINUTES HAVE PASSED. AT THAT TIME, YOU MUST STOP WRITING. IF YOU FINISH YOUR ESSAY BEFORE 25 MINUTES HAVE PASSED, YOU MAY NOT GO ON TO ANY OTHER SECTION OF THE EXAM. THE PROCTOR WILL ANNOUNCE WHEN TO START THE NEXT SECTION.

Analysis of Directions

1. You have 25 minutes to plan and write an essay on one assigned topic. You will have space for writing notes to help you organize your thoughts. (These notes will not be read by the persons grading your exam.)

2. Notice that this topic, or prompt, features a quote about an issue to which you are asked to respond. It is written with the intent that you will be able to respond quickly regardless of your background or interests.

3. A topic, or prompt, could feature a pair of quotes (two quotes) about an issue.

4. The assignment will ask you to give your view on a topic. Support your point of view with reasoning and specific details or examples.

5. Some assignments will include a "gloss" or quick paraphrase of the topic's main idea. This "gloss" is meant to assist you if you are not familiar with the quote or topic.

6. Spend 3 or 4 minutes making your notes and organizing your thoughts. Spend about 20 minutes writing your essay. Spend 1 or 2 minutes proofreading your essay.

7. Make sure that the essay you write is on the topic given.

8. The general instructions include the sentence suggesting that "you may want to write more than one paragraph." This remark is a polite way of saying that if you expect to score well, you had better write more than one paragraph. Very short essays usually receive very low scores. Aim for at least three paragraphs.

9. Be specific. Your readers are not, as you may suppose, combing your essay for split infinitives. They are looking for specific details, for concrete evidence of some kind used to support your points.

10. Don't use excessively large writing, don't leave wide margins, and don't skip any lines.

11. Remember: Your essay should be *clear* and *effective*.

Scoring the Essay

Your essay will be scored by experienced and trained high school and college teachers who teach English, writing, or language arts courses. Two teachers will score your essay on a 1–6 scale (6 is the highest score). The two readers will not know each other's scores. If their scores are more than two points apart, your essay will go to a third reader. The essay score of 2–12 will be scaled and factored in with the writing multiple-choice sections to give an overall writing skills score ranging from 200–800.

Analyzing the Scores

Since you have only 25 minutes to plan and write the essay, graders do not allow minor errors of grammar or mechanics to affect the score. The essays scored at 6 will not be errorless—they are, after all, first drafts—but they will be superior in content, organization, and development.

Score of 6

These clear and consistently competent essays have only minor errors and are characterized by the following:

- effective and insightful coverage of the tasks required by the exam question
- good organization and development, with relevant supporting details
- command of standard written English with a range of vocabulary and sentence variety

Score of 5

These competent essays have occasional errors or lapses in quality and are characterized by the following:

- effective coverage of the tasks required by the exam question
- generally good organization and development, with some supporting details
- good handling of standard written English with some range of vocabulary and sentence variety

Score of 4

These adequately competent essays have occasional errors or lapses in quality and are characterized by the following:

- coverage of the tasks required by the exam question
- adequate organization and development with some supporting details
- adequate handling of standard written English, but with minimal sentence variety and some grammar or diction errors

Score of 3

These marginal papers are characterized by the following:

- failure to fully cover the required tasks
- weak organization and/or development
- failure to use relevant supporting detail
- several errors of grammar, diction, and sentence structure

Score of 2

These inadequate papers are characterized by the following:

- failure to cover the assignment
- poor organization and development
- lack of supporting detail
- frequent errors of grammar, diction, and sentence structure

Score of 1

These incompetent papers are characterized by the following:

- failure to cover the assignment
- very poor organization and development
- errors of grammar, diction, and sentence structure so frequent as to interfere with meaning
- extreme brevity or shortness

There are a number of ways to approach writing a timed essay. If you've been practicing for this part of the exam in your English class, and you and your teacher are satisfied with the way you handle a 25-minute essay, you can skip or skim this section and continue to write your essays your way. If you aren't confident with your technique or wish to review the process with a few successful techniques, then read this section carefully.

Reviewing the Writing Process

For any timed writing task, you should envision three steps leading to the finished product:

1. Preparing to write (prewriting)
2. Writing
3. Proofreading (editing)

Preparing to Write (Prewriting)

Read the topic and the assignment very carefully. Circle or underline key words to help you focus on the assigned task. Reread the assignment. If there are several tasks given, number them and write them down. Let the nature of the assignment determine the structure of your essay.

Inventing and organizing information on short notice, given only a few minutes, can be difficult unless you are ready with an effective technique. Take time to organize your thoughts on paper before writing. The three basic techniques are brainstorming, clustering, and outlining.

Brainstorming

The process of creating and accumulating ideas and examples is called "brainstorming." Brainstorming is simply jotting down in the scratch area provided as many thoughts, ideas, and possibilities as you can remember, invent, or otherwise bring to mind to address the topic. Neatness, order, and spelling do not matter at this point.

After generating as many ideas or examples as you can within a few minutes, assess and organize your notes. Remember that development relies on specific examples: Decide which examples best enable you to support your points. Eliminate (cross out) those you don't wish to use, and number those you'll want to address in your response. Add any notes regarding more specific details or new thoughts that come to mind. However, don't worry about developing everything completely, because only you use these planning notes. Your time will be better spent developing these points in your writing and not in your notes.

Clustering

"Clustering" is a technique well suited to the timed essay. Use clustering as a way of organizing your thoughts before you write. Clustering provides a way to put all of your thoughts down on paper before you write so that you can quickly see the structure of the whole paper.

> "Work experience is the best teacher," say many sociologists. With this in mind, some parents encourage their high school students to get an after-school or weekend job. Other parents cite the importance of getting good grades to discourage their high school students from getting an after-school or weekend job.

Assignment: Which parents do you agree with? Using an example or examples from your reading, personal experiences, or observations, write an essay to support your position.

After you choose a topic, write it down in the prewriting area (given under the actual topic question) and draw a circle around that topic:

For a few moments, think of all the elements of that side of the issue and connect them to the central topic cluster:

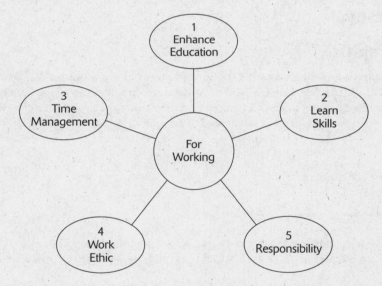

You can then number the parts of the cluster to give an order to your thoughts. You don't have to use all the elements of your cluster.

Outlining

Another technique well suited to the timed essay is the use of a simple, informal outline. A formal outline (using I., II., III., A., B., C., etc.) is not recommended and is not necessary. Your outline is meant to help you organize your thoughts and should be kept simple.

Introduction
> Working Beneficial
>> Learn Skills
>> Enhance education

Discussion or Body
> Learning Skills—Time management
> Enhance education—develop good work ethic

Conclusion or Summary
> Working depends on student
> Students can gain a lot

Notice that this outline is informal, but the basic parts, **Introduction, Discussion,** and **Conclusion,** help you focus and organize your response.

Remember, spend about 3 or 4 minutes prewriting and organizing your ideas before you start writing.

Writing the Essay

Opening Paragraph

A strong opening paragraph is essential for a well-developed response. One easy-to-master, yet extremely effective, type of introduction is a GENERALIZE-FOCUS-SURVEY structure. In this three- to four-sentence paragraph, the first sentence *generalizes* about the given topic, the second sentence *focuses* on what you have chosen to discuss, and the last one or two sentences *survey the particulars* you intend to present.

Remember:

- **Generalize**—address the question or topic
- **Focus**—state your position
- **Survey**—mention the points you will discuss (in order)

An effective first paragraph tells your reader what to expect in the body of the response. The GENERALIZE-FOCUS-SURVEY paragraph points toward the specifics you will discuss and suggests the order in which you will discuss them.

Body or Discussion

Writing the body of the response involves presenting specific details and examples that relate to the aspects you introduced in the first paragraph. The body may consist of one long paragraph or several short paragraphs. If you choose to break your discussion into several paragraphs, make sure that each paragraph consists of at least three sentences. Very short paragraphs may make your response appear insubstantial and scattered.

Be realistic about how much you can write. Although the readers want you to support your points adequately, they understand that you must write concisely to finish in time. Providing at least one substantial example, or "for instance," is important for each aspect you discuss in the body of your response.

Conclusion

As you prepare to write the conclusion, you should pay special attention to time. Having a formal conclusion to your response is unnecessary, but a conclusion should function to (1) complete your response to the question, (2) add information that you failed to introduce earlier, or (3) point toward the future.

Proofreading (Editing)

Always allow a few minutes to proofread your essay for errors in grammar, usage, and spelling. If you detect an error, either erase it cleanly or simply line it out carefully and insert the correction neatly. Keep in mind, both while you are writing and while you are correcting, that your handwriting should be legible. Even though readers are instructed to ignore the quality of handwriting, if the paper is too difficult to read, they may get a negative impression of the essay.

A Specific Approach: The "Why Essay"

One good way to approach a question that asks you to explain, analyze, or evaluate is to use a **"why essay"** format. A "why essay" is built around a thesis sentence. The thesis sentence begins with your opinion followed by the word "because" and then a list of the most important reasons the opinion is valid, reasonable, or well-founded.

For example, using the "work experience" sample topic below, a thesis statement could be:

> I think working while in school is beneficial to students because it provides skills that might enhance their formal education and teaches them a good work ethic.

The thesis statement would come at the end of the introductory paragraph followed by paragraphs that explain each supporting point. The paper ends with a summary of the reasons and a restatement of the thesis sentence. Each paragraph should contain approximately three to five sentences.

The introduction invites the reader to read on. The following reasons (three are usually sufficient) should give supporting examples or evidence. Your concluding paragraph can summarize your reasons, complete your response to the question, add information that you failed to introduce earlier, or point toward the future. You may wish to tie in a restatement of your thesis sentence.

The "why essay" format looks like the following table in outline form:

Paragraph Number	Why Essay Format	Examples by Paragraph
1	Introduction—Thesis Sentence	Paragraph 1
2	Reason 1	Paragraph 2
3	Reason 2	Paragraph 3
4	Reason 3	Paragraph 4
5	Conclusion	Paragraph 5

Now let's take a close look at a sample topic and two sample essays.

Directions: Read the following paragraph and assignment carefully. Then prepare and write a persuasive essay. Be sure to support your reasons with specific examples that will make your essay more effective.

"Work experience is the best teacher," say many sociologists. With this in mind, some parents encourage their high school students to get an after-school or weekend job. Other parents cite the importance of getting good grades to discourage their high school students from getting an after-school or weekend job.

Assignment: Which parents do you agree with? Using an example or examples from your reading, personal experiences, or observations, write an essay to support your position.

Two Well-Written Essays (with Comments)

The following two essays were written by students. The papers are reproduced exactly as they were written, so they contain some mechanical errors and some general writing mistakes. The students wrote the essays within the 25 minutes allotted.

Essay 1

> This is a good first paragraph. It clearly states the writer's position, and by suggesting that work can develop nonacademic skills, it prepares for the arguments of the next three paragraphs.

> Note how the repetition of the word "skills" links the second paragraph with the first.

> Paragraph three moves on to another advantage (development of a work ethic). The second sentence explains fully what the writer understands a "work ethic" to be.

> The last paragraph is the weakest paragraph of this essay. The writer has argued forcefully in favor of after-school work. There is no reason to weaken the argument with the trite suggestion that it will depend on the individual. What doesn't? In an argument essay like this, it is not necessary (and is usually a waste of time) to pay lip service to the opposing point of view.

There is a great deal of controversy among parents as to whether or not their children should hold a paying job while in high school. Some parents believe that working while in school is a valuable experience; others believe that the importance of good grades **superceeds** any value that a job might offer. **I think that working while in school can be very beneficial to students and provide them with skills that might enhance their "formal" education.**

One of the **skills** is time management. Learning how to balance your activities and obligations is essential as an adult. It is invaluable to know what you can handle and when you are taking on too much. **When I got a job in high school, I began to realize the importance of using my time wisely since I had less of it to throw around.** I think that I gained a lot from having to make those decisions as well as earning my own money.

Another benefit is that students can **develop a work ethic** which can be applied to their academic schooling or any task that they choose to take on. **Understanding the importance of working hard, doing a good job and being responsible are skills that are assets to any endeavor.** Students often develop **confidence** from being counted on to get something done and then rising to that challenge. **Additionally, learning to take pride in your work is really important.** When you care about something your performance often reflects that. Academic success largely depends upon this same kind of pride and confidence.

Ultimately, I believe that whether a child should work while in school **depends on the child.** Some children feel that they can't handle the responsibility while others are willing to try. I think **that students stand to gain a lot from working,** but should be able to **make that choice for themselves** in the end.

> A well-chosen word, but misspelled. It should be "supersede."

> The writer supports her argument (that part-time work develops the ability to manage time efficiently) by referring to personal experience.

> The move to a second point in this paragraph (increased confidence) would be clearer with the addition of a transitional word or phrase (such as "Further" or "Also") to begin the sentence. But, the writer rightly does include a transitional word ("Additionally") at the beginning of the next sentence.

Aside from the last paragraph, this is a very good essay, well-organized, well-supported, and specific. Its word choice, syntax, and mechanics are all competent.

Essay 2

Introduction is focused and states position *clearly* and *immediately*.

Some parents want their high school aged children to work part-time, while other parents prefer their children not to work and instead concentrate on studies. **I agree with the parents who want their children to get good grades, although I believe that after school work, sports or other activities are helpful in establishing good study habits** and creating a well-rounded, successful student.

Notice how it uses words from the counter-argument, "good grades," to support the position that part-time jobs are good because they lead to good grades.

The second paragraph supports the main position of the introduction—again supports the position that jobs can lead to good grades.

Life is not all study any more than it is all play. Students need to learn how to manage their time. They need to learn the organizational skills necessary to do a lot of different tasks in a timely manner. Work, sports, and other activities are necessary to provide a break from continual studying. **They also provide experiences that are essential to education and can lead to understanding and, therefore, better grades.**

The third paragraph gives supporting details from *experience* as asked for — personal experience *supports* the *position*.

Since my older brother was responsible for paying for his own college education, it was necessary for him to work part-time throughout his college years. He had to organize his work hours around class and study hours, so he found **a job in a grocery store** as this gave him the greatest flexibility. He organized his time and was able to work and keep up his grades.

The fourth paragraph shows that not working in part-time jobs doesn't mean that good grades will necessarily follow. Notice the supporting example from the experience and observation of the writer.

He told me that many of his college classmates came from wealthier backgrounds. **They didn't have to work and were able to concentrate full-time on their studies and their grades.** A lot of these kids took study breaks for coffee or beers or just chatting, and didn't organize their time well. **Some did quite poorly in school even though their parents did all they could to help them focus on grades.**

The conclusion:
• again restates the essay topic;
• uses support from observations to again support original restated position.

From my own observations and experience **I do not feel that after-school or weekend jobs hinder a student from getting good grades.** I feel that these activities can be more helpful than harmful by providing the student with the opportunity to organize their life activities. Whether in high school or in college **a student should be encouraged to engage in many activities and to organize their time so they can succeed in all they do. I plan to get a part-time job during my senior year in high school.**

Note: Since the question is "what is your opinion," it is quite permissible to write in the first person (I) and give your opinion without saying "in my opinion" or "I believe" or "my viewpoint is." Be personal and invent supporting examples!

Eight Important Points to Consider When Writing

1. Try to be genuinely interested in the topic.
2. Don't worry about the answer you think "they" want you to write.
3. Don't be afraid to be honest.
4. Avoid clichés.
5. Write naturally.
6. Choose your words with some thought and don't use words with meanings you're unsure about.
7. Don't be afraid to use contractions, figures of speech, even slang, but do so tactfully.
8. Don't be wishy-washy. Be confident as you support your position.

A Few Sample Topics for Practice

Topic 1

Directions: Think carefully about the issue presented in the following quotations and the assignment below.

"Save for a rainy day."

"Sacrificing for the future is fine for many, but for some of us, it may never come. Enjoy the present, for it is the only thing of which we *all* are certain."

Assignment: Is it important to save for the future? Plan and write an essay in which you develop your position on this issue. Use an example or examples from your reading, personal experiences, or observations, to support your position.

Evaluating Your Essay

When you practice, use the following checklist to evaluate the essay:

- Does the essay focus on the topic and complete the assigned task?
  (Circle one: Excellent   Average   Poor)

- Is the essay well organized, well developed, and consistent in argument?
  (Circle one: Excellent   Average   Poor)

- Does the essay use specific supporting details?
  (Circle one: Excellent   Average   Poor)

- Does the writing use correct grammar, usage, punctuation, and spelling?
  (Circle one: Excellent   Average   Poor)

- Is the handwriting legible?
  (Circle one: Excellent   Average   Poor)

Topic 2

Directions: Read the following quotation and assignment carefully. Then prepare and write an essay about the issue presented.

"Genius is one percent inspiration and ninety-nine percent perspiration."

—Thomas Edison

Assignment: Edison suggests that the major contributing factor of genius is hard work as opposed to thoughts and ideas. Do you agree or disagree with Edison? Using an example or examples from your reading or your personal observation, write an essay to support your position.

Evaluating Your Essay

When you practice, use the following checklist to evaluate the essay:

- Does the essay focus on the topic and complete the assigned task?
  (Circle one: Excellent   Average   Poor)

- Is the essay well organized, well developed, and consistent in argument?
  (Circle one: Excellent   Average   Poor)

- Does the essay use specific supporting details?
  (Circle one: Excellent   Average   Poor)

- Does the writing use correct grammar, usage, punctuation, and spelling?
  (Circle one: Excellent   Average   Poor)

- Is the handwriting legible?
  (Circle one: Excellent   Average   Poor)

A Summary of Strategies for Essay Writing

- Spend 3 or 4 minutes making your notes and organizing your thoughts. Spend about 20 minutes writing your essay. Spend 1 or 2 minutes proofreading your essay.

- Make sure that the essay you write is on the topic given.

- The general instructions include the sentence suggesting that "you may want to write more than one paragraph." Aim for at least three paragraphs.

- Be specific. Your readers are looking for specific details, for concrete evidence of some kind used to support your points.

- Don't use excessively large writing, don't leave wide margins, and don't skip any lines.

- Your essay should be *clear* and *effective*.

- Know how to use the writing process:

  Preparing to Write (Prewriting)

  Writing

  Proofreading (Editing)

- Keep the following questions in mind as you write and review your essay:

  Does the essay focus on the topic and complete the assigned task?

  Is the essay well organized, well developed, and consistent in argument?

  Does the essay use specific supporting details?

  Does the writing use correct grammar, usage, punctuation, and spelling?

  Is the handwriting legible?

Introduction to the Writing Section—Multiple Choice

There are three kinds of questions in the multiple-choice writing sections:

- Identifying Sentence Errors (sometimes called Usage)
- Improving Sentences (Sentence Correction)
- Improving Paragraphs (also called Revision in Context)

A typical exam will have two multiple-choice sections—one 25 minutes long and one 10 minutes long. A total of approximately 18 Identifying Sentence Error questions, approximately 25 Improving Sentence questions, and approximately 6 Improving Paragraphs questions will be spread between the two multiple-choice sections. The exact number of questions of each type may vary slightly; the total number of questions is approximately 49.

Common Errors to Watch For

Following is a list of the nearly thirty writing faults that are most likely to appear on the exam. Not all of them will turn up on the exam, but many of them will. Some of them may appear more than once (such as verb agreement) and some may appear in both the usage and the sentence correction sections.

The following chart lists the twenty-eight common writing faults most likely to be on the exam. The second column gives a simple sentence to illustrate the fault (on the exam, unfortunately, the errors will not be nearly so easy to see), with the error underlined. The third column gives the corrected version of the example.

Type of Error	Example of Error	Corrected Example
1. Noun agreement error	France and Italy are a country in Europe.	France and Italy are countries in Europe.
2. Subject-verb agreement error	The students of English is taking the test.	The students of English are taking the test.
3. Pronoun agreement error	Jack was late, so we left without them.	Jack was late, so we left without him.
4. Unclear pronoun reference	Jane, June, and Joan applied, and she got the job.	Jane, June, and Joan applied, and Jane got the job. (Joan or June)
5. Missing specific pronoun antecedent	Dave ate too fast which made him sick.	Dave ate too fast so he got sick.
6. Change of pronoun subjects	One needs a calculator, and you should bring two pens.	One needs a calculator, and one should bring two pens.
7. Wrong pronoun	She is the judge which sentenced the felon.	She is the judge who sentenced the felon.
8. Adjective/adverb error	His writing is carelessly because he writes too rapid.	His writing is careless because he writes too rapidly.
9. Comparative adjective error	Of the seven swimmers, she is the stronger.	Of the seven swimmers, she is the strongest.
10. Misplaced modifier	We saw the boy and his mother in a Batman costume.	We saw the boy in a Batman costume and his mother.

(continued)

Type of Error	Example of Error	Corrected Example
11. Dangling modifier	<u>Flowing from the mountain top, he</u> drank from the stream.	He drank from the stream that was flowing from the mountain top.
12. Double negative	There is <u>hardly no</u> coffee left in the pot.	There is hardly any coffee left in the pot.
13. Illogical comparison	In California, the <u>sun</u> rises <u>later than</u> New York.	In California, the sun rises later than in New York.
14. Verb tense sequence error	He <u>rang</u> the bell, <u>opened</u> the door, and <u>enters</u> the house.	He rang the bell, opened the door, and entered the house.
15. Verb tense error	Last week she <u>buys</u> a new car.	Last week she bought a new car.
16. Change of voice of verb	He <u>runs</u> a mile daily, and weights <u>are lifted</u> by him.	He runs a mile daily and lifts weights.
17. Verb form error	He has <u>brung</u> a bottle of wine.	He brought a bottle of wine.
18. Sentence fragment	<u>Having three sisters, two of them doctors.</u>	Having three sisters, two of them doctors, made her feel better.
19. Comma splice	She has three <u>sisters, two of</u> them are doctors.	She has three sisters, and two of them are doctors.
20. Fused (or run-on) sentences	She has <u>three sisters two of them are doctors.</u>	She has three sisters, and two of them are doctors.
21. Parallelism error	He is studying <u>biology, physics, and how to swim.</u>	He is studying biology, physics, and swimming.
22. Coordination error	Ames wrote only about Boston, <u>and</u> he was never there.	Ames wrote only about Boston, although he was never there.
23. Subordination error	Wilson sets many of his novels in Galway, <u>and he was born there</u>.	Wilson sets many of his novels in Galway where he was born.
24. Diction error	He will be <u>relapsed</u> from prison in June.	He will be released from prison in June.
25. Idiom error: gerund infinitive confusion	I am eager <u>in seeing</u> the film. He is incapable <u>to answer</u> the question.	I am eager to see the film. He is incapable of answering the question.
26. Idiom error: choice of preposition	They are in support <u>to</u> the idea.	They are in support of the idea.
27. Idiom error: choice of conjunction	He is as subtle <u>than</u> a fox.	He is as subtle as a fox.
28. Wordiness	Because <u>of the fact that</u> he failed to give <u>total and complete</u> attention, he missed the exit.	Because he failed to give complete attention, he missed the exit.

Identifying Sentence Error Questions (Usage)

You should have a total of about 17 to 19 usage questions.

Ability Tested

These questions test your ability to recognize errors in standard written English.

Basic Skills Necessary

Knowledge of some basic grammar and usage will help in this section. Review the rules of correct grammar and usage that have been emphasized in your high school English classes.

Directions

The following sentences many contain one error of grammar, usage, diction, or idiom. No sentence will contain more than one error, and some have no error. If there is an error, it will be underlined and have a letter beneath it. Sections of the sentence that are not underlined cannot be changed. In selecting your answer, observe the requirements of standard written English. If there is an error, choose the one underlined part that must be changed to correct the sentence. If there is no error, choose E.

Analysis of Directions

1. In this section, each question is a single complete sentence of fewer than thirty words (and usually fewer than twenty-five) with four underlined words or phrases lettered A, B, C, and D. A fifth choice, E, is for no error.

2. If there is an error, it will be underlined. Parts of the sentence that are not underlined are correct and cannot be changed.

3. No sentence will contain more than one error, so if you find an error don't keep looking; simply select the letter below the error.

4. If you cannot find a clear error in a sentence, do not hesitate to choose E (No Error).

5. Note that you do not have to correct the sentence; simply find the error if there is one.

6. Observe the rules of standard written English.

Suggested Approaches with Samples

The following are examples of the errors most often tested for in Usage or Identifying Sentence Error questions; strategies and explanations are included.

Subject-Verb Agreement Errors

An agreement error is the faulty combination of a singular and a plural, a singular subject and a plural verb or vice versa. Be sure you can identify the subject and the verb of the sentence. Do not let the intervening words distract you.

Samples

> **1.** The short stories of J. California Cooper <u>addresses</u> the black experience <u>with colloquial talk,</u>
>   A   B
>
> <u>dialect, dots, dashes,</u> and <u>even musical notes.</u> <u>No Error.</u>
>   C   D   E

The subject "stories" is a plural. To agree, the verb should be the plural "address." The correct answer is A.

> **2.** The increase in the number <u>of predators</u> that <u>carry infectious diseases</u> to the herds of zebra and gnu <u>are</u> a serious
>   A   B   C
>
> concern <u>to the park rangers.</u> <u>No Error.</u>
>   D   E

This is another error of agreement. The subject of the sentence is the singular noun "increase," and its verb, though widely separated from it, is the plural "are." It should read "the increase...is." The correct answer is C.

Pronoun Agreement Errors

Pronouns can be either singular or plural and must agree with the noun, verb, or other pronoun that they refer to.

Samples

> **1.** The greatest strength of the American political system <u>is</u> each voter's right <u>to determine</u> which way <u>they</u>
>   A   B   C
>
> <u>will vote.</u> <u>No Error.</u>
>   D   E

The singular "is" agrees with the singular "strength." The plural "they," however, does not agree with the singular "each voter." The correct answer is C.

> **2.** The governor <u>hopes</u> <u>to increase and redistribute</u> tax money, <u>raising</u> the expenditure on education and
>   A   B   C
>
> <u>equalizing them</u> throughout the state. <u>No Error.</u>
>   D   E

There are no errors in A, B, or C, but there is an error of agreement in D. The plural pronoun "them" refers to the singular "expenditure." The corrected sentence would have either "expenditures" and "them" or "expenditure" and "it." The correct answer is D.

Verb Tense Errors

The tenses (present, past, future) of the verbs in a sentence must be logical and consistent.

Samples

> **1.** When the bell rang, I <u>grabbed</u> my backpack and <u>run</u> <u>as fast as I could</u> <u>to catch</u> the first bus. <u>No Error.</u>
>   A   B   C   D   E

The first two verbs here ("rang," "grabbed") are in the past tense. To be consistent, "run" should be "ran." The correct answer is B.

2. Raul Julia won a Tony award in *The Three Penny Opera,* and he re-creates his role when the play became an

                       A   B   C

award-winning film. No Error.

  D   E

The verb "re-creates" should be "re-created," a past tense. The past tense is necessary to be consistent with the verb "became." The correct answer is A.

Case Errors

Pronouns in English have three cases: subjective (I, he), possessive (my, his) and objective (me, him). The function of the pronoun in the sentence determines its case.

Samples

1. When we were in elementary school, there was a competition between my sister and I that now seems

   A   B   C   D

ridiculous. No Error.

    E

The personal pronoun is the object of the preposition "between," so the phrase should be "between my sister and me." It is easy to see case errors like this when the pronoun immediately follows the preposition (to me, like him, without her), but it is harder when another object intercedes (to David and me, like Martha and him, with Iris and her). The correct answer is C.

2. According to the surgeon, the diagnosis of illness was not likely to alarm either she or her husband. No Error.

            A   B   C   D   E

The object of the infinitive "to alarm" is "she or her husband." The "she" should be the objective "her." The correct answer is C.

Ambiguous Pronoun Errors

The antecedent of a pronoun (the word the pronoun refers to) should be clear. Sentences in which a pronoun could have two or more different antecedents should be rewritten.

Samples

1. Many historians believe the Kennedy-Nixon election was decided by the television debate in which he appeared

        A   B   C   D

unshaven and humorless. No Error.

       E

The error is the ambiguous pronoun "he." A reader has no way of knowing whether the antecedent of this pronoun is Kennedy or Nixon. The correct answer is D.

2. In the 1840s, Dickens wrote the Christmas books *The Chimes* and *The Cricket on the Hearth,* but it did not

   A   B   C

attain the popularity of *A Christmas Carol.* No Error.

     D   E

There are two possible antecedents to the singular "it," *The Chimes,* and *The Cricket on the Hearth.* The correct answer is C.

105

Parallel Construction Errors

Errors of parallelism occur when two or more **linked** words or phrases are expressed in different grammatical structures. Parallelism errors may include unnecessary shifts in verb tenses (past to present, for example) or voice (active to passive, for example). They may also include shifts in pronouns (you to one, for example). Watch for these errors in lists or series.

Samples

> **1.** Miguel <u>enjoyed</u> <u>swimming</u>, <u>weight lifting</u>, and <u>to run</u>. <u>No Error.</u>
>   A   B   C   D   E

"To run" is incorrect; it should be an "-ing" word ("running") like the other items. The correct answer is D.

> **2.** <u>Working at a full-time job</u>, <u>helping to support a family</u>, and <u>a college education</u> added up to a <u>tremendous burden</u>
>   A   B   C   D
>
> for Tom. <u>No Error.</u>
>   E

An error in parallelism occurs with "a college education," which may be corrected by adding an "-ing" word, "completing." So the correct, parallel phrase is "completing a college education." The correct answer is C.

> **3.** Law school will <u>not only enable</u> one to pass the bar exam, <u>but also teach</u> <u>you</u> to <u>think clearly.</u> <u>No Error.</u>
>   A   B   C   D   E

The verbs "enable" and "teach" are correctly parallel, but the pronoun shift from "one" to "you" is an error. The correct answer is C.

Comparison Errors (Illogical Comparisons)

When making a comparison, be sure that the two compared elements are similar. Watch carefully for this error when a sentence begins with "Like." Note that the omission of necessary words can also make comparisons illogical. Though wordiness is a fault, some constructions require extra words to be clear and logical. A sentence like "I am interested in but uninformed about dinosaurs." would be incorrect without *both* the "in" and the "about."

Samples

> **1.** <u>Like Faulkner</u>, Eudora Welty's stories <u>give the reader</u> a sense <u>of what</u> life in the South <u>must have been like</u> in the
>   A   B   C   D
>
> thirties. <u>No Error.</u>
>   E

The problem in this sentence is at the beginning. As it now stands, the comparison is not Faulkner and Welty (two authors) or Faulkner's stories and Welty's fiction (two works), but Faulkner and Welty's stories (a writer and a writer's works). The corrected sentence would read "Like Faulkner's" or "Like those of Faulkner" or "Like the stories of Faulkner." The correct answer is A.

> **2.** Because the volcanoes on the island of Hawaii <u>are more active</u> <u>than other islands,</u> <u>it</u> is the center
>
        A   B   C
>
<u>for geological studies.</u> <u>No Error.</u>
>
    D   E

The comparison here is illogical. The sentence compares the more active volcanoes to other islands, not to volcanoes on the other islands. The corrected sentence would read "more active than those on other islands." The correct answer is B.

> **3.** The <u>organically grown</u> vegetables sold at this market <u>cost much more</u> than <u>the market</u> selling vegetables
>
      A   B   C
>
<u>grown with pesticides.</u> <u>No Error.</u>
>
    D   E

The sentence compares the cost of vegetables with the cost of a market. To make sense, it should read something like "cost much more than those grown with pesticides," or "cost much more than vegetables grown with pesticides." In sentences with comparisons, look carefully at exactly what two things are compared; be sure the comparison is a logical one. The correct answer is C.

Other Common Errors

Parts of Speech Errors

Be careful not to confuse adjectives (which modify nouns) with adverbs (which modify adjectives, verbs, and other adverbs).

Sample

> **1.** The great blue heron <u>has survived</u> because it is <u>difficult to stalk,</u> is <u>not particular tasty,</u> <u>and lacks</u> elegant
>
                   A   B   C   D
>
<u>plumage.</u> <u>No Error.</u>
>
    E

The error is the use of the adjective where an adverb is needed; to modify the adjective "tasty," the adjective "particular" should be replaced by the adverb "particularly." The correct answer is C.

Double Negative Error

Watch for double negatives. Keep in mind that words like "hardly," "never," and "neither" are negatives.

Samples

> **1.** Unaffected <u>by neither hunger nor cold,</u> Scott covered up to twenty miles <u>on each of the days</u> that the weather
>
               A   B
>
<u>permitted him</u> to <u>travel at all.</u> <u>No Error.</u>
>
    C   D   E

The error here is A, a double negative since "Unaffected" and "neither" are both negatives. To correct the usage, change "unaffected" to "affected" or "neither...nor" to "either...or." Since "Unaffected" is not underlined, choice A must be changed. The correct answer is A.

> **2.** Many psychologists <u>claim that</u> slips of the tongue do not mask <u>no deeply concealed wishes,</u> but are <u>simply</u> signs
>   A   B   C
> of <u>momentary confusion.</u> <u>No Error.</u>
>   D   E

The error here is the double negative: "do not mask"... "no." The correct answer is B.

Diction Errors

Diction errors (errors in the choice of word) are especially likely to show up with a word that looks or sounds very much like another: "sit" and "set," or "retain" and "detain," for example.

Samples

> **1.** <u>Setting at her typewriter</u> <u>almost every day</u> for fifty-five years, Agatha Christie <u>completed</u> eighty-six volumes
>   A   B   C
> of prose. <u>No Error.</u>
>   D   E

This is an error of diction, or choice of word. The writer has confused "to sit" (an intransitive verb) and "to set" (a verb that takes an object). The correct answer is A.

> **2.** <u>By prohibiting</u> <u>discounting by chain stores</u> and supermarkets, British book publishers <u>left</u> smaller private
>   A   B   C
> bookstores become <u>competitive with the larger distributors.</u> <u>No Error.</u>
>   D   E

This is another diction error, confusing "left" and "let." The correct answer is C.

Idiom Errors

Idiom errors are most likely to occur in sentences that require a choice between an infinitive and a gerund; "reluctant to speak" and "suspected of lying" are correct idioms. The items testing idiom errors will usually involve preposition choice.

Samples

> **1.** The prosecutor <u>feared</u> the showing of a teleplay <u>based on the defendant's life</u> would make <u>it</u> impossible
>   A   B   C
> <u>in selecting</u> a jury. <u>No Error.</u>
>   D   E

The error is the unidiomatic use of "in selecting" (a preposition followed by a gerund) instead of "to select" (an infinitive) after "impossible." The correct answer is D.

> **2.** Researchers <u>have extended</u> the life span of laboratory-grown cells, <u>a feat</u> <u>that</u> may shed light on the <u>process to age.</u>
>   A   B C   D
> <u>No Error.</u>
> E

The problem is in the phrase "process to age," a use of the infinitive when the correct idiom is "of aging." The correct answer is D.

3. <u>Based in</u> Oscar Hijuelos' prize-winning novel, *The Mambo Kings* <u>has a screenplay</u> <u>by</u> Cynthia Cidres, and <u>stars</u>
     A   B   C   D

Armand Assante. <u>No Error.</u>
               E

The correct preposition idiom here is "based on" or "based upon." The correct answer is A.

Sentences with No Errors

Do not hesitate to choose E when you cannot find a usage error that you are sure about. About one in five questions in this section of the exam will have no error.

Samples

1. The workers at the American embassy in Moscow <u>have been affected</u> in some way by radio waves, <u>but there is</u>
                                                 A   B

no certainty about <u>just what</u> <u>the effects have been.</u> <u>No Error.</u>
                 C   D   E

This is a sentence with no error. The correct answer is E.

2. The popularity <u>of many recent films</u> <u>is due</u> <u>not to their</u> sentiment or morality, <u>but to their</u> violence. <u>No Error.</u>
                   A   B   C   D   E

There is no error in this sentence. The singular "is" agrees with the singular "popularity," while the phrases "not to their" and "but to their" are correctly parallel. The correct answer is E.

A Summary of Strategies and Key Points for Identifying Sentence Error Questions

■ Focus on the underlined words or phrases looking for an obvious error.

■ You do not have to correct the sentence; simply find the error if there is one.

■ Remember, if there is an error, it will be underlined. Parts of the sentence that are not underlined are correct and cannot be changed.

■ Since no sentence will contain more than one error, if you find an error don't keep looking. Simply select the letter below the error.

■ If you cannot find a clear error in a sentence, do not hesitate to choose E (No Error).

■ Observe the rules of standard written English.

Improving Sentences Questions (Sentence Correction)

You will have a total of about 24 to 26 sentence correction questions.

Ability Tested

These questions test your ability to recognize and correct errors in standard written English.

Basic Skills Necessary

Knowledge of some basic grammar, usage, and punctuation will help in this section. Review the rules of correct grammar, usage, and punctuation that have been emphasized in your high school English classes.

Directions

The following questions test correctness and effective expression. In selecting the answer, pay attention to grammar, diction, sentence structure, and punctuation. In the following questions, part or all of each sentence is underlined. The A answer repeats the underlined portion of the original sentence, while the next four offer alternatives. Choose the answer that best expresses the meaning of the original sentence and at the same time is grammatically correct and stylistically superior. The correct choice should be clear, unambiguous, and concise.

Analysis of Directions

1. This question type presents a single sentence with all or part of it underlined.
2. The five lettered choices present five possible versions of the underlined part.
3. The rest of the sentence that is not underlined cannot be changed and must be used to determine which of the five answers is the best.
4. The first choice, A, repeats the original version, while the next four make changes.
5. Sometimes the original sentence is better than the four proposed alternatives. If you find no error and you feel the original sentence is best, select choice A.
6. Note that the correct choice should be clear, unambiguous, and concise.

Suggested Approaches with Samples

The sentences in this section of the test may have one or more of the same kind of errors found in the Identifying Sentence Errors (Usage) section.

The following are errors that are tested most frequently in the Improving Sentences section of the exam.

Misplaced Modifiers Errors, Dangling Phrases

Since a misplaced part is often awkward but not, strictly speaking, a grammatical error, the questions testing for misplaced parts will usually ask you to select the sentence that is not only grammatically correct, but also clear and exact, free from awkwardness and ambiguity. Watch for sentences that seem odd or have unnatural word order. Also watch for phrases that have nothing to modify; they are called "dangling modifiers."

Samples

---

1. <u>When she was only five, Janet's mother married for the third time.</u>

    A.   When she was only five, Janet's mother married for the third time.

    B.   When only five, Janet's mother married for the third time.

    C.   When Janet was only five, her mother married for the third time.

    D.   When Janet's mother married for the third time, she was only five.

    E.   Janet's mother married, when Janet was only five, for the third time.

The major problem in this sentence is the uncertainty about whom the "when she was only five" clause modifies, five-year-old Janet, or her mother. In choices A and D, the "she" appears to refer to the mother, while choice B, though the pronoun is missing, also seems to make the marrying mother five years old. Both C and E remove the ambiguity. In the choice between these two sentences, C is preferable, since E places the phrase "for the third time" awkwardly away from the verb "married," which it modifies. The correct answer is C.

---

2. Reacting to a false report of dangerous pesticides, <u>the cranberry harvest of 1999 went unsold to the nation's consumers.</u>

    A.   the cranberry harvest of 1999 went unsold to the nation's consumers.

    B.   the cranberry harvest of 1999 was not bought by the nation's consumers.

    C.   the nation's consumers do not buy the cranberry harvest in 1999.

    D.   the nation's consumers refused to buy the cranberry harvest of 1999.

    E.   the 1999 harvest of cranberries was not bought by the nation's consumers.

The participle that begins this sentence dangles; that is, it is placed to modify "the cranberry harvest," but it should be next to "consumers." It is the consumers, not the harvest, who reacted. Choice C avoids the dangling participle, but changes the past tense of the verb to the present. The correct answer is D.

---

3. <u>The caribou herds, for centuries, have supported the Gwich'in Indians</u> which migrate to feed in their summer range beside the Beaufort Sea.

    A.   The caribou herds, for centuries, have supported the Gwich'in Indians

    B.   For centuries, the caribou herds have supported the Gwich'in Indians

    C.   The caribou herds which have for centuries supported the Gwich'in Indians

    D.   The Gwich'in Indians have been supported by the caribou herds for centuries

    E.   For centuries, the Gwich'in Indians have been supported by the caribou herds,

---

Keep related words and phrases as close together as possible. The trouble with this sentence is a misplaced modifier; the clause about migrating to a summer range modifies the caribou, not the Indians. The best version will place herds as close to the "which" as possible. Choice C has no main verb. The correct answer is E.

---

4. Using Christian, West African, and Taino traditions, <u>ancient images are re-created in rare rain forest woods by George Crespo.</u>

    A.   ancient images are re-created in rare rain-forest woods by George Crespo.

    B.   rare rain-forest woods re-create ancient images by George Crespo.

    C.   George Crespo re-creates ancient images in rare rain-forest woods.

    D.   George Crespo is the creator of ancient images in rain-forest woods.

    E.   George Crespo re-creating ancient images of rare rain-forest woods.

When, like this one, a sentence begins with a participle, be on the alert for a dangling participle. Here it is the artist, Crespo, not the carvings, who uses the three traditions. Choices C, D, and E avoid the dangling modifier, but E has no main verb, and D is wordier than C and changes "re-creates" to "creates." The correct answer is C.

Parallel Construction Errors

Be especially careful with sentences that use *correlatives* (both . . . and; no . . . but; not only . . . but also; not . . . but; either . . . or; and others). Make sure that the construction that follows the second of the correlative conjunctions is like the construction that follows the first.

Samples

---

1. After he graduated from college, his parents gave him a new car, ten thousand dollars, and sent him on a trip around the world.

  A. After he graduated from college, his parents gave him a new car, ten thousand dollars, and sent him on a
  B. After graduating from college, his parents gave him a new car, ten thousand dollars, and a
  C. After he had graduated from college, his parents gave him a new car, ten thousand dollars, and a
  D. After he had graduated from college, his parents gave him a new car, ten thousand dollars, and sent him on a
  E. After graduating from college, his parents gave him a new car, ten thousand dollars, and sent him on a

---

The problem in the original sentence is parallelism. The verb "gave" begins a series with nouns as objects ("car," "dollars") but the third part of the series ("and sent him on") interrupts the series. Choices B and C correct this error by making "trip" a third object of "gave." Choice B cannot be right because it begins with a dangling participle; it appears that the parents are graduating from college. The correct answer is C.

---

2. To prune a rose is more dangerous than pruning an azalea.

  A. To prune a rose is more dangerous than pruning an azalea.
  B. Pruning a rose is more dangerous than pruning an azalea.
  C. To prune a rose is more dangerous than azalea pruning.
  D. It is much more dangerous to prune a rose than it is to prune an azalea.
  E. Pruning a rose is more dangerous than to prune an azalea.

The object here is to make the verbs on either side of the "than" parallel. You can use two infinitives ("to prune," "to prune") or two gerunds ("pruning," "pruning"), but not one of each as in choices A, C, and E. Choice D has the correct verb parallels, but changes the meaning. The correct answer is B.

---

3. Please remind me not only that I must cash a check, but also to have the car washed.

  A. that I must cash a check, but also to have the car washed.
  B. that I must cash a check, but also to wash the car.
  C. to cash a check, but also that the car needs washing.
  D. to cash a check, but also that I must have the car washed.
  E. to cash a check, but also to have the car washed.

The correlative here are "not only...but also." Choice E is the only answer that correctly uses a parallel construction ("not only to cash," "but also to have"). The correct answer is E.

Ambiguous Pronoun Errors

In the Identifying Sentence Errors section of the test there are ambiguous pronouns with more than one possible antecedent. In this part of the exam, the more common error is an ambiguous pronoun with no specific antecedent. You can correct this error by eliminating the pronoun or by supplying a specific antecedent, but not by substituting a different pronoun.

Samples

1. The whooping crane population has increased from only fifteen to about two hundred, <u>which is one of conservation's most encouraging stories.</u>

   A. which is one of conservation's most encouraging stories.
   B. which is one the most encouraging stories in conservation.
   C. and this is one of conservation's most encouraging stories.
   D. and this growth is one of conservation's most encouraging stories.
   E. and that appears to be encouraging to conservationists.

If it is possible, a pronoun should have a specific antecedent. In this sentence, choice D provides a noun as subject of the clause to replace the pronouns "which," "this," and "that." Changing the pronoun from "which" to "this" or "that," does nothing to correct the ambiguity of the pronoun. The correct answer is D.

2. <u>I came in fifteen minutes late which</u> made the whole class difficult to understand.

   A. I came in fifteen minutes late which
   B. I came in fifteen minutes late, and this
   C. I came in fifteen minutes late, and this is what
   D. By coming in fifteen minutes late, which
   E. Coming in fifteen minutes late

The pronoun "which" has no specific antecedent here, and the change of "which" to "this" does not correct the problem. Choice E eliminates the pronoun altogether and corrects the sentence. Choice D is a sentence fragment. The correct answer is E.

3. Ending the hope that a single genetic flaw might cause Alzheimer's disease, <u>they say the disorder apparently has multiple causes</u>, as do heart disease and cancer.

   A. they say the disorder apparently has multiple causes
   B. they say the disease has multiple apparent causes
   C. they say that it apparently has multiple causes
   D. researchers report the disease has many causes, apparent
   E. researchers report the disorder apparently has multiple causes

The vague "they" is the problem here. They who? Choices D and E replace the inexact pronoun with a specific noun. There is no important difference between "many" and "multiple," but E uses "apparently" correctly. The correct answer is E.

Pronoun Agreement Errors

Watch for change of pronoun subjects. If the pronoun "one" is used in a sentence, then the pronoun "you" should not be used (sometimes called parallel construction errors). Also make sure that the pronoun agrees in number (singular, plural) with the noun it represents.

Samples

1. When one reaches the first plateau, it does not guarantee that you will complete the climb to the summit.

   A.   When one reaches the first plateau, it
   B.   Because one reaches the first plateau, it
   C.   One's reaching the first plateau
   D.   That you have reached the first plateau
   E.   Reaching the first plateau

There is an inconsistency in the pronouns in this sentence. The part that cannot be changed uses "you," but the underlined section uses "one." A right answer will either use "you" or get rid of the pronoun altogether. Choices A, B, and C cannot be right, but D and E are both grammatically correct. In this case E is preferable because it is more direct.

2. Weaver's policy allowed a slave to earn cash if they were able to produce more than the average expected output each week.

   A.   if they were able to produce
   B.   if they produced
   C.   if they overproduced
   D.   by producing
   E.   producing

The error in choices A, B, and C is an agreement error; "slave" is singular, but the pronoun in all three is the plural "they." Choice D solves the problem by omitting the pronoun. The original meaning is unclear if the preposition "by" is dropped. The correct answer is D.

Verb Errors

There are many types of verb errors. Verb tense errors, verb sequence errors, change of voice errors, and subject-verb agreement errors are a few to watch for.

Samples

1. Four financial analysts prepare a summary of stock market activity each week, and it is broadcast by them on public radio.

   A.   each week, and it is broadcast by them
   B.   each week, and then it is broadcast
   C.   each week and it is broadcast by them
   D.   each week, and they broadcast it
   E.   broadcasting each week

The first clause of the sentence uses a verb in the active voice ("prepare"), but the second clause uses a passive ("is broadcast"). Choice D uses active verbs in both parts of the sentence, while A, B, and C keep the passive. C is also a run-on sentence. E is briefer but it loses some of the meaning of the sentence. The correct answer is D.

2. Using highly seasoned onions, green peppers, and celery in almost all of their recipes, <u>Creole cooking had</u> achieved a popularity throughout the country.

   A. Creole cooking had
   B. Creole cooking has
   C. Creole cooking have
   D. Creole cooks has
   E. Creole cooks have

The participle "using" should modify a plural noun, since the phrase also refers to "their recipes." Since "cooks" is plural, the plural verb "have" is the choice. The correct answer is E.

Connective Errors

Read two-part sentences carefully to be sure that the one or two words that connect the two parts (words like "but" or "and") indicate the relationship of the parts clearly.

Samples

1. According to the critics, the MTV awards ceremony <u>was tasteless, according to</u> the audience, it was better than ever.

   A. was tasteless, according to
   B. was tasteless according to
   C. was tasteless, and according to
   D. was tasteless, but according to
   E. was tasteless but to

There are two independent clauses here. They can be two separate sentences, or one sentence with either a semicolon or a conjunction and a comma. A and B leave the conjunction out, and E leaves out the comma. The punctuation is correct in C and D, but D is a better choice, since the two halves of the sentence contrast, and "but" denotes a contrary idea to follow. The correct answer is D.

2. Artist Christina Fernandez originally chose painting as her primary medium, <u>as she now works chiefly</u> in still photography and video.

   A. as she now works chiefly
   B. seeing as she now works chiefly
   C. working chiefly now
   D. but she now works chiefly
   E. because she now chiefly works

The two parts of the original sentence lack proper coordination. The two parts present a difference, which only the conjunction "but" makes clear. What the sentence is saying is *x* was true in the past, *but* is so no longer. The correct answer is D.

Sentence Fragments

Make sure that the answer you choose makes a complete sentence.

Sample

1. By the early eleventh century, Muslim scientists <u>knowing the rich medical literature of ancient Greece, as well as</u> arithmetic and algebra.

   A. knowing the rich medical literature of ancient Greece, as well as
   B. knew the rich medical literature of ancient Greece, as well as
   C. know the rich medical literature of ancient Greece, as well as
   D. having learned the rich medical literature of ancient Greece, as well as
   E. having been given knowledge of the rich medical literature of ancient Greece, as well as

As it stands, this is a sentence fragment, with a participle ("knowing") but no main verb. B supplies the missing verb. C eliminates the sentence fragment, but uses the present tense where past tense is required. D and E are just participles in a different tense. The correct answer is B.

Punctuation Errors

Look carefully at the punctuation. Before you begin, be sure to know the proper use of the comma and semicolon.

Samples

1. Each year about fifty thousand books are <u>published in Great Britain, that is as many as in</u> the four-times-larger United States.

   A. published in Great Britain, that is as many as in
   B. published in Great Britain; that is as many as in
   C. published in Great Britain; as many as in
   D. published in Great Britain; which is as many as in
   E. published in Great Britain as many as in

The error in the original sentence is the comma splice—joining the two independent clauses (or complete sentences) with just a comma. Correct the error by using a period, a comma with a conjunction, or, as here, a semicolon. Though C and D use semicolons, they no longer have independent second clauses, while E, which has made the second clause dependent, omits the comma. The correct answer is B.

2. George Eliot did not begin to write fiction until she was nearly <u>forty, this</u> late start accounts for the maturity of even her earliest works.

   A. forty, this
   B. forty this
   C. forty, and this
   D. forty, a
   E. forty, such a

This is a comma splice. It can be corrected by changing the comma to a semicolon, or by adding a conjunction like "and" in C. The correct answer is C.

3. In 1858, John Speke looked over the waters of <u>Lake Victoria he insisted that it was</u> the source of the Nile.

    A. Lake Victoria he insisted that it was
    B. Lake Victoria and he insisted it to be
    C. Lake Victoria and he insisted that they were
    D. Lake Victoria; insisting that they were
    E. Lake Victoria; he insisted that it was

The sentence is a *fused* or *run-on sentence,* joining two independent clauses with no punctuation or conjunctions. B and C add conjunctions, but fail to add the needed commas. D adds a semicolon, but makes the second clause dependent. Only E avoids a punctuation error. The correct answer is E.

Idiom Errors

As mentioned earlier, idiom errors are most likely to occur in sentences that require a choice between an infinitive and a gerund; "reluctant to speak" and "suspected of lying" are correct idioms. Most of the items testing idioms will usually involve preposition choice.

Sample

1. Exercising without proper warm-ups can be as harmful to the body <u>as if you didn't exercise at all.</u>

    A. as if you didn't exercise at all.
    B. as no exercise at all.
    C. than not exercising at all.
    D. than no exercise.
    E. as your not getting any exercise at all.

The idiom to use with the construction "as-adjective-... " is "as-adjective-as." B is better than A because it is shorter and does not change from a third person to a second person subject ("exercising" to "you"). The correct answer is B.

Wordiness

Sometimes, after eliminating three of the choices that are wrong, you will be left with two grammatically correct sentences. In this case, look for wordiness in one of the two and choose the other one.

Samples

1. <u>The Prado museum in Madrid has the largest collection of great Spanish paintings in the whole world.</u>

    A. The Prado museum in Madrid has the largest collection of great Spanish paintings in the whole world.
    B. The Prado museum in Madrid has the world's largest collection of great Spanish paintings.
    C. It is the Prado museum in Madrid that has the largest collection of the world's great Spanish paintings.
    D. The greatest collection of Spanish paintings in the world is held by the Prado museum in Madrid.
    E. In Madrid, it is the Prado museum that holds the world's largest collection of great Spanish paintings.

Although the original version is not ungrammatical, B is less wordy, replacing "in the whole world" with the more economical "the world's." C and E add the unnecessary "it is," while D uses the passive voice, always more wordy than the active. The correct answer is B.

2. Inhaling hot, steamy air to treat a cold will not make it <u>better, while possibly making it worse.</u>

    A. better, while possibly making it worse.
    B. better, and it may even make it worse.
    C. better, making it worse, possibly.
    D. better, even worsening it, perhaps.
    E. better, and it may even get worse than it is.

Choice B replaces the subordinated participial phrase with a clear independent clause coordinated by "and." E also has an independent clause, but it is more wordy than B. The correct answer is B.

Sentences with More than One Error

Many of the questions in this section of the test have several errors. The usual strategy in the answers is to give one choice that keeps both errors, and two others that correct only one of the two mistakes. Sometimes a choice will introduce a new kind of error. Be sure the answer you choose is grammatical, clear, and like the original in meaning.

Sample

1. The strike cannot be settled until the growers agree to improve health-care benefits <u>and improving the workers' housing.</u>

    A. and improving the workers' housing.
    B. and improving worker housing as well.
    C. and to improve the workers' housing.
    D. and the workers' housing.
    E. and also to the improvement of the housing of the workers.

The phrases "to improve health-care benefits" and "improving the workers' housing" are repetitive and not parallel. Choice B is wordy and not parallel. Choice C corrects the parallelism error, but not the repetition. Choice E is wordy. Choice D is brief and grammatical. The correct answer is D.

Sentences with No Errors

If you carefully read the original sentence a few times and just can't spot an error, there might not be one. Don't be afraid to select no error (choice A), if the original seems correct.

Samples

1. When swimming for Northwestern, <u>Debbie Holm set records that lasted for ten years.</u>

    A. Debbie Holm set records that lasted for ten years.
    B. the records Debbie Holm set lasted ten years.
    C. ten-year records were set by Debbie Holm.
    D. the records of Debbie Holm lasted ten years.
    E. Debbie Holm's records lasted ten years.

The phrase that begins this sentence has an understood but unwritten subject—the person who was swimming at Northwestern. The phrase will dangle unless this subject follows the comma. Only A puts the understood subject immediately after this phrase. Choices B, C, D, and E all make it look as if the "records" were the swimmers. The correct answer is A.

---

2. Carlos Fuentes sees Columbus' arrival in America <u>not as a cultural catastrophe, but as a seminal event</u> in a tragic and triumphant history.

   A.   not as a cultural catastrophe, but as a seminal event
   B.   not as a cultural catastrophe, but it is a seminal event
   C.   not as a cultural catastrophe, as a
   D.   as a seminal event, not as a cultural catastrophe
   E.   was not a cultural catastrophe, but it was a seminal event

---

The original version of the sentence is correct. The correlative conjunctions "not...but" should be followed by parallel constructions. There are parallelism errors in B and E. Choice C loses the contrast pointed by the use of "but." Choice D changes the meaning by separating "seminal event" from the phrase that completes it, "in a tragic and triumphant history." The correct answer is A.

A Summary of Strategies and Key Points for Improving Sentences Questions

◼ Focus on the underlined sentence or underlined part of the sentence.

◼ Remember, the rest of the sentence that is not underlined cannot be changed and must be used to determine which of the five answers is the best.

◼ The five lettered choices present five possible versions of the underlined part. The first choice, A, repeats the original version, while the next four make changes.

◼ Watch for errors in the choices and eliminate those choices.

◼ Sometimes the original sentence is better than the four proposed alternatives. If you find no error and you feel the original sentence is best, select choice A.

◼ Note that the correct choice should be clear, unambiguous, and concise.

◼ Observe the rules of standard written English.

Improving Paragraphs Questions (Revision in Context)

In this section of the exam, there are one or two sets of questions based on short samples of student writing. As a rule, each selection is about three paragraphs and about two hundred to three hundred words long. There are about four to seven questions on each passage.

Ability Tested

These questions test your ability to recognize and correct errors and revise paragraphs following the guidelines of standard written English.

Basic Skills Necessary

Applying basic grammar, sentence structure, and usage skills will help in this section. Another important skill involves the ability to deal with the organization, development, and language in a paragraph or complete essay. Review the rules of correct grammar and usage that have been emphasized in your high school English classes. Also review the elements of an outstanding essay.

Directions

The following passages are early drafts of student essays. Some parts of them need to be revised.

Read the selections carefully and answer the questions that follow. There will be questions about sentence structure, diction, and usage in individual sentences or parts of sentences. Other questions will deal with the whole essay or paragraphs and ask you to decide about the organization, development, and appropriate language. Choose the answer that follows the requirements of standard written English and most effectively expresses the intended meanings.

Analysis of Directions

1. Typically, one or two of the questions will ask you to combine two or three sentences.
2. One question may ask you to recognize and correct a usage error.
3. Other questions will deal with a variety of topics that arise from the selection.
4. There may be questions on sentence structure, on transitions from sentence to sentence or paragraph to paragraph, on the organization of the passage or a paragraph, on logic, on clarity, on rhetorical strategy, or on verbosity.
5. Some questions that deal with the whole essay or with individual paragraphs will focus on organization, development, and appropriate language.
6. Note the requirements of standard written English.
7. Keep in mind that the best answer is one that will most effectively express the intended meaning.

A Special Look at Sentence Combining

Let's take a closer look at sentence combining since about one-third or more of the questions may ask you to revise and combine sentences from a sample of student writing. Though your revision choices will be influenced by the rest of the paragraph, you can practice the technique with two or three sentences that are not part of a paragraph or essay.

The sentences the exam will ask you to work with will probably be grammatically correct, but they will be choppy, or wordy, or dull. There may be a series of very short sentences: "Iris is twenty. She is getting married in June. She is designing a dress. It is white." Or the sentences may be mindlessly coordinated: "Iris is twenty, and she is getting married in June, and she is designing a dress, and the dress is white." Your combined and revised version might read like this: "Twenty-year-old Iris is designing a white dress for her June wedding."

The purpose of sentence combining is to clarify the relationship between thoughts and to eliminate wordiness or choppiness. The techniques the exam questions will call for most often are *coordination* and *subordination*. To coordinate is to make equal; to subordinate is to place in a less important position. The parts of speech used to control sentence elements in these ways are the coordinating and subordinating conjunctions.

Coordinating Conjunctions

and	for	so
but	nor	yet

Subordinating Conjunctions

after	despite	though
although	how	unless
as	if	until
as...as	in order that	when
as if	provided that	whenever
as long as	since	where
as soon as	so...as	wherever
as though	so that	whereupon
because	than	while
before	that	why

The best way to begin a problem in combining sentences is to determine which thought you wish to emphasize. If the two ideas are equally significant, use the coordinating conjunction that best expresses their relationship. If one idea is more important, subordinate the other. If you have not already done so in your English class, practice different ways of combining sentences, especially sentences that seem awkward to you. It will help you on the multiple-choice section of the exam and will improve your writing.

On the exam, you may find a question which asks you to select the best coordinating or subordinating conjunction. The sentence-combining questions appear in two forms. In one, part of the end of one sentence and part of the beginning of the next will be underlined, and you will be given five revisions to choose from. In the second type, the question will ask for the best way to revise and combine two or three complete sentences from the passage.

Suggested Approaches with Samples

Following are two sets of Improving Paragraphs questions based on two separate passages from student essays. The question types are noted in these samples to help you focus on what to look for. Strategies are included with explanations of questions.

Questions 1–5 are based on the following passage.

(1) Is a man or a woman more likely to ask questions? (2) I think it depends on what the circumstances are and on who is around when a time to ask questions comes along. (3) In my family, my mother and I ask more questions than my brother or my father when all our family is together. (4) My father would never ask for directions when we're in the car, and this is when he is not sure of the way. (5) My mother would stop right away to ask, unless she was in an unsafe neighborhood.

(6) My brother tells me that he asks questions in school, and when he is at work after school, he doesn't. (7) It is because he thinks his boss will think he doesn't know his job. (8) He won't ask any questions at all. (9) At work he will ask questions only to his friend, Eddie. (10) Based on my brother and my father, men are more likely to not ask when they don't know something because they think it will hurt their image as able to do things well. (11) Women are more practical and will not drive around not knowing where you are.

Best Version Questions

---

1. Which of the following is the best version of the underlined portion of sentence 2 (reproduced below)?

> *I think it depends <u>on what the circumstances are and on who is around when a time to ask questions comes along.</u>*

    A. Leave it as it is.
    B. on the circumstances.
    C. on what the circumstances are and who is around at the time.
    D. on the circumstances and who is around when a time to ask questions comes along,
    E. on what the circumstances and the situation are for asking questions.

Since the word "circumstances" really includes "who is around," or "situation," there is no need to say more than what is said in B. All of the other choices are, by comparison, wordy. The correct answer is B.

---

2. Which of the following is the best version of the underlined portion of sentence 4 (reproduced below)?

> *My father would never ask for directions when we're in the <u>car, and this is when he is not sure</u> of the way.*

    A. Leave it as it is.
    B. car, and at a time when he is not sure
    C. car, even if he is not sure
    D. car, when he may not be sure
    E. car, because he is not sure

This section of the exam is likely to ask a question that depends on the careful choice of the right conjunctions. Here, the use of "even if" is both concise and fully expressive. The correct answer is C.

Revise and Combine Sentences

---

3. Which of the following is the best way to revise and combine sentences 7, 8, and 9 (reproduced below)?

> *It is because he thinks his boss will think he doesn't know his job. He won't ask any questions at all. At work he will ask questions only to his friend, Eddie.*

    A. Because he thinks his boss will think he doesn't know his job, he won't ask any questions at work unless he asks questions to his only friend, Eddie.
    B. At work, he will ask only his friend Eddie questions, otherwise his boss will think he doesn't know his job.
    C. He won't ask any questions at work at all, unless he asks his friend Eddie, because he thinks his boss will think he doesn't know his job.
    D. Because he doesn't want his boss to think he doesn't know his job, he won't ask any questions at all at work, but he will ask his friend Eddie questions.
    E. He will ask his friend at work, Eddie, questions, but not his boss, who will think he doesn't know his job.

In questions requiring sentence combining, try to avoid the repetition of words or phrases, like "ask" and "questions" here. Choices A and D repeat both words, and choice C repeats "ask." The word order of the first clause of choice E is awkward. The best choice is B—the shortest and the clearest version. The correct answer is B.

Phrases that Should Follow

> **4.** Which of the following phrases should follow "Based on my brother and my father" in sentence 10?
>
>   **A.** Leave it as it is.
>   **B.** it is more likely that men
>   **C.** my opinion is that men are more likely
>   **D.** men, unlike women are more likely
>   **E.** men are probably more likely

The problem in this sentence is the opening phrase will dangle unless it is followed by something that is "based on ...." The writer's opinion, not men, is based on her father and brother. The correct answer is C.

Technique Employed by Writer

> **5.** The writer of this passage employs all of the following EXCEPT
>
>   **A.** development of a contrast
>   **B.** employment of specific examples
>   **C.** chronological organization
>   **D.** raising and answering a question
>   **E.** reference to personal opinions

The writer contrasts men and women, using examples from her family. The passage opens with a question which the rest of the two paragraphs attempt to answer. Sentence 10, for example, is a personal opinion. The passage does not use a chronological organization. The correct answer is C.

Questions 6–10 are based on the following passage.

    (1) Many people think that they have insomnia. **(2)** If they haven't had eight hours of sleep, they think they have insomnia. **(3)** There is no evidence to support the common belief that you have to have eight hours of sleep every night. **(4)** Some people sleep as little as two hours a night. **(5)** They wake up the next morning, and they feel fine. **(6)** Some people need only five hours of sleep. **(7)** Some people must have more than eight hours of sleep to feel refreshed. **(8)** It is harder to keep track of time in a dark room than in the daylight. **(9)** It is easy to overestimate how long you have been awake, or underestimate how long you have been asleep.

Best Version

> **6.** As an introduction to the content of the paragraph as a whole, which of the following is the best version of the first sentence?
>
>   **A.** Leave it as it is.
>   **B.** Many people have insomnia.
>   **C.** Many people think they have insomnia, but they may be mistaken.
>   **D.** Why do so many people think that they have insomnia?
>   **E.** Is less than eight hours of sleep a sign of insomnia, as many believe?

As it stands, the first sentence raises questions about the content of the paragraph. Does it mean they do have insomnia or that they only think they do? Most of the paragraph—which is desperately in need of revision—is about the difficulty in determining what insomnia is, and why it is hard to define. Of the five possibilities, C does the best job of preparing a reader for the rest of the paragraph. B misleads the reader, and D and E ask questions the paragraph will not answer. The correct answer is C.

Combining Sentences

> **7.** Which of the following is the best way to combine sentences 1 and 2 (reproduced below)?
>
> *Many people think that they have insomnia. If they haven't had eight hours of sleep, they think they have insomnia.*
>
> **A.** Many people think that they have insomnia; if they haven't had eight hours of sleep, they think they have insomnia.
> **B.** If they haven't had eight hours of sleep, there are many people who think they have insomnia.
> **C.** Many people haven't had eight hours sleep, and they think they have insomnia.
> **D.** Many people, when they haven't had eight hours sleep, think they have insomnia.
> **E.** Many people who haven't had eight hours of sleep are the ones who think they have insomnia.

When combining sentences, try to consolidate words that are repeated once or twice. Here, the redundant phrase is "they think that they have insomnia." Choice B adds the unneeded "there are," and uses "they" twice. Choice C uses "they" twice, and choice E adds the wordy "are the ones who." The correct answer is D.

Best Version

> **8.** Which of the following is the best version of the underlined parts of sentences 4 and 5 (reproduced below)?
>
> *Some people sleep as little as two hours a <u>night. They wake up the next morning, and they feel fine.</u>*
>
> **A.** night; they wake up the next morning, and they feel fine.
> **B.** night, waking up the next morning and they feel fine.
> **C.** night, and they feel fine waking up the next morning.
> **D.** night, but they wake up the next morning and feel fine.
> **E.** night, yet wake up the next morning feeling fine.

Avoid the repetition of words. Here, the repeated "they" can be cut in A, B, C, and D. Since the sentences imply a contrast, the conjunctions "yet" or "but" are better than the "and." The correct answer is E.

Combining Sentences

> **9.** All of the following pairs of sentences would probably be improved by being combined EXCEPT
>
> **A.** 1 and 2
> **B.** 2 and 3
> **C.** 4 and 5
> **D.** 6 and 7
> **E.** 8 and 9

All of these pairs could be combined except sentences 2 and 3. Combining these sentences would greatly improve the writing. The correct answer is B.

Replacing Sentences

10. Which of the following would be the best replacement of sentences 8 and 9 (reproduced below) to make the conclusion of the paragraph more coherent?

> *It is harder to keep track of time in a dark room than in the daylight. It is easy to overestimate how long you have been awake or underestimate how long you have been asleep.*

  A. Because the number of hours asleep is difficult to estimate, many people have slept more than they think, and do not really need more.

  B. It is harder to keep track of time in a dark room than in the daylight; it is easy to overestimate how long you have been awake or underestimate how long you have been asleep.

  C. Because it is hard to keep track of time in the dark, people cannot really tell how long they have been asleep.

  D. Insomniacs cannot really tell how long they have slept.

  E. Insomniacs are more likely to overestimate their sleeplessness than to underestimate it.

The paragraph has moved from the varied number of hours of sleep people require to a slightly different topic: the difficulty of determining how long one has slept. Choices A, D, and E add new information not included in the original sentences. B is as wordy and unpointed as the original. Choice C is at least more concise and attempts to relate the idea to the difficulty of deciding what insomnia is, the notion hidden beneath the writing of the paragraph. The correct answer is C.

A Summary of Strategies and Key Points for Improving Paragraphs Questions

- Read the passage carefully, but don't get stuck on errors in the passage. The errors are intentional for later questions.

- Typically, one or two of the questions will ask you to combine two or three sentences.

- One question may ask you to recognize and correct a usage error.

- Other questions will deal with a variety of topics that arise from the selection.

- There may be questions on sentence structure, on transitions from sentence to sentence or paragraph to paragraph, on the organization of the passage or a paragraph, on logic, on clarity, on rhetorical strategy, or on verbosity.

- Some questions that deal with the whole essay or with individual paragraphs will focus on organization, development, and appropriate language.

- Keep in mind that the best answer is one that will most effectively express the intended meaning.

- Observe the rules of standard written English.

PART II

PRACTICE-REVIEW-ANALYZE-PRACTICE

Three Full-Length Practice Tests

This section contains three simulated full-length practice new SAT tests. The practice tests are followed by complete answers, explanations, and analysis techniques. The format, levels of difficulty, question structure, and number of questions are similar to those on the new SAT. Since the test is new, the number and order of question types may vary.

The SAT is copyrighted and may not be duplicated, and these questions are not taken directly from the actual tests or released sample problems. The sections in these practice exams are labeled by subject for your convenience in reviewing. They are not labeled on the actual SAT.

When you take these exams, try to simulate the test conditions by following the time allotments carefully.

Answer Sheets for Practice Test 1

(Remove These Sheets and Use Them to Write Your Essay and Mark Your Answers)

Section 1

Begin your essay on this page and continue on the next page if necessary. Do not write outside the essay boxes provided.

CUT HERE

CUT HERE

Section 2

1 Ⓐ Ⓑ Ⓒ Ⓓ Ⓔ
2 Ⓐ Ⓑ Ⓒ Ⓓ Ⓔ
3 Ⓐ Ⓑ Ⓒ Ⓓ Ⓔ
4 Ⓐ Ⓑ Ⓒ Ⓓ Ⓔ
5 Ⓐ Ⓑ Ⓒ Ⓓ Ⓔ
6 Ⓐ Ⓑ Ⓒ Ⓓ Ⓔ
7 Ⓐ Ⓑ Ⓒ Ⓓ Ⓔ
8 Ⓐ Ⓑ Ⓒ Ⓓ Ⓔ
9 Ⓐ Ⓑ Ⓒ Ⓓ Ⓔ
10 Ⓐ Ⓑ Ⓒ Ⓓ Ⓔ
11 Ⓐ Ⓑ Ⓒ Ⓓ Ⓔ
12 Ⓐ Ⓑ Ⓒ Ⓓ Ⓔ
13 Ⓐ Ⓑ Ⓒ Ⓓ Ⓔ
14 Ⓐ Ⓑ Ⓒ Ⓓ Ⓔ
15 Ⓐ Ⓑ Ⓒ Ⓓ Ⓔ
16 Ⓐ Ⓑ Ⓒ Ⓓ Ⓔ
17 Ⓐ Ⓑ Ⓒ Ⓓ Ⓔ
18 Ⓐ Ⓑ Ⓒ Ⓓ Ⓔ
19 Ⓐ Ⓑ Ⓒ Ⓓ Ⓔ
20 Ⓐ Ⓑ Ⓒ Ⓓ Ⓔ
21 Ⓐ Ⓑ Ⓒ Ⓓ Ⓔ
22 Ⓐ Ⓑ Ⓒ Ⓓ Ⓔ
23 Ⓐ Ⓑ Ⓒ Ⓓ Ⓔ
24 Ⓐ Ⓑ Ⓒ Ⓓ Ⓔ
25 Ⓐ Ⓑ Ⓒ Ⓓ Ⓔ
26 Ⓐ Ⓑ Ⓒ Ⓓ Ⓔ
27 Ⓐ Ⓑ Ⓒ Ⓓ Ⓔ
28 Ⓐ Ⓑ Ⓒ Ⓓ Ⓔ

Section 3

1 Ⓐ Ⓑ Ⓒ Ⓓ Ⓔ
2 Ⓐ Ⓑ Ⓒ Ⓓ Ⓔ
3 Ⓐ Ⓑ Ⓒ Ⓓ Ⓔ
4 Ⓐ Ⓑ Ⓒ Ⓓ Ⓔ
5 Ⓐ Ⓑ Ⓒ Ⓓ Ⓔ
6 Ⓐ Ⓑ Ⓒ Ⓓ Ⓔ
7 Ⓐ Ⓑ Ⓒ Ⓓ Ⓔ
8 Ⓐ Ⓑ Ⓒ Ⓓ Ⓔ
9 Ⓐ Ⓑ Ⓒ Ⓓ Ⓔ
10 Ⓐ Ⓑ Ⓒ Ⓓ Ⓔ
11 Ⓐ Ⓑ Ⓒ Ⓓ Ⓔ
12 Ⓐ Ⓑ Ⓒ Ⓓ Ⓔ
13 Ⓐ Ⓑ Ⓒ Ⓓ Ⓔ
14 Ⓐ Ⓑ Ⓒ Ⓓ Ⓔ
15 Ⓐ Ⓑ Ⓒ Ⓓ Ⓔ
16 Ⓐ Ⓑ Ⓒ Ⓓ Ⓔ
17 Ⓐ Ⓑ Ⓒ Ⓓ Ⓔ
18 Ⓐ Ⓑ Ⓒ Ⓓ Ⓔ
19 Ⓐ Ⓑ Ⓒ Ⓓ Ⓔ
20 Ⓐ Ⓑ Ⓒ Ⓓ Ⓔ

Section 4

1 Ⓐ Ⓑ Ⓒ Ⓓ Ⓔ
2 Ⓐ Ⓑ Ⓒ Ⓓ Ⓔ
3 Ⓐ Ⓑ Ⓒ Ⓓ Ⓔ
4 Ⓐ Ⓑ Ⓒ Ⓓ Ⓔ
5 Ⓐ Ⓑ Ⓒ Ⓓ Ⓔ
6 Ⓐ Ⓑ Ⓒ Ⓓ Ⓔ
7 Ⓐ Ⓑ Ⓒ Ⓓ Ⓔ
8 Ⓐ Ⓑ Ⓒ Ⓓ Ⓔ
9 Ⓐ Ⓑ Ⓒ Ⓓ Ⓔ
10 Ⓐ Ⓑ Ⓒ Ⓓ Ⓔ
11 Ⓐ Ⓑ Ⓒ Ⓓ Ⓔ
12 Ⓐ Ⓑ Ⓒ Ⓓ Ⓔ
13 Ⓐ Ⓑ Ⓒ Ⓓ Ⓔ
14 Ⓐ Ⓑ Ⓒ Ⓓ Ⓔ
15 Ⓐ Ⓑ Ⓒ Ⓓ Ⓔ
16 Ⓐ Ⓑ Ⓒ Ⓓ Ⓔ
17 Ⓐ Ⓑ Ⓒ Ⓓ Ⓔ
18 Ⓐ Ⓑ Ⓒ Ⓓ Ⓔ
19 Ⓐ Ⓑ Ⓒ Ⓓ Ⓔ
20 Ⓐ Ⓑ Ⓒ Ⓓ Ⓔ
21 Ⓐ Ⓑ Ⓒ Ⓓ Ⓔ
22 Ⓐ Ⓑ Ⓒ Ⓓ Ⓔ
23 Ⓐ Ⓑ Ⓒ Ⓓ Ⓔ
24 Ⓐ Ⓑ Ⓒ Ⓓ Ⓔ
25 Ⓐ Ⓑ Ⓒ Ⓓ Ⓔ
26 Ⓐ Ⓑ Ⓒ Ⓓ Ⓔ
27 Ⓐ Ⓑ Ⓒ Ⓓ Ⓔ
28 Ⓐ Ⓑ Ⓒ Ⓓ Ⓔ
29 Ⓐ Ⓑ Ⓒ Ⓓ Ⓔ
30 Ⓐ Ⓑ Ⓒ Ⓓ Ⓔ
31 Ⓐ Ⓑ Ⓒ Ⓓ Ⓔ
32 Ⓐ Ⓑ Ⓒ Ⓓ Ⓔ
33 Ⓐ Ⓑ Ⓒ Ⓓ Ⓔ
34 Ⓐ Ⓑ Ⓒ Ⓓ Ⓔ
35 Ⓐ Ⓑ Ⓒ Ⓓ Ⓔ

Section 5

1 Ⓐ Ⓑ Ⓒ Ⓓ Ⓔ
2 Ⓐ Ⓑ Ⓒ Ⓓ Ⓔ
3 Ⓐ Ⓑ Ⓒ Ⓓ Ⓔ
4 Ⓐ Ⓑ Ⓒ Ⓓ Ⓔ
5 Ⓐ Ⓑ Ⓒ Ⓓ Ⓔ
6 Ⓐ Ⓑ Ⓒ Ⓓ Ⓔ
7 Ⓐ Ⓑ Ⓒ Ⓓ Ⓔ
8 Ⓐ Ⓑ Ⓒ Ⓓ Ⓔ
9 Ⓐ Ⓑ Ⓒ Ⓓ Ⓔ
10 Ⓐ Ⓑ Ⓒ Ⓓ Ⓔ
11 Ⓐ Ⓑ Ⓒ Ⓓ Ⓔ
12 Ⓐ Ⓑ Ⓒ Ⓓ Ⓔ
13 Ⓐ Ⓑ Ⓒ Ⓓ Ⓔ
14 Ⓐ Ⓑ Ⓒ Ⓓ Ⓔ
15 Ⓐ Ⓑ Ⓒ Ⓓ Ⓔ
16 Ⓐ Ⓑ Ⓒ Ⓓ Ⓔ
17 Ⓐ Ⓑ Ⓒ Ⓓ Ⓔ
18 Ⓐ Ⓑ Ⓒ Ⓓ Ⓔ
19 Ⓐ Ⓑ Ⓒ Ⓓ Ⓔ
20 Ⓐ Ⓑ Ⓒ Ⓓ Ⓔ
21 Ⓐ Ⓑ Ⓒ Ⓓ Ⓔ
22 Ⓐ Ⓑ Ⓒ Ⓓ Ⓔ
23 Ⓐ Ⓑ Ⓒ Ⓓ Ⓔ
24 Ⓐ Ⓑ Ⓒ Ⓓ Ⓔ
25 Ⓐ Ⓑ Ⓒ Ⓓ Ⓔ
26 Ⓐ Ⓑ Ⓒ Ⓓ Ⓔ
27 Ⓐ Ⓑ Ⓒ Ⓓ Ⓔ

Section 6

1 Ⓐ Ⓑ Ⓒ Ⓓ Ⓔ
2 Ⓐ Ⓑ Ⓒ Ⓓ Ⓔ
3 Ⓐ Ⓑ Ⓒ Ⓓ Ⓔ
4 Ⓐ Ⓑ Ⓒ Ⓓ Ⓔ
5 Ⓐ Ⓑ Ⓒ Ⓓ Ⓔ
6 Ⓐ Ⓑ Ⓒ Ⓓ Ⓔ
7 Ⓐ Ⓑ Ⓒ Ⓓ Ⓔ
8 Ⓐ Ⓑ Ⓒ Ⓓ Ⓔ
9 Ⓐ Ⓑ Ⓒ Ⓓ Ⓔ
10 Ⓐ Ⓑ Ⓒ Ⓓ Ⓔ

11. (grid-in answer box)

12. (grid-in answer box)

13. (grid-in answer box)

Section 6 (continued)

14. – **17.** grid-in answer boxes

18. – **20.** grid-in answer boxes

Section 7

1 Ⓐ Ⓑ Ⓒ Ⓓ Ⓔ
2 Ⓐ Ⓑ Ⓒ Ⓓ Ⓔ
3 Ⓐ Ⓑ Ⓒ Ⓓ Ⓔ
4 Ⓐ Ⓑ Ⓒ Ⓓ Ⓔ
5 Ⓐ Ⓑ Ⓒ Ⓓ Ⓔ
6 Ⓐ Ⓑ Ⓒ Ⓓ Ⓔ
7 Ⓐ Ⓑ Ⓒ Ⓓ Ⓔ
8 Ⓐ Ⓑ Ⓒ Ⓓ Ⓔ
9 Ⓐ Ⓑ Ⓒ Ⓓ Ⓔ
10 Ⓐ Ⓑ Ⓒ Ⓓ Ⓔ
11 Ⓐ Ⓑ Ⓒ Ⓓ Ⓔ
12 Ⓐ Ⓑ Ⓒ Ⓓ Ⓔ
13 Ⓐ Ⓑ Ⓒ Ⓓ Ⓔ
14 Ⓐ Ⓑ Ⓒ Ⓓ Ⓔ
15 Ⓐ Ⓑ Ⓒ Ⓓ Ⓔ

Section 8

1 Ⓐ Ⓑ Ⓒ Ⓓ Ⓔ
2 Ⓐ Ⓑ Ⓒ Ⓓ Ⓔ
3 Ⓐ Ⓑ Ⓒ Ⓓ Ⓔ
4 Ⓐ Ⓑ Ⓒ Ⓓ Ⓔ
5 Ⓐ Ⓑ Ⓒ Ⓓ Ⓔ
6 Ⓐ Ⓑ Ⓒ Ⓓ Ⓔ
7 Ⓐ Ⓑ Ⓒ Ⓓ Ⓔ
8 Ⓐ Ⓑ Ⓒ Ⓓ Ⓔ
9 Ⓐ Ⓑ Ⓒ Ⓓ Ⓔ
10 Ⓐ Ⓑ Ⓒ Ⓓ Ⓔ
11 Ⓐ Ⓑ Ⓒ Ⓓ Ⓔ
12 Ⓐ Ⓑ Ⓒ Ⓓ Ⓔ
13 Ⓐ Ⓑ Ⓒ Ⓓ Ⓔ
14 Ⓐ Ⓑ Ⓒ Ⓓ Ⓔ
15 Ⓐ Ⓑ Ⓒ Ⓓ Ⓔ

Section 9

1 Ⓐ Ⓑ Ⓒ Ⓓ Ⓔ
2 Ⓐ Ⓑ Ⓒ Ⓓ Ⓔ
3 Ⓐ Ⓑ Ⓒ Ⓓ Ⓔ
4 Ⓐ Ⓑ Ⓒ Ⓓ Ⓔ
5 Ⓐ Ⓑ Ⓒ Ⓓ Ⓔ
6 Ⓐ Ⓑ Ⓒ Ⓓ Ⓔ
7 Ⓐ Ⓑ Ⓒ Ⓓ Ⓔ
8 Ⓐ Ⓑ Ⓒ Ⓓ Ⓔ
9 Ⓐ Ⓑ Ⓒ Ⓓ Ⓔ
10 Ⓐ Ⓑ Ⓒ Ⓓ Ⓔ
11 Ⓐ Ⓑ Ⓒ Ⓓ Ⓔ
12 Ⓐ Ⓑ Ⓒ Ⓓ Ⓔ
13 Ⓐ Ⓑ Ⓒ Ⓓ Ⓔ
14 Ⓐ Ⓑ Ⓒ Ⓓ Ⓔ
15 Ⓐ Ⓑ Ⓒ Ⓓ Ⓔ
16 Ⓐ Ⓑ Ⓒ Ⓓ Ⓔ
17 Ⓐ Ⓑ Ⓒ Ⓓ Ⓔ
18 Ⓐ Ⓑ Ⓒ Ⓓ Ⓔ
19 Ⓐ Ⓑ Ⓒ Ⓓ Ⓔ
20 Ⓐ Ⓑ Ⓒ Ⓓ Ⓔ

Section 10

1 Ⓐ Ⓑ Ⓒ Ⓓ Ⓔ
2 Ⓐ Ⓑ Ⓒ Ⓓ Ⓔ
3 Ⓐ Ⓑ Ⓒ Ⓓ Ⓔ
4 Ⓐ Ⓑ Ⓒ Ⓓ Ⓔ
5 Ⓐ Ⓑ Ⓒ Ⓓ Ⓔ
6 Ⓐ Ⓑ Ⓒ Ⓓ Ⓔ
7 Ⓐ Ⓑ Ⓒ Ⓓ Ⓔ
8 Ⓐ Ⓑ Ⓒ Ⓓ Ⓔ
9 Ⓐ Ⓑ Ⓒ Ⓓ Ⓔ
10 Ⓐ Ⓑ Ⓒ Ⓓ Ⓔ
11 Ⓐ Ⓑ Ⓒ Ⓓ Ⓔ
12 Ⓐ Ⓑ Ⓒ Ⓓ Ⓔ
13 Ⓐ Ⓑ Ⓒ Ⓓ Ⓔ
14 Ⓐ Ⓑ Ⓒ Ⓓ Ⓔ
15 Ⓐ Ⓑ Ⓒ Ⓓ Ⓔ

CUT HERE

Practice Test 1

Section 1: Writing—Essay

Time: 25 Minutes

1 Essay Question

You have 25 minutes to plan and write an essay on the topic below. DO NOT WRITE ON ANOTHER TOPIC. AN ESSAY ON ANOTHER TOPIC WILL NOT BE SCORED.

The essay is intended to give you the chance to show your writing skills. Be sure to express your ideas on the topic clearly and effectively. The quality of your writing is much more important than the quantity, but to cover the topic adequately, you may want to write more than one paragraph. Be specific.

Your essay must be written on the two lined pages provided. You will not be given any additional paper. If you keep your handwriting to a reasonable size, write on every line, and avoid wide margins, you should have enough space to complete your essay.

Directions: Read the following paragraph and assignment carefully. Then prepare and write a persuasive essay. Be sure to support your reasons with specific examples that will make your essay more effective.

> When Alexander Pope wrote, "A little learning is a dangerous thing," he was not recommending ignorance. His point is that incomplete or superficial knowledge may be harmful, especially if it encourages an unjustified certainty in private or public life.

Assignment: Using an example or examples from your reading or your personal observation, write an essay to support or to refute this paragraph.

THE PROCTOR WILL ANNOUNCE WHEN 25 MINUTES HAVE PASSED. AT THAT TIME, YOU MUST STOP WRITING. IF YOU FINISH YOUR ESSAY BEFORE 25 MINUTES HAVE PASSED, YOU MAY NOT GO ON TO ANY OTHER SECTION OF THE EXAM. THE PROCTOR WILL ANNOUNCE WHEN TO START THE NEXT SECTION.

Section 2: Critical Reading

Time: 25 Minutes

28 Questions

In this section, choose the best answer for each question and blacken the corresponding space on the answer sheet.

Directions: Each blank in the following sentences indicates that something has been omitted. Consider the lettered words beneath the sentence and choose the word or set of words that *best* fits the whole sentence.

EXAMPLE:

With a million more people than any other African nation, Nigeria is the most _____ country on the continent.

   A. impoverished
   B. successful
   C. populous
   D. developed
   E. militant

The correct answer is C.

---

1. Loved and hated by thousands, Dr. Lucy Bertram may well be the most _____ physician ever to become surgeon general.

   A. controversial
   B. popular
   C. successful
   D. well-trained
   E. professional

2. Over thousands of years, organisms have _____ many strategies to conserve water.

   A. administered
   B. evolved
   C. organized
   D. questioned
   E. considered

3. My cat is a creature of contradictions: _____ yet affectionate, _____ yet alert.

   A. aloof . . . dreamy
   B. cruel . . . shrewd
   C. quiet . . . lively
   D. selfish . . . nimble
   E. loving . . . sly

4. _____ for talking too much, the teacher _____ his reputation by keeping the class 30 minutes longer than the scheduled class time.

   A. Famous . . . evinced
   B. Renowned . . . overturned
   C. Notorious . . . verified
   D. Illustrious . . . rebutted
   E. Eminent . . . established

5. If Senator Montana runs for reelection next year, she will have the money-raising advantage of the _____.

   A. campaigner
   B. favorite
   C. underdog
   D. incumbent
   E. candidate

6. Using his own home as _____, Marlowe obtained a private loan that enabled him to _____ his financial obligations to the other partners and emerge free of debt.

   A. pledge . . . increase
   B. surety . . . augment
   C. collateral . . . discharge
   D. profit . . . eliminate
   E. deposit . . . endorse

7. The absurdist as opposed to the heroic treatment of war reached maturity in *Catch-22,* and the Vietnam War made this approach, which seemed so _____ and shocking, the only way to write about that conflict.

    A. banal
    B. radical
    C. plausible
    D. cozy
    E. familiar

8. Because the issue is so insignificant, it was surprising that the disagreement among city council members was so _____.

    A. tepid
    B. slovenly
    C. trivial
    D. acrimonious
    E. genial

9. Many thought Billy Eckstine's band _____ because its musicians were young, avant-garde jazzmen, while its lead singer crooned _____ popular ballads.

    A. progressive . . . romantic
    B. old-fashioned . . . unique
    C. inconsistent . . . conservative
    D. unmusical . . . familiar
    E. predictable . . . melodic

10. Hoping to escape detection, Minnie _____ placed an ace in her sleeve while Rance shuffled the cards.

    A. brazenly
    B. overtly
    C. furtively
    D. hopefully
    E. eagerly

GO ON TO THE NEXT PAGE

Directions: Questions follow each of the passages below. Using only the stated or implied information in each passage and in its introduction, if any, answer the questions.

Questions 11–12 are based on the following passage.

The doctrine of association has been the basis for explaining how one idea leads to another. Aristotle provided the basic law: association by contiguity. Seeing a shotgun may remind you of a
(5) murder, or it may remind you of a hunting experience in Wyoming, depending on your history. When you hear the word "table" you think of chair (or bench or Formica or something else in your history), carrots make you think of peas (or Bugs
(10) Bunny or vitamins) and so on. In each case, you experienced the two items contiguously in the same place or at the same time or both and they became linked in your mind. In psychology, word association tests are based on contiguity, the idea
(15) being that your response to a particular word is based on your personal history.

11. The author of the paragraph would agree with which of the following statements?

  A. No one thing is necessarily associated with any other particular thing.

  B. Aristotle posited associations which have become part of the modern experience.

  C. Some associations are fixed and unchangeable.

  D. Culture determines what associations a person makes.

  E. Word association is a poor test because people's associations vary so much.

12. Which of the following examples most strengthens the main point of the paragraph?

  A. Some people are able to experience more than two items contiguously.

  B. The smell of coffee makes everyone think of breakfast.

  C. Aristotle's writing is full of unexplained associations.

  D. People who make uncommon associations are often mentally disturbed, whereas people who make overly predictable associations lack creativity.

  E. Some Londoners who endured German bombings in World War II are still frightened by loud noises.

Questions 13–14 are based on the following passage.

Like many birds, the monarch butterfly is migratory. Each year more than 100 million of the insects fly from their summer homes in the north to areas in the south. Unlike migratory animals who learn their
(5) routes from their parents or other members of the species, the life span of monarchs is 90 days or less; an older generation cannot instruct a younger one. Not one of the insects that flew north in the spring is alive to fly south in the fall. Insect ecologists have
(10) recently established that monarchs use the position of the sun to determine their direction. It may also be that the butterflies can sense the force lines of the earth's magnetic field to use as a navigational aid, or that they find directional clues in the changing
(15) length of the days.

13. According to information in the paragraph, which of the following do butterflies use to help them find their way when they migrate?

  A. the prevailing winds

  B. one generation's teaching the next

  C. the position of the sun

  D. force lines of the earth's magnetic field

  E. the changing length of days and nights

14. Of the following general statements, which is best supported by the paragraph?

  A. Scientists have been unable to explain completely how monarch butterflies migrate successfully.

  B. Butterflies and other insects would be unable to navigate on cloudy days.

  C. Smaller animals like insects depend more on instincts than larger animals.

  D. Scientists know more about larger land and sea animals than they do about insects like the monarch butterfly.

  E. Scientists will never be able to explain how butterflies can find their way over long distances.

Questions 15–20 are based on the following passage.

The following passage is from a book about Paul Gauguin, the late 19th century artist who left France to live and paint on the Pacific island of Tahiti.

Gauguin decided to settle in Mataiea, some forty-five kilometers from Papeete, probably on the advice of a Tahitian chief whom he had befriended.
(5) There he rented a native-style oval bamboo hut, roofed with pandanu leaves. Once settled, he was in a position to begin work in earnest and to tackle serious figure studies. It was probably soon after this that he painted *Vahine no te tiare,* his first portrait of a Tahitian model.
(10) By the late summer of 1892 the completed canvas was back in Paris, hanging in the Goupil gallery. From the many subsequent references to this image in his correspondence, it is clear that Gauguin set considerable store by his "Tahitienne" and, by send-
(15) ing her on ahead to Paris, wanted her to serve as an ambassadress for the further images of Tahitian women he would be bringing back with him on his return. He pressed his male friends for their reactions to the girl, rather than to the picture, anxious to
(20) know whether they, like him, would be responsive to the beauty of her face: "And her forehead," he later wrote, "with the majesty of upsweeping lines, reminded me of that saying of Poe's, 'There is no perfect beauty without a certain singularity in the
(25) proportions.'" No one, it seems, was quite attuned to his emotional perception: while Aurier was enthusiastic, excited by the picture's rarity value, Schuffenecker was somewhat taken aback by the painting's lack of Symbolist character. Indeed, apart
(30) from the imaginary floral background which harked back to Gauguin's 1888 *Self-Portrait,* the image is a relatively straightforward one. Recent anthropological work, backed by the use of photography, had scientifically characterized the physical distinctions
(35) between the different races, distinctions that in the past had been imperfectly understood. Generally speaking, artists before Gauguin's time had represented Tahitians as idealized types, adjusting their features and proportions to accord with European
(40) taste. This meant that hitherto the Tahitian in Western art could scarcely be distinguished from his African or Asian counterpart.
Unfortunately, Charles Giraud's paintings have disappeared, so we cannot compare them with
(45) Gauguin's, but this first image by Gauguin suggests a desire to portray the Tahitian physiognomy naturalistically, without the blinkers of preconceived rules of beauty laid down by a classical culture. Naturalism as an artistic creed, though, was anathema to Gauguin;

(50) it made the artist a lackey of science and knowledge rather than a god-like creator. He wanted to go beyond empirical observation of this kind, to find a way of painting Tahiti that would accord with his Symbolist aspirations, that would embody the feel-
(55) ings he had about the place and the poetic image he carried with him of the island's mysterious past.

15. In line 13, the word "correspondence" means

A. correlation.
B. agreement.
C. conformity.
D. similarity.
E. letters.

16. Gauguin found the faces of Tahitian women beautiful because of their

A. elegant coloration.
B. unusual proportions.
C. refusal to wear makeup.
D. dark hair covering the forehead.
E. openness and innocence.

17. The passage suggests that a painter depicting a Tahitian in a period sometime before Gauguin would probably

A. rely on photographs for models.
B. make an image that was not in accord with European ideals of female beauty.
C. paint a picture that employed a symbolic landscape as background.
D. fail to differentiate a Tahitian from the inhabitants of Asian countries.
E. paint only models who were fully clothed in Western-style costume.

18. It can be inferred that the author would like to see the lost paintings of Charles Giraud in order to

A. determine whether they presented the Tahitians realistically.
B. determine whether they were better paintings than Gauguin's.
C. determine whether they deserve their high reputation.
D. compare the symbolism of these paintings with that of Gauguin's.
E. discover what subjects Giraud chose to paint.

GO ON TO THE NEXT PAGE

19. Of the following phrases, which does the author use to refer to the aspect of Gauguin's art that attempts to depict the real world accurately?

    I.   "the image is a relatively straightforward one" (lines 31–32)

    II. "desire to portray the Tahitian physiognomy naturalistically" (lines 46–47)

    III. "a way of painting Tahiti that would accord with his Symbolist aspirations" (lines 52–54)

    A. II only
    B. III only
    C. I and II only
    D. I and III only
    E. I, II, and III

20. The passage suggests that an important problem Gauguin would have to deal with in his paintings of Tahiti was how to

    A. reconcile his naturalistic and symbolistic impulses.
    B. make Europeans understand the beauty of Tahiti.
    C. find the necessary supplies in a remote location.
    D. earn enough money to support himself by selling his paintings in Paris.
    E. make artistic use of the new advances in photography.

Questions 21–28 are based on the following passage.

Jim Hansen, a climatologist at NASA's Goddard Space Institute, is convinced that the earth's temperature is rising and places the blame on the buildup of greenhouse gases in the atmosphere.
(5) Unconvinced, John Sununu, former White House chief of staff, doubts that the warming will be great enough to produce a serious threat and fears that measures to reduce the emissions would throw a wrench into the gears that drive the United States'
(10) troubled economy. The stakes in this debate are extremely high, for it pits society's short-term well-being against the future of all the planet's inhabitants. Our past transgressions have altered major portions of the earth's surface, but the effects have
(15) been limited. Now we can foresee the possibility that to satisfy the energy needs of an expanding human population, we will rapidly change the climate of the entire planet, with consequences for even the most remote and unspoiled regions of the globe.
(20) The notion that certain gases could warm the planet is not new. In 1896 Svante Arrhenius, a

Swedish chemist, resolved the long-standing question of how the earth's atmosphere could maintain the planet's relatively warm temperature when the
(25) oxygen and nitrogen that make up 99 percent of the atmosphere do not absorb any of the heat escaping as infrared radiation from the earth's surface into space. He discovered that even the small amounts of carbon dioxide in the atmosphere could absorb
(30) large amounts of heat. Furthermore, he reasoned that the burning of coal, oil, and natural gas could eventually release enough carbon dioxide to warm the earth. Hansen and most other climatologists agree that enough greenhouse gases have accumu-
(35) lated in the atmosphere to make Arrhenius's prediction come true. Burning fossil fuels is not the only problem; a fifth of our emissions of carbon dioxide now come from clearing and burning forests. Scientists are also tracking a host of other
(40) greenhouse gases that emanate from a variety of human activities; the warming effect of methane, chlorofluorocarbons, and nitrous oxide combined equals that of carbon dioxide.

Although the current warming from these gases
(45) may be difficult to detect against the background noise of natural climate variation, most climatologists are certain that as the gases continue to accumulate, increases in the earth's temperature will become evident even to skeptics. The battle lines
(50) for this particular skirmish are surprisingly well balanced. Those with concerns about global warming point to the recent report from the United Nations Intergovernmental Plan on Climate Change, which suggests that with "business as
(55) usual," emissions of carbon dioxide by the year 2025 will be 25 percent greater than previously estimated. On the other side, the George C. Marshall Institute, a conservative think tank, published a report warning that without greenhouse gases to
(60) warm things up, the world would become cool in the next century. Stephen Schneider, a leading computer modeler of future climate change, accused Sununu of "brandishing the [Marshall] report as if he were holding a crucifix to repel a
(65) vampire."

If the reality of global warming were put on trial, each side would have trouble making its case. Jim Hansen's side could not prove beyond a reasonable doubt that carbon dioxide and the other
(70) greenhouse gases have warmed the planet. But neither could John Sununu's side prove beyond a reasonable doubt that the warming expected from greenhouse gases has not occurred.

21. The purpose of the first paragraph (lines 1–19) of the passage is to

A. argue for the reduction of greenhouse gases in the atmosphere.

B. defend on economic grounds the reduction of greenhouse gases.

C. present two opposing positions on the subject of the earth's rising temperature.

D. lessen the concern of the public about the alleged buildup of greenhouse gases.

E. introduce the two most important spokesmen for and against ecological reforms.

22. In the first paragraph in line 11, the word "pits" means

A. removes the core of.

B. sets in competition.

C. depresses.

D. marks with small scars.

E. hardens.

23. From the information in the second paragraph of the passage, you can infer that a planet

A. whose atmosphere was made up entirely of oxygen would be warmer than a planet equally distant from the sun with an atmosphere made up entirely of nitrogen.

B. whose atmosphere was made up entirely of nitrogen would be warmer than a planet equally distant from the sun with an atmosphere made up entirely of oxygen.

C. with a larger amount of carbon dioxide in its atmosphere, other factors being equal, will be warmer than a planet with less carbon dioxide.

D. with a small amount of carbon dioxide in its atmosphere cannot increase this amount.

E. with little infrared radiation escaping from its surface is likely to be extremely cold.

24. The passage implies that a greenhouse gas is one that

I. forms a large part of the earth's atmosphere.

II. absorbs heat escaping from the earth's surface.

III. can be formed by the clearing and burning of forests.

A. III only

B. I and II only

C. I and III only

D. II and III only

E. I, II, and III

25. From the passage, it can be inferred that all the following are greenhouse gases EXCEPT

A. nitrogen.

B. carbon dioxide.

C. methane.

D. chlorofluorocarbons.

E. nitrous oxide.

26. Which of the following, if true, would call into question the argument of the Marshall report?

I. Since the earth's climate did not grow colder in the five hundred years since 1400 when the amount of greenhouse gases released by humans was small, there is no reason to expect a decrease in temperature when the amounts of gas released are now much larger.

II. The radical reduction of the emission of greenhouse gases will result in massive unemployment throughout the industrial world.

III. Some scientific studies have shown that the temperature of the earth is unaffected by the presence of oxygen in the atmosphere.

A. I only

B. II only

C. I and II only

D. I and III only

E. I, II, and III

GO ON TO THE NEXT PAGE

27. The word "skeptics" in line 49 most nearly means

    A. scientists.
    B. ecologists.
    C. opponents.
    D. doubters.
    E. politicians.

28. Stephen Schneider probably referred to Sununu's "brandishing the [Marshall] report as if he were holding a crucifix to repel a vampire" in order to

    I. amuse his audience.
    II. suggest that Sununu's claims are melodramatic.
    III. imply that the idea that greenhouse gases are dangerous is as imaginary as a vampire.

    A. III only
    B. I and II only
    C. I and III only
    D. II and III only
    E. I, II, and III

IF YOU FINISH BEFORE TIME IS CALLED, CHECK YOUR WORK ON THIS SECTION ONLY. DO NOT WORK ON ANY OTHER SECTION IN THE TEST.

Section 3: Mathematics

Time: 25 Minutes

20 Questions

Directions: Solve each problem in this section by using the information given and your own mathematical calculations, insights, and problem-solving skills. Then select the one correct answer of the five choices given and mark the corresponding circle on your answer sheet. Use the available space on the page for your scratch work.

Notes

1. All numbers used are real numbers.

2. Calculators may be used.

3. Some problems may be accompanied by figures or diagrams. These figures are drawn as accurately as possible EXCEPT when it is stated in a specific problem that a figure is not drawn to scale. The figures and diagrams are meant to provide information useful in solving the problem or problems. Unless otherwise stated, all figures and diagrams lie in a plane.

Data That Can Be Used for Reference

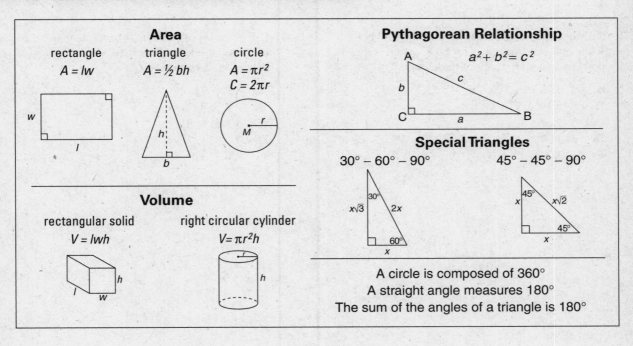

Area

rectangle
$A = lw$

triangle
$A = \frac{1}{2}bh$

circle
$A = \pi r^2$
$C = 2\pi r$

Volume

rectangular solid
$V = lwh$

right circular cylinder
$V = \pi r^2 h$

Pythagorean Relationship

$a^2 + b^2 = c^2$

Special Triangles

$30° - 60° - 90°$

$45° - 45° - 90°$

A circle is composed of 360°
A straight angle measures 180°
The sum of the angles of a triangle is 180°

GO ON TO THE NEXT PAGE

1. If $\frac{1}{5}$ of a number is 2, what is $\frac{1}{2}$ of the number?

- A. 10
- B. 5
- C. 3
- D. 2
- E. 1

3. If $x = -1$, then $x^4 + x^3 + x^2 + x - 3 =$

- A. −13
- B. −7
- C. −3
- D. −2
- E. 1

2. If a store purchases several items for $1.80 per dozen and sells them at 3 for $0.85, what is the store's profit on 6 dozen of these items?

- A. $ 4.20
- B. $ 5.70
- C. $ 9.60
- D. $10.60
- E. $20.40

4. If P is the set of prime numbers less than 10 and Q is the set of odd integers between 2 and 8, what is the union of sets P and Q?

- A. {3, 5, 7}
- B. {2, 3, 5, 7}
- C. {3, 5, 7, 9}
- D. {2, 3, 5, 7, 9}
- E. {1, 2, 3, 5, 7}

5. If $f(x) = 3^x + 5x$, then $f(3) =$

   A. 17
   B. 24
   C. 42
   D. 80
   E. 96

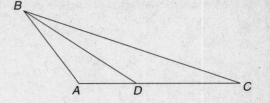

Note: Figure not drawn to scale.

7. In the preceding figure, $AB = AD$ and $BD = CD$. If $\angle C$ measures $19°$, what is the measure of $\angle A$ in degrees?

   A.   75°
   B.   94°
   C. 104°
   D. 114°
   E. 142°

6. The symbol $\otimes$ represents a binary operation defined as $a \otimes b = a^3 + b^2$. What is the value of $(-2) \otimes (-3)$?

   A.   17
   B.   1
   C.   0
   D. −1
   E. −17

8. Angela has nickels and dimes in her pocket. She has twice as many dimes as nickels. What is the best expression of the amount of money she has in cents if x equals the number of nickels she has?

   A. $25x$
   B. $10x + 5(2x)$
   C. $x + 2x$
   D. $5(3x)$
   E. $20(x + 5)$

GO ON TO THE NEXT PAGE

9. If $x - 4 = y$, what must $(y - x)^3$ equal?

   A.   −64
   B.   −12
   C.   12
   D.   64
   E.   128

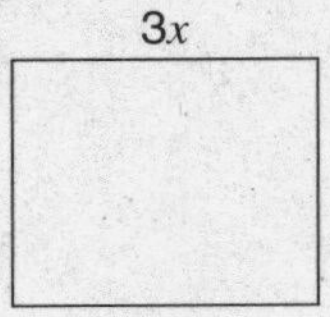

3x

10. The length of a rectangle is $3x$, and its perimeter is $10x + 8$. What is the width of the rectangle?

   A. $2x + 4$
   B. $2x + 8$
   C. $4x + 8$
   D. $4x + 4$
   E. $5x + 4$

11. If $\dfrac{3}{7} = \dfrac{10}{x - 4}$, then $x =$

   A. $8\frac{2}{7}$
   B.   11
   C. $19\frac{1}{3}$
   D. $24\frac{2}{3}$
   E. $27\frac{1}{3}$

12. A car travels 140 miles in 4 hours, while the return trip takes $3\frac{1}{2}$ hours. What is the average speed in miles per hour for the entire trip?

   A.   35
   B. $37\frac{1}{3}$
   C. $37\frac{1}{2}$
   D.   40
   E.   75

13. If $a > b$, and $ab > 0$, which of the following must be true?

   I. $a > 0$
   II. $b > 0$
   III. $a/b > 0$

   A. I only
   B. II only
   C. III only
   D. I and II only
   E. I and III only

15. Which of the following is equal to $\left(\dfrac{x^{-5} y^2}{x^{-2} y^{-3}} \right)^{-2}$?

   A. $x^6 y^2$

   B. $x^6 y^{10}$

   C. $\dfrac{x^6}{y^2}$

   D. $\dfrac{x^6}{y^{10}}$

   E. $\dfrac{x^3}{y^5}$

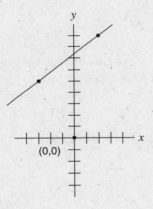

(0,0)

14. What is the slope of the line passing through the points $(-3, 5)$ and $(2, 9)$?

   A. -4

   B. $-\dfrac{5}{4}$

   C. $-\dfrac{4}{5}$

   D. $\dfrac{4}{5}$

   E. $\dfrac{5}{4}$

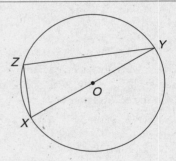

16. In circle O above, XY is a diameter, $OX = 8.5$, and $YZ = 15$. What is the area of $\triangle XYZ$ in square units?

   A. 40
   B. 60
   C. 120
   D. 127.5
   E. 180

GO ON TO THE NEXT PAGE

17. A bag contains 20 gumballs. If there are 8 red, 7 white, and 5 green, what is the minimum number of gumballs one must pick from the bag to be assured of one of each color?

    A.   16
    B.   9
    C.   8
    D.   6
    E.   3

18. If the five vowels are repeated continuously in the pattern *a, e, i, o, u, a, e, i, o, u*, and so on, what vowel will the 327th letter be?

    A.   *a*
    B.   *e*
    C.   *i*
    D.   *o*
    E.   *u*

19. The base of an isosceles triangle exceeds each of the equal sides by 8 feet. If the perimeter is 89 feet, what is the length of the base in feet?

    A.   27
    B. $29\frac{2}{3}$
    C.   35
    D.   54
    E.   70

20. What is the area of a rhombus with a perimeter of 40 and a diagonal of 10?

    A. $50\sqrt{3}$
    B.   100
    C. $100\sqrt{5}$
    D.   200
    E.   400

IF YOU FINISH BEFORE TIME IS CALLED, CHECK YOUR WORK ON THIS SECTION ONLY. DO NOT WORK ON ANY OTHER SECTION IN THE TEST.

Section 4: Writing—Multiple Choice

Time: 25 Minutes

35 Questions

In this section, choose the best answer for each question and blacken the corresponding space on the answer sheet.

Directions: The following questions test correctness and effective expression. In selecting the answer, pay attention to grammar, diction, sentence structure, and punctuation. In the following questions, part or all of each sentence is underlined. The A answer repeats the underlined portion of the original sentence, while the next four offer alternatives. Choose the answer that best expresses the meaning of the original sentence, and at the same time is grammatically correct, and stylistically superior. The correct choice should be clear, unambiguous, and concise.

EXAMPLE:

The forecaster predicted <u>rain and the sky was clear.</u>

- **A.** rain and the sky was clear.
- **B.** rain but the sky was clear.
- **C.** rain the sky was clear.
- **D.** rain, but the sky was clear.
- **E.** rain being as the sky was clear.

The correct answer is D.

---

1. Some players have no trouble seeing the weaknesses <u>in other people's game and they</u> are quite unable to see faults of their own.

   - **A.** in other people's game and they
   - **B.** in other games and they
   - **C.** in other players' games, and they
   - **D.** in other people's game, but they
   - **E.** in other games, but they

2. The Socialist Party is now powerful enough to worry the governing Christian Democrats, <u>and they may win</u> fifty seats in the next election.

   - **A.** and they may win
   - **B.** and they might win
   - **C.** and the Socialists may win
   - **D.** and the party
   - **E.** winning

3. The Medical Board is supposed to protect consumers from <u>incompetent, grossly negligent, unlicensed, and unethical practitioners.</u>

   - **A.** incompetent, grossly negligent, unlicensed, and unethical practitioners.
   - **B.** incompetent, grossly negligent practitioners who are unlicensed or unethical.
   - **C.** the incompetent and grossly negligent who practice without ethics or a license.
   - **D.** incompetent practitioners, gross and negligent, unlicensed and unethical.
   - **E.** those practitioners who are incompetent, grossly negligent, unlicensed, and unethical.

4. The wall is a continually evolving work of <u>art, it is a</u> forum for messages against violence, war, and cruelty.

   - **A.** art, it is a
   - **B.** art; it is a
   - **C.** art, in that it is a
   - **D.** art it is a
   - **E.** art a forum

GO ON TO THE NEXT PAGE

5. Before 1984, Australia had a strong tradition of private <u>medical care, but even conservatives now accepting</u> the national health care plan.

- **A.** medical care, but even conservatives now accepting
- **B.** medical care; but even conservatives now accepting
- **C.** medical care, but now with even conservatives accepting
- **D.** medical care, conservatives now accepting
- **E.** medical care, but now even conservatives accept

6. In the play, <u>great care is given to present the workers' oppression, and the author is uninterested</u> in the psychology of his characters.

- **A.** great care is given to present the workers' oppression, and the author is uninterested
- **B.** great care is given to present the workers' oppression, but the author is uninterested
- **C.** great care is given to the presentation of the workers' oppression, but the author is uninterested
- **D.** the author takes great care to present the workers' oppression, but is uninterested
- **E.** the author is very careful to present the workers' oppression, and he is uninterested

7. <u>Twenty-five thousand troops went to Somalia, and they failed to disarm the warring clans and failed</u> to create a secure environment.

- **A.** Twenty-five thousand troops went to Somalia, and they failed to disarm the warring clans and failed
- **B.** Twenty-five thousand troops went to Somalia, but they failed to disarm the warring clans and so they failed
- **C.** Twenty-five thousand troops went to Somalia, but they failed to disarm the warring clans and
- **D.** Twenty-five thousand troops went to Somalia, failing to disarm the warring clans and failing
- **E.** There were twenty-five thousand troops who went to Somalia, and they failed to disarm the warring clans, also failing

Directions: The following sentences may contain one error of grammar, usage, diction, or idiom. No sentence will contain more than one error, and some have no error. If there is an error, it will be underlined with a letter. Sections of the sentence that are not underlined cannot be changed. In selecting your answer, observe the requirements of standard written English. If there is an error, choose the one underlined part that must be changed to correct the sentence. If there is no error, choose E.

EXAMPLE:

The film <u>tell the story</u> of a cavalry captain and <u>his wife</u> who <u>try to</u> <u>rebuild their lives</u> after the Civil War.
        A   B   C   D
<u>No Error.</u>
 E

The correct answer is A.

---

8. The owners hired <u>my husband and I</u> to
                       A
<u>manage the inn</u> because <u>we had</u> more experience
     B   C
<u>than the other applicants.</u> <u>No Error.</u>
      D   E

9. Pistachios <u>imported from Asia</u> <u>cost more than</u>
             A   B
<u>the orchards of</u> California but <u>they are</u> larger
     C   D
and have more flavor. <u>No Error.</u>
               E

10. <u>There are</u> in the House and Senate general
   A
agreement <u>about the farm bill,</u> but <u>they are</u> far
        B   C
<u>from agreeing about</u> the budget. <u>No Error.</u>
   D   E

11. Early tomorrow morning, <u>weather permitting,</u>
                      A
he <u>departed on</u> an <u>around-the-state run</u> to
    B   C
<u>raise money</u> for the disabled. <u>No Error.</u>
  D   E

12. When they <u>had completed</u> the lay-out
            A
of the <u>paper's front page,</u> the editors
        B
<u>considered the problems</u> of the <u>sports page.</u>
      C   D
<u>No Error.</u>
 E

13. The volleyball players <u>which arrived</u> for
                A
the team picture <u>in the uniforms</u> that they
         B
<u>had worn to practice</u> were <u>irritable and tired.</u>
   C   D
<u>No Error.</u>
 E

14. The soil conditions <u>beneath structures</u> may cause
             A
<u>more worse</u> damage <u>in an earthquake</u> than the
   B   C
temblor <u>itself.</u> <u>No Error.</u>
      D   E

15. The debate <u>appeared to be stalemated,</u> since
           A
<u>there was</u> no possibility of the conservatives'
  B
<u>conceding with</u> their opponents' offer
  C
<u>to compromise.</u> <u>No Error.</u>
  D   E

GO ON TO THE NEXT PAGE

16. The region is <u>so dry</u> that <u>there are</u> <u>hardly any</u>
              A   B   C

    animals, and <u>scarcely no</u> plant life in the dunes.
               D

    <u>No Error.</u>
     E

17. Either <u>the allied bombing</u> or the subsequent
            A

    Iraqi attempt <u>to quell</u> the Shiite uprising
             B

    <u>are responsible for</u> the <u>damage to the shrines.</u>
       C   D
    <u>No Error.</u>
     E

18. Japanese defense policy <u>was changed completely</u>
                   A

    when the Socialist Party <u>scrapped</u> <u>its age-old</u>
               B   C

    insistence <u>to dismantle</u> the armed forces.
           D

    <u>No Error.</u>
     E

19. The election of a <u>separatist-dominated</u>
             A

    Parliament <u>has alarmed</u> those <u>who will believe</u>
         B   C

    Quebec <u>must not secede</u> from Canada. <u>No Error.</u>
         D   E

20. The engineers <u>have designed</u> an offshore drilling
            A

    platform <u>strong enough</u> <u>to withstand not only</u>
         B   C
    Atlantic storms <u>but also the occasional iceberg.</u>
              D
    <u>No Error.</u>
     E

21. In Britain, <u>a nationwide</u> business
           A

    <u>in buying and selling</u> special license plates
       B

    <u>have developed,</u> and <u>prices rise</u> each year.
      C   D
    <u>No Error.</u>
     E

22. If <u>we plan carefully</u> and waste no time
       A

    <u>on irrelevant topics,</u> you should <u>be able</u> to
         B   C

    <u>finish the essay</u> in twenty minutes. <u>No Error.</u>
       D   E

23. <u>Desperately trying</u> <u>to lead</u> the cat away from the
       A   B

    nest, the bird <u>had flew</u> within inches of <u>its</u> claw.
            C   D
    <u>No Error.</u>
     E

24. The citizens of Berlin <u>bid</u> a <u>fondly good-bye</u> to
              A   B

    the American troops <u>who had occupied</u> much of
              C

    the city <u>since the war ended.</u> <u>No Error.</u>
         D   E

25. When the new ambassador <u>first arrived</u>
               A

    <u>in the capital,</u> though <u>late in May,</u> <u>they found</u>
      B   C   D

    that the larger lakes were still frozen. <u>No Error.</u>
                      E

26. <u>Encouraged by</u> the success of <u>its</u> weekly
      A   B

    Spanish-language programs, MTV <u>will launch</u>
                      C

    a <u>twenty-four hour</u> Spanish language cable
       D

    network. <u>No Error.</u>
         E

Directions: The following passages are early drafts of student essays. Some parts of them need to be revised.

Read the selections carefully and answer the questions that follow. There will be questions about sentence structure, diction, and usage in individual sentences or parts of sentences. Other questions will deal with the whole essay or paragraphs, and ask you to decide about organization, development, and appropriate language. Choose the answer that follows the requirements of standard written English, and most effectively expresses the intended meanings.

Questions 27–31 are based on the following passage.

(1) Separation is to pass from one stage of life as we prepare for another stage of life. (2) It is a process that occurs in life all throughout one's development. (3) The process of separation is a large part of the rebellious stage of adolescence. (4) The adolescent struggles with establishing his own identity, and to separate from his parents by rejecting parental rules and expectations. (5) The rejection and struggles are parts of this separation process. (6) Unusual clothing, hair-styles and color are frequently the first signs to appear indicating a separation process is taking place. (7) They are an outward display declaring their independence and separation.

(8) A mature adult experiences separation in many areas of life. (9) For example, separation from a job, career, marriage, community, and also by death from a parent or loved one are inescapable events. (10) A separation from a job may be devastating if it is unplanned or a decision made by another. (11) Even a planned job or career change brings on a certain amount of anxiety, especially if the change requires a relocation. (12) Many adults become depressed and have difficulty dealing with separation. (13) A career change is not well planned if it occurs at the same time as other separations like divorce or the death of a parent.

(14) The death of parent, spouse or loved one brings us to a more terrifying separation anxiety. (15) The healing process is longer and anxiety is high. (16) It awakens our rational and irrational emotions. (17) I can clearly remember being angry when my father died. (18) I was angry at him for leaving, yet I know he did not choose his time of death. (19) It was a totally irrational feeling, yet it was very real. (20) Fortunately, as we develop our courage to handle separation also grows. (21) Separation never becomes mundane; it always remains a challenge.

27. Which of the following is the best revision of the underlined portions of sentences 1 and 2 below?

> *Separation is to pass from one stage of life as we prepare for another stage of life. It is a process that occurs in life all throughout one's development.*

A. is to pass from one stage of life as we prepare for another stage, and it is a process that occurs in life throughout one's development.

B. is passing from one stage of life in a process that occurs all throughout one's development.

C. is to pass from one stage in the process of life's development as we prepare for another stage.

D. occurs when we pass from one stage in preparation for another stage of life's development.

E. is a life-long process of passing from one stage of development to another.

28. Which of the following is the best version of the underlined portion of sentence 4?

> *The adolescent struggles with establishing his own identity, and to separate from his parents by rejecting parental rules and expectations.*

A. Leave it as it is.

B. with establishing their own identity and separating themselves from parents by rejecting parental

C. with establishing identity, and separating themselves from parents by rejecting parental

D. to establish his own identity, and to separate from his parents by rejecting their

E. to establish their own identity, and to separate from their parents by rejecting parental

GO ON TO THE NEXT PAGE

29. Unlike the first paragraph, the second paragraph deals with separations

    A. that are literal, rather than figurative.

    B. that can occur only to adults.

    C. that may involve unhappiness.

    D. that mark a passage from one stage of life to another.

    E. that are exclusively male.

30. Which of the following sentences could be deleted with the least disturbance to the sense of the passage?

    A. sentence 8

    B. sentence 9

    C. sentence 10

    D. sentence 12

    E. sentence 13

31. Which of the following changes would make sentence 20 clearer?

    A. Combine sentence 20 with sentence 19.

    B. Combine sentence 20 with sentence 21.

    C. Delete the comma after "Fortunately."

    D. Add a comma after "develop."

    E. Change "to handle" to "in handling."

Questions 32–35 are based on the following passage.

(1) Almost every week I am guilty of procrastination. (2) The dictionary definition of "procrastination" is "habitually putting off doing something that should be done." (3) For me, the act of procrastinating is a series of excuses for avoiding assigned tasks. (4) I can't say exactly why I go through the agony of waiting till the very last moment of all to begin my chore. (5) But though I always ask "Why do you wait so long?" I keep putting things off to the last minute.

(6) The reasons for procrastinating vary and I am not always sure which category of reasons the enterprise falls into. (7) The easiest reason of all to recognize is that of simply trying to avoid an unpleasant chore. (8) It is not surprising that I would want to put off doing something that would cause emotional distress. (9) Another reason for procrastinating is facing a task that seems insurmountable. (10) "It's too much," I tell myself. (11) Sometimes it is the unfamiliarity that causes this behavior. (12) After all the fear of the unknown requires taking a risk. (13) Taking a risk requires the possibility of failure—could that be the real reason for procrastinating?

(14) Whatever the reasons, the result is the same: a sleepless night filled with guilt and anxiety. (15) Guilt and its by-product anxiety become the major components of the effects of procrastination. (16) I know that I can avoid all the psychological imbalances associated with procrastination. (17) Logically, I can take out my planning calendar and schedule my time to accommodate any task, any chores, or any assignment. (18) And once again procrastination overpowers logic and the last minute rush begins.

32. Which of the following is the best version of sentence 6 (reproduced below)?

    The reasons for procrastinating vary and I am not always sure which category of reasons the enterprise falls into.

    A. Leave it as it is.

    B. The reasons for procrastination vary, and into which category of reasons the enterprise falls is not always sure.

    C. The reasons for procrastinating are varied and which category fits the enterprise is uncertain.

    D. The reasons vary, and I am not always sure why I procrastinate.

    E. The categories of reasons for procrastination vary, and which fits an enterprise is not always sure.

33. Sentence 7 (reproduced below) could be made more concise by deleting all of the following words EXCEPT

    The easiest reason of all to recognize is that of simply trying to avoid an unpleasant chore.

    A. reason

    B. of all

    C. that of

    D. simply

    E. to avoid

34. Which of the following best describes the writer's intention in the second paragraph?

    A. to suggest reasons to explain behavior

    B. to summarize evidence of irrational behavior

    C. to give specific details

    D. to point a moral conclusion

    E. to evaluate evidence of irrational behavior

35. Which of the following sentences could be eliminated from the third paragraph without seriously affecting its meaning or coherence?

    A. sentence 14
    B. sentence 15
    C. sentence 16
    D. sentence 17
    E. sentence 18

IF YOU FINISH BEFORE TIME IS CALLED, CHECK YOUR WORK ON THIS SECTION ONLY. DO NOT WORK ON ANY OTHER SECTION IN THE TEST.

Section 5: Critical Reading

Time: 25 Minutes

27 Questions

In this section, choose the best answer for each question and blacken the corresponding space on the answer sheet.

Directions: Each blank in the following sentences indicates that something has been omitted. Consider the lettered words beneath the sentence and choose the word or set of words that best fits the whole sentence.

EXAMPLE:

With a million more people than any other African nation, Nigeria is the most _____ country on the continent.

    A. impoverished
    B. successful
    C. populous
    D. developed
    E. militant

The correct answer is C.

---

1. It is _____ to assume that if aspirin can prevent second heart attacks, it can also _____ an attack in the first place.

    A. fanciful . . . eliminate
    B. logical . . . ward off
    C. sensible . . . encourage
    D. reasonable . . . foment
    E. idle . . . defend against

2. Cigars are not a safe _____ to cigarettes because, though cigar smokers do not inhale, they are still _____ higher rates of lung and mouth cancers than nonsmokers.

    A. answer . . . responsible for
    B. preference . . . free from
    C. alternative . . . subject to
    D. rejoinder . . . involved in
    E. accent . . . victimized by

3. Justices Marshall and Brennan opposed the death penalty on the grounds that it failed to _____ crimes, since all the available evidence made it clear that far more murders per capita were committed in states or countries with capital punishment than in those without it.

    A. explain
    B. augment
    C. foster
    D. deter
    E. exculpate

4. After the smoke and _____ of the city, Mr. Fitzgerald was glad to return to the _____ air and peace of the mountains.

    A. hubbub . . . turbid
    B. grime . . . murky
    C. tranquility . . . effulgent
    D. composure . . . brisk
    E. hustle-bustle . . . exhilarating

5. A strike by Ford workers in Mexico poses a(n) _____ for the ruling party, which must choose between alienating its union ally or undermining its fight against inflation.

A. enigma
B. dilemma
C. problem
D. option
E. riddle

6. By combining an American cartoon character with Japanese traditions, the popular comic by Stan Sakai presents as a hero a samurai rabbit, a unique _____ of East and West.

A. fusion
B. division
C. rejection
D. exclusion
E. query

7. A _____ that allowed voters to decide on the legality of casino gambling was passed by a(n) _____ 9-to-1 margin.

A. statute . . . meager
B. referendum . . . overwhelming
C. prohibition . . . huge
D. bill . . . narrow
E. ban . . . sizable

8. The _____ upon which this fine novel is developed with great _____ and intelligence is that no males live beyond the age of 18.

A. theory . . . fatuity
B. plot . . . understanding
C. idea . . . recalcitrance
D. premise . . . subtlety
E. solution . . . cleverness

9. The _____ use of washing machines and automobiles in the Middle Ages is part of the comedy of this high-spirited film.

A. untimely
B. anachronistic
C. unconvincing
D. archaic
E. supposed

GO ON TO THE NEXT PAGE

Directions: Questions follow the passage below. Using only the stated or implied information in the passage and in its introduction, if any, answer the questions.

Questions 10–11 are based on the following passage.

Jonas Salk, who developed the first successful polio vaccine, became involved in polio research only as a means of obtaining funding for his new laboratory in Pittsburgh. This laboratory was one of

(5) four receiving grants for the polio virus typing project, which began in 1948. Salk originally believed that the project was a "dull but dependable investment that would provide money for his lab." Perhaps Salk's newness to the study of polio bene-

(10) fited him because he started fresh, without preconceived ideas. He was the only researcher to use the newly developed tissue culture method of working with the virus. Other researchers, including Albert Sabin, who later developed the oral polio vaccine,

(15) did their work with monkeys infected with the virus, a more difficult process.

10. The main purpose of the paragraph is to

   A. criticize Salk for his interest in funding rather than finding a polio vaccine.

   B. compare the research methods of Jonas Salk and Albert Sabin.

   C. indicate how desperate the medical community was to find a polio vaccine.

   D. criticize Albert Sabin for clinging to outmoded forms of virus research.

   E. suggest that Salk's newness to polio research may have been an advantage.

11. Given the information in the passage, which of the following can best be described as ironic?

   A. "Albert Sabin, who later developed the oral polio vaccine. . . ." (lines 13–14)

   B. ". . . originally believed that the project was a 'dull but dependable investment'" (lines 6–8)

   C. "He was the only researcher to use the newly developed tissue culture . . . ." (lines 11–12)

   D. ". . . he started fresh, without preconceived ideas." (lines 10–11)

   E. "This laboratory was one of four receiving grants for the polio typing project, which began in 1948." (lines 4–6)

Questions 12–15 are based on the following pair of passages.

Passage 1

The boob tube hasn't done much for national elections. Political ads are sound bites, and televised debates have become less and less informative. Generally, candidates are elliptical in expressing

(5) their convictions. In the 1960 Kennedy-Nixon debates both candidates were relatively forthright. Both candidates agreed they'd be willing to raise taxes in the interest of national defense, something politicians wouldn't do today for fear an opponent

(10) would focus on the statement in a negative campaign commercial. The amount of time each candidate spends making a point and answering questions has decreased from election to election. Is this because the audience's attention span is getting shorter or is

(15) it because neither candidate wants to be too specific about issues on the chance that someone's feathers might get ruffled?

Passage 2

Television has become an integral part of the political process in America. In 1992, the audience

(20) for the first presidential debate was larger than the audience for the Super Bowl. Many people regard television debates as the most effective way we have of choosing a leader, and the popularity of the town-meeting style of television debates may sig-

(25) nal Americans' desire to enter the political process and become more active in making their choices. Because of television, candidates are less dependent on party infrastructure to disseminate their messages. They can appeal to people directly. A

(30) good example is the 1992 independent candidacy of Ross Perot. Although losing the election, Perot garnered 19 percent of the popular vote, and for much of this, he had television to thank.

12. According to the author of Passage 1, television debates

    A. have improved since the Kennedy-Nixon debates in 1960.

    B. are of little interest to most Americans.

    C. provide valuable information to the electorate.

    D. encourage the candidates to be forthright in their responses.

    E. give candidates less time to speak than they did in 1960.

13. In Passage 1, the word "elliptical" (line 4) most nearly means

    A. redundant.

    B. sincerely felt.

    C. deliberately obscure.

    D. terse and to the point.

    E. quietly persuasive.

14. According to the author of Passage 2, all of the following are positive results of televised debates EXCEPT

    A. greater voter turnout at the polls.

    B. greater interest in taking an active role in elections.

    C. greater availability of information for voters.

    D. less importance of political party infrastructure.

    E. greater visibility for independent candidates.

15. Which of the following best characterizes the difference between Passage 1 and Passage 2?

    A. Passage 1 is light-hearted and Passage 2 is philosophical.

    B. The two passages are alike in tone but different in point of view.

    C. Passage 1 is colloquial and sarcastic and Passage 2 is straightforward.

    D. While Passage 2 is literary and pompous, Passage 1 is objective and journalistic.

    E. Passage 1 focuses on facts, whereas Passage 2 focuses on ideas.

Questions 16–27 are based on the following passage.

Early in the day Dorothea had returned from the infant school which she had set going in the village, and was taking her usual place in the pretty sitting-room which divided the bedrooms of the
(5) sisters, bent on finishing a plan for some buildings (a kind of work which she delighted in), when Celia, who had been watching her with a hesitating desire to propose something, said—"Dorothea dear, if you don't mind—if you are not very busy—
(10) suppose we looked at mamma's jewels today, and divided them? It is exactly six months today since uncle gave them to you, and you have not looked at them yet."

Celia's face had the shadow of a pouting
(15) expression in it, the full presence of the pout being kept back by an habitual awe of Dorothea. To her relief, Dorothea's eyes were full of laughter as she looked up.

"What a wonderful little almanac you are,
(20) Celia! Is it six calendar or six lunar months?"

"It is the last day of September now, and it was the first of April when uncle gave them to you. You know, he said that he had forgotten them till then. I believe you have never thought of them since you
(25) locked them up in the cabinet here."

"Well, dear, we should never wear them, you know." Dorothea spoke in a full cordial tone, half caressing, half explanatory. She had her pencil in her hand, and was making tiny side-plans on a
(30) margin.

Celia coloured, and looked very grave. "I think, dear, we are wanting in respect to mamma's memory, to put them by and take no notice of them. And," she added, after hesitating a little, "necklaces
(35) are quite usual now; and Madame Poinçon, who was stricter in some things even than you are, used to wear ornaments. And Christians generally— surely there are women in heaven now who wore jewels." Celia was conscious of some mental
(40) strength when she really applied herself to argument.

"You would like to wear them?" exclaimed Dorothea, an air of astonished discovery animating her whole person. "Of course, then, let us have them
(45) out. Why did you not tell me before? But the keys, the keys!" She pressed her hands against the sides of her head and seemed to despair of her memory. "They are here," said Celia, with whom this explanation had been long meditated and prearranged.

GO ON TO THE NEXT PAGE

(50)   The casket was soon open before them, and the various jewels spread out on the table. It was no great collection, but a few of the ornaments were really of remarkable beauty, the finest that was obvious at first being a necklace of purple amethysts set
(55) in exquisite gold work, and a pearl cross with five brilliants in it. Dorothea immediately took up the necklace and fastened it round her sister's neck, where it fitted almost as closely as a bracelet; but the circle suited the style of Celia's head and neck, and
(60) she could see that it did, in the pier-glass opposite.

"There, Celia! You can wear that with your Indian muslin. But this cross you must wear with your dark dresses."

Celia was trying not to smile with pleasure.
(65) "O Dodo, you must keep the cross yourself."

"No, no, dear, no," said Dorothea, putting up her hand with careless deprecation.

"Yes, indeed you must; it would suit you—in your black dress, now," said Celia, insistingly.
(70) "You *might* wear that."

"Not for the world, not for the world. A cross is the last thing I would wear as a trinket." Dorothea shuddered slightly.

"Then you will think it wicked in me to wear it,"
(75) said Celia, uneasily.

"No, dear, no," said Dorothea, stroking her sister's cheek. "Souls have complexions too: what will suit one will not suit another."

"But you might like to keep it for mamma's
(80) sake."

"No, I have other things of mamma's—her sandal-wood box which I am so fond of—plenty of things. In fact, they are all yours, dear. We need discuss them no longer.
(85) There—take away your property."

Celia felt a little hurt. There was a strong assumption of superiority in this Puritanic toleration, hardly less trying to the blond flesh of an unenthusiastic sister than a Puritanic persecution.

16. From the details of the passage, it can be learned or inferred that

I.   Dorothea and Celia are sisters.
II. Dorothea and Celia may be orphans.
III. Dorothea and Celia are temperamentally very alike.

A. III only
B. I and II only
C. I and III only
D. II and III only
E. I, II, and, III

17. The first paragraph of the passage refers to the "infant school" and "plan for some buildings" in order to suggest that Dorothea is

A. prying and interfering.
B. rich and idle.
C. self-centered and ambitious.
D. active and unselfish.
E. philanthropic and ineffectual.

18. In line 20, Dorothea asks Celia whether it is "six calendar or six lunar months" because she

A. wants to know exactly how many days have passed.
B. is good-humoredly teasing Celia.
C. had hoped to keep the jewels from Celia.
D. wants to demonstrate the scientific precision of her mind.
E. has forgotten what the current month is.

19. In line 32, the phrase "wanting in respect" can be best understood to mean

A. obliged to be more deferential.
B. desirous to esteem.
C. lewd in regard.
D. deficient in regard.
E. eager for consideration.

20. The "argument" to which Celia has "really applied herself" (lines 40–41) is intended to convince Dorothea to

A. show greater respect for their dead mother.
B. give all the jewels to her.
C. give the most valuable of the jewels to her.
D. agree to sharing and wearing the jewels.
E. examine the jewels and lock them up again.

21. Although in lines 26–27 Dorothea has said, "we should never wear them, you know," she changes her opinion because she

A. is moved by Celia's appeal to the memory of their mother.
B. is convinced by Celia's reference to Madame Poinçon.
C. realizes that Celia wants to wear the jewels.
D. sees how becoming the jewels are to Celia.
E. can appear superior to Celia by refusing to wear them herself.

22. In line 67, the word "deprecation" means

    A. protest.

    B. lessening.

    C. indifference.

    D. removal.

    E. agreement.

23. The word "trying" in line 88 means

    A. irksome.

    B. attempting.

    C. effortful.

    D. experimental.

    E. determining.

24. In line 87, "Puritanic toleration" is a reference to

    A. Celia's awe of Dorothea.

    B. Celia's acceptance of Dorothea's foibles.

    C. Celia's love of jewels and finery.

    D. Dorothea's hypocritical indifference to finery.

    E. Dorothea's self-denial and generosity.

25. In the last sentence of the passage, the word "unenthusiastic" refers to

    A. Dorothea's refusal to wear jewels.

    B. Dorothea's giving her permission for Celia to wear jewels.

    C. Celia's attitude toward self-denial.

    D. Celia's attitude toward wearing jewels.

    E. the author's attitude toward Dorothea.

26. The inconsistency in Dorothea's reasoning that the passage reveals is her

    A. forgetting about when the jewels were given to her.

    B. losing the keys to the cabinet holding the jewels.

    C. insistence that Christians cannot wear jewels.

    D. wanting Celia to wear jewels but refusing to wear them herself.

    E. deceitful claim that she honors the memory of her mother.

27. The purpose of the passage as a whole is to

    A. reveal the likeness of Celia and Dorothea.

    B. expose the submerged ill feelings between Celia and Dorothea.

    C. reveal the differences in the natures of Celia and Dorothea.

    D. demonstrate the dangers of materialism.

    E. satirize the hypocrisy of the two young women.

IF YOU FINISH BEFORE TIME IS CALLED, CHECK YOUR WORK ON THIS SECTION ONLY. DO NOT WORK ON ANY OTHER SECTION IN THE TEST.

STOP

Section 6: Mathematics

Time: 25 Minutes

20 Questions

Directions: This section is composed of two types of questions. Use the 25 minutes allotted to answer both question types. For questions 1–10, select the one correct answer of the five choices given and mark the corresponding circle on your answer sheet. Your scratch work should be done on any available space in the section.

Notes

1. All numbers used are real numbers.

2. Calculators may be used.

3. Some problems may be accompanied by figures or diagrams. These figures are drawn as accurately as possible EXCEPT when it is stated in a specific problem that a figure is not drawn to scale. The figures and diagrams are meant to provide information useful in solving the problem or problems. Unless otherwise stated, all figures and diagrams lie in a plane.

Data That Can Be Used for Reference

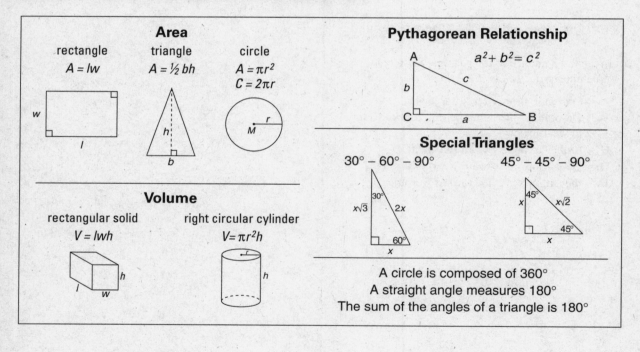

Area

rectangle
$A = lw$

triangle
$A = \frac{1}{2}bh$

circle
$A = \pi r^2$
$C = 2\pi r$

Volume

rectangular solid
$V = lwh$

right circular cylinder
$V = \pi r^2 h$

Pythagorean Relationship

$a^2 + b^2 = c^2$

Special Triangles

$30° - 60° - 90°$

$45° - 45° - 90°$

A circle is composed of 360°
A straight angle measures 180°
The sum of the angles of a triangle is 180°

8, 9, 12, 17, 24, . . .

1. In the preceding sequence, a certain pattern determines each of the subsequent numbers. What is the next number in the sequence?

   A.   41
   B.   35
   C.   33
   D.   30
   E.   29

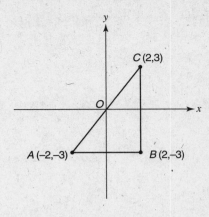

3. What is the area of $\triangle ABC$ in the figure above?

   A.   3
   B.   6
   C.   12
   D.   18
   E.   24

2. What is $\frac{1}{4}$ of 0.03 percent?

   A.   0.75
   B.   0.075
   C.   0.0075
   D.   0.00075
   E.   0.000075

The product of two numbers is equal to twice the difference of the two numbers.

4. Which equation best represents the preceding situation?

   A. $x + y = 2(x - y)$
   B. $x + y = 2(x \div y)$
   C. $(x)(y) = 2(x \div y)$
   D. $(x)(y) = 2(x - y)$
   E. $(x)(y) = 2(x + y)$

GO ON TO THE NEXT PAGE

5. If $4^n = 64$, what is the value of 3^{n+2}?

   A.   15
   B.   27
   C.   54
   D.   81
   E.   243

7. If D is between A and B on $\overleftrightarrow{AB}$, then which of the following must be true?

   A. $AD = DB$
   B. $DB = AB - AD$
   C. $AD = AB + DB$
   D. $DB = AD + AB$
   E. $AB = AD - BD$

6. For what values of z is $f(z) = \dfrac{3z^3 + z - 7}{z^2 - 25}$ undefined?

   A.   25
   B.   5
   C.   0
   D.   −5
   E.   −5, 5

8. If $x - 3 = \dfrac{18}{x}$, then $x =$

   A.   −9 or 9
   B.   −6 or −3
   C.   6 or −3
   D.   −6 or 3
   E.   6 or 3

9. For all integers z,

$\boxed{z} = z^2 - 1$, if z is an even integer and
$\boxed{z} = z^2 + 1$, if z is an odd integer.

What is the value $\boxed{7} - \boxed{6}$?

A. −2
B. 2
C. 4
D. 11
E. 15

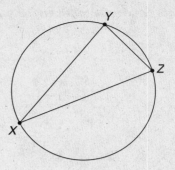

10. What is the length of the diameter $\overline{XZ}$ of the circle above if $XY = 15$ and $YZ = 8$?

A. 17
B. 23
C. 46
D. 289
E. Cannot be determined from the given information.

GO ON TO THE NEXT PAGE

Directions for Student-Produced Response Questions (Grid-ins): Questions 11–20 require you to solve the problem and enter your answer by carefully marking the circles on the special grid. Examples of the appropriate way to mark the grid follow.

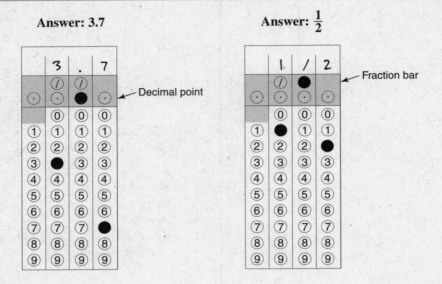

Answer: 3.7

Decimal point

Answer: $\frac{1}{2}$

Fraction bar

Answer: $1\frac{1}{2}$

Do not grid in mixed numbers in the form of mixed numbers. Always change mixed numbers to improper fractions or decimals.

Answer: 123

Space permitting, answers may start in any column. Each grid-in answer below is correct.

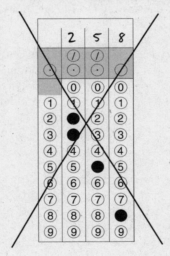

Note: Circles must be filled in correctly to receive credit. Mark only one circle in each column. No credit will be given if more than one circle in a column is marked. Example:

Answer: 258 (no credit)

GO ON TO THE NEXT PAGE

Answer: $\frac{8}{9}$

Accuracy of decimals: Always enter the most accurate decimal value that the grid will accommodate. For example: An answer such as .8888. . . can be gridded as .888 or .889. Gridding this value as .8, .88, or .89 is considered inaccurate and therefore not acceptable. The acceptable grid-ins of $\frac{8}{9}$ are:

Be sure to write your answers in the boxes at the top of the circles before doing your gridding. Although writing out the answers above the columns is not required, it is very important to ensure accuracy. Even though some problems may have more than one correct answer, grid only one answer. Grid-in questions contain no negative answers.

11. What is the value of $5x^2 - 3x + 2$ when $x = -4$?

12. A long-distance telephone call costs $2.45 for the first 3 minutes and $.32 per minute for each additional minute. What is the cost in dollars and cents for a 25-minute call? (Disregard the $ sign when gridding your answer.)

13. A jacket sold for $56, which was 80% of the original price. What was the original price in dollars and cents? (Disregard the $ sign when gridding your answer.)

14. What is the length of the side of a cube whose volume is 64 cubic units?

16. If the numerator of a fraction is tripled, and the denominator of a fraction is doubled, the resulting fraction will reflect an increase of what percent? (Disregard the % sign when gridding your answer.)

BILL FOR PURCHASE

Science Textbooks	$840
Lab Equipment	$460
Formaldehyde	$320
Teacher's Manuals	$120
TOTAL	$2220

15. Scholastic Supplies, Inc. sends the bill above to Zither Junior High School. Although the bill includes the cost of science lab workbooks, Scholastic Supplies forgot to list them on the bill. How much did the science lab workbooks cost Zither High School? (Disregard the $ sign when gridding your answer.)

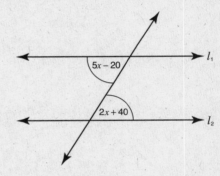

17. In the figure above $l_1 \| l_2$, what is the value of x?

GO ON TO THE NEXT PAGE

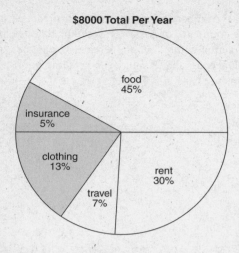

$8000 Total Per Year

food
45%

insurance
5%

clothing
13%

travel
7%

rent
30%

18. Based on the chart above, how much more money was spent on clothing than on insurance?

20. A bus leaves from Burbank at 9:00 a.m. traveling east at 50 miles per hour. At 1:00 p.m., a plane leaves Burbank traveling east at 300 miles per hour. How many minutes will it take the plane to overtake the bus?

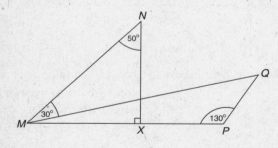

19. In the figure above, what is the ratio of the degree measure of ∠MQP to the degree measure of ∠PXN?

IF YOU FINISH BEFORE TIME IS CALLED, CHECK YOUR WORK ON THIS SECTION ONLY. DO NOT WORK ON ANY OTHER SECTION IN THE TEST.

STOP

Section 7: Critical Reading

Time: 20 Minutes

15 Questions

In this section, choose the best answer for each question and blacken the corresponding space on the answer sheet.

Directions: Questions follow the two passages below. Using only the stated or implied information in each passage and in its introduction, if any, answer the questions.

Questions 1–15 are based on the following passages.

The two passages that follow are taken from recent historical studies of Christopher Columbus.

Passage 1

In his history published in 1552, Francisco Lopez de Gomara wrote: "The greatest event since the creation of the world (excluding the incarnation and death of Him who created it) is the discovery of
(5) the Indies." On the strength of this realization, Columbus emerged from the shadows, reincarnated not so much as a man and historical figure as he was as a myth and symbol. He came to epitomize the explorer and discoverer, the man of vision and audac-
(10) ity, the hero who overcame opposition and adversity to change history. By the end of the sixteenth century, English explorers and writers acknowledged the primacy and inspiration of Columbus. He was celebrated in poetry and plays, especially by the
(15) Italians. Even Spain was coming around. In a popular play, Lope de Vega in 1614 portrayed Columbus as a dreamer up against the stolid forces of entrenched tradition, a man of singular purpose who triumphed, the embodiment of that spirit driving hu-
(20) mans to explore and discover.

Historians cannot control the popularizers of history, mythmakers, or propagandists, and in post-Revolutionary America the few historians who studied Columbus were probably not disposed to
(25) try. Even if they had been, there was little information available on which to assess the real Columbus and distinguish the man from the myth. With the discovery and publication of new Columbus documents by Martin Fernandez de Navarrete in 1825,
(30) this was less of an excuse, and yet the material only provided more ammunition to those who would embellish the symbolic Columbus through the nineteenth century.

Washington Irving mined the new documents to
(35) create a hero in the romantic mold favored in the century's literature. Irving's Columbus was "a man of great and inventive genius" and his "ambition was lofty and noble, inspiring him with high thoughts, and an anxiety to distinguish himself by
(40) great achievements." Perhaps. But an effusive Irving got carried away. He said that Columbus's "conduct was characterized by the grandeur of his views and the magnanimity of his spirit . . . . Instead of ravaging the newly found countries . . . he sought
(45) to colonize and cultivate them, to civilize the natives." Irving acknowledged that Columbus may have had some faults, such as his part in enslaving and killing people, but offered the palliating explanation that these were "errors of the times."

(50) William H. Prescott, a leading American historian of the conquest period, said of Columbus that "the finger of the historian will find it difficult to point to a single blemish in his moral character." Writers and orators of the nineteenth century as-
(55) cribed to Columbus all the human virtues that were most prized in that time of geographic and industrial expansion, heady optimism, and an unquestioning belief in progress as the dynamic of history.

Most people living in America four centuries
(60) after the voyages of discovery had created the Columbus they wanted to believe in and were quite satisfied with their creation. But scholars were already finding grounds for a major reassessment of Columbus's reputation in history.

Passage 2

(65) Why should one suppose that a culture like Europe's, steeped as it was in the ardor of wealth, the habit of violence, and the pride of intolerance, dispirited and adrift after a century and more of disease and famine and death beyond experience,
(70) would be able to come upon new societies in a fertile world, innocent and defenseless, and not displace and subdue, if necessary destroy, them? Why should one suppose such a culture would pause there to observe, to learn, to borrow the wisdom
(75) and the ways of a foreign, heathen people, half naked and befeathered, ignorant of cities and kings

GO ON TO THE NEXT PAGE

and metal and laws, and unschooled in all that the
Ancients held virtuous? Was not Europe in its
groping era of discovery in the fifteenth century in
(80) fact in search of salvation, as its morbid sonnets
said, or of that regeneration which new lands and
new peoples and of course new riches would be
presumed to provide?

And there was salvation there, in the New
(85) World, though it was not of a kind the Europeans
then understood. They thought first that exploitation was salvation, and they went at that with a
vengeance, and found new foods and medicines
and treasures, but that proved not to be; that colo-
(90) nization and settlement was salvation, and they
peopled both continents with conquerors, and it
was not that either. The salvation there, had the
Europeans known where and how to look for it,
was obviously in the integrative tribal ways, the
(95) nurturant communitarian values, the rich interplay
with nature that made up the Indian cultures—as it
made up, for that matter, the cultures of ancient
peoples everywhere, not excluding Europe. It was
there especially in the Indian consciousness, in
(100) what Calvin Martin has termed "the biological outlook on life," in which patterns and concepts and
the large teleological constructs of culture are not
human-centered but come from the sense of being
at one with nature, biocentric, ecocentric.

(105) However one may cast it, an opportunity there
certainly was once, a chance for the people of
Europe to find a new anchorage in a new country,
in what they dimly realized was the land of
Paradise, and thus find finally the way to redeem
(110) the world. But all they ever found was half a world
of nature's treasures and nature's peoples that
could be taken, and they took them, never knowing,
never learning the true regenerative power there,
and that opportunity was lost. Theirs was indeed a
(115) conquest of Paradise, but as is inevitable with any
war against the world of nature, those who win will
have lost—once again lost, and this time perhaps
forever.

1. In lines 15–20 of the first paragraph, the reference to the play by Lope de Vega serves to

   I. give an example of Columbus's reputation in Spain.
   II. demonstrate how widespread Columbus's reputation had become.
   III. exemplify how Columbus was already a myth and symbol of the discoverer.

   A. I only
   B. II only
   C. I and III only
   D. II and III only
   E. I, II, and III

2. In Passage 1 (line 24), the word "disposed" means

   A. arranged.
   B. employed.
   C. settled.
   D. inclined.
   E. given away.

3. In Passage 1 (line 35), the phrase "romantic mold" most nearly means

   A. pattern concerned with love.
   B. idealized manner.
   C. visionary model.
   D. fictitious shape.
   E. escapist style.

4. Of the following words used in the third paragraph of Passage 1, which most clearly reveals a judgment of the modern author as opposed to that of Washington Irving?

   A. "mined" (line 34)
   B. "ambition" (line 37)
   C. "Perhaps" (line 40)
   D. "magnanimity" (line 43)
   E. "palliating" (line 48)

5. The major purpose of Passage 1 is to

- **A.** praise the daring and accomplishments of Columbus.
- **B.** survey the reputation of Columbus from the sixteenth through the nineteenth century.
- **C.** contrast the real Columbus of history with the mythic Columbus of the nineteenth century.
- **D.** describe the benefits and the damage of Columbus's voyages.
- **E.** reveal the unforeseen and harmful consequences of Columbus's voyages.

6. With which of the following generalizations would the author of Passage 1 be most likely to agree?

- I. The values of a historical period are usually reflected by the heroes people of that time choose to idolize.
- II. What people believe about historical figures is usually what they want to believe.
- III. Written history is usually a record of the truth as it is known at the time of writing.

- **A.** I only
- **B.** I and II only
- **C.** I and III only
- **D.** II and III only
- **E.** I, II, and III

7. The questions of the first paragraph of Passage 2 (lines 65–83) serve chiefly to

- **A.** raise doubts about issues that cannot be explained.
- **B.** defend and justify the actions of Europeans in the age of discovery.
- **C.** suggest areas that future historians might profitably explore.
- **D.** show how much easier it is to understand issues of the distant past with the objectivity given by time.
- **E.** reveal the author's ideas about the nature of Europeans at the time of Columbus's voyages.

8. In Passage 2 (lines 77–78), the phrase "unschooled in all that the Ancients held virtuous" is used to

- I. reflect the European view of the American natives.
- II. reveal a significant foundation of European culture in the period.
- III. give a reason for the European contempt for the native Americans.

- **A.** III only
- **B.** I and II only
- **C.** I and III only
- **D.** II and III only
- **E.** I, II, and III

9. Which of the following does Passage 2 present as discovered and understood by the Europeans in America?

- **A.** Human-centered cultures
- **B.** New foods and medicines
- **C.** Communitarian values
- **D.** An Indian consciousness
- **E.** An ecocentric culture

10. According to Passage 2, a "biological outlook on life" would be best defined as one in which

- **A.** the interdependence of all life forms is understood.
- **B.** humans are the measure of all things.
- **C.** the needs of rich and poor are equally considered.
- **D.** the economic well-being of all races is emphasized.
- **E.** the primary motivation is survival of the species.

11. The major purpose of Passage 2 is to

- **A.** describe the benefits and damage of Columbus's discovery.
- **B.** present Columbus's discovery as a tragically missed opportunity to regenerate Europe.
- **C.** attack the greed and cruelty that inspired the European colonization of America.
- **D.** defend the European colonization of America as historically determined and unavoidable.
- **E.** evaluate as objectively as possible the meaning of the European incursion into the Americas.

GO ON TO THE NEXT PAGE

12. Of the five paragraphs in Passage 1, which one best prepares the reader for the contents of Passage 2?

    A. The first (lines 1–20)
    B. The second (lines 21–33)
    C. The third (lines 34–49)
    D. The fourth (lines 50–58)
    E. The fifth (lines 59–64)

13. Compared to Passage 1, Passage 2 may be described by all the following EXCEPT

    A. more personal.
    B. more philosophical.
    C. more judgmental.
    D. more historical.
    E. more emotional.

14. Compared to that of Passage 1, the prose of Passage 2 makes greater use of all the following EXCEPT

    A. words in series.
    B. rhetorical questions.
    C. understatements.
    D. repetitions.
    E. parallel phrases.

15. Which of the following aptly describes a relationship between Passage 1 and Passage 2?

    I. Passage 1 predicts a reevaluation of Columbus's accomplishments, and Passage 2 makes that reevaluation.
    II. Passage 1 calls attention to the way the image of Columbus in each period reflects the values of that period, and Passage 2 presents an image that reflects late twentieth-century ideas.
    III. Passage 1 focuses on the reputation of Columbus, and Passage 2 emphasizes his unique character.

    A. III only
    B. I and II only
    C. I and III only
    D. II and III only
    E. I, II, and III

IF YOU FINISH BEFORE TIME IS CALLED, CHECK YOUR WORK ON THIS SECTION ONLY. DO NOT WORK ON ANY OTHER SECTION IN THE TEST.

Section 8: Mathematics

Time: 20 Minutes

15 Questions

Directions: Solve each problem in this section by using the information given and your own mathematical calculations, insights, and problem-solving skills. Then select the one correct answer of the five choices given and mark the corresponding circle on your answer sheet. Use the available space on the page for your scratch work.

Notes

1. All numbers used are real numbers.

2. Calculators may be used.

3. Some problems may be accompanied by figures or diagrams. These figures are drawn as accurately as possible EXCEPT when it is stated in a specific problem that a figure is not drawn to scale. The figures and diagrams are meant to provide information useful in solving the problem or problems. Unless otherwise stated, all figures and diagrams lie in a plane.

Data That Can Be Used for Reference

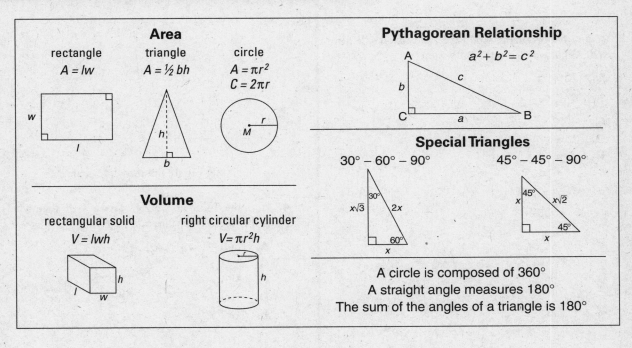

GO ON TO THE NEXT PAGE

1. If $2x + 13$ represents an odd number, what must the next consecutive odd number be?

   A. $2x + 15$
   B. $2x + 14$
   C. $3x + 13$
   D. $3x + 15$
   E. $4x + 1$

2. A suit that originally sold for $120 was on sale for $90. What was the rate of discount?

   A. 75%
   B. $33\frac{1}{3}\%$
   C. 30%
   D. 25%
   E. 20%

3. If $\sqrt{\dfrac{81}{x}} = \dfrac{9}{5}$, then $x =$

   A. 5
   B. 9
   C. 25
   D. 50
   E. 53

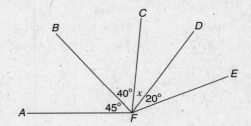

Note: Figure not drawn to scale.

4. If, in the figure above $\angle CFD = \angle AFB$, then what is the degree measure of $\angle AFE$?

   A. 40°
   B. 45°
   C. 150°
   D. 160°
   E. 180°

5. What is the value of x if the average of 93, 82, 79, and x is 87?

    A.   87

    B.   90

    C.   93

    D.   94

    E.   348

7. Gasoline varies in cost from \$0.96 to \$1.12 per gallon. If a car's mileage varies from 16 to 24 miles per gallon, what is the difference between the most and the least that the gasoline for a 480-mile trip will cost?

    A.   \$ 5.12

    B.   \$ 7.04

    C.   \$11.52

    D.   \$14.40

    E.   \$52.80

SCHOOLWIDE EYE COLOR SURVEY

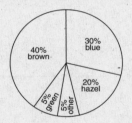

6. Annette does a schoolwide survey and publishes her results in the preceding circle graph. If 62 people at Annette's school have hazel eyes, how many have brown eyes?

    A.   20

    B.   40

    C.   62

    D.   124

    E.   248

8. If the length and width of a rectangle are increased by x units, its perimeter is increased by how many units?

    A. $4x$

    B. $2x$

    C. x^2

    D. x

    E. $x + 4$

GO ON TO THE NEXT PAGE

9. If $\dfrac{x^2 - 5x + 7}{x^2 - 4x + 10} = 1$, then $x =$

A. -3

B. $\dfrac{1}{3}$

C. $\dfrac{7}{10}$

D. $\dfrac{17}{9}$

E. 3

10. Harriet planned to complete a certain task on Wednesday, January 1, but because of illness, the completion date was postponed 48 days. On which day of the week in February was the task completed?

A. Monday

B. Tuesday

C. Wednesday

D. Thursday

E. Friday

11. One angle of a triangle is 68°. The other two angles are in the ratio of 3:4. Which of the following is the number of degrees in the smallest angle of the triangle?

A. 16

B. 34

C. 48

D. 64

E. 68

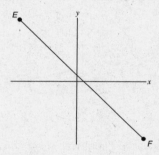

Note: Figure not drawn to scale.

12. If, in the preceding graph, point E has coordinates $(-3, 5)$ and point F has coordinates $(6, -7)$, then the length of $EF =$

A. 21

B. 15

C. 7

D. 5

E. 3

13. A random poll of 2,500 moviegoers throughout New York found that 1,500 preferred comedies, 500 preferred adventure films, and 500 preferred dramas. Of the 8,000,000 moviegoers in New York, which of the following is (are) the most reasonable estimate(s) drawn from the poll?

   I.   1,500,000 prefer comedies.

   II. 500,000 prefer dramas.

   III. 1,600,000 prefer dramas.

   A.   I only

   B.   II only

   C.   III only

   D.   I and II only

   E.   I and Ill only

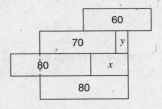

14. The horizontal length of each rectangle above is marked within. What is the total horizontal length of $x + y$?

   A.   40

   B.   50

   C.   80

   D.   90

   E.   It cannot be determined from the information given.

15. How will the graph of $g(x) = (x + 5)^2$ differ from the graph of $f(x) = x^2$?

   A. $g(x)$ will be 5 units above $f(x)$.

   B. $g(x)$ will be 5 units below $f(x)$.

   C. $g(x)$ will be 5 units to the right of $f(x)$.

   D. $g(x)$ will be 5 units to the left of $f(x)$.

   E. $g(x)$ will be 25 units above $f(x)$.

IF YOU FINISH BEFORE TIME IS CALLED, CHECK YOUR WORK ON THIS SECTION ONLY. DO NOT WORK ON ANY OTHER SECTION IN THE TEST.

Section 9: Mathematics

Time: 25 Minutes

20 Questions

Directions: Solve each problem in this section by using the information given and your own mathematical calculations, insights, and problem-solving skills. Then select the one correct answer of the five choices given and mark the corresponding circle on your answer sheet. Use the available space on the page for your scratch work.

Notes

1. All numbers used are real numbers.
2. Calculators may be used.
3. Some problems may be accompanied by figures or diagrams. These figures are drawn as accurately as possible EXCEPT when it is stated in a specific problem that a figure is not drawn to scale. The figures and diagrams are meant to provide information useful in solving the problem or problems. Unless otherwise stated, all figures and diagrams lie in a plane.

Data That Can Be Used for Reference

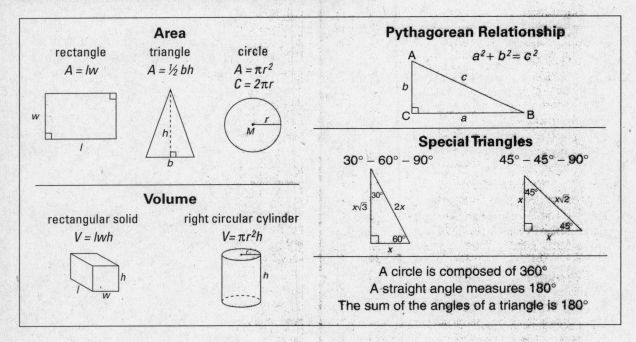

1. If $2x - 5 = 9$, then $3x + 2 =$

   A. 44
   B. 23
   C. 16
   D. 14
   E.   7

3. If $x = 3$, $y = 4$, and $z = -1$, what is the value of $2x + 3y^2 - z?$

   A. 151
   B. 149
   C.   55
   D.   53
   E.   19

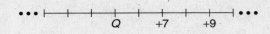

2. On the above number line, what is the point 15 units to the left of point Q?

   A.   10
   B.   5
   C.   0
   D.   −9
   E. −10

4. If cassette tapes cost $2.98 for a package of two tapes, how much change will Roy receive from a twenty-dollar bill if he purchases 12 tapes?

   A. $2.02
   B. $2.12
   C. $2.18
   D. $2.22
   E. $3.02

GO ON TO THE NEXT PAGE

5. $\dfrac{6^4 + 6^5}{6^4} =$

    A.   36

    B.   31

    C.   30

    D.   7

    E.   6

6. Ernie cut a yardstick into two pieces, the larger piece being six inches more than the smaller. How could Ernie compute the size of the smaller piece, x?

    A. $x + 6 = 36$

    B. $2x = 36$

    C. $x + x + 6 = 36$

    D. $2x - 6 = 36$

    E. $2x + 6 = 30$

$$\begin{array}{r} \square\square 4 \\ \times\ \ 8 \\ \hline 5\,3\,9\,\square \end{array}$$

7. The sum of the digits in the three boxes equals

    A.   5

    B.   7

    C.   9

    D.   13

    E.   15

8. Which of the following ordered pairs (a, b) is NOT a member of the solution set of $2a - 3b = 6$?

    A. $(6, 2)$

    B. $(-3, -4)$

    C. $(3, 0)$

    D. $\left(4, \dfrac{2}{3}\right)$

    E. $(0, 2)$

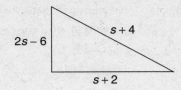

9. Which of the following expresses the perimeter of the preceding triangle?

    A. $(2s-6)(s-4)$

    B. $\frac{1}{2}(2s-6)(s+4)$

    C. $4s$

    D. $4s+12$

    E. $4s-12$

10. What percent of $\frac{2}{3}$ is $\frac{1}{2}$?

    A. 300%

    B. $133\frac{1}{3}$%

    C. 75%

    D. 50%

    E. $33\frac{1}{3}$%

11. A house is on the market for a selling price of $64,000. The buyer made a $1,500 deposit, but fifteen percent of the selling price is needed for the down payment. How much more money does the buyer need for the down payment?

    A. $ 3,200

    B. $ 6,400

    C. $ 8,100

    D. $ 9,600

    E. $11,100

12. The average of 9 numbers is 7, and the average of 7 other numbers is 9. What is the average of all 16 numbers?

    A. 8

    B. $7\frac{7}{8}$

    C. $7\frac{1}{2}$

    D. $7\frac{1}{4}$

    E. $7\frac{1}{8}$

GO ON TO THE NEXT PAGE

13. If the volume and the total surface area of a cube are equal, then what is the length of one edge of the cube?

    A.   2 units

    B.   3 units

    C.   4 units

    D.   5 units

    E.   6 units

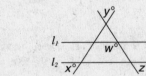

14. If $l_1 \parallel l_2$, $x = 60°$, and $w = 2z$, then $y + w =$

    A.   60°

    B.   90°

    C.   120°

    D.   150°

    E.   180°

15. If # is a binary operation such that $a \# b$ is defined as $\dfrac{a^2 + b^2}{a^2 - b^2}$ and $(a^2 - b^2 \neq 0)$, then what is the value of $a \# b$ if $2a = b$ and $a \neq 0$?

    A. $1\dfrac{1}{3}$

    B. $\dfrac{3}{5}$

    C. $-\dfrac{1}{2}$

    D. $-\dfrac{3}{5}$

    E. $-1\dfrac{2}{3}$

16. If a pipe can drain a tank in t hours, what part of the tank does it drain in 3 hours?

    A. $3t$

    B. $\dfrac{t}{3}$

    C. $t + 3$

    D. $\dfrac{3}{t}$

    E. $t - 3$

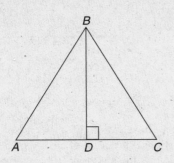

Note: Figure not drawn to scale.

17. In the preceding figure, $BD \perp AC$, $AB = 34$, $BD = 30$, and $BC = 34$. What is the length of AC?

   A.   8
   B.   18
   C.   30
   D.   32
   E.   34

18. What is the area of a square inscribed in a circle whose circumference is 16π?

   A.   512
   B.   256
   C.   128
   D.   64
   E.   32

19. 750 times 45 equals P. Therefore, 750 times 44 equals

   A. $P - 45$
   B. $P - 750$
   C. $P - 1$
   D. $44P$
   E. $750P$

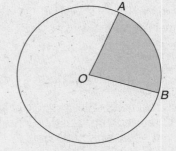

20. What is the probability that a dart thrown in the circle with center O above will land in the shaded region, if the measure of $\angle AOB$ is $60°$?

   A. $\dfrac{1}{2}$

   B. $\dfrac{1}{3}$

   C. $\dfrac{1}{4}$

   D. $\dfrac{1}{6}$

   E. $\dfrac{1}{8}$

IF YOU FINISH BEFORE TIME IS CALLED, CHECK YOUR WORK ON THIS SECTION ONLY. DO NOT WORK ON ANY OTHER SECTION IN THE TEST.

STOP

Section 10: Writing—Multiple Choice

Time: 10 Minutes

15 Questions

In this section, choose the best answer for each question and blacken the corresponding space on the answer sheet.

Directions: The following questions test correctness and effective expression. In selecting the answer, pay attention to grammar, diction, sentence structure, and punctuation. In the following questions, part or all of each sentence is underlined. The A answer repeats the underlined portion of the original sentence, while the next four offer alternatives. Choose the answer that best expresses the meaning of the original sentence, and at the same time is grammatically correct, and stylistically superior. The correct choice should be clear, unambiguous, and concise.

EXAMPLE:

The forecaster predicted <u>rain and the sky was clear.</u>

A. rain and the sky was clear.
B. rain but the sky was clear.
C. rain the sky was clear.
D. rain, but the sky was clear.
E. rain being as the sky was clear.

The correct answer is D.

---

1. <u>Scott saw that novels had ceased to paint idealized figures of romance, reviewing Jane Austen's *Emma,* and would henceforth copy real life.</u>

A. Scott saw that novels had ceased to paint idealized figures of romance, reviewing Jane Austen's *Emma,* and would henceforth copy real life.
B. Scott saw that novels had ceased to paint idealized figures of romance and would henceforth copy real life, reviewing Jane Austen's *Emma.*
C. Scott saw that by copying real life novels had ceased to paint idealized figures of romance, reviewing Jane Austen's *Emma.*
D. Reviewing Jane Austen's *Emma,* Scott saw that novels had ceased to paint idealized figures of romance, and would henceforth copy real life.
E. Reviewing Jane Austen's *Emma,* that the novel had ceased to paint idealized figures of romance and would henceforth copy real life was seen by Scott.

2. Immobilizing animals through anesthesia is not a new <u>technique zoos</u> have used this procedure for decades.

A. technique zoos
B. technique; zoos
C. technique, zoos
D. technique although zoos
E. technique for the reason that zoos

3. Many small seed companies were privately owned, but they have been taken over by chemical giants and they depend on large pesticide sales.

A. Many small seed companies were privately owned, but they have been taken over by chemical giants and they depend on large pesticide sales.

B. Many small seed companies were privately owned, have been taken over by chemical giants, and they depend on large pesticide sales.

C. Many small seed companies are privately owned, and they have been taken over by chemical giants that depend on large pesticide sales.

D. Many small privately owned seed companies depending on large sales of pesticides have been taken over by chemical giants.

E. Chemical giants that depend on large pesticide sales have taken over many small privately owned seed companies.

4. Drawing on resources that include unpublished letters and manuscripts, Anne Atkinson has written a thorough and original biography of Emily Dickinson.

A. Drawing on resources that include unpublished letters and manuscripts

B. Drawn on resources that include unpublished letters and manuscripts

C. She has drawn on resources that include unpublished letters and manuscripts, and so

D. Unpublished letters and manuscripts are the resources used, and

E. Drawing on unpublished letters and manuscripts as her resources

5. The rites of how an adolescent female is initiated becoming a member of adult society have never been photographed.

A. of how an adolescent female is initiated becoming

B. initiating an adolescent female so that she becomes

C. of the adolescent female's initiation becoming

D. which initiate an adolescent female and she becomes

E. by which the adolescent female is initiated and becomes

6. Manning's book on *Nicholas Nickleby* is the most dependable guide to this difficult novel, and it is also the wittiest account.

A. guide to this difficult novel, and it is also the wittiest account.

B. guide, and it is also the wittiest account of this difficult novel.

C. guide to this difficult novel, and the wittiest.

D. guide and also the wittiest account of this difficult novel.

E. and wittiest guide to this difficult novel.

7. To lose weight rapidly, one must weigh every food portion carefully, exercise regularly, and you should only drink water, black coffee, or diet soda.

A. and you should only drink

B. and you should drink only

C. only drinking

D. and drink only

E. and one should drink only

8. Different from any other designs in the show, Orlando Fashions Company exhibited a collection made entirely of nylon.

A. Different from any other designs in the show,

B. Different from any designs in the show,

C. With designs different from any others in the show,

D. Designed differently from others in the show,

E. Different from other designs in the show,

9. As Gordon's army advanced farther into the interior, and its supply line from the coast became more and more vulnerable.

A. and its supply line from the coast became more and more vulnerable.

B. its supply line from the coast became more and more vulnerable.

C. its supply line from the coast becoming more and more vulnerable.

D. while its supply line from the coast became more and more vulnerable.

E. and its supply line from the coast becoming more and more vulnerable.

GO ON TO THE NEXT PAGE

10. The crowned crane lives in the marshlands and meadows of West Africa, <u>and you can find them in the open grasslands as well.</u>

    A. and you can find them in the open grasslands as well.

    B. and they also live in the open grasslands.

    C. and they also can be found in the open grasslands.

    D. and in the open grasslands, as well.

    E. and they live also in the open grasslands.

11. The banking system is stronger now than it has been in many <u>years, which may encourage bankers</u> to reduce their reserves.

    A. years, which may encourage bankers

    B. years, and this may encourage bankers

    C. years, a condition that may encourage bankers

    D. years, and because of this, bankers may be encouraged

    E. years; this may encourage bankers

12. This summer, Las Vegas will see a record number of visitors, <u>and a very high percentage of them will be children.</u>

    A. and a very high percentage of them will be children.

    B. being children in a very high percentage.

    C. and children will be among them in a very high percentage.

    D. among whom a very high percentage of them will be children.

    E. and among them will be children in a very high percentage.

13. <u>Nature has provided so that nearly every plant-eating insect has a natural enemy, but</u> most insecticides kill both.

    A. Nature has provided so that nearly every plant-eating insect has a natural enemy, but

    B. Nature has seen to it that nearly every plant-eating insect has a natural enemy, and

    C. Nature provides that nearly every plant-eating insect has a natural enemy, but

    D. Nearly every plant-eating insect has a natural enemy, but

    E. Natural enemies of nearly every plant-eating insect have been provided by nature, but

14. By mid-October, black oaks, dogwood, and big-leaf <u>maples which form splashes</u> of yellow, red and orange.

    A. maples which form splashes

    B. maples form splashes

    C. maples which are forming splashes

    D. maples forming splashes

    E. maples that form splashes

15. <u>Throughout the entire work, Huxley is constantly repeating</u> that we have become the slaves of machines.

    A. Throughout the entire work, Huxley is constantly repeating

    B. Throughout the entire work, Huxley states repeatedly

    C. Constantly throughout the entire work, Huxley states

    D. Throughout, Huxley repeatedly states

    E. Huxley states

IF YOU FINISH BEFORE TIME IS CALLED, CHECK YOUR WORK ON THIS SECTION ONLY. DO NOT WORK ON ANY OTHER SECTION IN THE TEST.

Scoring Practice Test 1

Answer Key for Practice Test 1

Section 2: Critical Reading

1. A	9. C	17. D	25. A
2. B	10. C	18. A	26. A
3. A	11. A	19. C	27. D
4. C	12. E	20. A	28. B
5. D	13. C	21. C	
6. C	14. A	22. B	
7. B	15. E	23. C	
8. D	16. B	24. D	

Section 3: Mathematics

1. B	6. B	11. E	16. B
2. C	7. C	12. B	17. A
3. C	8. A	13. C	18. B
4. B	9. A	14. D	19. C
5. C	10. A	15. D	20. A

Section 4: Writing—Multiple Choice

1. D	10. A	19. C	28. D
2. C	11. B	20. E	29. A
3. A	12. E	21. C	30. D
4. B	13. A	22. A	31. D
5. E	14. B	23. C	32. D
6. D	15. C	24. B	33. E
7. C	16. D	25. D	34. A
8. A	17. C	26. E	35. B
9. C	18. D	27. E	

Section 5: Critical Reading

1. B	8. D	15. C	22. A
2. C	9. B	16. B	23. A
3. D	10. E	17. D	24. E
4. E	11. B	18. B	25. C
5. B	12. E	19. D	26. D
6. A	13. C	20. D	27. C
7. B	14. A	21. C	

Section 6: Mathematics

1. C	6. E	11. 94	16. 50
2. E	7. B	12. 9.49	17. 20
3. C	8. C	13. 70	18. 640
4. D	9. E	14. 4	19. 4/9
5. E	10. A	15. 480	20. 48

Section 7: Critical Reading

1. E	5. B	9. B	13. D
2. D	6. B	10. A	14. C
3. B	7. E	11. B	15. B
4. C	8. E	12. E	

Section 8: Mathematics

1. A	5. D	9. A	13. C
2. D	6. D	10. B	14. E
3. C	7. D	11. C	15. D
4. C	8. A	12. B	

Section 9: Mathematics

1. B	6. C	11. C	16. D
2. E	7. E	12. B	17. D
3. C	8. E	13. E	18. C
4. B	9. C	14. E	19. B
5. D	10. C	15. E	20. D

Section 10: Writing—Multiple Choice

1. D	5. E	9. B	13. D
2. B	6. E	10. D	14. B
3. E	7. D	11. C	15. D
4. A	8. C	12. A	

Analyzing Your Test Results

The charts on the following pages should be used to carefully analyze your results and spot your strengths and weaknesses. The complete process of analyzing each subject area and each individual problem should be completed for each practice test. These results should then be reexamined for trends in types of errors (repeated errors) or poor results in specific subject areas. *This reexamination and analysis is of tremendous importance to you in assuring maximum test preparation benefit.*

Reviewing the Essay

Have an English teacher, tutor, or someone else with good writing skills read and evaluate your essay using the Essay Checklist given below. Have your reader evaluate the complete essay as good, average, or marginal. Note that your paper would actually be scored from 1 to 6 by two trained readers (actual total score 2–12). But since we are trying only for a rough approximation, the simple good, average, or marginal overall evaluation will give you a general feeling for your score range.

Use the following checklist to evaluate your essay:

- Does the essay focus on the topic and complete the assigned task?
  (Circle one: Excellent   Average   Poor)

- Is the essay well organized, well developed, and consistent in argument?
  (Circle one: Excellent   Average   Poor)

- Does the essay use specific supporting details?
  (Circle one: Excellent   Average   Poor)

- Does the writing use correct grammar, usage, punctuation, and spelling?
  (Circle one: Excellent   Average   Poor)

- Is the handwriting legible?
  (Circle one: Excellent   Average   Poor)

Critical Reading Analysis Sheet

Section 2	Possible	Completed	Right	Wrong
Sentence Completion	10			
Short Reading Passages	4			
Long Reading Passages	14			
Subtotal	28			
Section 5	**Possible**	**Completed**	**Right**	**Wrong**
Sentence Completion	9			
Short Reading Passages	6			
Long Reading Passages	12			
Subtotal	27			
Section 7	**Possible**	**Completed**	**Right**	**Wrong**
Long Reading Passages	15			
Subtotal	15			
Overall Critical Reading Totals	70			

Mathematics Analysis Sheet

Section 3	Possible	Completed	Right	Wrong
Multiple Choice	20			
Subtotal	20			
Section 6	**Possible**	**Completed**	**Right**	**Wrong**
Multiple Choice	10			
Grid-Ins	10			
Subtotal	20			
Section 8	**Possible**	**Completed**	**Right**	**Wrong**
Multiple Choice	15			
Subtotal	15			
Section 9	**Possible**	**Completed**	**Right**	**Wrong**
Multiple Choice	20			
Subtotal	20			
Overall Math Totals	**75**			

Note: Only 3 math sections (about 55 questions) count on your actual exam in the new SAT.

Writing—Multiple-Choice Analysis Sheet

Section 4	Possible	Completed	Right	Wrong
Improving Sentences	7			
Identifying Sentence Errors	19			
Improving Paragraphs	9			
Subtotal	35			
Section 10	**Possible**	**Completed**	**Right**	**Wrong**
Improving Sentences	15			
Subtotal	15			
Overall Writing— Multiple-Choice Totals	**50**			

Analysis/Tally Sheet for Problems Missed

One of the most important parts of test preparation is analyzing why you missed a problem so that you can reduce the number of mistakes. Now that you have taken the practice test and checked your answers, carefully tally your mistakes by marking them in the proper column.

Reason for Mistakes					
	Total Missed	Simple Mistake	Misread Problem	Lack of Knowledge	Lack of Time
Section 2: Critical Reading					
Section 5: Critical Reading					
Section 7: Critical Reading					
Subtotal					
Section 3: Mathematics					
Section 6: Mathematics					
Section 8: Mathematics					
Section 9: Mathematics					
Subtotal					
Section 4: Writing—Multiple Choice					
Section 10: Writing—Multiple Choice					
Subtotal					
Total Reading, Math and Writing					

Reviewing the preceding data should help you determine *why* you are missing certain problems. Now that you've pinpointed the type of error, compare it to other practice tests to spot other common mistakes.

Complete Answers and Explanations for Practice Test 1

Section 2: Critical Reading

Sentence Completion

1. **A.** The adjective here should pick up the implications of "loved" and "hated," not just one or the other. The word "controversial," A, accounts for both. The other choices are not specifically related in any way to the rest of the sentence.

2. **B.** You need a verb here describing the action of organisms with a meaning like "developed" or "discovered." The best choice is B, "evolved," developed gradually, which also fits well with the detail of "thousands of years." The wrong answers describe too conscious an action.

3. **A.** Here you need words that are contradictory to the two givens: "affectionate" and "alert." "Aloof" A, "cruel" B, or "selfish" D are possible first words, but "shrewd" B, "lively" C, and "nimble" D are not contradictions of "alert," so the only possible right answer is A.

4. **C.** The first adjective offers a choice among five, any one of which would fit the first phrase. Because this fame is for an unfavorably regarded trait, however, the best choice is "notorious." A hero is "famous," "renowned," "illustrious," or "eminent," but a man who talks too much is "notorious." Because the action described confirms the reputation for long-windedness, "verified" is the only possible choice of the verbs.

5. **D.** You know that Montana already is a senator who may run for reelection. Therefore, she is the "incumbent," the holder of an office. The details of the sentence support this choice. Although the other nouns are not wholly unsuitable, none of them has any real connection with the details in the rest of the sentence.

6. **C.** The first noun must be a term that refers to what is pledged to obtain a loan, a word like "pledge," or "surety," or "collateral," or "deposit." Only "profit," D, can be eliminated. The verb must mean liquidate or get rid of because he emerges "free of debt." Only "discharge," C, is left when you eliminate A, B, and E. This confirms the sense of "collateral" being the best of the four available nouns.

7. **B.** The missing word describes "absurdist" fiction and is parallel to the word shocking. Clearly, "banal," A, "plausible," C, "cozy," D, and "familiar," E, will not do. The adjective "radical" means favoring fundamental change or very leftist.

8. **D.** The sense of the sentence calls for an adjective expressing strong feelings because the writer is surprised by this response to an "insignificant" issue. D is the only logical answer.

9. **C.** The sentence describes a division in the band, avant-garde instrumentalists, and a popular-ballad crooner, so the first adjective should account for this split. The word "progressive," A, fits only the band, and "old-fashioned," B, and "predictable," E, fit the singer. The word "inconsistent" is the best of the choices. The second adjective should describe "popular ballads," and all except B, "unique," will do.

10. **C.** Because she hoped to be undetected, she had to hide the card "furtively," that is, stealthily or surreptitiously. The words "brazenly," A, and "overtly," B, contradict the opening phrase.

Short Reading Passages

11. **A.** The fact that associations vary from person to person, depending on personal history, is the point of the paragraph. C contradicts this point, and D, while a tempting answer, is incorrect. Your culture may help determine your associations, but it is your own history which is the prime determiner, according to the passage. B is meaningless here. The reverse of E is true; word association tests are valuable because people's associations vary and can therefore provide clues to their psychological state.

12. **E.** This example illustrates how personal history creates associations. B may seem correct, but to some people, coffee might be associated with a cigarette, inability to sleep, etc. "Everyone" is the problem word here. A and C are irrelevant. D draws a conclusion that is not warranted, nor does it strengthen the main point of the paragraph.

13. **C.** Lines 9–11 state that this fact has been "recently established." D and E are presented as possibilities, not certainties. Nothing in the paragraph suggests A, and, according to the paragraph, B is simply untrue because of the butterfly's short life span.

14. **A.** The point of the paragraph is that scientists cannot yet fully explain how the migrating butterfly finds its way. They don't know enough about how the butterfly navigates to know whether B is correct. Nothing in the passage either supports or refutes C and D, and E may or may not be true. (Beware of words like "never" and "always" in answer choices.)

Long Reading Passages

15. **E.** Although "correspondence" can mean correlation, agreement, or similarity, here it means communication by letters. Gauguin's "correspondence" refers to the letters he wrote to France from the South Pacific.

16. **B.** Gauguin's letter refers to the quotation from Poe that finds "singularity" (oddness, uniqueness, strangeness) in perfect beauty, and he is reminded of these lines by the beauty of his first Tahitian model.

17. **D.** The passage points out that most of the artists before Gauguin had not painted Tahitians realistically, but as "idealized types," altered to fit European tastes, just the opposite of choice B. The passage goes on to point out that the Tahitian could "scarcely be distinguished from his African or Asian counterpart."

18. **A.** The reader can infer that Charles Giraud painted Tahitians before Gauguin did, but because the paintings have not survived, the author cannot know whether Giraud followed other artists and painted to suit European ideas of beauty or if, like Gauguin, he painted the Tahitians as they really were. It is for this reason the author would like to see Giraud's work.

19. **C.** The passage opposes the terms "Naturalism" and "Symbolism." The naturalistic or realistic in Gauguin is alluded to in lines 31–32 ("straightforward") and lines 46–47 ("naturalistically"), and lines 52–54 refer to the nonrealistic "Symbolist aspirations."

20. **A.** The two impulses in Gauguin that appear to be at odds are his wish to render the Tahitians as they really are and at the same time to reveal a "poetic image" of the "island's mysterious past." The problem is discussed in the last 32 lines of the passage.

21. **C.** The first paragraph is introductory and presents the opposing positions on global warming and greenhouse gases represented by the climatologist Jim Hansen and the politician John Sununu.

22. **B.** Although "pit" (the verb) can mean to scar or remove the core of, the meaning here is sets in opposition or sets in competition.

23. **C.** Because neither oxygen nor nitrogen absorbs heat, neither A nor B is likely. The amount of carbon dioxide in the atmosphere can be increased by burning of fossil fuels, D. In choice E, the opposite is more likely to be true because heat escapes as infrared radiation. Because carbon dioxide absorbs heat, a planet with more in its atmosphere would be warmer.

24. **D.** Because oxygen and nitrogen, which are not greenhouse gases, form 99 percent of the atmosphere according to the second paragraph, the passage does not imply that greenhouse gases make up a large part of the atmosphere. The second paragraph also tells us that carbon dioxide absorbs large amounts of heat and that the release of carbon dioxide can lead to warming. The third paragraph adds that clearing and burning forests create carbon dioxide.

25. **A.** If greenhouse gases absorb heat and nitrogen does not absorb heat (paragraph 2), then nitrogen is not a greenhouse gas. The other four are mentioned in the second and third paragraphs of the passage.

26. **A.** The first statement makes a point that logically questions the Marshall report theory that "without greenhouse gases to warm things up, the world would become cool in the next century." If so, why was it not cool before there were greenhouse gases? The passage does not give us any information about economic predictions in the Marshall report, and in any case, because the report advocates the encouragement of greenhouse gases, this idea would not undermine its conclusions. Similarly, the third statement would not affect the arguments of the report because oxygen is not a greenhouse gas.

27. **D.** The word "skeptic" now usually means a person who habitually questions or doubts even matters generally accepted.

28. **B.** The image of Mr. Sununu as a character in a Dracula film was probably intended to amuse the audience and to make the opponent seem a bit ridiculous. It would also suggest that the claims are melodramatic. A believer in the danger of too much greenhouse gas in the atmosphere would not be likely to suggest that the danger is imaginary, so the third statement is very unlikely.

Section 3: Mathematics

1. **B.** Setting up an equation gives $\frac{1}{5}x = 2$. Multiplying both sides by 5,

$$(5)\frac{1}{5}x = 2(5)$$

Then

$$x = 10$$

And $\frac{1}{2}$ of 10 is 5.

2. C. The selling price for 1 dozen at 3 for $0.85 is

$$3 \times 4 = 12 = 1 \text{ dozen} = \$0.85 \times 4 = \$3.40$$

Therefore, 6 dozen will yield $\$3.40 \times 6 = \$20.40$.

The store's cost for 6 dozen at $1.80 per dozen is $\$1.80 \times 6 = \$10.80$.

Therefore, the profit on 6 dozen of these items will be $20.40 – $10.80, or $9.60.

3. C. If $x = -1$,

$$
\begin{aligned}
x^4 + x^3 &+ x^2 + x - 3 \\
&= (-1)^4 + (-1)^3 + (-1)^2 + (-1) - 3 \\
&= 1 + (-1) + 1 + (-1) - 3 \\
&= 0 + 1 + (-1) - 3 \\
&= 1 + (-1) - 3 \\
&= 0 - 3 \\
&= -3
\end{aligned}
$$

4. B. The union of two sets is the set of elements belonging to set P or set Q or to both sets P and Q.

$$P = \{2,3,5,7\} \text{ and } Q = \{3,5,7\}$$
$$P \cup Q = \{2,3,5,7\}$$

5. C. Substitute 3 for x.

$$
\begin{aligned}
f(x) &= 3^x + 5x \\
f(x) &= 3^3 + 5(3) \\
&= 27 + 15 \\
&= 42
\end{aligned}
$$

6. B. Since $a \otimes b = a^3 + b^2$,

$$
\begin{aligned}
(-2) \otimes (-3) &= (-2)^3 + (-3)^2 \\
&= (-8) + 9 \\
&= 1
\end{aligned}
$$

7. C. Since $BD = CD$, $\angle CBD = \angle C = 19°$

Therefore,
$$
\begin{aligned}
\angle BDC &= 180° - (\angle CBD - \angle C) \\
&= 180° - (19° + 19°) \\
&= 180° - 38° \\
&= 142°
\end{aligned}
$$

Then
$$
\begin{aligned}
\angle BDA &= 180° - \angle BDC \\
&= 180° - 142° \\
&= 38°
\end{aligned}
$$

Since $AB = AD$, $\qquad \angle ABD = \angle BDA = 38°$

Therefore,

$$\angle A = 180° - (\angle BDA + \angle ABD)$$
$$= 180° - (38° + 38°)$$
$$= 180° - 76°$$
$$= 104°$$

8. A. The number of nickels that Angela has is x. Therefore, the total value of those nickels (in cents) is $5x$. Angela also has twice as many dimes as nickels, or $2x$. The total value in cents of those dimes is $2x(10)$, or $20x$. Adding together the value of the nickels and dimes gives $5x + 20x$, or $25x$.

9. A. If $x - 4 = y$, then $y - x = -4$. Therefore, $(y - x)^3 = (-4)^3 = -64$.

10. A. The perimeter of a rectangle with length l and width w is $2l + 2w$. Because the perimeter of the rectangle is $10x + 8$ and its length is $3x$,

$$\text{perimeter} = 2l + 2w$$
$$10x + 8 = 2(3x) + 2w$$
$$10x + 8 = 6x + 2w$$
$$10x + 8 - 6x = 6x + 2w - 6x$$
$$4x + 8 = 2w$$
$$2x + 4 = w$$

Therefore, the width of the rectangle is $2x + 4$.

11. E. If $\frac{3}{7} = \frac{10}{x - 4}$, then cross multiplying yields

$$3(x - 4) = (7)(10)$$
$$3x - 12 = 70$$
$$3x - 12 + 12 = 70 + 12$$
$$3x = 82$$
$$\frac{3x}{3} = \frac{82}{3}$$
$$x = \frac{82}{3}, \text{ or } 27\frac{1}{3}$$

12. B. The car travels a total distance of 280 miles in $7\frac{1}{2}$ hours for the round trip. Its average speed in miles per hour is

$$280 \div 7\frac{1}{2} = \frac{280}{1} \div \frac{15}{2}$$
$$= \frac{280}{1} \times \frac{2}{15} = \frac{560}{15} = \frac{112}{3}$$
$$= 37\frac{1}{3}$$

You could have used your calculator here and simply divided 280 by 7.5, getting 37.333, or $37\frac{1}{3}$.

13. C. Because a and b must both be positive or both be negative, choice C, III only, is the only answer that *must* be true.

14. D. The slope (m) of a line passing through the points (x_1, y_1) and (x_2, y_2) is

$$m = \frac{y_2 - y_1}{x_2 - x_1}$$

The line passes through (–3, 5) and (2, 9), so

$$m = \frac{9-5}{2-(-3)} = \frac{4}{5}$$

Note that you could eliminate choices A, B, and C because they are all negative slopes, and the diagram shows a line with a positive slope.

15. D.

$$\left(\frac{x^{-5}y^2}{x^{-2}y^{-3}}\right)^{-2} = \frac{x^{10}y^{-4}}{x^4 y^6}$$
$$= x^{10-4}y^{-4-6}$$
$$= x^6 y^{-10}$$
$$= \frac{x^6}{y^{10}}$$

16. B. $\angle XYZ$ is inscribed in a semicircle and is therefore a right angle. Therefore, $\triangle XYZ$ is a right triangle and the Pythagorean theorem states

$$(XY)^2 = (XZ)^2 + (YZ)^2$$
$$(17)^2 = (XZ)^2 + (15)^2 \, (XY \text{ is a diameter})$$
$$289 = (XZ)^2 + 225$$
$$289 - 225 = (XZ)^2$$
$$(XZ)^2 = 64$$
$$XZ = \sqrt{64}$$
$$XZ = 8$$
$$\text{area of } \triangle XYZ = \frac{1}{2}bh$$
$$= \frac{1}{2}(XZ)(YZ)$$
$$= \frac{1}{2}(8)(15)$$
$$= (4)(15)$$
$$= 60$$

17. A. If 15 gumballs were picked from the bag, it is possible that 8 of them are red and 7 are white. On the next pick (the 16th), however, one is assured of having one gumball of each color.

18. B. Because each letter repeats after every five vowels, divide 327 by 5, and the remainder will determine the vowel in that place of the pattern. Since $327 \div 5 = 65$ with a remainder of 2, the remainder of 2 indicates that the second vowel (e) will be the 327th letter.

19. C. Let x = length of equal sides in feet and $x + 8$ = length of base in feet.

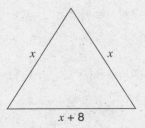

Since the perimeter is 89 feet,

$$x + x + x + 8 = 89$$
$$3x + 8 = 89$$
$$3x + 8 - 8 = 89 - 8$$
$$3x = 81$$
$$\frac{3x}{3} = \frac{81}{3}$$
$$x = 27$$

Therefore, the length of the base is $x + 8$, or 35 feet.

20. **A.** Because the perimeter of the rhombus is 40, each side has length 10. Because the diagonals of a rhombus are perpendicular and bisect each other,

$$x^2 + 5^2 = 10^2$$
$$x^2 + 25 = 100$$
$$x^2 = 75$$
$$x = \sqrt{75}$$
$$x = 5\sqrt{3}$$

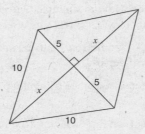

The area of a quadrilateral with perpendicular diagonals d_1 and d_2 is

$$\text{area} = \frac{1}{2} d_1 \cdot d_2$$
$$= \frac{1}{2}(10)(10\sqrt{3})$$
$$= 50\sqrt{3}$$

Section 4: Writing—Multiple Choice

Improving Sentences

1. **D.** The correct version should include either "people's" or "players'" to keep from changing the meaning. Since the word "players" has already been used in the sentence, "people's" is the better choice. The second part of the sentence specifically contrasts the two behaviors, so "but" is a better choice of conjunction than "and." The sentence contains two independent clauses which should be separated by a conjunction *and* a comma.

2. **C.** The problem in this sentence is the ambiguous "they." To which of the two parties does it refer? C uses more words, but makes clear which party will win the election. Both D and E are also ambiguous.

3. **A.** The original version is correct. It consists of a series of four adjectives, with one adverbial modifier ("grossly"). It is also the most concise of the five versions of the sentence. There is no need to break up the series of adjectives, and the other versions add unnecessary words. Choice D, by changing "grossly" to "gross," changes the meaning of the sentence.

4. **B.** The error in the original sentence is a comma splice, the use of a comma to join two complete sentences. D, omitting the comma, is even worse. B's use of a semicolon corrects the sentence. Remember that the semicolon is usually the equivalent of a period, not a comma. E needs a comma to be correct; C is wordy and awkward, though the punctuation is not wrong.

5. **E.** Up to the comma, this is a complete sentence, but the second half has a subject but no main verb. Choices A, B, C, and D have only the participle "accepting" (a verbal adjective, not a verb). E has a main verb, "accept," and is the only version that is not a sentence fragment.

6. **D.** The conjunction "but" is a better choice than "and," because the two parts of the sentence present a contrast. In A, B, and C, the sentence needlessly shifts from the passive ("is given") to the active voice.

7. **C.** Again, the "but" is a better conjunction choice than the "and." Although B is not grammatically wrong, it is wordier than C, the most concise of the five choices. The shift from the active verbs to the participles in D and E disrupts the parallel structure.

Identifying Sentence Errors

8. **A.** There is an error in the case of the pronoun "I." It is the object of the verb "hired" and should be "me." "The owners hired I," would be easy to spot as an error. Don't let words between related parts of a sentence distract you.

9. **C.** As it stands, two unlike objects are compared. The sentence says pistachios cost more than orchards; what it intended to say was imported pistachios cost more than California pistachios.

10. **A.** The verb "are" (a plural) does not agree with the singular "agreement." Again, the error would be easy to see if the two words were together. The plural "they" is correct, as it refers to "House" and "Senate."

11. **B.** The verb tense is wrong here. The use of "tomorrow" tells us the action is to take place in the future, but "departed" is a past tense. It should be "will depart."

12. **E.** The sentence has no errors. The verb tense sequence using the past perfect "had completed" followed by the past "considered" is correct.

13. **A.** The pronoun "who" should replace the pronoun "which." To refer to persons, use "who;" to refer to things or animals, use "which."

14. **B.** The comparative here repeats itself, since "worse" already means "more bad." You could say something like "more harmful" or "worse," but not "more worse."

15. **C.** The choice of preposition here is not idiomatic. We say "concede to," not "with."

16. **D.** The error is a double negative. The "hardly any" avoids the error, but "scarcely no" has two negatives. A sentence testing this error will probably use either "hardly" or "scarcely" as one of the negatives. A "not" and a "no" ("I don't have no money.") is too easy.

17. **C.** This is an agreement error, common in constructions using "either/or." Here the subject of the plural verb "are" is the singular "attempt," or the singular "bombing." It cannot be both, since the point of the sentence is that one or the other is responsible.

18. **D.** An often-tested idiom error is the interchange of an infinitive ("to dismantle") and a prepositional phrase with a gerund ("on dismantling"). Here, the noun "insistence" requires the prepositional phrase. If, however, the sentence had read "refusal" instead of "insistence," the infinitive would be correct.

19. **C.** The use of the future tense of the verb ("will believe") makes no sense in this context. The present tense, "believe," should have been used.

20. **E.** The sentence uses the correlative "not only...but also" which often introduces errors of parallelism, but here there are no errors.

21. **C.** This is another agreement error; the singular subject "business" requires the singular verb "has developed."

22. **A.** The subject of the second half of the sentence is "you," and since it is not underlined, it cannot be changed. To keep the pronouns consistent, the "we" at the beginning must also be "you."

23. **C.** The verb form "had flew" is the error here. Either the past tense "flew" or the past perfect "had flown" would be correct.

24. **B.** There is an adverb-adjective confusion here. The adjective "fond" should be used to modify the noun "good-bye."

25. **D.** The sentence begins with a singular "ambassador," but changes to an unspecified plural "they" in the main clause. They who?

26. **E.** The sentence is correct. The singular "its" refers to the singular MTV and the verb tense is reasonable.

Improving Paragraphs

27. **E.** Both sentences are very wordy: "stage of life" is used twice, "life," three times, and "all throughout" is redundant. The revision in B and E gets rid of the repetitions of "stage," but B keeps the wordy "that occurs all." The best choice is E.

28. **D.** There are two problems here: the lack of parallelism in "with establishing" and "to separate," and the pronoun agreement with the singular "adolescent." B and E make the phrases parallel, but use the plural pronoun "their." D has the singular "his," and parallel infinitives "to establish" and "to separate."

29. **A.** One problem with this essay is its vague use of the word "separation." In the second paragraph, the essay deals with the literal separation caused by events like divorce or death. But the first paragraph is not concerned with a physical separation. The adolescent may be psychologically distanced from his parents, but the separation is metaphorical. Choices B, C, and D are not "unlike the first paragraph" and E is untrue.

30. **D.** The twelfth sentence is not really needed here. It repeats what is implicit in sentence 11. The rest of the paragraph is about kinds of separation, rather than their effect.

31. **D.** Without the comma we may read "our courage" as the object of the verb "develop:" "as we develop our courage." In this sentence, "develop" is intransitive, that is, does not take an object.

32. **D.** A good revision of this sentence will eliminate the repetition of "reasons", as well as the vague and pompous "category of reasons" and "enterprise." D keeps the meaning intact, and does so with the greatest clarity and fewest words.

33. **E.** The sentence could do without A, B, C, and D, and the word "trying" as well. The slimmed-down sentence will read: The easiest to recognize is to avoid an unpleasant chore.

34. **A.** The paragraph offers three plausible reasons to explain why the writer procrastinates.

35. **B.** The paragraph still reads smoothly without sentence 15, which does little more than repeat the content of sentence 14: that procrastination produces guilt and anxiety.

Section 5: Critical Reading

Sentence Completion

1. **B.** The "also" in the second half of the sentence signals that the verb is parallel to "prevent" in the first half. You can eliminate C and D. The first adjective must mean something like reasonable or sensible, so B "logical" is a better choice than A "fanciful" or E "idle," which mean just the opposite.

2. **C.** The first noun must mean something like substitute but a word that will fit with the preposition "to." Choice A "answer" is possible, C "alternative" is a good answer, and D "rejoinder" might work. The phrase "responsible for" A makes little sense in this context, and "involved in" D is awkward. The phrase "subject to" is clearly the best of the three and C the best of the five choices.

3. **D.** The logic of the sentence suggests that the missing verb must mean something like prevent or decrease. Choices B "augment" (increase) and C "foster" are the opposite of what is needed. Neither "explain" A nor "exculpate" (excuse) E makes much sense, although "deter" (discourage, keep from doing) fits well.

4. **E.** The sentence opposes the unpleasant "smoke and _____ of the city," with the "_____ air and peace of the mountains," so the first blank must be a noun similar in effect to "smoke," and the second blank requires an adjective with pleasant denotation. In A and B the nouns are possible, but the adjectives are not. In C and D, the noun choices cannot fit. Choice E correctly has the bad "hustle-bustle" and the good "exhilarating."

5. **B.** A situation requiring the choice between two unpleasant alternatives is the definition of the word "dilemma" and what this sentence describes. Some of the other choices are plausible, but because "dilemma" so exactly fits the situation, it is clearly the best.

6. **A.** The word "combining" should alert you to look for a noun here that denotes a coming together of East and West. Choices B, C, and D are clearly wrong. Choice A "fusion," the union of different things, fits well.

7. **B.** The noun referring to what "allowed voters to decide" on an issue could be "statute" A, "referendum" B (the most precise word), or "bill" D. The missing adverb that describes the 9-to-1 win must denote a very resounding margin of victory. Neither "meager" A nor "narrow" D will do. Again, the best answer uses the most specific noun as well as the most suitable adverb.

8. **D.** The first blank requires a noun describing something a novel is based on. Choices A, C, and D are possible. B and E are eliminated by the use of "upon which." The second word must praise the book because it is parallel with "intelligence" and the novel has been called "fine." Choices A and C must be eliminated, and only D remains.

9. **B.** The adjective "anachronistic" means representing something as existing at other than its proper time, such as a washing machine in the Middle Ages or a knight in armor at a football game. Choice A is a possibility, although B is more exact.

Short Reading Passages

10. **E.** Note lines 9–11. The tone of the passage is not critical, and therefore A and D are not good answers. B is a secondary point, not the main purpose of the paragraph. C, while it may be a true statement, is not relevant to this passage.

11. **B.** What Salk originally believed was "a dull but dependable investment" became a milestone in medical history that made him famous; his original belief was therefore ironic in terms of the results. The other answers are straightforward and contain no ironies.

12. **E.** See lines 11–13. The author believes the opposite of A, C, and D, and does not express an opinion on B. The point of the passage is that debates have become less and less informative and the candidates less and less forthright.

13. **C.** Even without knowing the definition of the word, you can determine that this is the only choice that makes sense in context. B, D, and E all contradict the picture the author gives of candidates who are less than forthright and who are afraid of saying anything that might "ruffle feathers." A is completely unrelated to "elliptical."

14. **A.** The author of Passage 2 cites B (lines 7–8), C (lines 5–6), D (lines 10–11), and E (lines 12–14). The author does NOT cite, however, any evidence that these positive effects have increased voter turnout.

15. **C.** For example, Passage 1 uses words like "boob tube" and "sound bites" and asks a sarcastic rhetorical question at the end of the passage. Passage 2, on the other hand, presents points in a straightforward fashion. A is not accurate because "philosophical" is an inappropriate characterization of Passage 2. The tone used in Passage 1 is not like the tone in Passage 2, B, and D isn't an accurate characterization of either passage. E is simply too vague.

Long Reading Passages

16. **B.** The passage explicitly refers to Celia and Dorothea as sisters. Although it does not mention their father's death, you know that the jewels belonged to their mother, and because an uncle, not her father, gave them to Dorothea, it may be that the father is dead and they are in the uncle's care.

17. **D.** That Dorothea has started an "infant school" in the village and is busy with plans for some buildings tells you at once that she is active and generous. No details in the passage suggest that she is prying, idle, ambitious, or ineffectual, although she may be rich or philanthropic.

18. **B.** The preceding sentence tells you that Dorothea's eyes are "full of laughter," and her tone when she speaks again is "full" and "cordial." She is teasing Celia good-naturedly, making fun of her sister's remark that it is exactly "six months today." In this dialogue, it is Celia who has planned what she will say, and Dorothea speaks spontaneously. Dorothea has probably forgotten all about the jewels, and Celia has probably been thinking about them for some time.

19. **D.** The phrase means disrespectful or lacking in respect. The reader must recognize that the verb "want" here means to lack, not the more common to wish for. Choice C confuses "wanting" and "wanton."

20. **D.** Celia does not wish to have all the jewels, although she does want a share, and she expects to wear them. Unlike Dorothea, she is not at all Puritanical. She correctly anticipates that Dorothea might object to wearing jewelry, so she has prepared this defense on the moral grounds that she thinks will best convince Dorothea.

21. **C.** Dorothea, who does not care about the jewels herself, has simply not realized that Celia really wants to wear them. In lines 42–45, the reader is told that this "discovery" is astonishing to her, and the moment she realizes Celia's true feeling, she rushes to open the cabinet. Celia's arguments would have been more effective if she had simply told Dorothea of her real wishes because Dorothea loves her sister and is eager to make her happy. Notice that Dorothea has said that the jewels would not be worn only before she realizes what Celia really wishes.

22. **A.** "Deprecation" is disapproval, or protest, as is suggested in this sentence by Dorothea's saying "no." A lessening is a "depreciation," and a removal is a "deprivation."

23. **A.** The adjective in this context comes from the verb meaning to annoy, to irk, as in to try one's patience. In some contexts, "trying" might mean attempting or determining, but here, irksome is the best definition.

24. **E.** The "Puritanic toleration" is Dorothea's. She has given up all the jewels to Celia and even encouraged her to wear them. Although this is in one way pleasing to Celia, it does put Dorothea in a position of moral superiority, which Celia finds annoying.

25. **C.** Dorothea is the Puritan, and Celia is the "unenthusiastic sister"; that is, one who has not adopted the religious extremes of self-denial, such as not wearing jewels.

26. **D.** Although some answers here describe Dorothea accurately, only D points to an inconsistency. Dorothea regards wearing jewelry as somehow immoral, and yet, because she sees that Celia really wants to wear the jewels, she encourages her to do so. What is right for her sister would not be right for her.

27. **C.** The passage is centrally concerned with delineating the two sisters. Although there is some mild comedy at the expense of both, the passage is not satiric, and it reveals as much love as friction between the sisters. They are not alike, and though Celia may take pleasure in jewels, the passage is not about the dangers of materialism. The author, the reader senses, is amused by and fond of both of these young women.

Section 6: Mathematics

1. **C.** In the series 8, 9, 12, 17, 24. . . ,

$$9 - 8 = 1$$
$$12 - 9 = 3$$
$$17 - 12 = 5$$
$$24 - 17 = 7$$

Therefore, the difference between the next term and 24 must be 9, or

$$x - 24 = 9$$
$$x = 33$$

Therefore, the next term in the series must be 33.

2. **E.** $\frac{1}{4}$ of 0.03% =

Change $\frac{1}{4}$ to .25 and 0.03% to 0.0003.

$$(.25)(0.0003) = 0.000075$$

3. E. The area of a triangle is $\frac{1}{2} \times$ base $\times$ height

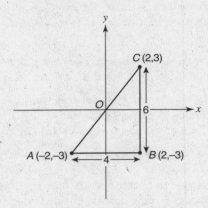

Base AB of the triangle is 4 units (because from A to the y-axis is 2 units and from the y-axis to B is 2 units). Height BC of the triangle is 6 units (3 units from B to the x-axis and another 3 units to C). Note that $\angle B$ is a right angle. So

$$\text{Area of triangle} = \frac{1}{2} \times 4 \times 6$$
$$= \frac{1}{2} \times 24$$
$$= 12$$

4. D. You should have a working knowledge of these expressions:

Sum: The result of addition.

Difference: The result of subtraction.

Product: The result of multiplication.

Quotient: The result of division.

Therefore, the *product of two numbers* may be represented as $(x)(y)$. The *difference of the two numbers* may be either $x - y$ or $y - x$. The term twice indicates that the expression is to be multiplied by 2. Therefore, the entire expression breaks down as follows:

$$\underbrace{\text{The product of two numbers}}_{(x)(y)} \underbrace{\text{is equal to}}_{=} \underbrace{\text{twice}}_{2} \underbrace{\text{the difference of the two numbers}}_{(x-y)}$$

5. E. If $4^n = 64$, then $n = 3$ (since $4 \times 4 \times 4 = 64$)

Now plug 3 in for n.

$$3^{n+2} = 3^{3+2} = 3^5 = 243$$

6. E. $f(z) = \dfrac{3z^3 + z - 7}{z^2 - 25}$ is undefined when $z^2 - 25 = 0$, since the denominator of a fraction cannot be equal to 0.

So set $z^2 - 25$ equal to 0 and solve.

$$z^2 - 25 = (z + 5)(z - 5) = 0$$
$$z + 5 = 0 \text{ or } z - 5 = 0$$
$$z = -5 \text{ or } z = 5$$

7. B. Because D is between A and B on $\overleftrightarrow{AB}$, you know that the sum of the lengths of the smaller segments AD and DB is equal to the length of the larger segment AB.

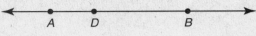

Therefore,

$$AB = AD + DB$$
$$AB - AD = AD + DB - AD$$
$$AB - AD = DB$$

8. C. Solve the equation as follows:

$$x - 3 = \frac{18}{x}$$
$$x(x - 3) = x \cdot \frac{18}{x}$$
$$x(x - 3) = 18$$
$$x^2 - 3x = 18$$
$$x^2 - 3x - 18 = 0$$
$$(x - 6)(x + 3) = 0$$
$$x - 6 = 0 \quad \text{or} \quad x + 3 = 0$$
$$x = 6 \quad \text{or} \quad x = -3$$

9. E. $\boxed{6} = 6^2 - 1, \ z$ is even and $\boxed{7} = 7^2 + 1, \ z$ is odd

$$\boxed{7} - \boxed{6} = (7^2 + 1) - (6^2 - 1)$$

So,
$$= 50 - 35$$
$$= 15$$

10. A. Since $\angle Y$ is inscribed in a semicircle, $\angle Y$ is a right angle. So using the Pythagorean theorem you get,

$$(XY)^2 + (YZ)^2 = (XZ)^2$$
$$15^2 + 8^2 = (XZ)^2$$
$$225 + 64 = (XZ)^2$$
$$289 = (XZ)^2$$
$$\sqrt{289} = XZ$$
$$XZ = 17$$

Grid-In Questions

11. Answer: 94. Since $x = -4$,

$$5x^2 - 3x + 2 = 5(-4)^2 - 3(-4) + 2$$
$$= 5(16) + 12 + 2$$
$$= 80 + 12 + 2$$
$$= 94$$

12. Answer: 9.49. For a 25-minute call, the first 3 minutes will cost $2.45, and the additional 22 minutes will cost $.32 per minute. The cost *(C)* for the call will be

$$C = \$2.45 + (22)(\$.32)$$
$$= \$2.45 + \$7.04$$
$$= \$9.49$$

13. Answer: 70. Let n = the original price of the jacket. 80% of n is $56.

$$(0.80) \cdot n = \$56$$
$$n = \$56 \div 0.80$$
$$n = \$70$$

14. Answer: 4. The volume of a cube with side of length x is x^3. Therefore,

$$x^3 = 64$$
$$x = \sqrt[3]{64}$$
$$x = 4$$

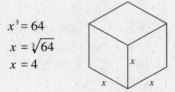

15. Answer: 480. You can quickly solve this problem by using your calculator. Total the four listed items: $840 + $460 + $320 + $120 = $1,740. Subtract $1,740 from the given total: $2,220 – $1,740 = $480. The lab workbooks cost $480.

16. Answer: 50. Begin by choosing a simple fraction, $\frac{100}{100}$, for example. If the numerator is tripled and the denominator is doubled, the resulting fraction is $\frac{300}{200}$, or $1\frac{1}{2}$. So the new fraction represents a 50% increase over the original fraction.

17. Answer: 20. Since $l_1 \| l_2$, the alternate interior angles have the same measure and

$$5x - 20 = 2x + 40$$
$$3x - 20 = 40$$
$$3x = 60$$
$$x = 20$$

18. Answer: 640. The phrase *how much more* indicates subtraction. Clothing was 13% of the total. Insurance was 5% of the total. So 13% – 5%, or 8%, more of the total of $8,000 was spent on clothing than on insurance.

$$.08 \times \$8,000 = \$640$$

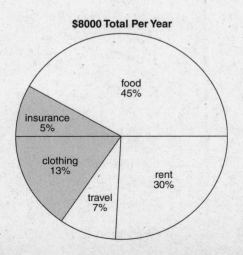

19. Answer: 4/9. In $\triangle MXN$, $\angle MNX = 50°$, $\angle MXN = 90°$, and $\angle NMQ = 30°$

$$\angle NMQ + \angle QMX = \angle NMX$$

So $$50° + 90° + 30° + \angle QMX = 180°$$

$$170° + \angle QMX = 180°$$

$$\angle QMX = 10°$$

In $\triangle MPQ$, $$\angle QMP + \angle MPQ + \angle MQP = 180°$$

$$10° + 130° + \angle MQP = 180°$$

$$140° + \angle MQP = 180°$$

$$\angle MQP = 40°$$

Angle PXN is 90°, so the ratio of $\angle MQP$ to $\angle PXN$ is 40/90, or 4/9.

20. Answer: 48. Set up the equations as follows: Let t be the length of time it will take the plane to overtake the bus. Then $t + 4$ is the time that the bus has traveled before the plane starts. The distance the bus has traveled by 1:00 p.m. is $50(t + 4)$ because distance equals rate times time ($d = rt$). The distance the plane will travel is $300t$. Now, equating these two (they will have to travel the same distance for one to overtake the other) gives $50(t + 4) = 300t$.

Solve the equation as follows.

$$50(t + 4) = 300t$$

$$50t + 200 = 300t$$

$$200 = 250t$$

Therefore, $$\frac{4}{5} = t$$

Four-fifths of an hour ($\frac{4}{5} \times 60$) is 48 minutes. Therefore, it will take 48 minutes for the plane to overtake the bus.

Section 7: Critical Reading

Long Reading Passages

1. E. The sentence on Lope de Vega's play does all three. It gives an example of a play by a Spanish playwright using Columbus as a hero; it shows that Columbus's reputation had reached to the popular theater; and it gives an example of Columbus in his symbolic role as the "embodiment of that spirit driving humans to explore and discover."

2. D. The best of the five definitions here is "inclined." Although the verb "dispose" can mean to arrange or to give away, the context here makes clear that the meaning is something like not inclined to struggle against the myth of Columbus, and the next sentence, as well as the rest of the paragraph, confirms this meaning.

3. B. The nouns used for "mold" here—pattern, manner, model, shape, or style—are all adequate; "romantic" here is best defined by idealized. The word is explained further by the phrase "favored in the century's literature," and the quotations from Irving that follow depict an idealized rather than a visionary, fictitious, or escapist hero.

4. C. Since "ambition" and "magnanimity" are direct quotations from Irving, neither is possible. The word "mined" expresses no judgment, and "palliating" refers neutrally to Irving's inadequate explanation. The use of "Perhaps" expresses the author's reluctance to accept Irving's assessment of Columbus.

5. B. The first paragraph surveys Columbus's reputation in the sixteenth and seventeenth centuries; the second, third, and fourth deal with the nineteenth century. Although the last paragraph predicts a reevaluation in the twentieth century, the passage does not deal with the hostile criticism of the explorer.

6. B. The fourth paragraph explains how the nineteenth-century Columbus reflected what that period most valued, and the last paragraph refers to people creating "the Columbus they want to believe in." The account of nineteenth-century historians' indifference to the Columbus documents discovered in 1825 contradicts the notion that history is truth as it is known at the time of writing.

7. E. Each of the questions reveals more of the author's ideas about the Europeans at the time of Columbus's voyages. The passage goes on to show how these limitations led to the exploitation of the New World. The paragraph does not defend or justify their actions.

8. E. All three are accurate descriptions of the effects of the phrase. The phrase "a foreign, heathen people, half naked and befeathered, ignorant of cities and kings and metal and laws, and unschooled in all that the Ancients held virtuous" is the European view of the native Americans as inferior, contemptuous of their ignorance of Greece and Rome, which had become important to Europe in the age of discovery. The point of view of this phrase is that of the fifteenth-century European, not that of the twentieth-century author.

9. B. The second paragraph refers to new foods and medicines found in the New World.

10. A. The passage presents the biological outlook as one in which humans have a sense of being at one with nature, where humans' relation to earth and all its life forms is more important than their relation to other humans. Choices B and E are just what the biological outlook is not. Choices C and D are concerned with economic rather than ecological well-being.

11. B. The passage argues that, properly understood, the discovery might have brought regeneration to Europe, but the Europeans, tragically, could only exploit and destroy the new-found lands. The passage does criticize this European failure, but this criticism is not its real point. The passage does not describe the benefits of the discovery A, and it is by no means objective E.

12. E. The last paragraph of Passage 1 refers to "a major reassessment of Columbus's reputation," and Passage 2 presents a view of the consequences of Columbus's voyages totally unlike the heroic adulation of the first four paragraphs of the first passage.

13. D. Passage 2 presents a highly personal, highly emotional, judgmental, philosophical view of Columbus's discovery. But it is not more historical than Passage 1. In fact, it presents only the view of its twentieth-century author, and Passage 1 samples opinions from several periods.

14. C. The style of Passage 2 is characterized by its use of words in series, repetition, parallel phrases, and rhetorical questions. It does not use understatement. Some readers, no doubt, would argue that it depends on overstatement.

15. B. The first two statements are just, but although Passage 1 focuses on Columbus's reputation, Passage 2 does not even mention Columbus by name. The second passage does reevaluate the discovery of America. The second passage also presents an interpretation of the voyages of discovery that reflects the late twentieth-century concern for the wisdom of ancient cultures, for ecology, and for the dangers of warring against nature.

Section 8: Mathematics

1. A. Since the difference between any two consecutive odd numbers is 2, the next odd number after $2x + 13$ would be

$$2x + 13 + 2 = 2x + 15$$

2. D. The amount of discount was $120 - $90 = $30. The rate of discount is a percent, so

$$\frac{percent}{100} = \frac{is\ number}{of\ number}$$

$$\frac{x}{100} = \frac{30}{120}$$

Cross multiplying

$$120x = 3000$$

$$\frac{120x}{120} = \frac{3000}{120}$$

$$x = 25$$

Therefore, the rate of discount was 25%.

3. C. $\sqrt{\frac{81}{x}} = \frac{9}{5}$

Squaring both sides,

$$\frac{81}{x} = \frac{81}{25}$$

Therefore, $x = 25$.

4. C. Since $\angle CFD = \angle AFB$, then $\angle CFD = 45°$ and $\angle AFE = 45° + 40° + 45° + 20° = 150°$.

5. D.
$$\text{Average} = \frac{93 + 82 + 79 + x}{4} = 87$$
$$93 + 82 + 79 + x = 87 \cdot 4$$
$$254 + x = 348$$
$$x = 94$$

6. D. According to the graph, 20% have hazel eyes and 40% have brown eyes. This means that there are twice as many brown-eyed people as there are hazel-eyed people.

$$62 = \text{people with hazel eyes}$$
$$2 \times 62 = 124 \text{ people with brown eyes}$$

7. D. The most the trip would cost is when gas costs $1.12 and the mileage is 16 mpg. Therefore, $1.12 \times (480/16) = $33.60. The least would be $0.96 \times (480/24) = $19.20. The difference is therefore $14.40.

8. A. The perimeter of a rectangle equals $2l + 2w$, where l is the length and w is the width. If the length and width are increased by x, the perimeter will be

$$2(l + x) + 2(w + x)$$
$$= 2l + 2x + 2w + 2x$$
$$= 2l + 2w + 4x$$

which is an increase of $4x$ units.

9. A. Since $\frac{x^2 - 5x + 7}{x^2 - 4x + 10} = 1 = \frac{1}{1}$, cross multiply to get

$$x^2 - 5x + 7 = x^2 - 4x + 10$$
$$x^2 - 5x + 7 - x^2 = x^2 - 4x + 10 - x^2$$
$$-5x + 7 = -4x + 10$$
$$-5x + 7 + 4x = -4x + 10 + 4x$$
$$-x + 7 = 10$$
$$-x + 7 - 7 = 10 - 7$$
$$-x = 3$$
$$x = -3$$

10. B. Forty-eight days late is one day shy of exactly 7 weeks (7 weeks = $7 \times 7 = 49$ days). If the job were finished in 49 days, then it would have been completed on the same day, Wednesday. Because 48 is one day less than 7 weeks, however, the job was completed one day earlier than Wednesday: Tuesday.

11. C. Let $3x$ = one angle and $4x$ = other angle.

$$3x + 4x + 68 = 180$$
$$7x + 68 = 180$$
$$7x = 112$$
$$x = 16$$
$$3x = 48$$
$$4x = 64$$

Therefore, the smallest angle of the triangle is 48°.

12. B. If two points have coordinates (x_1, y_1) and (x_2, y_2), the distance, d, between these points is defined to be

$$d = \sqrt{(x_1 - x_2)^2 + (y_1 - y_2)^2}$$

Since E has coordinates $(-3, 5)$ and F has coordinates $(6, -7)$, the distance between E and F is

$$EF = \sqrt{(-3 - 6)^2 + [5 - (-7)]^2}$$
$$= \sqrt{(-9)^2 + (12)^2}$$
$$= \sqrt{81 + 144}$$
$$= \sqrt{225}$$
$$= 15$$

13. C. III only. The random sample indicates that 1,500 out of 2,500 New York moviegoers prefer comedies, or 60% of those polled prefer comedies. Of those polled, 500 out of 2,500, or 20%, prefer dramas. Therefore, out of 8,000,000 total New York moviegoers, 60% should be found to prefer comedies (4,800,000), and 20% (1,600,000) should be found to prefer dramas. Only III reflects either of these estimates.

14. E. The horizontal length of x cannot be determined because there is no indication of the overlapping length of the rectangle to the left of x. If x cannot be determined, then $x + y$ cannot be determined.

15. D. Adding a positive number to the domain variable shifts the graph of a function to the left.

Hence $g(x)$ will be 5 units to the left of $f(x)$.

Section 9: Mathematics

1. B. Solve for x.

$$2x - 5 = 9$$
$$2x = 14$$

Then $x = 7$

Now substitute 7 for x.

$$3x + 2 = 3(7) + 2$$
$$= 21 + 2$$
$$= 23$$

2. E. Note that since there is a mark between +7 and +9, that mark must equal +8. Therefore, each mark equals 1. Counting back, point Q is at +5. Therefore, 15 units to the left of +5 would be $+5 - 15 = -10$.

3. C.
$$2x + 3y^2 - z = (2)(3) + 3(4)^2 - (-1)$$
$$= 6 + 3(16) + 1$$
$$= 6 + 48 + 1$$
$$= 55$$

4. B. To purchase twelve tapes, Roy must buy six packages. At \$2.98 per package, he spends \$17.88. His change from a twenty-dollar bill will be \$20.00 − \$17.88 = \$2.12.

5. D.
$$\frac{6^4 + 6^5}{6^4} = \frac{6^4}{6^4} + \frac{6^5}{6^4}$$
$$= 1 + 6$$
$$= 7$$

6. C. If we call the smaller piece x, then the larger piece (6 inches bigger) must be $x + 6$. Since the two pieces together equal a yardstick,
$$x + (x + 6) = 36$$
$$x + x + 6 = 36$$

7. E. For the multiplication problem to work correctly, the figures must be

$$\begin{array}{r} \boxed{6}\,\boxed{7}\,4 \\ \times\qquad 8 \\ \hline 5\,3\,9\,\boxed{2} \end{array}$$

Therefore, the sum of the boxed digits is 15.

8. E. In the ordered pair (0, 2), $a = 0$ and $b = 2$. For $2a − 3b$,
$$2(0) - 3(2) = 0 - 6 = -6 \neq 6$$

Therefore, the ordered pair (0, 2) is not a member of the solution sets of $2a − 3b = 6$.

9. C. The perimeter is the sum of all sides. Therefore,
$$(2s - 6) + (s + 4) + (s + 2) = \text{perimeter}$$
$$\begin{array}{r} 2s - 6 \\ s + 4 \\ \underline{s + 2} \\ 4s + 0 = 4s \end{array}$$

10. C.
$$\frac{\text{is number}}{\text{of number}} = \frac{\text{percent}}{100}$$
$$\frac{\frac{1}{2}}{\frac{2}{3}} = \frac{x}{100}$$

Cross multiplying,
$$\frac{2}{3}x = 50$$
$$x = \frac{150}{2} = 75\%$$

11. C. Fifteen percent of the selling price is needed for a down payment. Since the selling price of the house is $64,000, 15% of the selling price equals

$$(.15)(\$64,000) = \$9,600$$

The buyer has already paid $1,500 toward the deposit. To figure how much more money is needed for the down payment, subtract $1,500 from $9,600.

$$\$9,600 - \$1,500 = \$8,100$$

12. B. If the average of 9 numbers is 7, then the sum of these numbers must be 9×7, or 63. If the average of 7 numbers is 9, then the sum of these numbers must be 7×9, or 63. The sum of all 16 numbers must be $63 + 63$, or 126. Therefore, the average of all 16 numbers must be

$$126 \div 16 = \frac{126}{16} = 7\frac{14}{16} = 7\frac{7}{8}$$

13. E. Let x equal the length of a side of the cube. The volume $V = x^3$, and the surface area $S = 6x^2$. Therefore, $x = 6$.

14. E. Since $l_1 \| l_2$, the corresponding angles formed on lines l_1 and l_2 are equal.

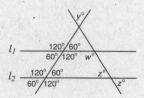

In any quadrilateral, the sum of interior degrees equals 360°. Therefore, $\angle w + \angle z = 180°$. If $w = 2z$, $\angle w = 120°$, and $\angle z = 60°$. Therefore,

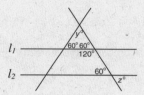

$\angle y = 60°$ (since there are 180° in a triangle). So the sum of $y + w = 60° + 120° = 180°$.

15. E. The value of $a \# b$ is

$$\frac{a^2 + b^2}{a^2 - b^2}$$

If $2a = b$, plug in $2a$ for b.

$$\frac{a^2 + (2a)^2}{a^2 - (2a)^2} = \frac{a^2 + 4a^2}{a^2 - 4a^2} = -\frac{5a^2}{3a^2} = -\frac{5}{3} = -1\frac{2}{3}$$

16. D. Since it takes the pipe t hours to drain the tank completely, it will drain $1/t$ part of the tank each hour. Therefore, in three hours, it will drain $3(\cdot 1/t)$, or $3/t$, part of the tank.

17. D. Since $AB = BE = 34$, $\triangle ABC$ is an isosceles triangle and altitude BD will bisect AC. Since $\triangle BDC$ is a right triangle, use the Pythagorean theorem, which says

$$(BC)^2 = (BD)^2 + (CD)^2$$
$$(34)^2 = (30)^2 + x^2$$
$$1156 = 900 + x^2$$
$$x^2 = 1156 - 900$$
$$x^2 = 256$$
$$x = \sqrt{256} = 16$$

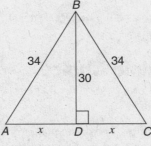

Therefore,

$$CD = 16 = AD$$
$$AC = AD + DC$$
$$= 16 + 16$$
$$= 32$$

18. C. Circumference $= \pi d$.

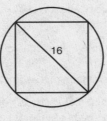

$$16\pi = \pi d$$
$$d = 16$$

diameter of circle = diagonal of square

area of square $= \frac{1}{2}$(product of diagonals)

$$= \frac{1}{2} d_1 \times d_2$$
$$= \frac{1}{2}(16)(16) = 128$$

Therefore, the area of the square is 128.

Alternate method: Using the Pythagorean theorem for isosceles right triangles gives $x^2 + x^2 = 16^2$, $2x^2 = 256$, and $x^2 = 128$, which is the area of the square.

19. B. Drawing a picture may be helpful. 750×45 equals P.

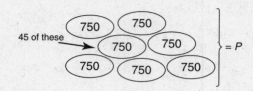

Note that 750 times 44 is the same as above but with one less circle. Therefore, it equals $P - 750$. If this concept is still difficult to understand, think in terms of dollars. You are paid $750 each week for 45 weeks. Therefore, your total pay (P) is $750 times 45. Suppose that you work only 44 weeks, however. Then your total pay will be P – one week's pay, or $P - \$750$.

20. D. Since there are 360° in a circle, the shaded region represents 60°/360° or $\frac{1}{6}$ of the circle. Hence the probability that a dart will land in the shaded region is $\frac{1}{6}$.

Section 10: Writing—Multiple Choice

Improving Sentences

1. D. The problem here is a misplaced modifier. The participial phrase "reviewing Jane Austen's *Emma,* modifies "Scott," and should appear as close to the noun it modifies as possible. The solution is D, which puts the phrase at the beginning of the sentence, immediately followed by the word it modifies.

2. B. There are two complete sentences here, but no conjunction or punctuation to join them. The run-on sentence can be corrected by putting a period or a semicolon at the end of the first sentence (after "technique"). Choices D and E change the meaning of the sentence, and need a comma.

3. E. The original version has an ambiguous pronoun (does the second "they" refer to the seed or the chemical companies?), is wordy ("they" is used twice), and shifts from active to passive voice. B has the ambiguous pronoun and the active-passive shift. C is wordy and has the active-passive shift. D corrects these problems but distorts the meaning. E solves all the problems.

4. A. Though the sentence begins with a participle, "Drawing" does not dangle, but modifies Anne Atkinson, which immediately follows. The original version is the best of the five, avoiding the verbosity of C, the passive voice of D, the awkward tense change of B, and the slight change of meaning in E.

5. E. C is attractively concise, but is so shortened that it doesn't quite make sense. The two verbs here, "initiate" and "become," are equally important, and can be made parallel as in E; A and B subordinate one or the other.

6. E. All of these sentences are grammatical, but E is the most concise in normal word order. C uses the same words, but the word order is unconventional, making "wittiest" an afterthought.

7. D. We can eliminate A and B because they use "you"; but the sentence began with the pronoun "one" (the third, not the second person) as the subject. E corrects this error, but the repetition of the "one should" breaks the parallel verbs without a repeated subject. D keeps the parallel use of active verbs, while C replaces the verb with a participle.

8. C. Choices A, B, D, and E are adjectival phrases that modify the designs or collection, not the company. The designs, not the company, are "different." With the "with designs" phrase, the phrase now logically refers to Orlando Fashions Company, which follows it.

9. B. The sentence is a fragment in all four versions except B. Here the first clause is dependent, and the main clause has a subject ("supply line") and a main verb ("became"). Though both A and D also use "became," the clauses are still dependent, because the conjunctions ("and," and "while") join them to the initial dependent clause. The "becoming" is a participle, not a verb.

10. D. The original version needlessly shifts from a third person subject ("the crane") to a second person ("you"). C shifts from an active to a passive verb. Using the prepositional phrase, as in D, eliminates the need for the "they."

11. C. Strict grammarians favor a pronoun having a single word as its antecedent. In this sentence, the pronouns "which" and "this" refer to the idea that the banking system is stronger but not to a single word. A, B, D, and E are alike in this reference. Given the choice, C is preferable since its pronoun, "that," does refer to a single word: "condition."

12. A. The original version is the best choice here. B is the only one that is shorter, but it is too short to make sense. The other choices are not bad, but they are wordier than A. So long as you can be sure the meaning is the same and the grammar is right, choose the version with the fewest words.

13. D. The issue here is does the omission of a phrase like "nature has provided" or its equivalent change the meaning of the sentence. Clearly D is the most concise, and "but" is preferable to "and." Since the clause also uses the adjective "natural," the "nature has provided" phrase is redundant.

14. B. As it stands, this is a sentence fragment; it has no main verb, since "form" is in a dependent clause. The same problem exists in C and E, while D is a participle not a verb. In B, "form" is the main verb of a sentence with "maples" the subject.

15. D. This is another verbose sentence. If you say "throughout," there is no need to say "the entire work" also, since "throughout" means "all the way through." Choice E pares too much from the sentence, losing the sense of both "throughout" (where) and "constantly" (how often).

Answer Sheets for Practice Test 2

(Remove These Sheets and Use Them to Write Your Essay and Mark Your Answers)

Section 1

Begin your essay on this page and continue on the next page if necessary. Do not write outside the essay boxes provided.

CUT HERE

CUT HERE

CUT HERE

Section 2

1 Ⓐ Ⓑ Ⓒ Ⓓ Ⓔ
2 Ⓐ Ⓑ Ⓒ Ⓓ Ⓔ
3 Ⓐ Ⓑ Ⓒ Ⓓ Ⓔ
4 Ⓐ Ⓑ Ⓒ Ⓓ Ⓔ
5 Ⓐ Ⓑ Ⓒ Ⓓ Ⓔ
6 Ⓐ Ⓑ Ⓒ Ⓓ Ⓔ
7 Ⓐ Ⓑ Ⓒ Ⓓ Ⓔ
8 Ⓐ Ⓑ Ⓒ Ⓓ Ⓔ
9 Ⓐ Ⓑ Ⓒ Ⓓ Ⓔ
10 Ⓐ Ⓑ Ⓒ Ⓓ Ⓔ
11 Ⓐ Ⓑ Ⓒ Ⓓ Ⓔ
12 Ⓐ Ⓑ Ⓒ Ⓓ Ⓔ
13 Ⓐ Ⓑ Ⓒ Ⓓ Ⓔ
14 Ⓐ Ⓑ Ⓒ Ⓓ Ⓔ
15 Ⓐ Ⓑ Ⓒ Ⓓ Ⓔ
16 Ⓐ Ⓑ Ⓒ Ⓓ Ⓔ
17 Ⓐ Ⓑ Ⓒ Ⓓ Ⓔ
18 Ⓐ Ⓑ Ⓒ Ⓓ Ⓔ
19 Ⓐ Ⓑ Ⓒ Ⓓ Ⓔ
20 Ⓐ Ⓑ Ⓒ Ⓓ Ⓔ
21 Ⓐ Ⓑ Ⓒ Ⓓ Ⓔ
22 Ⓐ Ⓑ Ⓒ Ⓓ Ⓔ
23 Ⓐ Ⓑ Ⓒ Ⓓ Ⓔ
24 Ⓐ Ⓑ Ⓒ Ⓓ Ⓔ
25 Ⓐ Ⓑ Ⓒ Ⓓ Ⓔ
26 Ⓐ Ⓑ Ⓒ Ⓓ Ⓔ
27 Ⓐ Ⓑ Ⓒ Ⓓ Ⓔ
28 Ⓐ Ⓑ Ⓒ Ⓓ Ⓔ
29 Ⓐ Ⓑ Ⓒ Ⓓ Ⓔ
30 Ⓐ Ⓑ Ⓒ Ⓓ Ⓔ
31 Ⓐ Ⓑ Ⓒ Ⓓ Ⓔ
32 Ⓐ Ⓑ Ⓒ Ⓓ Ⓔ
33 Ⓐ Ⓑ Ⓒ Ⓓ Ⓔ
34 Ⓐ Ⓑ Ⓒ Ⓓ Ⓔ

Section 3

1 Ⓐ Ⓑ Ⓒ Ⓓ Ⓔ
2 Ⓐ Ⓑ Ⓒ Ⓓ Ⓔ
3 Ⓐ Ⓑ Ⓒ Ⓓ Ⓔ
4 Ⓐ Ⓑ Ⓒ Ⓓ Ⓔ
5 Ⓐ Ⓑ Ⓒ Ⓓ Ⓔ
6 Ⓐ Ⓑ Ⓒ Ⓓ Ⓔ
7 Ⓐ Ⓑ Ⓒ Ⓓ Ⓔ
8 Ⓐ Ⓑ Ⓒ Ⓓ Ⓔ
9 Ⓐ Ⓑ Ⓒ Ⓓ Ⓔ
10 Ⓐ Ⓑ Ⓒ Ⓓ Ⓔ
11 Ⓐ Ⓑ Ⓒ Ⓓ Ⓔ
12 Ⓐ Ⓑ Ⓒ Ⓓ Ⓔ
13 Ⓐ Ⓑ Ⓒ Ⓓ Ⓔ
14 Ⓐ Ⓑ Ⓒ Ⓓ Ⓔ
15 Ⓐ Ⓑ Ⓒ Ⓓ Ⓔ
16 Ⓐ Ⓑ Ⓒ Ⓓ Ⓔ
17 Ⓐ Ⓑ Ⓒ Ⓓ Ⓔ
18 Ⓐ Ⓑ Ⓒ Ⓓ Ⓔ
19 Ⓐ Ⓑ Ⓒ Ⓓ Ⓔ
20 Ⓐ Ⓑ Ⓒ Ⓓ Ⓔ
21 Ⓐ Ⓑ Ⓒ Ⓓ Ⓔ
22 Ⓐ Ⓑ Ⓒ Ⓓ Ⓔ
23 Ⓐ Ⓑ Ⓒ Ⓓ Ⓔ
24 Ⓐ Ⓑ Ⓒ Ⓓ Ⓔ
25 Ⓐ Ⓑ Ⓒ Ⓓ Ⓔ
26 Ⓐ Ⓑ Ⓒ Ⓓ Ⓔ
27 Ⓐ Ⓑ Ⓒ Ⓓ Ⓔ
28 Ⓐ Ⓑ Ⓒ Ⓓ Ⓔ

Section 4

1 Ⓐ Ⓑ Ⓒ Ⓓ Ⓔ
2 Ⓐ Ⓑ Ⓒ Ⓓ Ⓔ
3 Ⓐ Ⓑ Ⓒ Ⓓ Ⓔ
4 Ⓐ Ⓑ Ⓒ Ⓓ Ⓔ
5 Ⓐ Ⓑ Ⓒ Ⓓ Ⓔ
6 Ⓐ Ⓑ Ⓒ Ⓓ Ⓔ
7 Ⓐ Ⓑ Ⓒ Ⓓ Ⓔ
8 Ⓐ Ⓑ Ⓒ Ⓓ Ⓔ
9 Ⓐ Ⓑ Ⓒ Ⓓ Ⓔ
10 Ⓐ Ⓑ Ⓒ Ⓓ Ⓔ
11 Ⓐ Ⓑ Ⓒ Ⓓ Ⓔ
12 Ⓐ Ⓑ Ⓒ Ⓓ Ⓔ
13 Ⓐ Ⓑ Ⓒ Ⓓ Ⓔ
14 Ⓐ Ⓑ Ⓒ Ⓓ Ⓔ
15 Ⓐ Ⓑ Ⓒ Ⓓ Ⓔ
16 Ⓐ Ⓑ Ⓒ Ⓓ Ⓔ
17 Ⓐ Ⓑ Ⓒ Ⓓ Ⓔ
18 Ⓐ Ⓑ Ⓒ Ⓓ Ⓔ
19 Ⓐ Ⓑ Ⓒ Ⓓ Ⓔ
20 Ⓐ Ⓑ Ⓒ Ⓓ Ⓔ

Section 5

1 Ⓐ Ⓑ Ⓒ Ⓓ Ⓔ
2 Ⓐ Ⓑ Ⓒ Ⓓ Ⓔ
3 Ⓐ Ⓑ Ⓒ Ⓓ Ⓔ
4 Ⓐ Ⓑ Ⓒ Ⓓ Ⓔ
5 Ⓐ Ⓑ Ⓒ Ⓓ Ⓔ
6 Ⓐ Ⓑ Ⓒ Ⓓ Ⓔ
7 Ⓐ Ⓑ Ⓒ Ⓓ Ⓔ
8 Ⓐ Ⓑ Ⓒ Ⓓ Ⓔ
9 Ⓐ Ⓑ Ⓒ Ⓓ Ⓔ
10 Ⓐ Ⓑ Ⓒ Ⓓ Ⓔ
11 Ⓐ Ⓑ Ⓒ Ⓓ Ⓔ
12 Ⓐ Ⓑ Ⓒ Ⓓ Ⓔ
13 Ⓐ Ⓑ Ⓒ Ⓓ Ⓔ
14 Ⓐ Ⓑ Ⓒ Ⓓ Ⓔ
15 Ⓐ Ⓑ Ⓒ Ⓓ Ⓔ
16 Ⓐ Ⓑ Ⓒ Ⓓ Ⓔ
17 Ⓐ Ⓑ Ⓒ Ⓓ Ⓔ
18 Ⓐ Ⓑ Ⓒ Ⓓ Ⓔ
19 Ⓐ Ⓑ Ⓒ Ⓓ Ⓔ
20 Ⓐ Ⓑ Ⓒ Ⓓ Ⓔ
21 Ⓐ Ⓑ Ⓒ Ⓓ Ⓔ
22 Ⓐ Ⓑ Ⓒ Ⓓ Ⓔ
23 Ⓐ Ⓑ Ⓒ Ⓓ Ⓔ
24 Ⓐ Ⓑ Ⓒ Ⓓ Ⓔ
25 Ⓐ Ⓑ Ⓒ Ⓓ Ⓔ
26 Ⓐ Ⓑ Ⓒ Ⓓ Ⓔ
27 Ⓐ Ⓑ Ⓒ Ⓓ Ⓔ
28 Ⓐ Ⓑ Ⓒ Ⓓ Ⓔ

Section 6

1 Ⓐ Ⓑ Ⓒ Ⓓ Ⓔ
2 Ⓐ Ⓑ Ⓒ Ⓓ Ⓔ
3 Ⓐ Ⓑ Ⓒ Ⓓ Ⓔ
4 Ⓐ Ⓑ Ⓒ Ⓓ Ⓔ
5 Ⓐ Ⓑ Ⓒ Ⓓ Ⓔ
6 Ⓐ Ⓑ Ⓒ Ⓓ Ⓔ
7 Ⓐ Ⓑ Ⓒ Ⓓ Ⓔ
8 Ⓐ Ⓑ Ⓒ Ⓓ Ⓔ
9 Ⓐ Ⓑ Ⓒ Ⓓ Ⓔ
10 Ⓐ Ⓑ Ⓒ Ⓓ Ⓔ

11. [grid-in answer box with columns containing /, ., and digits 0–9]

12. [grid-in answer box with columns containing /, ., and digits 0–9]

13. [grid-in answer box with columns containing /, ., and digits 0–9]

14.

15.

16.

17.

18.

19.

20.

Section 7

```
1  Ⓐ Ⓑ Ⓒ Ⓓ Ⓔ
2  Ⓐ Ⓑ Ⓒ Ⓓ Ⓔ
3  Ⓐ Ⓑ Ⓒ Ⓓ Ⓔ
4  Ⓐ Ⓑ Ⓒ Ⓓ Ⓔ
5  Ⓐ Ⓑ Ⓒ Ⓓ Ⓔ
6  Ⓐ Ⓑ Ⓒ Ⓓ Ⓔ
7  Ⓐ Ⓑ Ⓒ Ⓓ Ⓔ
8  Ⓐ Ⓑ Ⓒ Ⓓ Ⓔ
9  Ⓐ Ⓑ Ⓒ Ⓓ Ⓔ
10 Ⓐ Ⓑ Ⓒ Ⓓ Ⓔ
11 Ⓐ Ⓑ Ⓒ Ⓓ Ⓔ
12 Ⓐ Ⓑ Ⓒ Ⓓ Ⓔ
13 Ⓐ Ⓑ Ⓒ Ⓓ Ⓔ
14 Ⓐ Ⓑ Ⓒ Ⓓ Ⓔ
```

Section 8

```
1  Ⓐ Ⓑ Ⓒ Ⓓ Ⓔ
2  Ⓐ Ⓑ Ⓒ Ⓓ Ⓔ
3  Ⓐ Ⓑ Ⓒ Ⓓ Ⓔ
4  Ⓐ Ⓑ Ⓒ Ⓓ Ⓔ
5  Ⓐ Ⓑ Ⓒ Ⓓ Ⓔ
6  Ⓐ Ⓑ Ⓒ Ⓓ Ⓔ
7  Ⓐ Ⓑ Ⓒ Ⓓ Ⓔ
8  Ⓐ Ⓑ Ⓒ Ⓓ Ⓔ
9  Ⓐ Ⓑ Ⓒ Ⓓ Ⓔ
10 Ⓐ Ⓑ Ⓒ Ⓓ Ⓔ
11 Ⓐ Ⓑ Ⓒ Ⓓ Ⓔ
12 Ⓐ Ⓑ Ⓒ Ⓓ Ⓔ
13 Ⓐ Ⓑ Ⓒ Ⓓ Ⓔ
14 Ⓐ Ⓑ Ⓒ Ⓓ Ⓔ
15 Ⓐ Ⓑ Ⓒ Ⓓ Ⓔ
```

Section 9

```
1  Ⓐ Ⓑ Ⓒ Ⓓ Ⓔ
2  Ⓐ Ⓑ Ⓒ Ⓓ Ⓔ
3  Ⓐ Ⓑ Ⓒ Ⓓ Ⓔ
4  Ⓐ Ⓑ Ⓒ Ⓓ Ⓔ
5  Ⓐ Ⓑ Ⓒ Ⓓ Ⓔ
6  Ⓐ Ⓑ Ⓒ Ⓓ Ⓔ
7  Ⓐ Ⓑ Ⓒ Ⓓ Ⓔ
8  Ⓐ Ⓑ Ⓒ Ⓓ Ⓔ
9  Ⓐ Ⓑ Ⓒ Ⓓ Ⓔ
10 Ⓐ Ⓑ Ⓒ Ⓓ Ⓔ
11 Ⓐ Ⓑ Ⓒ Ⓓ Ⓔ
12 Ⓐ Ⓑ Ⓒ Ⓓ Ⓔ
13 Ⓐ Ⓑ Ⓒ Ⓓ Ⓔ
14 Ⓐ Ⓑ Ⓒ Ⓓ Ⓔ
15 Ⓐ Ⓑ Ⓒ Ⓓ Ⓔ
16 Ⓐ Ⓑ Ⓒ Ⓓ Ⓔ
17 Ⓐ Ⓑ Ⓒ Ⓓ Ⓔ
18 Ⓐ Ⓑ Ⓒ Ⓓ Ⓔ
19 Ⓐ Ⓑ Ⓒ Ⓓ Ⓔ
20 Ⓐ Ⓑ Ⓒ Ⓓ Ⓔ
21 Ⓐ Ⓑ Ⓒ Ⓓ Ⓔ
22 Ⓐ Ⓑ Ⓒ Ⓓ Ⓔ
23 Ⓐ Ⓑ Ⓒ Ⓓ Ⓔ
24 Ⓐ Ⓑ Ⓒ Ⓓ Ⓔ
25 Ⓐ Ⓑ Ⓒ Ⓓ Ⓔ
26 Ⓐ Ⓑ Ⓒ Ⓓ Ⓔ
27 Ⓐ Ⓑ Ⓒ Ⓓ Ⓔ
28 Ⓐ Ⓑ Ⓒ Ⓓ Ⓔ
```

Section 10

```
1  Ⓐ Ⓑ Ⓒ Ⓓ Ⓔ
2  Ⓐ Ⓑ Ⓒ Ⓓ Ⓔ
3  Ⓐ Ⓑ Ⓒ Ⓓ Ⓔ
4  Ⓐ Ⓑ Ⓒ Ⓓ Ⓔ
5  Ⓐ Ⓑ Ⓒ Ⓓ Ⓔ
6  Ⓐ Ⓑ Ⓒ Ⓓ Ⓔ
7  Ⓐ Ⓑ Ⓒ Ⓓ Ⓔ
8  Ⓐ Ⓑ Ⓒ Ⓓ Ⓔ
9  Ⓐ Ⓑ Ⓒ Ⓓ Ⓔ
10 Ⓐ Ⓑ Ⓒ Ⓓ Ⓔ
11 Ⓐ Ⓑ Ⓒ Ⓓ Ⓔ
12 Ⓐ Ⓑ Ⓒ Ⓓ Ⓔ
13 Ⓐ Ⓑ Ⓒ Ⓓ Ⓔ
14 Ⓐ Ⓑ Ⓒ Ⓓ Ⓔ
15 Ⓐ Ⓑ Ⓒ Ⓓ Ⓔ
```

CUT HERE

Practice Test 2

Section 1: Writing—Essay

Time: 25 Minutes

1 Essay Question

You have 25 minutes to plan and write an essay on the topic below. DO NOT WRITE ON ANOTHER TOPIC. AN ESSAY ON ANOTHER TOPIC WILL NOT BE SCORED.

The essay is intended to give you the chance to show your writing skills. Be sure to express your ideas on the topic clearly and effectively. The quality of your writing is much more important than the quantity, but to cover the topic adequately, you may want to write more than one paragraph. Be specific.

Your essay must be written on the two lined pages provided. You will not be given any additional paper. If you keep your handwriting to a reasonable size, write on every line, and avoid wide margins, you should have enough space to complete your essay.

Directions: Read the following paragraph and assignment carefully. Then prepare and write a persuasive essay. Be sure to support your reasons with specific examples that will make your essay more effective.

> "There is no compelling reason for 'live' television to be live. If all programs made use of the available five-minute delay such as is now in use on some talk radio broadcasts, we could be sure that children would not be exposed to profanity, lewdness, or extreme violence."

Assignment: What questions does this passage raise? Write an essay in which you evaluate this quotation. Give your opinion about this matter and support your view with specific evidence.

THE PROCTOR WILL ANNOUNCE WHEN 25 MINUTES HAVE PASSED. AT THAT TIME, YOU MUST STOP WRITING. IF YOU FINISH YOUR ESSAY BEFORE 25 MINUTES HAVE PASSED, YOU MAY NOT GO ON TO ANY OTHER SECTION OF THE EXAM. THE PROCTOR WILL ANNOUNCE WHEN TO START THE NEXT SECTION.

Section 2: Writing—Multiple Choice

Time: 25 Minutes

34 Questions

In this section, choose the best answer for each question and blacken the corresponding space on the answer sheet.

Directions: The following questions test correctness and effective expression. In selecting the answer, pay attention to grammar, diction, sentence structure, and punctuation. In the following questions, part or all of each sentence is underlined. The A answer repeats the underlined portion of the original sentence, while the next four offer alternatives. Choose the answer that best expresses the meaning of the original sentence, and at the same time is grammatically correct and stylistically superior. The correct choice should be clear, unambiguous, and concise.

EXAMPLE:

The forecaster predicted <u>rain and the sky was clear.</u>

   A.   rain and the sky was clear.
   B.   rain but the sky was clear.
   C.   rain the sky was clear.
   D.   rain, but the sky was clear.
   E.   rain being as the sky was clear.

The correct answer is D.

---

1. As they crossed the Atlantic, <u>cheeses were probably made in the galley by the colonists on the *Mayflower.*</u>

   A.   cheeses were probably made in the galley by the colonists on the *Mayflower.*
   B.   probably cheeses were made in the galley by the colonists of the *Mayflower.*
   C.   cheese was made, probably in the galley, by the colonists on the *Mayflower.*
   D.   the colonists of the *Mayflower* probably made cheeses in the galley.
   E.   in the galley of the *Mayflower,* the colonists probably made cheese.

2. The series of articles is about the sicknesses of a violent society, <u>and also about how these ills can be remedied.</u>

   A.   and also about how these ills can be remedied.
   B.   and as well about the ways of remedying these ills.
   C.   and remedies for these ills.
   D.   and its remedy.
   E.   and about remedying these ills.

3. This year's alumni and alumnae differ from <u>last year's they support</u> the funding campaign for the new library.

   A.   last year's they support
   B.   last year's; they support
   C.   last year's, they support
   D.   last year's supporting
   E.   last year's in the support they give to

4. In addition to those of gasoline and sugar, <u>the higher grain prices which lead to more expensive meat and poultry.</u>

   A.   the higher grain prices which lead to more expensive meat and poultry.
   B.   the higher prices of meat and poultry caused by more expensive grain.
   C.   the higher prices in grain, meat and poultry.
   D.   higher grain prices leading to more expensive meat and poultry.
   E.   the higher grain prices will lead to more expensive meat and poultry.

5. The workers remain in the fields until they are <u>exhausted; and this,</u> in time, will seriously injure their health.

    A.   exhausted; and this,

    B.   exhausted; it,

    C.   exhausted, which,

    D.   exhausted, a practice that,

    E.   exhausted, and it,

6. When you see, instead of read, a play, <u>it sometimes reveals new strengths or weaknesses.</u>

    A.   it sometimes reveals new strengths or weaknesses.

    B.   new strengths or weaknesses are sometimes revealed to you.

    C.   you sometimes see new strengths or weaknesses.

    D.   sometimes new strengths or weaknesses are revealed.

    E.   new strengths or weaknesses can be seen sometimes.

7. Carrying the warm water across the yard to melt the ice on the <u>bird bath, the sparrows were gathered in groups</u> a few feet away.

    A.   bird bath, the sparrows were gathered in groups

    B.   bird bath, the sparrows gathered in groups

    C.   bird bath, the groups of sparrows gathered

    D.   bird bath, the groups of sparrow were gathering

    E.   bird bath, I saw groups of sparrows gathered

GO ON TO THE NEXT PAGE

Directions: The following sentences may contain one error of grammar, usage, diction, or idiom. No sentence will contain more than one error, and some have no error. If there is an error, it will be underlined with a letter. Sections of the sentence that are not underlined cannot be changed. In selecting your answer, observe the requirements of standard written English. If there is an error, choose the one underlined part that must be changed to correct the sentence. If there is no error, choose E.

EXAMPLE:

The film <u>tell the story</u> of a cavalry captain and <u>his wife</u> who <u>try to</u> <u>rebuild their lives</u> after the Civil War.
　　　A　　　　　　　　　　　　　　　　B　　　　C　　　D

<u>No Error.</u>
E

The correct answer is A.

---

8. <u>By paying</u> very close attention to the shape of the
　　A
gem and <u>looking carefully</u> at the setting, you
　　　　　B
<u>can clearly see</u> that the ring <u>will not be</u> an
　C　　　　　　　　　　　　　D
antique. <u>No Error.</u>
　　　　　E

9. If the election results are <u>as Harris predicts,</u> the
　　　　　　　　　　　　　　　A
new senator will be the man <u>which</u> the people
　　　　　　　　　　　　　B
<u>believed</u> made the <u>better showing</u> in the televised
　C　　　　　　　D
debate. <u>No Error.</u>
　　　　　E

10. Not one of the sixty-five students
<u>majoring in economics</u> <u>were prepared for</u> the
　　A　　　　　　B
<u>teacher's</u> <u>asking about</u> Marx on the examination.
　C　　　D
<u>No Error.</u>
　E

11. If the <u>best-selling book</u> always won the award,
　　　　A
the publishers <u>who pay for the publicity</u> would
　　　　　　B
withdraw <u>their support,</u> and there wouldn't be
　　　　　C
<u>no award at all.</u> <u>No Error.</u>
　D　　　　　E

12. It <u>must be she</u> he had in mind when he spoke
　　A
of a <u>well-trained athlete</u> <u>who has won</u> a place
　　　B　　　　　C
<u>on the Olympic squad.</u> <u>No Error.</u>
　D　　　　　E

13. The reasons for <u>his looking so young</u> are
　　　　　A
<u>his low-fat diet,</u> <u>his daily exercise,</u> and his
　B　　　　C
<u>regularity to follow his doctor's recommendations.</u>
　　　　D
<u>No Error.</u>
　E

14. I <u>sincerely believe that</u> a person
　　A
<u>intelligent enough</u> to be in business
　B
<u>by themselves</u> should have the ability
　C
<u>to recognize a dangerous investment.</u> <u>No Error.</u>
　D　　　　　E

15. The jury must first <u>decide whether or not</u> the
　　　　　A
defendant <u>was</u> in New York, and then how he
　　　B
<u>can have had</u> the strength <u>to carry</u> a 200-pound
　C　　　　　D
body. <u>No Error.</u>
　　　E

16. The art of American morticians paints death
    —————————————————————
    A
    to look like life, sealed it away in watertight
    —————————— ————
    B   C
    caskets, and spirits it away to graveyards
                 ———————————
                 D
    camouflaged as gardens. No Error.
                            ————————
                            E

17. Many of the compounds that can
    ——————————————
    A
    be produced from the leaves of this plant
    —————————————
    B
    are dangerous, but the plant themselves cannot
    —————————   ——————————
    C   D
    be called toxic. No Error.
                    ————————
                    E

18. Most of the survivors now recovering neither
                         ——————————
                         A
    heard and saw anything unusual just before the
          ———————   ——————————
          B   C
    plane crashed. No Error.
          ———————— ————————
          D   E

19. *The Young Visitors* is an unusually powerful novel
                            ————————————————————
                            A
    about a group of cruel and idle young boys who
                    ——————————————————————
                    B
    destruct an old man's home for no other reason
    ————————
    C
    than that it is beautiful. No Error.
    ——————————————————   ————————
    D   E

20. The state legislature has recommended a bill
                         —————————————
                         A
    that allows a married couple not to declare the
    ——————————   ———————————
    B   C
    income of either the husband or the wife,
    depending upon which income is more lower.
                    ——————————————————————————
                    D
    No Error.
    ————————
    E

21. It seems increasingly obvious that men's clothes
    ————————————————————————
    A
    are designed not to please the men who will wear
    them, but to impress the people who will see them.
    ————   —————————   —————————————
    B   C   D
    No Error.
    ————————
    E

22. Unlike Monet, Graham's oil paintings have
    ——————————————
    A
    few bright colors, are small, and depict only
    ————————————————— —————————   ——————————
    B   C   D
    urban scenes. No Error.
                 ————————
                 E

23. When my broken arm was in a cast, neither the
    ————————————————————————————————
    A
    nurse nor I were able to shave my face without
                ————————— —————————————————
                B   C
    one or two cuts. No Error.
        ——————————— ————————
        D   E

24. If I had my way, the driver would be charged for
         —————————   ——————————
         A   B
    criminal negligence and drunk driving,
    and spend at least a year in jail. No Error.
    —————————   ————————————   ————————
    C   D   E

25. There are at most colleges the requirement that
                                 ——————————————————
                                 A
    students take standardized tests to be used by
             ————   —————————
             B   C
    admissions committees to evaluate applicants
                          ——————————
                          D
    for entrance. No Error.
                 ————————
                 E

26. If westerners acknowledge that the eastern
                 ————————————————
                 A
    United States has wilderness areas,
                 ——————————————————
                 B
    one probably thinks of the Blue Ridge
    —————————————————
    C
    Mountains or perhaps Maine. No Error.
                —————————————— ————————
                D   E

GO ON TO THE NEXT PAGE

Directions: The following passages are early drafts of student essays. Some parts of them need to be revised.

Read the selections carefully and answer the questions that follow. There will be questions about sentence structure, diction, and usage in individual sentences or parts of sentences. Other questions will deal with the whole essay or paragraphs, and ask you to decide about organization, development, and appropriate language. Choose the answer that follows the requirements of standard written English, and most effectively expresses the intended meanings.

Questions 27–30 are based on the following passage.

The Majority Is Often Wrong

(1) I agree with the statement the majority is often wrong. (2) The idea that the majority is always right has been disproved by every bad or dishonest politician who has been elected to any political office by the votes of the majority. (3) It is disproved by every jury decision where it turns out later that the prisoner they found guilty was really innocent. (4) It is frequently disproved in high school. (5) It is disproved in Germany when they elected Hitler.

(6) In my school when I was a sophomore there was an election of the student body president. (7) Two boys (who I'll call Jack and Dave) and one girl (Jane) were running for president. (8) Dave was bad student, and he was popular and a good basketball player. (9) Jack was active in a lot of clubs and in music, and Jane was by far the best student of the three. (10) Dave won by a landslide, but never even finished his sophomore year when he was in a drunk driving accident. (11) This shows how wrong the majority can be.

(12) These examples show how the majority is often wrong is true. (13) The old saying, the majority is always right, is wrong.

27. Which of the following is the best version of sentence 5 (reproduced below)?

> *It is disproved in Germany when they elected Hitler.*

A. Leave it as it is.
B. It is disproved by Germany where they elected Hitler.
C. It is disproved when the Germans elected Hitler.
D. Hitler disproves it in Germany.
E. It was disproved when the Germans elected Hitler.

28. The first paragraph would be most improved by the removal of which of the following sentences?

A. Sentence 1.
B. Sentence 2.
C. Sentence 3.
D. Sentence 4.
E. Sentence 5.

29. Which of the following does the first paragraph make use of?

A. emphatic repetition of a phrase
B. rhetorical question
C. definition of a term
D. specific example of a personal experience
E. elaboration of an example

30. Which of the following is the best version of sentence 6 (reproduced below)?

> *In my school when I was a sophomore there was an election of the student body president.*

A. Leave it as it is.
B. When I was a sophomore, my school held an election for student body president.
C. In my school, they held an election for student body president when I was a sophomore.
D. A student body president election was held by my school when I was a sophomore.
E. When I was a sophomore, they held a student body president election at my school.

Questions 31–34 are based on the following passage.

Are Americans Getting Lazier?

(1) Too many people today are trying to get what they want by using the least effort the fastest way. (2) Technology has helped this. (3) Calculators now give you the solution to complex equations in seconds, even watches have calculators on them. (4) People drive their cars to the corner to drop off mail because they are too lazy to walk even if it is healthy and possibly faster to just walk.

(5) Americans used to want a house in the suburbs, a family, a job, and something to look forward to when the kids were grown up. (6) Now they want quick money without taking risks, get rich overnight, and live the life of luxury. (7) They no longer plan ahead. (8) They think about today. (9) They don't think about tomorrow at all. (10) People are lazier than ever.

(11) They turn to television and radio for the news. (12) They don't read newspapers. (13) They depend more and more on automation doing things for you. (14) With more things voice automated, Americans will no longer need their remote controls. (15) Without some change, our future may be a nightmare of sloth.

31. Which of the following is the best combined version of sentences 1 and 2 (reproduced below)?

> *Too many people today are trying to get what they want by using the least effort the fastest way. Technology has helped this.*

A. Leave it as it is.
B. Too many people today are trying to get what they want by using the least effort the fastest way, and technology is helping them.
C. With the help of technology, there are too many people today who are trying to get what they want by using the least effort the fastest way.
D. Technology is helping too many people who are trying to get what they want by using the least effort in the fastest way.
E. Helped by technology, too many people today are trying to get what they want in the fastest way using the least effort.

32. Which of the following is the best version of sentence 2 (reproduced below)?

> *Technology has helped this.*

A. Leave it as it is.
B. This has been helped by technology.
C. Technology has helped this effort.
D. Technology is helping this to happen.
E. But technology has helped this.

33. Which of the following is the best version of sentence 6 (reproduced below)?

> *Now they want quick money without taking risks, get rich overnight, and live the life of luxury.*

A. Leave it as it is.
B. They now want quick money without taking risks, riches overnight, and to live the life of luxury.
C. Now they want to earn money quickly without risk, to get rich overnight, and to live a life of luxury.
D. They want quick money now, without taking risks, and they want riches overnight and to live a life of luxury.
E. What they want now is quick money, no risks, riches overnight, and to live a life of luxury.

34. To eliminate the series of very short sentences in the second paragraph, which of the following is the best way to combine sentences 7, 8, and 9 (reproduced below)?

> *They no longer plan ahead. They think about today. They don't think about tomorrow at all.*

A. They no longer plan ahead or think about tomorrow; they think about today.
B. It is today, not tomorrow that they think about; they never plan ahead.
C. They plan ahead no longer, thinking only of today and not thinking about tomorrow at all.
D. No longer planning ahead, they think about today, and not at all about tomorrow.
E. They no longer plan ahead, but think only of today.

IF YOU FINISH BEFORE TIME IS CALLED, CHECK YOUR WORK ON THIS SECTION ONLY. DO NOT WORK ON ANY OTHER SECTION IN THE TEST.

Section 3: Critical Reading

Time: 25 Minutes

28 Questions

In this section, choose the best answer for each question and blacken the corresponding space on the answer sheet.

Directions: Each blank in the following sentences indicates that something has been omitted. Consider the lettered words beneath the sentence and choose the word or set of words that *best* fits the whole sentence.

EXAMPLE:

With a million more people than any other African nation, Nigeria is the most _____ country on the continent.

  A. impoverished
  B. successful
  C. populous
  D. developed
  E. militant

The correct answer is C.

---

1. Understanding the _____ that separate us from each other can also enable us to _____ the complex fabric of our society.

  A. differences . . . appreciate
  B. truths . . . combat
  C. traditions . . . resolve
  D. similarities . . . enrich
  E. fears . . . complete

2. What is most needed in a discussion of immigration are solid facts, not wishful thinking; realities, not _____.

  A. explanations
  B. reasons
  C. ideas
  D. fears
  E. myths

3. South Korea's industrial production fell 6 percent last year, the largest annual _____ since 1980, fueling fears that the _____ economy is slipping deeper into recession.

  A. figure . . . flourishing
  B. decrease . . . steady
  C. decline . . . sagging
  D. change . . . lethargic
  E. drop . . . booming

4. By gradually winning the support of both liberals and conservatives, both rich and poor, the governor has demonstrated that her remarkable _____ skills go side by side with her willingness to speak openly and _____ on controversial issues.

  A. interpersonal . . . equivocally
  B. diplomatic . . . frankly
  C. organizational . . . covertly
  D. personal . . . deceptively
  E. intimidating . . . obscurely

5. Slander and libel laws stand as a protection of an individual's reputation against the _____ dissemination of falsehoods.

   A. unintentional
   B. inevitable
   C. inferential
   D. irresponsible
   E. incontestable

6. Presenting love as foolish, compromised, or dangerous, his love songs are frankly _____.

   A. lyrical
   B. antiromantic
   C. conventional
   D. melodic
   E. sentimental

7. By showing that the trainer's voice _____ gave commands to the horse, he was able to _____ the clever ruse which contended that an animal could add and subtract.

   A. ostensibly . . . confirm
   B. never . . . debunk
   C. covertly . . . unmask
   D. unwittingly . . . prove
   E. potentially . . . defend

8. For an actor so changeable and unpredictable, even the word _____ seems inadequate.

   A. immutable
   B. mercurial
   C. stoical
   D. placid
   E. obstinate

9. A _____ is distrustful of human goodness and sincerity, and a _____ has a hatred of people in general.

   A. pessimist . . . ingrate
   B. siren . . . tyrant
   C. altruist . . . anarchist
   D. cynic . . . misanthrope
   E. philanthropist . . . misogynist

10. Though she was _____ by the medical establishment, Dr. Sandstrom bravely continued her work until other doctors could no longer deny the _____ of her theories.

   A. ignored . . . conviction
   B. vilified . . . probability
   C. encouraged . . . originality
   D. supported . . . credibility
   E. attacked . . . tenets

GO ON TO THE NEXT PAGE

Directions: Questions follow each of the passages below. Using only the stated or implied information in each passage and in its introduction, if any, answer the questions.

Questions 11–12 are based on the following passage.

Though most slang expressions have short lives—"groovy," for example—"cool" has lasted for more than fifty years. The word was used, as it is today, to describe large sums of money ("a cool mil-
(5) lion") as long ago as 1730, while its common modern usage (in fashion) is believed to have been coined by jazz musicians in the twentieth century. The large number of definitions in almost any dictionary makes it clear that "cool" is an example of an "unspecified" word," while a word like "wrath-
(10) ful" is highly determined. The more unspecified a word is, the more chances it has of survival. Several linguists argue that "cool" is still used because of its connection to jazz, and they cite Miles Davis' *Birth of the Cool*. On the other hand, it may simply be the
(15) sound of the word—because it is so easy to say.

11. According to the passage, which of the following words would be the best example of a "highly determined" word?

A. conduct
B. influence
C. assassinate
D. flower
E. handle

12. The passage suggests that the slang usage of the word "cool" has remained in the language because

A. it has a large number of meanings
B. it cannot be used as a verb, noun, or adjective
C. jazz has increased in popularity since mid-century
D. it is the opposite of warm
E. it has one syllable

Questions 13–14 are based on the following passage.

The poet Homer, about whom little is known, can be seen as the parent of all Greek literature. Later epic poets of Western literature viewed him as the undisputed master. However, for his most suc-
(5) cessful followers, curiously enough, his work was as much a target as a model. The Roman poet Virgil's *Aeneid,* for example, is a refutation of the individualistic value system of the Homeric epic, and the stanzas describing the battle in Heaven in
(10) John Milton's *Paradise Lost* (1667), while Homeric

in style, are essentially comic. Cervantes' *Don Quixote* (1605) and James Joyce's *Ulysses* (1921), both of which owe much to Homer, lean towards parody and mock epic. No serious author since
(15) Homer has combined his unabashed heroic ethos and erudition.

13. In line 8, the "individualistic value system of the Homeric epic" most likely refers to a belief in the

A. rules of Greek warfare
B. values of personal heroism
C. importance of epic combat
D. values of the Greek political system
E. principles of democracy

14. The phrase "curiously enough" in line 5 serves to

A. emphasize Homer's superiority
B. present an unsolved puzzle
C. point to a paradox
D. introduce a critical point of view
E. mock the heroic ethos

Questions 15–20 are based on the following passage.

The following passage is from The Autobiography of Benjamin Franklin.

In 1732 I first publish'd my Almanack, under the name of Richard Saunders; it was continu'd by me about twenty-five years, commonly call'd Poor Richard's Almanack. I endeavor'd to make it both
(5) entertaining and useful, and it accordingly came to be in such demand, that I reap'd considerable profit from it, vending annually near ten thousand. And observing that it was generally read, scarce any neighborhood in the province being without it, I
(10) consider'd it as a proper vehicle for conveying instruction among the common people, who bought scarcely any other books; I therefore filled all the little spaces that occurr'd between the remarkable days in the calendar with proverbial sentences,
(15) chiefly such as inculcated industry and frugality, as the means of procuring wealth, and thereby securing virtue; it being more difficult for a man in want, to act always honestly, as, to use here one of those proverbs, it is hard for an empty sack to stand
(20) upright.

These proverbs, which contained the wisdom of many ages and nations, I assembled and form'd into

a connected discourse prefix'd to the Almanack of 1757, as the harangue of a wise old man to the peo-
(25) ple attending an auction. The bringing all these scattered counsels thus into a focus enabled them to make greater impression. The piece, being universally approved, was bought by the clergy and gentry, to distribute gratis among their poor parishioners
(30) and tenants. In Pennsylvania, as it discouraged useless expense in foreign superfluities, some thought it had its share of influence in producing that growing plenty of money which was observable for several years after its publication.
(35)   I considered my newspaper, also, as another means of communicating instruction, and in that view frequently reprinted in it extracts from the Spectator, and other moral writers; and sometimes publish'd little pieces of my own. Of these are a
(40) Socratic dialogue, tending to prove that, whatever might be his parts and abilities, a vicious man could not properly be called a man of sense; and a discourse on self-denial, showing that virtue was not secure till its practice became a habitude, and was
(45) free from the opposition of contrary inclinations.
    In the conduct of my newspaper, I carefully excluded all libelling and personal abuse. Whenever I was solicited to insert any thing of that kind, and the writers pleaded, as they generally did, the lib-
(50) erty of the press, and that a newspaper was like a stage-coach, in which any one who would pay had a right to a place, my answer was, that I would print the piece separately if desired, but that I would not take upon me to spread his detraction; and that,
(55) having contracted with my subscribers to furnish them with what might be either useful or entertaining, I could not fill their papers with private altercation, in which they had no concern, without doing them manifest injustice.

15. In line 17, the word "want" means

A. custom.
B. captivity.
C. covetousness.
D. desire.
E. need.

16. According to the passage, the best way to become virtuous is to first become

A. wealthy.
B. educated.
C. self-knowing.
D. reasonable.
E. self-serving.

17. With which of the following ideas about the freedom of the press would Franklin be likely to disagree?

I.   A person who is willing to pay for printing in a newspaper should be allowed to publish whatever he or she chooses.
II. The primary obligation of the free press is to its subscribers.
III. Personal disputes do not belong in the public press.

A. I only
B. II only
C. III only
D. I and II only
E. I and III only

18. Franklin's refusal to publish in his newspaper any personal abuse was based on his belief that

A. the newspaper might be prosecuted for libel.
B. personal abuse should not be printed for any price.
C. false personal attacks are too difficult to distinguish from attacks that are based on fact.
D. a newspaper's responsibility is to furnish its subscribers with worthy reading matter.
E. anyone who has paid for an item has the right to have it printed.

19. The passage suggests that Franklin's principal profession was as a(n)

A. politician.
B. inventor.
C. printer.
D. scientist.
E. novelist.

20. According to the passage, in both his almanac and newspaper, Franklin hoped to combine

A. profit and religion.
B. wisdom and appeal to a large public.
C. ideas of thrift and virtue.
D. instruction and entertainment.
E. comedy and tragedy.

Practice Test 2

GO ON TO THE NEXT PAGE

Questions 21–28 are based on the following passage.

Immediately after Hubble's launch, operators at the National Aeronautics and Space Administration Goddard Space Flight Center and at the Space Telescope Science Institute began an extensive se-
(5) ries of systems checks and calibrations. The first test images revealed an inherent focusing problem, technically known as spherical aberration. A close examination of the images revealed that the telescope's main mirror had been ground to the wrong
(10) shape: it is two microns flatter at the edges than stipulated by design (a micron is one millionth of a meter). Small though the error may seem, it is a gross mistake by the standards of modern precision optics. The shape of the mirror makes it impossible
(15) to focus all the light collected by Hubble to a single point. Hubble's designers intended that the telescope should be able to concentrate 70 percent of the light of a point source—a distant star, for example— into a spot 0.1 arcsecond across (an arcsecond is a
(20) tiny angle, equal to 1/1,800 the apparent diameter of the moon). Actually, only 15 percent of the light falls into this central image; the other 85 percent spills over into an unwanted halo several arcseconds in diameter.
(25) Various other difficulties have surfaced. Twice each orbit, when Hubble passes in and out of the earth's shadow, the sudden temperature change causes the telescope's large solar cell panels to flap up and down about 30 centimeters every 10 sec-
(30) onds. The resulting jitter can disrupt the telescope's pointing system and cause additional blurring of astronomical images. Two of Hubble's six gyroscopes have failed, and a third works only intermittently; the telescope needs at least three gyroscopes
(35) to perform its normal science operations. Faulty electrical contacts threatened to shut down the High-Resolution Spectrograph.

NASA hopes to address some of these problems in 1994, when astronauts are scheduled to visit
(40) Hubble. They will attempt to replace the telescope's solar panels and two of the gyroscopes. The astronauts may also try to install a package of corrective optics and an upgraded Wide Field and Planetary Camera if the new devices are completed
(45) by then.

In the meantime, scientists have quickly learned how to wring as much performance from the space telescope as possible. Because Hubble's mirror was ground to fine precision and because its error is
(50) well understood, computer enhancement can restore many images to their intended sharpness. The resulting astronomical views have eloquently refuted some early pessimism about the telescope's scientific capabilities. Regrettably, attaining such
(55) resolution often involves discarding the smeared halos that appear around celestial targets, literally throwing away most of the light captured by Hubble.

The greatest blow to Hubble's scientific mission
(60) therefore has been not a loss of resolution but a loss of sensitivity. Hubble was designed to be able to detect objects a billion times fainter than those visible to the human eye. At present, the telescope is limited to observing objects roughly 20 times
(65) brighter than intended. Hubble cannot detect some particularly elusive targets, such as extremely distant galaxies and quasars or possible planets around nearby stars. Astronomers have had to postpone many of their potentially most significant ob-
(70) servations until the telescope is fixed.

Although designed to home in on some of the most remote cosmic objects, Hubble has proved well suited to studying objects within the solar system. For example, it has captured stunning views of
(75) the giant planets, Jupiter and Saturn. NASA's two Voyager space probes closely scrutinized Jupiter in 1979 and Saturn in 1980 and 1981. The space telescope can routinely produce images of Jupiter and Saturn comparable in detail to those obtained by
(80) the Voyagers only a few days before their closest approaches to the two planets.

21. In line 6, the word "inherent" means

   A.   correctable, insignificant.
   B.   theoretical, hypothetical.
   C.   serious, grave.
   D.   innate, basic.
   E.   suppressing, holding back.

22. How much greater a percentage of the light of a point source would have been concentrated into an arcsecond spot if the mirror of the Hubble telescope had been ground correctly?

   A.   15 percent
   B.   30 percent
   C.   55 percent
   D.   70 percent
   E.   80 percent

23. It can be inferred from the third paragraph that the telescope is subjected to sharp temperature changes because the temperature is

    A. affected by its proximity to the moon.
    B. affected by the presence of the earth's shadow.
    C. affected by the proximity of other planets to the earth.
    D. affected by the earth's atmosphere.
    E. much higher as the telescope moves away from the sun.

24. According to the passage, all of the following have been troubled or defective EXCEPT

    A. solar cell panels.
    B. gyroscopes.
    C. main mirror.
    D. High-Resolution Spectrograph.
    E. lens.

25. The word "address" as used in line 38 means

    A. write to.
    B. use a proper form.
    C. apply itself.
    D. take a stand.
    E. repair.

26. Which of the following best describes the difference between a telescope's sensitivity and its resolution?

    A. Sensitivity is response to light or sound waves; resolution is its ability to separate an image into parts.
    B. Sensitivity is the condition of receiving accurately outside stimuli; resolution is the capability of making darker shades lighter.
    C. Sensitivity is its ability to perceive light; resolution is its ability to make the parts of an image visible.
    D. Sensitivity is the distance at which a telescope can pick up foreign objects; resolution is the image of these objects.
    E. Sensitivity is what is always lost in an image when resolution is gained.

27. The last paragraph of the passage provides

    A. a summary of the arguments of the whole passage.
    B. an irrelevant comparison of the Hubble telescope and the Voyager probes.
    C. a personal anecdote of the author.
    D. a contradiction of the assertions of the third paragraph (lines 38–45) of the passage.
    E. a rebuttal of media claims that the Hubble telescope is a failure.

28. The purpose of the passage as a whole is to

    A. assess the accomplishments and shortcomings of the Hubble telescope.
    B. compare the successes of the Hubble telescope with those of other space telescopes.
    C. explain why the media disappointment with the Hubble telescope is unjustified.
    D. remind readers of what the Hubble telescope may accomplish after repairs are made.
    E. explain why the loss of sensitivity in the Hubble telescope is compensated by a gain in resolution.

IF YOU FINISH BEFORE TIME IS CALLED, CHECK YOUR WORK ON THIS SECTION ONLY. DO NOT WORK ON ANY OTHER SECTION IN THE TEST.

Section 4: Mathematics

Time: 25 Minutes

20 Questions

Directions: Solve each problem in this section by using the information given and your own mathematical calculations, insights, and problem-solving skills. Then select the one correct answer of the five choices given and mark the corresponding circle on your answer sheet. Use the available space on the page for your scratch work.

Notes

1. All numbers used are real numbers.

2. Calculators may be used.

3. Some problems may be accompanied by figures or diagrams. These figures are drawn as accurately as possible EXCEPT when it is stated in a specific problem that a figure is not drawn to scale. The figures and diagrams are meant to provide information useful in solving the problem or problems. Unless otherwise stated, all figures and diagrams lie in a plane.

Data That Can Be Used for Reference

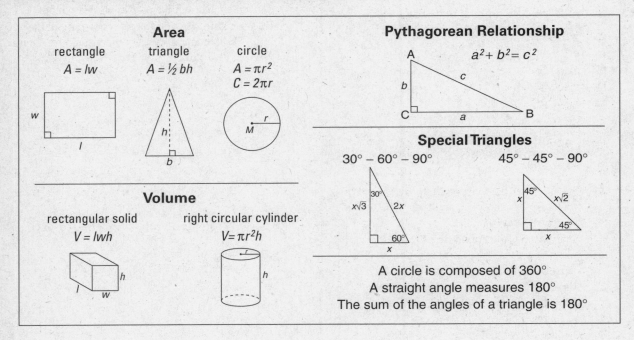

Area

rectangle
$A = lw$

triangle
$A = \frac{1}{2}bh$

circle
$A = \pi r^2$
$C = 2\pi r$

Volume

rectangular solid
$V = lwh$

right circular cylinder
$V = \pi r^2 h$

Pythagorean Relationship

$a^2 + b^2 = c^2$

Special Triangles

30° – 60° – 90°

45° – 45° – 90°

A circle is composed of 360°
A straight angle measures 180°
The sum of the angles of a triangle is 180°

1. A man purchased 4 pounds of steak priced at $3.89 per pound. How much change did he receive from a $20 bill?

    A. $44.66

    B. $15.56

    C. $ 4.46

    D. $ 4.44

    E. $ 4.34

2. If a number is divisible by 7 but is not divisible by 21, then the number cannot be divisible by

    A.   2

    B.   3

    C.   5

    D.   8

    E.   10

3. If $.0039y = 39$, then $y =$

    A.   10

    B.   100

    C.   1000

    D.   10,000

    E.   100,000

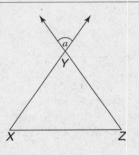

4. In $\triangle XYZ$, $XY = 10$, $YZ = 10$, and $\angle a = 84°$. What is the degree measure of $\angle Z$?

    A.   96°

    B.   84°

    C.   48°

    D.   42°

    E.   24°

GO ON TO THE NEXT PAGE

5. If $a = \sqrt{b}$ and $b = 81$, what is the value of $\sqrt{a}$?

   A. $\dfrac{1}{3}$

   B.   3

   C.   9

   D.   81

   E.   100

6″	2″	10″	2″	5″

6. Above are the measures of rainfall for five consecutive days during the winter. For the measure of those five days, which of the following is true?

   I.   The median equals the mode.

   II.   The median equals the arithmetic mean.

   III.   The range equals the median.

   A.   I only

   B.   II only

   C.   III only

   D.   I and II only

   E.   I and III only

7. Three-fifths of a geometry class is made up of female students. What is the ratio of male students to female students?

   A. $\dfrac{2}{5}$

   B. $\dfrac{3}{5}$

   C. $\dfrac{2}{3}$

   D. $\dfrac{5}{3}$

   E. $\dfrac{3}{2}$

8. What is the slope of the line for the equation $6x + y = 3$?

   A.   6

   B.   3

   C.   −2

   D.   −6

   E.   −9

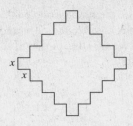

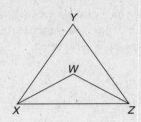

9. In the figure above, all line segments meet at right angles, and each segment has a length of x. What is the area of the figure in terms of x?

A. $25x$
B. $36x$
C. $36x^2$
D. $41x^2$
E. $41x^3$

11. WX and WZ are angle bisectors of the base angles of isosceles triangle XYZ above. If $Y = 80°$, what is the degree measure of $\angle XWZ$?

A. $65°$
B. $80°$
C. $100°$
D. $130°$
E. $160°$

10. If $x - y = 15$ and $3x + y = 13$, then $y =$

A. -8
B. -7
C. 7
D. 8
E. 15

12. If $m^2 + n^2 = 12$ and $mn = 9$, then $(m + n)^2 =$

A. 12
B. 24
C. 30
D. 42
E. 48

GO ON TO THE NEXT PAGE

13. If x, y, and z are consecutive positive integers greater than 1, not necessarily in that order, which of the following is (are) true?

   I. $x > z$
  II. $x + y > z$
 III. $yz < xz$
 IV. $xy < y + z$

  A. I only
  B. II only
  C. II and III only
  D. II and IV only
  E. III and IV only

14. The area of a square is 72 square feet. What is the length of a diagonal of the square?

  A. 36 feet
  B. $18\sqrt{2}$ feet
  C. 12 feet
  D. $6\sqrt{2}$ feet
  E. 6 feet

15. In a triangle, the ratio of two angles is 5:2, and the third angle is equal to the difference between the other two. What is the number of degrees in the smallest angle?

  A. 36
  B. $25\frac{5}{7}$
  C. $25\frac{2}{7}$
  D. 18
  E. 9

16. If $(a, b) \oplus (c, d) = (ac - bd, ad)$, then $(-2, 3) \oplus (4, -1) =$

  A. $(-5, 2)$
  B. $(-5, -2)$
  C. $(-11, 2)$
  D. $(-11, -2)$
  E. $(-5, -3)$

17. A collection of 25 coins consists of nickels, dimes, and quarters. There are three times as many dimes as nickels and three more dimes than quarters. What is the total value of the collection in dollars and cents?

A. $3.65
B. $3.25
C. $2.25
D. $1.65
E. $1.25

19. If m and n are integers and $\sqrt{mn} = 10$, which of the following CANNOT be a value of $m + n$?

A. 25
B. 29
C. 50
D. 52
E. 101

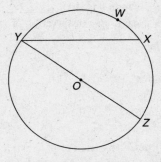

18. On the circle above with center O, arc YWX equals 100°. Which of the following is the degree measure of $\angle XYZ$?

A. 130°
B. 100°
C. 80°
D. 50°
E. 40°

20. What are the y-intercepts for the hyperbola $2y^2 - 5x^2 = 50$?

A. $\left(0, \pm 5\sqrt{2}\right)$
B. $\left(0, \pm \sqrt{10}\right)$
C. $\left(0, \pm \sqrt{5}\right)$
D. $\left(0, \pm 25\right)$
E. $\left(0, \pm 5\right)$

IF YOU FINISH BEFORE TIME IS CALLED, CHECK YOUR WORK ON THIS SECTION ONLY. DO NOT WORK ON ANY OTHER SECTION IN THE TEST.

Practice Test 2

Section 5: Critical Reading

Time: 25 Minutes

28 Questions

In this section, choose the best answer for each question and blacken the corresponding space on the answer sheet.

Directions: Each blank in the following sentences indicates that something has been omitted. Consider the lettered words beneath the sentence and choose the word or set of words that *best* fits the whole sentence.

EXAMPLE:

With a million more people than any other African nation, Nigeria is the most _____ country on the continent.

    A.   impoverished
    B.   successful
    C.   populous
    D.   developed
    E.   militant

The correct answer is C.

---

1. With the benefit of _____, it is easy to see the mistakes we made last week or last year.

    A.   hindsight
    B.   prophecy
    C.   insight
    D.   tactfulness
    E.   nostalgia

2. The pamphlet argues that imagination is not a gift _____ to poets, but something everyone possesses.

    A.   relevant
    B.   inimical
    C.   unique
    D.   unrestricted
    E.   conducive

3. That "less is more" is a(n) _____ upon which all of the governor's conservation program is based.

    A.   hope
    B.   question
    C.   enigma
    D.   image
    E.   paradox

4. Though McCarthy tried to provoke a _____, Eisenhower ignored all the senator's _____ as if he had not heard them.

    A.   fight . . . avocations
    B.   compromise . . . overtures
    C.   confrontation . . . accusations
    D.   condemnation . . . motives
    E.   consensus . . . implications

5. Again and again, out of indifference or sheer stupidity, we have _____ our resources, assuming that there was no end to the earth's _____ to recover from our mistakes.

- **A.** invested . . . resolve
- **B.** expanded . . . ability
- **C.** wasted . . . failure
- **D.** husbanded . . . inability
- **E.** squandered . . . capacity

6. Despite _____ reports of freewheeling spending on political candidates by large corporations, most business contributions are _____ divided between the two major parties.

- **A.** lurid . . . equitably
- **B.** shocking . . . unfairly
- **C.** unfair . . . secretly
- **D.** favorable . . . evenly
- **E.** encouraging . . . carefully

7. With characteristic understatement, Webster called his client's embezzlement of 4 million dollars a regretted _____.

- **A.** peccadillo
- **B.** crime
- **C.** atrocity
- **D.** theft
- **E.** enormity

8. Keynes's theory that unemployment is caused by a(n) _____ disposition to save cannot explain the high unemployment in _____ countries that have no savings at all.

- **A.** simple . . . wealthy
- **B.** bizarre . . . prosperous
- **C.** orderly . . . rich
- **D.** individualistic . . . successful
- **E.** excessive . . . indigent

9. His biographer believed that Pierce's _____ was caused by his _____ to travel and his refusal to read about any position different from his own.

- **A.** parochialism . . . reluctance
- **B.** insularity . . . readiness
- **C.** bigotry . . . zeal
- **D.** narrow-mindedness . . . eagerness
- **E.** magnanimity . . . failure

GO ON TO THE NEXT PAGE

Directions: Questions follow the passage below. Using only the stated or implied information in the passage and in its introduction, if any, answer the questions.

Questions 10–11 are based on the following passage.

    In the early 1800s, a group of English workers known as the Luddites protested the effects of the Industrial Revolution on their jobs. They claimed as their leader Ned Ludd, also known as "King
(5) Ludd," who supposedly destroyed two large machines that produced inexpensive stockings, undercutting the stockings produced by skilled knitters. The Luddite movement grew in England to the point where many wool and cotton mills were
(10) destroyed. In response, the British government harshly suppressed Luddites, making "machine breaking" a capital crime and executing 17 men in 1813. In today's world, the term Luddite is used to describe anyone who opposes the advance of in-
(15) dustrial technology, although according to some historians, this unfairly characterizes the original movement.

10. The paragraph suggests that

  A. many people are as opposed to workers' protests today as they were in the 19th century.

  B. advances in technology have caused widespread destruction throughout history.

  C. today's understanding of the Luddite movement may be oversimplified.

  D. the British government unfairly executed people for speaking out against industrial changes.

  E. people don't appreciate craftsmanship and much as they do low prices.

11. From details in the paragraph, which of the following statements is accurate?

  A. The Luddite movement grew in the textile industry.

  B. Both men and women participated in the Luddite movement.

  C. Luddites believed in a socialistic society.

  D. The protests conducted by the Luddites didn't affect production.

  E. Most British citizens supported the government against the Luddites.

Questions 12–13 are based on the following passage.

    The neutrino, a subatomic particle named by physicist Enrico Fermi in 1931, was actually first hypothesized by Wofgang Pauli. In the physical universe, what goes in always equals what comes
(5) out, in one form or another. But when radioactive atoms spat out electrons and changed into other kinds of atoms, some energy appeared to be missing, which led Pauli to propose that the energy was carried away by a virtually invisible particle. He
(10) was almost embarrassed by his theory: "I have done a terrible thing. I have postulated a particle that cannot be detected." And when Fermi submitted a paper on the possibility of such a particle, it was rejected as "remote from reality." The first for-
(15) mal experiment to hunt for neutrinos was in 1956, when physicists Clyde Cowan and Fred Reines found a definite trace of the particles in the intense wash of radiation emitted from newly commissioned nuclear reactors.

12. According to the paragraph, Pauli thought that neutrinos might explain

  A. intense radiation.

  B. missing energy.

  C. formation of electrons.

  D. mysterious events in the universe.

  E. loss of radiation.

13. Of the following statements, which is best supported by the paragraph?

  A. The scientific community resists new theories.

  B. Scientists are competitive and are not comfortable sharing their hypotheses.

  C. Neither Pauli nor Fermi made an attempt to find a neutrino.

  D. Scientists are mistrustful of explanations that rely on "invisible" elements.

  E. Nuclear reactors were made possible by the discovery of neutrinos.

Questions 14–16 are based on the following pair of passages.

Passage 1

Urban renewal was supposed to revitalize cities by redeveloping slums and blighted commercial areas. But it failed because of the introduction of eminent domain into the land development process.
(5) Normally, buildings are demolished only when developers have acquired the properties, and only after they know demand exists for more profitable developments in their place. Market forces ensure that there are few properties which end up vacant
(10) for long. But because of urban renewal, governments used eminent domain to condemn too much property, whether demand existed or not. As so often happens, government interference created a major problem. In many cities, it left undeveloped,
(15) "unrenewed" vacant lots, which are not only eyesores but also hangouts for criminal elements.

Passage 2

Urban renewal is an opportunity to develop better communities. In its original form, many projects failed—for a number of reasons—and many
(20) city planners and civic leaders judged the idea a failure. But the concept now focuses not on the destruction of vibrant (if run-down) communities but more on renovation, selective demolition, commercial development and tax incentives. It is still
(25) not without its critics or its problems. For example, when areas are "gentrified," poorer residents can be "priced out" and forced to move into even more depressed areas of cities. But the concept of urban renewal continues to evolve as successes and fail-
(30) ures are examined. Encouraging more community involvement in development projects is a sure way to increase the successes.

14. The author of Passage 1 would most likely favor which of the following?

A. more prosecutions of slum landlords
B. increased government funding in depressed areas
C. less involvement of the government in development projects
D. fewer restrictions on private developers
E. more traffic control and public parking lots in depressed downtown areas.

15. In Passage 2, line 26, the word "gentrified" most nearly means

A. patrolled by special police units.
B. redeveloped for middle- and upper-class residents.
C. taken over by the federal government and demolished.
D. "spruced up" superficially.
E. turned into housing for the poor.

16. On which one of the following points would the authors of Passage 1 and Passage 2 be most likely to agree?

A. Government involvement is the major cause of the failure of urban renewal.
B. Urban renewal has been good for the middle class but not for the poor.
C. Most urban renewal projects have failed.
D. Demolition and rebuilding should be done selectively.
E. Tax incentives shouldn't be used to encourage urban renewal.

Questions 17–28 are based on the following passage.

Playfully, we call them "shrinks," acknowledging each time we do so that the psychiatrist's precursor was the head-shrinking witchdoctor, the original healer of souls. Often we use the name sardonically,
(5) implying that a certain residue of mumbo-jumbo still clings to our supposedly enlightened science of the mind. But by the same token might there not be something of at least marginal value to be found in the supposedly superstitious practice of witch-
(10) doctoring? Have traditional cultures anything to teach our industrial society about the meaning of sanity? The anthropologist Marshall Sahlins, assembling a composite picture of life among the hunters and gatherers, once undertook to reconstruct a
(15) "stone-age economics" from which he believed we might learn something about the meaning of wealth and poverty. Is there a "stone-age psychiatry" that can be mined for similarly heuristic insights?
Until well into this century, even trained anthro-
(20) pological observers tended to regard tribal healers as charlatans whose practices were mere quackery. Some scholars classified all shamans as psychotics whose practices were "witchcraft" in the most pejorative meaning of the word. The terms used ranged
(25) from the politely technical ("neurotic–epileptoid

GO ON TO THE NEXT PAGE

(30) type") to the bluntly dismissive ("veritable idiots"), but all came down to regarding tribal therapy as the mad treating the mad. Thanks largely to the work of Claude Levi–Strauss and subsequent studies in transcultural psychiatry, we have since come to see that tribal societies possess spiritual and psychotherapeutic traditions that may be more effective in the treatment of their own people than Western medicine, especially when it comes to mental and emotional disorders. The anthropologist I. M. Lewis,

(35) standing the question on its head, has gone so far as to suggest that our psychotherapy might be viewed as a scaled-down subspecies of traditional healing. "The more meaningful equivalence," he observes,

(40) "is that psychiatry, and especially psychoanalysis, as Jung would perhaps have admitted much more freely than most Freudians would care to, represent limited and imperfect forms of shamanism." The remark is not entirely fair to Freud, who readily

(45) acknowledged that tribal healers can be as adept as many psychiatrists at creating a "condition of expectant faith" that can have great therapeutic effect.

Perhaps the most marked difference between psychotherapy old and new is the complexity and

(50) breadth of traditional healing. In tribal societies, the distinction between the physical and psychic is far less rigid than we understand it to be. One might almost say that traditional medicine regards all disease as psychosomatic, in the sense that the

(55) psyche is implicated in its etiology. Even a frozen foot may be treated by Eskimo shamans as a psychic disturbance.

Therefore, thoughts, dreams, memories, emotions must be mobilized in its cure. The province of

(60) stone-age psychiatry is a broad one.

E. Fuller Torrey, taking issue with the "psychiatric imperialism" of Western society, points out that healing has everything to do with the cultural bond that unites therapist and client. A common

(65) worldview, a shared diagnostic vocabulary, mutually respected ideas and principles make for the trust and conviction without which healing may be impossible. But if we have learned that tribal techniques can be more effective than modern psychia-

(70) try in treating native people, this knowledge may have little direct value for us—unless we can find some common ground with tribal peoples that allows us to borrow a portion of their culture. That common ground may be the ground of desperation.

(75) If our relations with nature are as deeply failed as the environmental crisis suggests, we may have to look for help wherever we can find it, including insights long absent from our own society. Where else are these to be found but in the experience of

(80) our fellow humans living different lives in a different world?

Traditional therapy can be stubbornly parochial; it is embedded in a place and a history, in the rhythms of climate, in the contours of a landscape

(85) where the birds and beasts have been close companions for centuries. In local lore, a river, a mountain, a grove may take on the personality of a tribal elder, a presence named and known over the generations. Artifacts assume a peculiarly evocative

(90) power. The manangs of Borneo come to their patients bearing a bundle filled with strange implements: the horns of the giant beetle, a quartz amulet that is "the stone of light," a wild boar's tusk that can retrieve lost souls. What can these things mean

(95) to us? They seem like the proverbial "eye of newt and toe of frog" that make witchcraft appear so ludicrous. Yet the effectiveness of the shaman's method largely lies in its emotional specificity. What we as modern observers achieve by our efforts

(100) to universalize is, at last, something of our own, a new creation that may lack the color and force of the original.

17. In the first paragraph, the author uses the word "shrinks" (line 1) in order to

   I. jokingly refer to the forerunners of the contemporary psychiatrist.
   II. suggest a distrust of contemporary psychiatry.
   III. remind readers of the potential value in the traditional practices.

   A. I only
   B. I and II only
   C. I and III only
   D. II and III only
   E. I, II, and III

18. The first paragraph cites the work of anthropologist Marshall Sahlins in order to suggest that

   A. if the stone age can teach us about economics, perhaps it can teach us about psychiatry.
   B. the problems of poverty in our era can be solved by consulting stone-age economics.
   C. the stone-age notions of rich and poor are irrelevant in today's complex civilization.
   D. modern anthropologists need not limit their studies to the lifestyles of lost civilizations.
   E. modern psychiatry is dependent on ancient ideas.

19. The passage argues that tribal medical treatment may be

    A. more universally effective than modern methods.

    B. more effective in treating people living in civilized countries than modern methods.

    C. about as effective as Western methods in treating members of tribal societies.

    D. more effective than Western methods in treating mental disorders of tribal members.

    E. more effective than Western methods in treating mental disorders of non-Western nations.

20. The passage implies that one reason for the success within a tribe of tribal medicine is that

    A. some tribal doctors may use curative herbs.

    B. the patient expects to be cured.

    C. some tribal doctors have Western training.

    D. the patients are not really sick.

    E. some tribal doctors refuse to use amulets.

21. Which of the following would be likely to be treated by ancient psychotherapy but not by modern?

    A. Depression

    B. Broken arm

    C. Fear of crowds

    D. Schizophrenia

    E. Mental illness

22. The word "marked" in line 48 means

    A. signaled.

    B. indicated.

    C. scored.

    D. conspicuous.

    E. recorded.

23. Which of the following best expresses the meaning of the phrase "between the physical and psychic" in line 51?

    A. Between body and mind

    B. Between the sensual and sensuous

    C. Between the real and supernatural

    D. Between logic and the uncanny

    E. Between sensory and extrasensory perception

24. In line 54, the word "psychosomatic" can be best defined as

    A. curable by herbal medicine or spells.

    B. contagious.

    C. originating in the mind.

    D. imaginary.

    E. subject to treatment by witchcraft.

25. Freud and E. Fuller Torrey agree on the importance in

    A. mutual trust between doctor and patient.

    B. a conviction of the superiority of shamanism to psychiatry.

    C. the patient's desire to be cured.

    D. a conviction of the superiority of psychiatry to shamanism.

    E. a genuine belief in the efficacy of witchcraft.

26. In line 61, the phrase "taking issue with" can be best defined as

    A. departing from.

    B. resulting from.

    C. disagreeing with.

    D. proceeding with.

    E. siding with.

27. Anticipating the skepticism that might arise from taking ancient medicine seriously, the author has deliberately used all the following words and phrases to mock ancient medicine or its practitioners EXCEPT

    A. "mumbo-jumbo" (line 5).

    B. "charlatans" (line 21).

    C. "psychotics" (line 22).

    D. "eye of newt and toe of frog" (lines 95–96).

    E. "shaman's method" (lines 97–98).

28. The purpose of the passage as a whole is to

    A. question the usefulness of modern psycho-therapy as opposed to tribal healing methods.

    B. assert the superiority of tribal methods to Western psychiatric procedures.

    C. urge the study of tribal medicine and tribal ways to abet Western psychiatry.

    D. criticize Western civilization's arrogant dismissal of tribal lore.

    E. reconstruct as far as it is possible some principles of stone-age mental therapy.

Practice Test 2

IF YOU FINISH BEFORE TIME IS CALLED, CHECK YOUR WORK ON THIS SECTION ONLY. DO NOT WORK ON ANY OTHER SECTION IN THE TEST.

Section 6: Mathematics

Time: 25 Minutes

20 Questions

Directions: This section is composed of two types of questions. Use the 25 minutes allotted to answer both question types. For questions 1–10, select the one correct answer of the five choices given and mark the corresponding circle on your answer sheet. Your scratch work should be done on any available space in the section.

Notes

1. All numbers used are real numbers.

2. Calculators can be used.

3. Some problems may be accompanied by figures or diagrams. These figures are drawn as accurately as possible EXCEPT when it is stated in a specific problem that a figure is not drawn to scale. The figures and diagrams are meant to provide information useful in solving the problem or problems. Unless otherwise stated, all figures and diagrams lie in a plane.

Data That Can Be Used for Reference

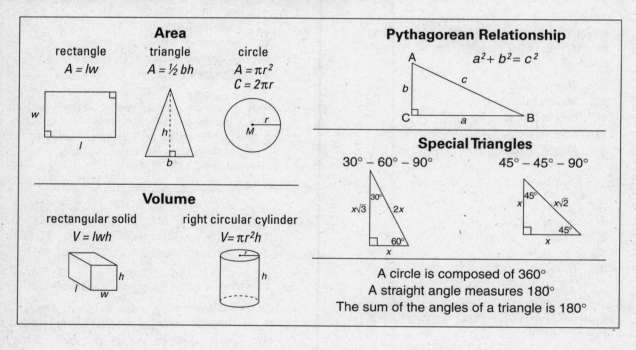

Area

rectangle
$A = lw$

triangle
$A = \frac{1}{2}bh$

circle
$A = \pi r^2$
$C = 2\pi r$

Pythagorean Relationship

$a^2 + b^2 = c^2$

Special Triangles

$30° - 60° - 90°$

$45° - 45° - 90°$

Volume

rectangular solid
$V = lwh$

right circular cylinder
$V = \pi r^2 h$

A circle is composed of 360°
A straight angle measures 180°
The sum of the angles of a triangle is 180°

1. What is the value of $(3 + 5)^2$?

   A.   8
   B.   9
   C.   16
   D.   34
   E.   64

3. If $y + 2$ is a positive integer, then y must be

   A.   even
   B.   odd
   C.   greater than –2
   D.   less than 2
   E.   positive

2. In the arithmetic sequence 4, 8, 12, 16, 20, . . . , which of the following could not be a term in the sequence?

   A.   760
   B.   656
   C.   512
   D.   438
   E.   392

4. A plumber charges $45 for the first hour of work and $20 per hour for each additional hour of work after the first. What would be the total bill for labor if the plumber works for 6 consecutive hours?

   A. $ 65
   B. $120
   C. $145
   D. $165
   E. $180

GO ON TO THE NEXT PAGE

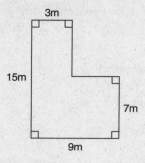

3m

15m

7m

9m

5. What is the perimeter, in meters, of the figure above?

    A.   40

    B.   42

    C.   48

    D.   58

    E.   Cannot be determined from the given information

6. If $a = p + prt$, then $r =$

    A. $\dfrac{a-1}{t}$

    B. $\dfrac{a-p}{pt}$

    C. $a - p - pt$

    D. $\dfrac{a}{t}$

    E. $\dfrac{a+p}{pt}$

7. Rajiv will be y years old x years from now. How old will he be z years from now?

    A. $y - x + z$

    B. $y + x + z$

    C. $y + x - z$

    D. $y - x - z$

    E. $x + z - y$

8. Which of the following is equivalent to $z^{\frac{5}{2}}$?

    A. $\sqrt[5]{z^2}$

    B. $\sqrt[5]{z}$

    C. $\sqrt{z^5}$

    D. $\sqrt{z}$

    E. $\sqrt{5z}$

9. The average of three numbers is 55. The second is 1 more than twice the first, and the third is 4 less than three times the first. What is the largest number?

A. 165
B. 88
C. 80
D. 57
E. 28

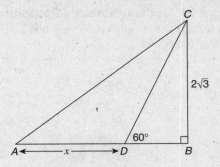

10. In the figure above, the area of $\triangle ABC = 6\sqrt{3}$. What is the value of x?

A. 2
B. $2\sqrt{3}$
C. 4
D. $4\sqrt{2}$
E. 6

GO ON TO THE NEXT PAGE

Directions for Student-Produced Response Questions (Grid-ins): Questions 11–20 require you to solve the problem and enter your answer by carefully marking the circles on the special grid. Examples of the appropriate way to mark the grid follow.

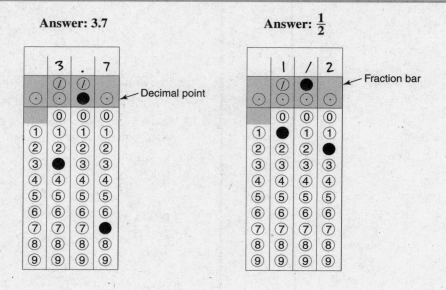

Answer: 3.7   Answer: $\frac{1}{2}$

Answer: $1\frac{1}{2}$

Do not grid in mixed numbers in the form of mixed numbers. Always change mixed numbers to improper fractions or decimals.

Change to 1.5   or   Change to $\frac{3}{2}$

Answer: 123

Space permitting, answers can start in any column. Each grid-in answer that follows is correct.

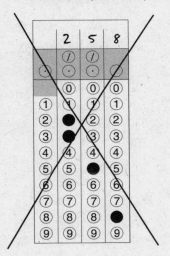

Note: Circles must be filled in correctly to receive credit. Mark only one circle in each column. No credit will be given if more than one circle in a column is marked. Example:

Answer: 258 (no credit)

GO ON TO THE NEXT PAGE

Answer: $\frac{8}{9}$

Accuracy of decimals: Always enter the most accurate decimal value that the grid will accommodate. For example: An answer such as .8888 . . . can be gridded as .888 or .889. Gridding this value as .8, .88, or .89 is considered inaccurate and therefore not acceptable. The acceptable grid-ins of $\frac{8}{9}$ are:

Be sure to write your answers in the boxes at the top of the circles before doing your gridding. Although writing out the answers above the columns is not required, it is very important to ensure accuracy. Even though some problems may have more than one correct answer, grid only one answer. Grid-in questions contain no negative answers.

11. If $x + \frac{3}{5}x = 1$, then $x =$

13. What is the average of $\frac{1}{4}$, $\frac{1}{6}$, and $\frac{1}{12}$?

12. In a class of 35 students, 60% are girls. How many boys are in the class?

14. If a car averages 317.9 miles on 17 gallons of gas, how many miles will it travel on 5 gallons of gas?

Springfield High School's average SAT scores over a five-year period were

	Math	Verbal
1989	520	540
1990	515	532
1991	518	528
1992	510	525
1993	507	510

15. What was the mean (average) of the verbal SAT scores for the five-year period 1989 through 1993?

16. The ratio of the measures of the angles of a quadrilateral is 3:5:7:9. What is the degree measure of the smallest angle?

17. If Jim takes 6 days to paint a house alone and Mike takes 8 days to paint the same house alone, what part of the job will be completed if both boys work for 2 days?

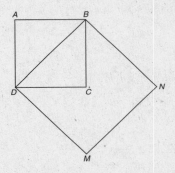

18. In square *ABCD* in the figure above, *AB* = 5. What is the area of square *BDMN*?

GO ON TO THE NEXT PAGE

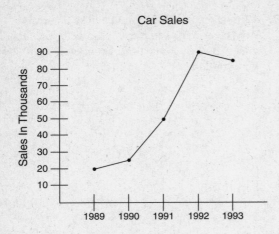

Car Sales

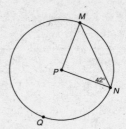

19. In the graph above, if each point aligns exactly with a grid mark or aligns halfway between two grid marks, what was the greatest percentage increase between two consecutive years? (Disregard the % sign when you are gridding your answer.)

20. What is the measure in degrees of arc *MQN* in the circle above with center *P*?

IF YOU FINISH BEFORE TIME IS CALLED, CHECK YOUR WORK ON THIS SECTION ONLY. DO NOT WORK ON ANY OTHER SECTION IN THE TEST.

Section 7: Critical Reading

Time: 20 Minutes

14 Questions

In this section, choose the best answer for each question and blacken the corresponding space on the answer sheet.

Directions: Questions follow the two passages below. Using only the stated or implied information in each passage and in its introduction, if any, answer the questions.

Questions 1–14 are based on the following passages.

The two passages that follow are about the conductor of the modern symphony orchestra. The first was written in the 1950s by a well-known composer-conductor. The second was written in the 1960s by a well-known composer.

Passage 1

There was an era of the so-called violin-conductor, whose main duty was to start and stop the orchestra and generally keep the flow of the music going. This was all well and good as long as orches-
(5) tras were small enough. But around Beethoven's time, orchestras began getting larger and larger, and it soon became apparent that somebody had to be up there to keep the players together. So conducting as we know it is actually less than 150 years old.
(10) The first real conductor in our sense of the word was Mendelssohn, who founded a tradition of conducting based on the concept of precision, as symbolized in the wooden stick we call the baton. Mendelssohn dedicated himself to an exact realiza-
(15) tion of the score he was conducting, through manipulation of that baton. There soon arrived, however, a great dissenter named Richard Wagner who declared that everything Mendelssohn was doing was wrong and that any conductor worth his salt should person-
(20) alize the score he was conducting by coloring it with his own emotions and his own creative impulse. And so out of the clash of these two points of view the history of conducting was born; and there arose all those great names in conducting, as well as all the
(25) fights that go on about them right up to our own time. Mendelssohn fathered the "elegant" school, whereas Wagner inspired the "passionate" school of conducting. Actually, both attitudes are necessary, the Apollonian and the Dionysian, and neither one is
(30) completely satisfactory without the other. Both of them can be badly abused, as we know from having heard performances that seemed clear but were dry as dust, and others in which passion became simple distortion.

(35) The ideal modern conductor is a synthesis of the two attitudes, and this synthesis is rarely achieved. In fact, it's practically impossible. Almost any musician can be a conductor, even a pretty good one; but only a rare musician can be a great one. This is
(40) not only because it is so hard to achieve the Mendelssohn-Wagner combination, but also because the conductor's work encompasses such a tremendous range. Unlike an instrumentalist or a singer, he has to play on an orchestra. His instru-
(45) ment is one hundred human instruments, each one a thorough musician, each with a will of his own; and he must cause them to play like one instrument with a single will. Therefore, he must have enormous authority, to say nothing of psychological insight in
(50) dealing with this large group and all this is just the beginning. He must be a master of the mechanics of conducting. He must have an inconceivable amount of knowledge. He must have a profound perception of the inner meanings of music, and he must have
(55) uncanny powers of communication. If he has all this, he is the ideal conductor.

Passage 2

Conducting, like politics, rarely attracts original minds, and the field is more for the making of careers and the exploitation of personalities—another
(60) resemblance to politics—than a profession for the application of exact and standardized disciplines. A conductor may actually be less well equipped for his work than his players, but no one except the players need know it, and his career is not depen-
(65) dent on them in any case, but on the society women (including critics) to whom his musical qualities are of secondary importance. The successful conductor can be an incomplete musician, but he must be a complete angler. His first skill *has* to be power
(70) politics.

In such people the incidence of ego disease is naturally high to begin with, and I hardly need add that the disease grows like a tropical weed under the

GO ON TO THE NEXT PAGE

(75) sun of a pandering public. The results are that the conductor is encouraged to impose a purely egotistical, false, and arbitrary authority, and that he is accorded a position out of all proportion to his real value in the musical, as opposed to the music-business, community. He soon becomes a "great"

(80) conductor, in fact, or as the press agent of one of them recently wrote me, a "titan of the podium," and as such is very nearly the worst obstacle to genuine music-making. "Great" conductors, like "great" actors, are unable to play anything but

(85) themselves; being unable to adapt themselves to the work, they adapt the work to themselves, to their "style," their mannerisms. The cult of the "great" conductor also tends to substitute looking for listening, so that to conductor and audience

(90) alike (and to reviewers who habitually fall into the trap of describing a conductor's appearance rather than the way he makes music sound, and of mistaking the conductor's gestures for the music's meanings), the important part of the performance

(95) becomes the gesture. If you are incapable of listening, the conductor will show you what to feel. Thus, the film-actor type of conductor will act out a life of Napoleon in "his" *Eroica*[1], wear an expression of noble suffering on the retreat from Moscow

(100) (TV having circumvented the comparatively merciful limitation to the dorsal view) and one of ultimate triumph in the last movement, during which he even dances the Victory Ball. If you are unable to listen to the music, you watch the corybantics[2],

(105) and if you *are* able, you had better not go to the concert.

[1] *Eroica* = a symphony by Beethoven originally dedicated to Napoleon
[2] corybantics = dancing

1. From Passage 1, the reader can infer that in the seventeenth century

  I. orchestras did not employ a conductor.
  II. orchestras were smaller than they are today.
  III. orchestral players were better trained and more skillful.

  A. I only
  B. II only
  C. I and II only
  D. I and III only
  E. I, II, and III

2. From its use in Passage 1 (line 29) it can be inferred that the word "Apollonian" means

  A. sunny and optimistic.
  B. Wagnerian.
  C. emotionally intense.
  D. Bacchic.
  E. clear and elegant.

3. According to Passage 1, instrumentalists and singers have an advantage over a conductor because they

  A. have only to do what the conductor directs.
  B. need not master the mechanics of conducting.
  C. must cope with only one instrument, not a hundred.
  D. must be able to read music.
  E. need not understand the meaning of a score.

4. Of which of the following kinds of conductor described in Passage 1 would the author of that passage be most likely to approve?

  A. One "dedicated . . . to an exact realization of the score" (lines 14–15)
  B. One "coloring [the score] with his own emotions and his own creative impulse" (lines 20–21)
  C. One whose performances "seemed clear but were dry as dust" (lines 32–33)
  D. One in whose performances "passion became simple distortion" (lines 33–34)
  E. One who is both "elegant" and "passionate" and can "personalize the score" (lines 26–28 and 19–20)

5. By adding the parenthetical phrase "including critics" (line 66) the author of Passage 2 suggests all of the following EXCEPT

  A. Music critics and society women are alike.
  B. Music critics are more interested in orchestras than in orchestra conductors.
  C. Music critics are more important to a conductor's success than are the conductor's musical abilities.
  D. Music critics are less interested in musical ability than are orchestra players.
  E. Music critics are less able to judge musical qualities than are musicians.

6. The author of Passage 2 believes that politicians are

    A. original thinkers.
    B. career-minded.
    C. highly disciplined professionals.
    D. modest and self-effacing.
    E. indifferent to power.

7. By the phrase "the incidence of ego disease is naturally high" (lines 71–72), the author of the Passage 2 means

    A. there is a great deal of illness among musicians.
    B. conductors are rarely sick.
    C. conducting is a dangerous and demanding profession.
    D. conductors are very self centered.
    E. orchestras are likely to thrive in tropical countries.

8. In Passage 2, the distinction implied in lines 78–79 between the "music-business community" and the "musical community" is that

    A. in the music-business community, conductors are undervalued.
    B. in the music-business community, composers are overvalued.
    C. in the musical community, music is more important than personality.
    D. only the music-business community is concerned with money.
    E. the music-business community is concerned with popular music, and the musical community with classical music.

9. The phrase "TV having circumvented the comparatively merciful limitation to the dorsal view" (lines 100–101) in Passage 2 can be best understood to mean

    A. television has brought conductors to a much larger audience than ever before.
    B. television allows the viewer to see and hear details of a performance that are not clear in the concert hall.
    C. television distorts both the sound and the appearance of a symphony concert.
    D. television unfortunately allows the viewers to see the front of the conductor.
    E. television programs have the fortunate advantage of being easily turned off.

10. In the last paragraph of Passage 2, the phrase "if you *are* able" refers to

    I. visualize the "Victory Ball."
    II. "listen to the music."
    III. "watch the corybantics."

    A. II only
    B. III only
    C. I and III only
    D. II and III only
    E. I, II, and III

11. The author of Passage 2 either directly or obliquely makes fun of all the following EXCEPT

    A. conductors.
    B. politicians.
    C. the musical public.
    D. music critics.
    E. orchestral players.

12. Of the following kinds of conductor described in Passage 1, which would the author of Passage 2 be most likely to approve?

    A. One "dedicated . . . to an exact realization of the score" (lines 14–15)
    B. One "coloring [the score] with his own emotions and his own creative impulse" (lines 20–21)
    C. One whose performances "seemed clear but were dry as dust" (lines 32–33)
    D. One in whose performances "passion became simple distortion" (lines 33–34)
    E. One who is both "elegant" and "passionate" and can "personalize the score" (lines 33, 26–28 and 19–20)

13. Which of the following words is used in both passages but with totally different connotations?

    A. "conductor"
    B. "exact"
    C. "music"
    D. "great"
    E. "orchestra"

GO ON TO THE NEXT PAGE

14. That both passages were written at mid-century rather than very recently is suggested by their

    I.   assumption that an orchestra will be led by a conductor rather than by a concert-master.

    II.   assumption that a conductor is a male.

    III.   assumption that a performance may be reviewed by a music critic.

    A.   I only
    B.   II only
    C.   III only
    D.   I and II only
    E.   I, II, and III

IF YOU FINISH BEFORE TIME IS CALLED, CHECK YOUR WORK ON THIS SECTION ONLY. DO NOT WORK ON ANY OTHER SECTION IN THE TEST.

Section 8: Mathematics

Time: 20 Minutes

15 Questions

Directions: Solve each problem in this section by using the information given and your own mathematical calculations, insights, and problem-solving skills. Then select the one correct answer of the five choices given and mark the corresponding circle on your answer sheet. Use the available space on the page for your scratch work.

Notes

1. All numbers used are real numbers.
2. Calculators can be used.
3. Some problems may be accompanied by figures or diagrams. These figures are drawn as accurately as possible EXCEPT when it is stated in a specific problem that a figure is not drawn to scale. The figures and diagrams are meant to provide information useful in solving the problem or problems. Unless otherwise stated, all figures and diagrams lie in a plane.

Data That Can Be Used for Reference

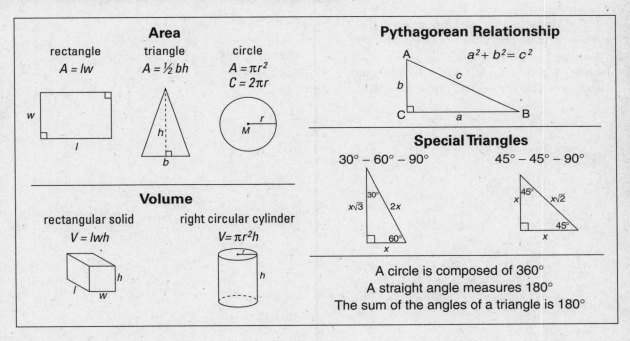

Area

rectangle
$A = lw$

triangle
$A = \frac{1}{2}bh$

circle
$A = \pi r^2$
$C = 2\pi r$

Volume

rectangular solid
$V = lwh$

right circular cylinder
$V = \pi r^2 h$

Pythagorean Relationship

$a^2 + b^2 = c^2$

Special Triangles

$30° - 60° - 90°$

$45° - 45° - 90°$

A circle is composed of 360°
A straight angle measures 180°
The sum of the angles of a triangle is 180°

GO ON TO THE NEXT PAGE

1. What is .25% of 12?

A. $\frac{3}{100}$

B. $\frac{3}{10}$

C. $\frac{1}{3}$

D. 3

E. 300

2. A square 4 inches on a side is cut up into smaller squares 1 inch on a side. What is the maximum number of such squares that can be formed?

A. 4
B. 8
C. 16
D. 36
E. 64

3. If a book costs \$5.70 after a 40% discount, what was its original price?

A. \$2.28
B. \$6.10
C. \$7.98
D. \$9.12
E. \$9.50

4. $\dfrac{\frac{2}{3} + \frac{1}{2}}{\frac{1}{6} + \frac{1}{4} + \frac{2}{3}} =$

A. $\frac{2}{13}$

B. $\frac{2}{9}$

C. $\frac{13}{20}$

D. $1\frac{1}{13}$

E. $3\frac{1}{4}$

**Number of Wild Bear Sightings Before and After
Conservation Measures in Five Different Counties**

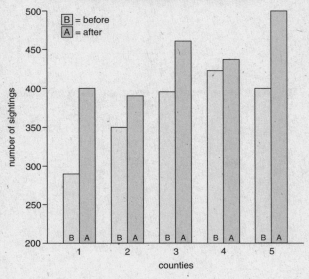

5. According to the graph above, which county had
the most bear sightings before the conservation
measures?

A.   1
B.   2
C.   3
D.   4
E.   5

6. If $(x + 1)$ times $(2x + 1)$ is an odd integer, then x
must be

A.   an odd integer.
B.   an even integer.
C.   a prime number.
D.   a composite number.
E.   a negative number.

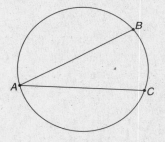

7. If $\angle A = 40°$ *and* $\overset{\frown}{AC} = 130°$, then $\overset{\frown}{AB} =$

A.   60°
B.   80°
C.   150°
D.   190°
E.   Cannot be determined from the given
information.

GO ON TO THE NEXT PAGE

8. A certain geometry class has 36 students. If two-thirds of the students are boys and three-fourths of the boys are under six feet tall, how many boys in the class are under six feet tall?

A. 6
B. 12
C. 18
D. 24
E. 27

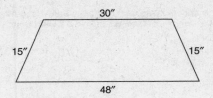

10. What is the area of the trapezoid above in square inches?

A. 108
B. 234
C. 368
D. 468
E. 585

9. If $|3x + 6| = 15$, then $x =$

A. 3
B. −3
C. −3, 3
D. −7, 3
E. −7, 7

11. If $f(x) = 3^x + 4$ and x is an integer, then which of the following could be a value of $f(x)$?

A. 3
B. 4
C. $4\frac{1}{9}$
D. $5\frac{1}{3}$
E. 9

12. If $y = \dfrac{1-x}{x}$, then $x =$

   A. $\dfrac{1}{y+1}$

   B. $\dfrac{1-y}{y}$

   C. $\dfrac{y}{1-y}$

   D. $y+1$

   E. $\dfrac{1}{y-1}$

14. If $4\sqrt{y+3} + 14 = 50$, then $y =$

   A. 81

   B. 78

   C. -9

   D. -81

   E. -84

13. Three factories of Conglomerate Corporation are capable of manufacturing hubcaps. Two of the factories can each produce 100,000 hubcaps in 15 days. The third factory can produce hubcaps 30% faster. Approximately how many days would it take to produce a million hubcaps with all three factories working simultaneously?

   A. 38

   B. 42

   C. 44

   D. 46

   E. 50

15. What is the area in square yards of an equilateral triangle if the length of one of its sides is 12 yards?

   A. $18\sqrt{3}$

   B. $36\sqrt{3}$

   C. 72

   D. $72\sqrt{3}$

   E. 216

IF YOU FINISH BEFORE TIME IS CALLED, CHECK YOUR WORK ON THIS SECTION ONLY. DO NOT WORK ON ANY OTHER SECTION IN THE TEST.

STOP

Section 9: Critical Reading

Time: 25 Minutes

28 Questions

In this section, choose the best answer for each question and blacken the corresponding space on the answer sheet.

Directions: Each blank in the following sentences indicates that something has been omitted. Consider the lettered words beneath the sentence and choose the word or set of words that best fits the whole sentence.

EXAMPLE:

With a million more people than any other African nation, Nigeria is the most _____ country on the continent.

    A.   impoverished
    B.   successful
    C.   populous
    D.   developed
    E.   militant

The correct answer is C.

---

1. In poor and politically unsettled countries, trucks are the only means of getting in or out, public transportation being virtually _____.

    A.   indecipherable
    B.   ubiquitous
    C.   indifferent
    D.   inadequate
    E.   nonexistent

2. Parker is known for the _____ of her stories, many of them less than three pages long.

    A.   wit
    B.   sincerity
    C.   cynicism
    D.   economy
    E.   development

3. Because most parents who watched *Sesame Street* as children are likely to regard the show as _____ viewing for their children, an advertiser can _____ a very large young audience.

    A.   educational . . . alienate
    B.   obligatory . . . rely on
    C.   compulsory . . . avoid
    D.   required . . . apprehend
    E.   habitual . . . expect

4. A fiscal _____, Lloyd would sell shares when all the best economic advisors were recommending against doing so.

    A.   conservative
    B.   maverick
    C.   investor
    D.   Tory
    E.   moderate

5. The clothes she designs for men are conservative, but her fashions for women are more _____.

A. liberal
B. flamboyant
C. tasteful
D. expensive
E. conventional

6. His _____ protests against elephant poaching, an illegal but enormously _____ pursuit, put the warden at risk.

A. vigorous . . . unpopular
B. realistic . . . costly
C. unregarded . . . profitable
D. outspoken . . . lucrative
E. tactful . . . popular

7. Although it is _____ that scientists will discover even smaller particles, we have theoretical reasons to believe that we _____ or are very close to a knowledge of nature's ultimate building blocks.

A. unlikely . . . have misapprehended
B. uncertain . . . have approached
C. possible . . . have reached
D. probable . . . have avoided
E. moot . . . have acquired

8. Contrary to several sports writers' opinions, Valdez is neither _____ nor _____, but an affable and articulate young man.

A. sullen . . . winsome
B. genial . . . quiet
C. morose . . . reticent
D. gracious . . . impolite
E. aggressive . . . well spoken

9. In 1900, Spanish operatic composers faced a problem of language, for if works were not written in Italian, singers of international stature _____ to sing them.

A. refused
B. hoped
C. vocalized
D. desired
E. preferred

10. The reason for reduced spending on arms throughout the world is not _____, but _____, not a change in thinking, but a shortage of money.

A. ideological . . . economic
B. personal . . . political
C. pacifist . . . practical
D. local . . . universal
E. liberal . . . conservative

GO ON TO THE NEXT PAGE

Directions: Questions follow the passage below. Using only the stated or implied information in the passage and in its introduction, if any, answer the questions.

Questions 11–12 are based on the following passage.

Native American oral tradition includes legends, trickster tales, and "coup" stories. Legends differ from myths in that they arise from historical events and are exaggerated over time. (In American folk-
(5) lore, Daniel Boone supposedly could kill a bear with his bare hands.) A common Native American figure is Trickster, who takes on different shapes, depending on a tribe's location—for example, Coyote in the Southwest, Raven in the Northwest,
(10) and Jay or Wolverine in Canada. Trickster tales are used, depending on tribal tradition, to instruct, inspire, entertain or present a culture hero who may save the world. "Coup" stories are warriors' tales of their brave deeds in battle. These warriors are also
(15) culture heroes, but the truth of a "coup" story must be verified by other warriors who were present.

11. The sentence in parentheses in lines 4–6 is included primarily to

  A. provide for the reader a familiar example of a legend.
  B. add humor to the passage.
  C. suggest the similarity between Trickster and Daniel Boone.
  D. show the difference between legend and "coup" stories.
  E. explain the relationship between American folklore and Native American oral tradition.

12. According to information in the passage, which of the following statements is accurate?

  A. Legends are more important to Native Americans than myths.
  B. Trickster varies in form from location to location, but the tales serve the same purposes.
  C. Myths and legends are designed to entertain, whereas "coup" stories are used to instruct.
  D. "Coup" stories are more exciting and interesting than legends because they are true.
  E. The oldest form in the Native American tradition is the myth.

Questions 13–14 are based on the following passage.

At the outset of the Civil War, the North possessed a large population, a superior rail system, a greater industrial capacity, greater capital assets, and a larger food-production capability than did the
(5) South. Despite the North's apparent economic superiority, the South did possess a few military advantages. Among them were fighting a defensive war on their home ground and an established military tradition. Most of the leaders of the pre-War army
(10) were from the South, whereas the North had to train a new military leadership.

13. The final sentence of the paragraph

  A. supports the contention that most of the talent in the United States is concentrated in the South.
  B. hints that the North found its military leaders in the South.
  C. criticizes the North for entering the war without trained leadership.
  D. supports the statement that the South had an established military tradition.
  E. indicates that the South should have won the war.

14. The author implies which of the following points in the passage?

  A. The North didn't have an economic advantage at the end of the war.
  B. Previous to the beginning of the war, the South was already fighting another war and seasoning its leaders.
  C. Almost all the banks in the United States were located in the North.
  D. Military advantages are much more important that economic advantages.
  E. The North had a greater capacity for enduring a prolonged conflict.

Questions 15–16 are based on the following passage.

In the middle of the 20th century, as television became more and more popular, pundits predicted that the new medium would be instrumental in promoting greater understanding among the people of
(5) the world. If war correspondents could show pictures of the horror and devastation of war, surely nations would renounce violence. If viewers were shown the lives of average people torn apart by conflict, surely they would insist that their leaders
(10) make peace. Television, they predicted, would increase our knowledge and understanding, and by the year 2000 the world would be free from war, and its inhabitants would be better educated, more tolerant, and happier than ever before in history.

15. This paragraph is most likely the introduction to a(n)

    A. account of the increasing popularity of television.

    B. recounting of the early days of television.

    C. criticism of an overly optimistic view of television.

    D. questioning of the value of "reality" television.

    E. study of the limitations of print journalism.

16. The pundits of line 2 have assumed that

    A. the nature of man is essentially unchanging.

    B. television would replace film as the most popular form of entertainment.

    C. a television image is more powerful than a voice on the radio.

    D. there is no scale to measure degrees of happiness in men.

    E. television is a more democratic medium than print journalism.

Questions 17–28 are based on the following passage.

Acid rain, in the past half decade, has been added to the technological world's litany of fears. Like carbon dioxide, it is an unintended by-product of the Industrial Revolution. Evidence strongly
(5) suggests that pollutants in the atmosphere are acidifying rains, lakes, and streams.

The problem is not well understood. It is not even well named. The words would sound less sinister if it were commonly known that all rains and
(10) snows are naturally acidic. A substance's acidity is measured on the pH scale, in which 7 is perfectly neutral, neither acidic nor alkaline. Speaking very

roughly, the average pH of rain in nature—though
(15) it varies from place to place on the globe—is thought to be 5.6, which is slightly acidic.

In many parts of the industrial world, however, and in forested country far downwind of factory country, the pH of rains and snows is much lower.
(20) Rainfall in the eastern United States is currently estimated by the Environmental Protection Agency to be about pH 4.5. The pH scale is logarithmic, which means that as one counts down the scale, each integer is 10 times more acidic than normal.
(25) And they often become worse. "One long rainfall in the autumn of 1978 holds a dubious national record," environmentalist and writer John Luoma reports in his book *Troubled Skies, Troubled Waters.* "Instruments registered values less than pH
(30) 2, a level six to eight times more acidic than vinegar and some five thousand times more acidic than normal rain." The pollutants responsible for this increase are chiefly sulfur dioxide and the oxides of nitrogen. Swirled and cooked together with other
(35) gases and chemicals in the atmosphere, they can combine to form, among other things, sulfuric acid, which then falls on our country's soil and gathers in our lakes. Those lakes most at risk are in territory that was scraped clean of topsoil during the last ad-
(40) vances and retreats of the ice age. In the great chain of wilderness lakes that extends from northern Minnesota into Canada, in the Appalachians, and in much of Scandinavia, the ice scoured right down to the bedrock, and the new soil that has collected
(45) there is still quite thin. These regions are poor in the kind of natural alkaline rock, like limestone, that elsewhere helps to neutralize acid rain. Many of their lakes have been greatly acidified, altering their chemistry in complex ways that are only be-
(50) ginning to be understood. Fish in these lakes have died off. The water is eerily clear and clean, because in it so little life survives.

Ironically, part of the problem is an engineering feat that was once seen as the problem's solution.
(55) Coal-burning plants such as Kyger Creek, and the General James M. Gavin plant, both in Cheshire, Ohio, have built huge smokestacks (Gavin's is over 1,000 feet high) to loft their emissions of sulfur dioxide and nitrogen oxides high into the atmos-
(60) phere and keep these wastes from sickening their neighbors in Cheshire. The gases are borne extraordinary distances in the upper atmosphere, where they have plenty of time and space to recombine into sulfuric acid, which then falls thousands of
(65) miles from Kyger Creek and Gavin. Tall stacks help convert acid rain from a local to an environmental problem.

GO ON TO THE NEXT PAGE

Environmentalists and industrialists agree that acid rain is poorly understood and must be studied (70) further. But they disagree about what to do in the meantime. Some argue for several kinds of preventive action now. For instance, expensive "scrubbers" could be installed immediately by plants such as Kyger Creek and Gavin to clean sulfur (75) dioxides from the stacks' emissions. But many other people—including most of those who would have to pay to install the scrubbers—think the expense premature. The issue has as many sides as any in climatology. Some of the chemical emis- (80) sions in question even make good fertilizer. Notes climatologist Reid Bryson of the University of Wisconsin, "It may be the old saying about a silver lining to every cloud—but here in Wisconsin, when they cleaned up the sulfur emissions from one of (85) our local power plants, the farmers in the area had to start adding sulfur to their fields."

Though the debate continues, Jon Luoma says, "the difficulties in the way of reducing acid rain are not so much scientific as political."

17. The second paragraph describes acid rain as "not even well named" because

A. rain is naturally acidic.
B. no liquids are perfectly neutral.
C. some rains are alkaline.
D. the public cannot understand the meaning of the phrase.
E. the phrase makes acid rain appear to be a serious problem.

18. The first sentence of the third paragraph refers to "forested country far downwind of factory country" as having rains and snows of low pH because

A. industrial pollution travels upwind.
B. the pH scale is logarithmic.
C. rainfall is heavier in forested country.
D. all rainfall is acidic.
E. pollution from factories is blown here by winds.

19. From the information in the third paragraph, it can be inferred that the pH of vinegar is probably

A. 2
B. 4
C. 6
D. 7
E. 8

20. In the third paragraph, the phrase "a dubious national record" is best taken to mean a

A. record not scientifically confirmed.
B. record not generally accepted as a record.
C. record not expected to endure.
D. local rather than an international record.
E. record not worth achieving.

21. Of the following, which would be the most alkaline?

A. A liquid with a pH of 3
B. A liquid with a pH of 5
C. A liquid with a pH of 7
D. A liquid with a pH of 9
E. A liquid with a pH of 11

22. The passage suggests that an area with limestone may be harmed less by acid rain because

A. no rain will run off into lakes and streams.
B. streams will be more abundant and faster flowing.
C. the limestone may neutralize the acid.
D. the limestone will absorb less water than other rocks.
E. limestone is a natural by-product of coal burning.

23. As it is used in line 51, the word "eerily" means

A. scrupulously
B. immaculately
C. strangely
D. partially
E. ostensibly

24. In line 53, the adverb "ironically" is used because

A. the smokestacks failed to protect Cheshire.
B. the result is the opposite of what was expected.
C. the builders of the smokestacks failed to consider the problems of acid rain.
D. smokestacks cannot solve the problems of acid rain.
E. engineers, rather than scientists, were responsible for the construction.

25. Near the end of the fifth paragraph, the reference to "the old saying about a silver lining to every cloud" is used because

    A. some effects of acid rain are beneficial.

    B. there is hope that someday acid rain problems will be eliminated.

    C. acid rain falls far from the source of pollution.

    D. the solution to the problem of acid rain is political, not scientific.

    E. lakes in some regions are now clear and clean because of acid rain.

26. The chief antagonists in the debate about how to deal with causes of acid rain are most likely to be

    A. industrial polluters and farmers.

    B. industrialists and environmentalists.

    C. the federal government and private landowners.

    D. farmers whose soils benefit from acid rain and farmers whose soils do not.

    E. foresters and fishermen.

27. The passage implies that acid rain could be reduced by all of the following EXCEPT

    A. emission controls on smokestacks.

    B. reduction of coal burning in industry.

    C. reduction of sulfur dioxide in the atmosphere.

    D. reduction of the use of sulfur as fertilizer.

    E. reduction of oxides of nitrogen in the atmosphere.

28. That "the difficulties in the way of reducing acid rain are not so much scientific as political" is due chiefly to the fact that

    A. scientists do not yet fully understand acid rain.

    B. the side effects of acid rain can be beneficial as well as harmful.

    C. many scientists believe preventive measures should be undertaken immediately.

    D. acid rain falls on areas at great distances from the source of pollution.

    E. the cost of cleaning sulfur dioxides from smokestacks may be paid by the federal government.

Practice Test 2

IF YOU FINISH BEFORE TIME IS CALLED, CHECK YOUR WORK ON THIS SECTION ONLY. DO NOT WORK ON ANY OTHER SECTION IN THE TEST.

Section 10: Writing—Multiple Choice

Time: 10 Minutes

15 Questions

In this section, choose the best answer for each question and blacken the corresponding space on the answer sheet.

Directions: The following questions test correctness and effective expression. In selecting the answer, pay attention to grammar, diction, sentence structure, and punctuation. In the following questions, part or all of each sentence is underlined. The A answer repeats the underlined portion of the original sentence, while the next four offer alternatives. Choose the answer that best expresses the meaning of the original sentence, and at the same time is grammatically correct and stylistically superior. The correct choice should be clear, unambiguous, and concise.

EXAMPLE:

The forecaster predicted <u>rain and the sky was clear.</u>

- **A.** rain and the sky was clear.
- **B.** rain but the sky was clear.
- **C.** rain the sky was clear.
- **D.** rain, but the sky was clear.
- **E.** rain being as the sky was clear.

The correct answer is D.

---

1. The operas of Mozart are very frequently performed in <u>Austria; Verdi operas</u> are the favorites in Italy.

- **A.** Austria; Verdi operas
- **B.** Austria Verdi operas
- **C.** Austria, although Verdi operas
- **D.** Austria; while Verdi operas
- **E.** Austria the operas of Verdi

2. The book argues that *Othello* is the better play <u>because of its construction, which is more careful that that of *King Lear.*</u>

- **A.** because of its construction, which is more careful than that of *King Lear.*
- **B.** because its construction, which is more careful than *King Lear*'s.
- **C.** because of its construction, more careful than *King Lear*'s construction.
- **D.** because it is more carefully constructed than *King Lear.*
- **E.** because its construction is more careful than *King Lear.*

3. A valuable device taking advantage of the remarkable sensitivity of cesium has just been <u>constructed, and scientists have known of this capability for many years.</u>

- **A.** constructed, and scientists have known of this capability for many years.
- **B.** constructed, which scientists have known about for many years.
- **C.** constructed, although scientists have known of this capability for many years.
- **D.** constructed, and this capability has been known to scientists for many years.
- **E.** constructed, a capability about which scientists have known for many years.

4. The doctor visits her patients in intensive care once every three hours, <u>which can be decreased</u> as danger lessens.

- **A.** which can be decreased
- **B.** a schedule that can be altered
- **C.** which can be altered
- **D.** to be decreased
- **E.** and can be altered

5. <u>Enjoying the look of a movie musical—its sets, costumes, and dances—is</u> as important as enjoying its songs.

   A   Enjoying the look of a movie musical—its sets, costumes, and dances—is

   B.   The look of a movie musical—its sets, costumes, and dances—is

   C.   The look of a movie musical—its sets, costumes, and dances—are

   D.   In a movie musical, the sets costumes and dances are

   E.   The sets, costumes and dances of a movie musical are

6. Ardmore has been cheated several times <u>because of his being of a trusting nature.</u>

   A.   because of his being of a trusting nature.

   B.   because of his trustworthiness.

   C.   because his nature is trusting.

   D.   because he is trusting.

   E.   being trusting by nature.

7. A very old plant in our gardens, <u>the cornflower appears in paintings made as early as the fourth century.</u>

   A.   the cornflower appears in paintings made as early as the fourth century.

   B.   cornflowers appear in paintings made as early as the fourth century.

   C.   fourth-century-made paintings show cornflowers.

   D.   paintings of cornflowers were made as early as the fourth century.

   E.   paintings of cornflowers made as early as the fourth century.

8. <u>Tomoka Seki studied ballet in France for two years, and now she is</u> studying Balinese dancing and Asian art.

   A.   Tomoka Seki studied ballet in France for two years, and now she is

   B.   Having studied ballet in France for two years, Tomoka Seki is now

   C.   Ballet was studied in France for two years by Tomoka Seki who is now

   D.   She studied ballet in France for two years, and now Tomoka Seki is

   E.   For two years, Tomoka Seki studies ballet in France now she is

9. Struggling with every word, <u>the essay was completed by John</u> at the expense of several hours sleep.

   A.   the essay was completed by John

   B.   John completed the essay

   C.   the essay John completed

   D.   the essay completed itself

   E.   the essay itself was completed

10. <u>Like the mountains that are found in Switzerland,</u> the mountains of Colorado and Wyoming keep their snows for ten months.

   A.   Like the mountains that are found in Switzerland,

   B.   Like the mountains located in Switzerland,

   C.   Like the mountains found in Switzerland,

   D.   Like those in Switzerland,

   E.   Like mountains which are Swiss,

11. <u>In the *Trenton News,* they report that</u> there are as many as 10,000 homeless people in Washington, D.C.

   A.   In the *Trenton News,* they report that

   B.   In the *Trenton News,* it is reported that

   C.   In the *Trenton News,* they issued the report that

   D.   The *Trenton News* reports that

   E.   The *Trenton News* makes the report that

GO ON TO THE NEXT PAGE

12. Paris Mayor Jacques Chirac after a multi-million dollar face-lift dedicated the refurbished Champs Elysees.

- **A.** Paris Mayor Jacques Chirac after a multi-million dollar face-lift dedicated the refurbished Champs Elysees.
- **B.** After a multi-million dollar face-lift, Jacques Chirac, mayor of Paris, dedicated the refurbished Champs Elysees.
- **C.** A multi-million dollar face-lift completed, Paris Mayor Jacques Chirac dedicated the refurbished Champs Elysees.
- **D.** After Jacques Chirac, Paris Mayor, completed a multi-million dollar face-lift, he dedicated the refurbished Champs Elysees.
- **E.** Paris Mayor Jacques Chirac dedicated the refurbished Champs Elysees after a multi-million dollar face-lift.

13. Completing the film on time was as satisfying to the director of *Beneath the Sea,* as mastering the underwater camera techniques.

- **A.** as mastering
- **B.** as his being able to master
- **C.** as it was when mastering
- **D.** than the mastery of
- **E.** the fact that he mastered

14. Lured by the Florida sun, Canadians by the thousands descend annually into St. Petersburg each year.

- **A.** Canadians by the thousands descend annually into St. Petersburg each year.
- **B.** St. Petersburg receives thousands of Canadians each year.
- **C.** St. Petersburg annually receives thousands of Canadians.
- **D.** Canadians by the thousands descend on St. Petersburg each year.
- **E.** thousands of Canadians descend into St. Petersburg each year.

15. At the door of the kitchen, he stopped to wipe the mud from his boots, ran a comb through his hair, and knocks loudly at the door.

- **A.** and knocks loudly at the door.
- **B.** and knocks loud at the door.
- **C.** and knocked loudly at the door.
- **D.** and then knocks loudly on the door.
- **E.** knocking at the door loudly.

IF YOU FINISH BEFORE TIME IS CALLED, CHECK YOUR WORK ON THIS SECTION ONLY. DO NOT WORK ON ANY OTHER SECTION IN THE TEST.

STOP

Scoring Practice Test 2

Answer Key for Practice Test 2

Section 2: Writing—Multiple Choice

1. D	10. B	19. C	28. D
2. C	11. D	20. D	29. A
3. B	12. E	21. E	30. B
4. E	13. D	22. A	31. E
5. D	14. C	23. B	32. C
6. C	15. E	24. B	33. C
7. E	16. C	25. A	34. E
8. D	17. D	26. C	
9. B	18. B	27. E	

Section 3: Critical Reading

1. A	8. B	15. E	22. C
2. E	9. D	16. A	23. B
3. C	10. B	17. A	24. E
4. B	11. C	18. D	25. C
5. D	12. A	19. C	26. C
6. B	13. B	20. D	27. E
7. C	14. C	21. D	28. A

Section 4: Mathematics

1. D	6. B	11. D	16. A
2. B	7. C	12. C	17. A
3. D	8. D	13. B	18. E
4. C	9. D	14. C	19. C
5. B	10. A	15. A	20. E

Section 5: Critical Reading

1. A	8. E	15. B	22. D
2. C	9. A	16. D	23. A
3. E	10. C	17. E	24. C
4. C	11. A	18. A	25. A
5. E	12. B	19. D	26. C
6. A	13. D	20. B	27. E
7. A	14. C	21. B	28. C

Section 6: Mathematics

1. E	6. B	11. 5/8	16. 45
2. D	7. A	12. 14	17. 7/12
3. C	8. C	13. 1/6	18. 50
4. C	9. C	14. 93.5	19. 100
5. C	10. C	15. 527	20. 264

Section 7: Critical Reading

1. C	5. B	9. D	13. D
2. E	6. B	10. A	14. B
3. C	7. D	11. E	
4. E	8. C	12. A	

Section 8: Mathematics

1. A	5. D	9. D	13. D
2. C	6. B	10. D	14. B
3. E	7. C	11. C	15. B
4. A	8. C	12. A	

Section 9: Critical Reading

1. E	8. C	15. C	22. C
2. D	9. A	16. C	23. C
3. B	10. A	17. A	24. B
4. B	11. A	18. E	25. A
5. B	12. B	19. A	26. B
6. D	13. D	20. E	27. D
7. C	14. E	21. E	28. D

Section 10: Writing—Multiple Choice

1. A	5. A	9. B	13. A
2. D	6. D	10. D	14. D
3. C	7. A	11. D	15. C
4. B	8. B	12. E	

Analyzing Your Test Results

The charts on the following pages should be used to carefully analyze your results and spot your strengths and weaknesses. The complete process of analyzing each subject area and each individual problem should be completed for each practice test. These results should then be reexamined for trends in types of errors (repeated errors) or poor results in specific subject areas. *This reexamination and analysis is of tremendous importance to you in assuring maximum test preparation benefit.*

Reviewing the Essay

Have an English teacher, tutor, or someone else with good writing skills read and evaluate your essay using the Essay Checklist given below. Have your reader evaluate the complete essay as good, average, or marginal. Note that your paper would actually be scored from 1 to 6 by two trained readers (actual total score 2–12). But since we are trying only for a rough approximation, the simple good, average, or marginal overall evaluation will give you a general feeling for your score range.

Use the following checklist to evaluate your essay:

- Does the essay focus on the topic and complete the assigned task?
  (Circle one: Excellent   Average   Poor)

- Is the essay well organized, well developed, and consistent in argument?
  (Circle one: Excellent   Average   Poor)

- Does the essay use specific supporting details?
  (Circle one: Excellent   Average   Poor)

- Does the writing use correct grammar, usage, punctuation, and spelling?
  (Circle one: Excellent   Average   Poor)

- Is the handwriting legible?
  (Circle one: Excellent   Average   Poor)

Critical Reading Analysis Sheet

Section 3	Possible	Completed	Right	Wrong
Sentence Completion	10			
Short Reading Passages	4			
Long Reading Passages	14			
Subtotal	28			
Section 5	Possible	Completed	Right	Wrong
Sentence Completion	9			
Short Critical Reading Passages	7			
Long Reading Passages	12			
Subtotal	28			

(continued)

Critical Reading Analysis Sheet *(continued)*

Section 7	Possible	Completed	Right	Wrong
Long Reading Passages	14			
Subtotal	14			
Section 9	Possible	Completed	Right	Wrong
Sentence Completion	10			
Short Reading Passages	6			
Long Reading Passages	12			
Subtotal	28			
Overall Critical Reading Totals	98			

Note: Only 3 Critical Reading sections (approximately 70 questions) count toward your actual score on the new SAT.

Mathematics Analysis Sheet

Section 4	Possible	Completed	Right	Wrong
Multiple Choice	20			
Subtotal	20			
Section 6	Possible	Completed	Right	Wrong
Multiple Choice	10			
Grid-Ins	10			
Subtotal	20			
Section 8	Possible	Completed	Right	Wrong
Multiple Choice	15			
Subtotal	15			
Overall Math Totals	55			

Writing—Multiple-Choice Analysis Sheet

Section 2	Possible	Completed	Right	Wrong
Improving Sentences	7			
Identifying Sentence Errors	19			
Improving Paragraphs	8			
Subtotal	34			
Section 10	**Possible**	**Completed**	**Right**	**Wrong**
Improving Sentences	15			
Subtotal	15			
Overall Writing— Multiple-Choice Totals	49			

Analysis/Tally Sheet for Problems Missed

One of the most important parts of test preparation is analyzing *why* you missed a problem so that you can reduce the number of mistakes. Now that you have taken the practice test and checked your answers, carefully tally your mistakes by marking them in the proper column.

Reason for Mistakes					
	Total Missed	Simple Mistake	Misread Problem	Lack of Knowledge	Lack of Time
Section 3: Critical Reading					
Section 5: Critical Reading					
Section 7: Critical Reading					
Section 9: Critical Reading					
Subtotal					
Section 4: Mathematics					
Section 6: Mathematics					
Section 8: Mathematics					
Subtotal					
Section 2: Writing—Multiple Choice					
Section 10: Writing—Multiple Choice					
Subtotal					
Total Reading, Math, and Writing					

Reviewing the preceding data should help you determine *why* you are missing certain problems. Now that you've pinpointed the type of error, compare it to other practice tests to spot other common mistakes.

Complete Answers and Explanations for Practice Test 2

Section 2: Writing—Multiple Choice

Improving Sentences

1. **D.** The subject of the dependent clause that begins this sentence is the pronoun "they." What should follow is a noun to explain who the "they" are. It is not "cheeses" or "cheese" as in A, B, and C. D correctly puts "the colonists" first in the main clause, and also gets rid of the passive verbs of A, B, and C. D is preferable to E, because it avoids the separation of the modifying phrase and what it modifies.

2. **C.** The original sentence is not grammatically wrong, but it is wordy. It repeats the preposition "about," and uses the passive voice. B is even wordier, though it does get rid of the passive. D uses the fewest words, but it is ungrammatical. The pronoun should refer to the plural "sicknesses"; it appears to refer to the singular "society." E repeats the "about" needlessly; all other things being equal, "remedies" is probably better than "remedying" since it is a noun like "sicknesses," rather than a gerund.

3. **B.** There are two complete sentences here with no punctuation or conjunction to join them. The easiest way to correct the run-on sentence is with the semicolon. E is not wrong, but it is wordier.

4. **E.** The original sentence has a subject, but no main verb, since "lead" is in a dependent clause. C has no verb or verbals. B and D have participles, that is, adjectives, not verbs. Only E is a complete sentence with its main verb ("will lead") in the future tense.

5. **D.** This sentence uses a pronoun ("this") without a specific antecedent; "this" refers to the general idea of the whole first clause. To use a different pronoun, as B, C, and E do, without supplying the missing specific antecedent does not correct the sentence. Only D solves the problem. The specific antecedent for the pronoun "that" is the noun "practice."

6. **C.** The original sentence begins with a second person subject ("you"), but switches to the third person ("it"). Only C keeps "you" as the subject of the main clause, and also uses a verb in the active voice. B, D, and E all use the passive.

7. **E.** As soon as you see a sentence that begins, like this one, with a participle, look to see if it dangles. Who is carrying the warm water? Not the "sparrows." Not the "groups." The only possible right answer is E.

Identifying Sentence Errors

8. **D.** The sentence begins with two gerunds and a main verb all in the present tense. To keep the sequence of verb tenses consistent, the last verb must be the present "is," not the future "will be."

9. **B.** The choice of pronoun is in error here. Since the pronoun refers to a man, "who" rather than "which" is the right word.

10. **B.** This is the subject-verb agreement error, disguised by the separation of the singular subject "one" and the interrupting plurals "of the sixty-five students majoring in economics." The right verb is the singular "was."

11. **D.** Since "wouldn't" contains a negative, the second "no" makes a double negative. The corrected sentence can read "would be no" or "wouldn't be any."

12. **E.** You should think twice about the case of the pronouns here, but remember that "who" and "whom" are not likely to appear on the test. The "who" here is right. The "she" is also right. The verb "to be" does not take an object. Don't forget that each test will contain several sentences with no error.

13. **D.** The sentence confuses an idiom, using an infinitive ("to follow") where the conventional usage calls for the prepositional phrase ("regularity in following").

14. **C.** This is a pronoun agreement error. The sentence begins with the singular noun "a person," but instead of saying "by himself" or "by herself" switches to the plural "themselves."

15. E. The sentence is correct. Though the verb tenses vary, they present a logical time scheme.

16. C. Here the verb tenses are not coherent. Two of the verbs ("paints" and "spirits") are in the present tense, but "sealed" for no reason is a past tense.

17. D. This is another pronoun agreement error, easy to miss even though the singular noun ("plant") and the erring plural pronoun ("themselves") are together.

18. B. The idiom is "neither...nor," not the "neither...and" we have here.

19. C. The use of "destruct" as the main verb is an error of diction. A better choice would be "destroy."

20. D. The comparison that ends this sentence is needlessly doubled. Since "lower" means "more low," the "more" should be deleted.

21. E. This sentence appears to be testing parallelism, but the parallel construction "not to please" with "but to impress" is right. The future tenses of the verbs are also correct.

22. A. The comparison here is not logical. Monet (a painter) is compared to paintings. The correct sentence should read "Unlike Monet's."

23. B. With the "neither... nor" construction here, the subject is a singular (either "nurse" or "I"). The verb should be "was able."

24. B. In this context, the correct idiom meaning "accused of" is "charged with," rather than "charged for."

25. A. With the plural "There are," the noun must also be plural to agree; "the requirement" should be "requirements."

26. C. The antecedent of the pronoun "one" is the plural "westerners"; the pronoun should be "they."

Improving Paragraphs

27. E. The problem with this sentence is the tense of the verb. The other two sentences in the paragraph that begin with "It is disproved" deal with situations in the past that continue to occur: dishonest politicians are still elected, and juries still make mistakes. For this reason, the use of the present tense is correct. Hitler, however, is no longer elected, so the verb should be in the past tense. Option E corrects the tense, and at the same time keeps the rhetorical balance of repeating "It...disproved."

28. D. Sentence 4 is an anticlimax. It is vague (What high school? What happened?) and more relevant to the next paragraph. The three other examples in this paragraph are more specific and more cogent.

29. A. The deliberate repetition of the phrase "it is disproved" is an effective way of emphasizing how often the majority may be wrong. There are no instances of the other choices in the paragraph.

30. B. Though several of these sentences are not wrong, B, with its subject-verb-object word order, is preferable to the expletive "there was" of A or the passive verb of D. In C and E, the "they" is a vague pronoun, with no specific antecedent.

31. E. There are two problems in these sentences. The phrase "the fastest way" is too far away from "trying to get" which it modifies. The "this" in the second sentence is a vague pronoun. Option E corrects both by moving "the fastest way" ahead of "by using" and by eliminating "this."

32. C. The original version of sentence 2 uses a pronoun ("this") with no specific antecedent. Options A, B, D, and E may move the "this" to different parts of the sentence, but unless there is a specific noun for the pronoun to refer to, the error is still there. Add a word like "tendency," "problem," "attempt," or "effort" and the pronoun is no longer vague.

33. C. The original version uses verbs for nouns in a series that lacks parallelism. The best choice must make all three elements parallel; here, C uses three infinitives ("to earn," "to get," and "to live").

34. E. If you think only about today, you cannot be thinking about tomorrow, so to say so is redundant. The use of "but" is preferable to "and" in this context.

Section 3: Critical Reading

Sentence Completion

1. **A.** The first noun could be any of the five except "similarities," although at first glance, A "differences" looks like the best. The second blank needs a verb that follows from "understanding," and A "appreciate" is the closest to the earlier word. Choices B and C make little sense with the fabric metaphor (how can one "resolve" or "combat" a "fabric"?).

2. **E.** The phrase "facts, not wishful thinking" is parallel to "realities, not _____," so you need a word that is opposite to "realities" and similar in effect to "wishful thinking." Only "myths" describes something that contrasts with "realities."

3. **C.** The verb "fell" tells you that the first noun must mean "decline" or fall. Choices B "decrease," C "decline," and E "drop" are all possibilities. The adjective describing this economy must also denote falling, so you can eliminate "steady" B and "booming" E, but C "sagging" is appropriate.

4. **B.** The first adjective must be consistent with the information that the skills have won over both liberals and conservatives. Choices A, B, and D would fit, and "organizational" C or "intimidating" E would not. The second blank requires an adverb that parallels or accords with "openly." Both "equivocally" (ambiguously) and "deceptively" are clearly the opposite of what is needed. The correct choice is B "frankly."

5. **D.** The missing adjective here should describe the actions of a slanderer. The noun "dissemination" means spreading abroad; the action of spreading a "libel" or "slander" is not well described by any of these choices except by D "irresponsible."

6. **B.** The final adjective must describe songs that satirize love as "foolish" or "compromised." The best choice is "antiromantic." The four other choices conflict with the assertion of the first half of the sentence.

7. **C.** If signaling the horse by the voice is part of a "clever ruse," the missing adverb must be something signifying "secretly" or "without being observed." Only C "covertly" has this meaning. The verb that fills the second blank must mean something like expose, and C "unmask" fits the requirement.

8. **B.** The needed word here is a strong way of saying "changeable" or "unpredictable." Of the five choices, "mercurial" (volatile, "changeable") is clearly the best.

9. **D.** The sentence presents two related definitions and is a straightforward test of vocabulary. A "cynic" distrusts "human goodness"; a "misanthrope" hates "people in general." A "pessimist" looks on the dark side of things and expects the worst; an "ingrate" is an ungrateful person. A "siren" is a temptress; a "tyrant" is an absolute ruler, usually a cruel or despotic one. An "altruist" is unselfishly concerned for the welfare of others; an "anarchist" opposes all forms of government. A "philanthropist" is a generous lover of humankind; a "misogynist" is a person who hates women.

10. **B.** If the doctor must be brave to continue her work, the missing verb must describe something to be resisted. The best choices are "vilified," B, and "attacked," E. The result of the brave work is acceptance by other doctors of the "probability" or the "tenets" of her theories. "Tenets" usually refers to doctrines or principles of a school of thought and is not quite right in this context. But both "vilified" (reviled, defamed) and "probability" fit well.

Short Reading Passages

11. **C.** From the passage it is clear that words that have only one meaning, such as "wrathful," are called "highly determined." All of the other answers here can have more than one meaning.

12. **A.** See lines 3–10. B is simply wrong; "cool" can be used as a verb, noun, and adjective. Although, according to the passage, some linguists suggest that "cool" has lasted because of its connection to jazz, nothing indicates that jazz has "increased in popularity," C. E, which is the second best answer, may be related to the point in the passage that "cool" has lasted because it is easy to say. However, "easy to say" and "one syllable" are not the same thing.

13. B. The word "individualistic" is a clue, as is the phrase "unabashed heroic ethos" in line 15. The "heroic ethos" is the only specific value system mentioned in the paragraph. Nothing suggests that an "individualistic value system" is associated with warfare, combat, or the Greek political system, which in fact is not considered in the passage (A, C, D). E is too vague.

14. C. A paradox is a statement that is seemingly contradictory but perhaps true. Here, the paradox is that while writers viewed Homer as the master and admired his great epics, they also targeted his works by parodying them (that is, creating mock epics) and using them for comic effect. The phrase does not mock the heroic ethos, and no critical point of view is presented (D, E). It also doesn't emphasize Homer's superiority, A. B might seem a tempting choice, but there is no "unsolved puzzle," only the observation of a paradox.

Long Reading Passages

15. E. As it is used here, "want" means need or poverty rather than a wish or desire for something.

16. A. Franklin's first paragraph makes the point that procuring wealth will secure virtue because it is much harder for a person in need to resist a temptation to act dishonestly than for one who has no worry about the next meal. Although Franklin would no doubt encourage self knowledge, education, and reason, the passage specifically cites wealth as security for virtue.

17. A. Although Franklin was willing to print personal abuse for a fee, he insisted on doing so separately from his newspaper. He did so because he believed in his obligation to the subscribers of his newspaper, who had no concern with private altercations. He would "disagree" only with the first of these three statements.

18. D. Franklin believed that his obligation to his subscribers required him to print material that was useful or entertaining, materials worth their subscription fees.

19. C. Although Franklin is remembered as a statesman, scientist, and inventor, his chief means of support, as this passage implies, was as a printer.

20. D. The first and last paragraphs refer to Franklin's wish to make his publications "entertaining and useful" (line 5) and "useful or entertaining" (lines 56–57).

21. D. The word "inherent" means innate, inborn, existing in something as a basic characteristic. The problem is "inherent" because the mirror had been ground to the wrong shape.

22. C. If the mirror had been ground correctly, it would have concentrated 70 percent rather than 15 percent of the light—that is, 55 percent more than the present 15 percent.

23. B. The passage refers to sudden temperature changes when the telescope passes in and out of the earth's shadow.

24. E. The passage makes no mention of defects in the lens of the telescope.

25. C. As it is used here, the verb means to apply (oneself) to, to deal with, to encounter.

26. C. A telescope's sensitivity is its ability to respond to light (rather than to sound), and the resolution, which can be computer-enhanced, is the ability to make the image that it detects visible and clear. Of the five choices, C offers the best definitions.

27. E. The last paragraph deals chiefly with the telescope's success with objects within the solar system. This success is sufficient to rebut media claims of failure because Hubble makes it possible for astronomers to see the planets well whenever they want to do so.

28. A. The passage as a whole gives a balanced view of the "Hubble space telescope." It admits the disappointments and specifies several tasks that the instrument is not yet able to handle. But it also points out the areas in which the telescope has been successful—not "revolutionary," but useful to astronomers.

Section 4: Mathematics

1. **D.** The 4 pounds of steak would cost

$$4 \times \$3.89 = \$15.56$$

The change from a $20 bill would be

$$\begin{array}{r} \$20.00 \\ -15.56 \\ \hline \$\ 4.44 \end{array}$$

2. **B.** For a number to be divisible by 21, it must be divisible by 3 and by 7 because $21 = 3 \times 7$. Therefore, if a number is divisible by 7 but not by 21, it cannot be divisible by 3.

3. **D.**

$$.0039y = \frac{39}{10,000} \ y = 39$$
$$y = \frac{10,000}{39} \times 39$$
$$y = 10,000$$

Or, using your calculator, divide 39 by .0039.

4. **C.** Since $XY = YZ = 10$, $\triangle XYZ$ is an isosceles triangle and $\angle X = \angle Z$. $\angle Y = 84°$ because it forms a vertical angle with the given angle.

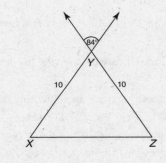

$$\angle X + \angle Y + \angle Z = 180°$$
$$\angle X + 84° + \angle Z = 180°$$
$$2(\angle Z) + 84° = 180°$$
$$2(\angle Z) = 96°$$
$$\angle Z = 48°$$

Therefore, the measure of $\angle Z = 48°$.

5. **B.** If $a = \sqrt{b}$ and $b = 81$, then $a = \sqrt{81}$ or $a = 9$. So the value of $\sqrt{a}$ is $\sqrt{9} = 3$.

6. **B.** II only. The arithmetic mean is the average (sum divided by number of items), or $6 + 2 + 10 + 2 + 5 = 25$ divided by $5 = 5$.

The median is the middle number after the numbers have been ordered: 2, 2, 5, 6, 10. The median is 5.

The mode is the most frequently appearing number: 2.

The range is the highest minus the lowest, or $10 - 2 = 8$.

Therefore, only II is true: The median (5) equals the mean (5).

7. C. Since three-fifths of the class are females, two-fifths of the class are males. Therefore, the ratio of males to females is

$$\frac{2}{5} \text{ to } \frac{3}{5} = \frac{\frac{2}{5}}{\frac{3}{5}}$$

$$= \frac{2}{5} \div \frac{3}{5}$$

$$= \frac{2}{5} \cdot \frac{5}{3}$$

$$= \frac{2}{3}$$

8. D. First change the equation to slope-intercept form $y = mx + b$, where m is the slope and b is the y intercept.

$$6x + y = 3$$
$$\underline{-6x \qquad\quad -6x}$$
$$y = 3 - 6x \quad \text{or} \quad -6x + 3$$

Next, you can see that in the equation $y = -6x + 3$, -6 is in the m position and is therefore the slope.

9. D. Breaking the figure into squares of side x by adding lines gives

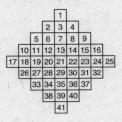

Remember that each square has area x^2. Then the total area is $41x^2$. Choices A, B, and E are not possible because area must be in square units.

10. A. Adding the two equations,

$$x - y = 15$$
$$\underline{3x + y = 13}$$
$$4x \qquad = 28$$
$$\frac{4x}{4} = \frac{28}{4}$$
$$x = 7$$

Since $x = 7$	or	Since $x = 7$
and $x - y = 15$		and $3x + y = 13$
$7 - y = 15$		$3(7) + y = 13$
$7 - 7 - y = 15 - 7$		$21 + y = 13$
$-y = 8$		$21 - 21 + y = 13 - 21$
$y = -8$		$y = -8$

Therefore, $x = 7$ and $y = -8$.

11. D. In isosceles $\triangle XYZ$, $\angle X = \angle Z$.

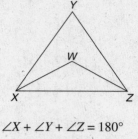

$$\angle X + \angle Y + \angle Z = 180°$$

$$\angle X + 80° + \angle Z = 180°$$

$$\angle X + \angle Z = 100°$$

$$\angle X = \angle Z = 50°$$

Since WX bisects $\angle YXZ$ and WZ bisects $\angle YZX$,

$$\angle YXW = \angle WXZ = \angle YZW = \angle WZX = 25°$$

Therefore, on $\triangle XWZ$,

$$\angle XWZ + \angle WXZ + \angle WZX = 180°$$

$$\angle XWZ + 25° + 25° = 180°$$

$$\angle XWZ + 50° = 180°$$

$$\angle XWZ = 130°$$

12. C.

$$(m + n)^2 = (m + n)(m + n)$$

$$= m^2 + mn + mn + n^2$$

$$= m^2 + 2mn + n^2$$

$$= (m^2 + n^2) + (2mn)$$

Since $m^2 + n^2 = 12$ and $mn = 9$,

$$(m^2 + n^2) + (2mn) = 12 + 2(9)$$

$$= 12 + 18$$

$$= 30$$

13. B. Adding any two of three consecutive positive integers greater than 1 will always be greater than the other integer. Therefore, II is true. The others cannot be determined because they depend on values and/or the order of x, y, and z.

14. C. Area of the square

$$= \frac{1}{2} \times \text{product of diagonals}$$

$$= \frac{1}{2} d_1 d_2$$

$$= \frac{1}{2} d^2 \ \left(\text{because } d_1 = d_2 \text{ in a square}\right)$$

Therefore,

$$\frac{1}{2} d^2 = 72$$

$$d^2 = 144$$

$$d = 12 \text{ feet}$$

15. A. Let $5x$ = first angle, $2x$ = second angle, and $5x - 2x = 3x$ = third angle. Since the sum of the angles in any triangle is $180°$,

$$5x + 2x + 3x = 180°$$
$$10x = 180°$$
$$\frac{10x}{10} = \frac{180°}{10}$$
$$x = 18°$$

Therefore,

$$5x = 90°$$
$$2x = 36°$$
$$3x = 54°$$

The smallest angle will have a measure of $36°$.

16. A.

$$(-2, 3) \oplus (4, -1) = [(-2)(4) - (3)(-1), (-2)(-1)]$$
$$= [(-8) - (-3), (2)]$$
$$= (-5, 2)$$

17. A. Let n = number of nickels, $3n$ = number of dimes, and $3n - 3$ = number of quarters. Since 25 coins are in the collection,

$$n + 3n + (3n - 3) = 25$$
$$7n - 3 = 25$$
$$7n = 28$$
$$n = 4 \text{ nickels} = \$0.20$$
$$3n = 12 \text{ dimes} = \$1.20$$
$$3n - 3 = 9 \text{ quarters} = \$2.25$$

Therefore, the total value of the collection is $\$0.20 + \$1.20 + \$2.25 = \$3.65$

18. E. Since arc YXZ is a semicircle, its measure is $180°$.

$$\text{arc } XZ = \text{arc } YXZ - \text{arc } YWX$$
$$= 180° - 100°$$
$$= 80°$$

Since an inscribed angle $= \frac{1}{2}$(intercepted arc),

$$\angle XYZ = \frac{1}{2} \text{ (arc } XZ)$$
$$= \frac{1}{2} (80°)$$
$$= 40°$$

Therefore, $\angle XYZ$ has a measure of $40°$.

19. C. Since $\sqrt{mn} = 10$, $mn = 100$, and the possible values for m and n would be

$$1 \text{ and } 100$$
$$2 \text{ and } 50$$
$$4 \text{ and } 25$$
$$5 \text{ and } 20$$
$$10 \text{ and } 10$$

Since none of these combinations yields $m + n = 50$, choice C is correct.

20. E. To find the y-intercepts, set $x = 0$ and solve for y.

$$2y^2 - 5(0^2) = 50$$
$$2y^2 = 50$$
$$\frac{2y^2}{2} = \frac{50}{2}$$
$$y^2 = 25$$
$$y = \pm\sqrt{25}$$
$$y = \pm 5$$

Section 5: Critical Reading

Sentence Completion

1. A. The informative phrase here is "mistakes we made last week or last year." These mistakes we understand by looking back, by "hindsight." None of the other choices fits the rest of the sentence so well.

2. C. The parallel phrases here are "something everyone possesses" and "imagination is not a gift _____ to poets." The right word must be the opposite of universal, since the word "not" precedes it. The best choice is "unique," different from all others. With "not," this is equivalent to "something everyone possesses."

3. E. The phrase "less is more" is not a "hope," a "question" (that would be "is less more?"), an "enigma" (riddle), or an "image." It is a "paradox," an apparent self-contradiction, since less *should* be less, not more.

4. C. Choices A, C, and D would seem to fit the first blank, but the second noun, which describes something the senator did that the president ignored, could be only B or C, and B has already been eliminated. Both of the nouns in C make very good sense in this context.

5. E. Since the action is described as stupid and indifferent, it cannot be something that has helped our resources, so we are left with two possible answers: "wasted" C or "squandered" E. The second blank must be a word meaning "ability; capacity" E makes good sense, but "failure" C does not.

6. A. Reports of "freewheeling" corporate spending are unlikely to be "favorable" or "encouraging," but choices A and B fit well, and C is a possibility. The "despite" at the beginning of the sentence tells us that the reports are not true, and the missing adverb should be very different from "freewheeling." Both B "unfairly" and C "secretly" contradict the "despite," but A makes good sense. The reports must be "lurid," that is, sensational or startling, and the adverb is "equitably," that is, fairly or even-handedly.

7. A. The first phrase tells us the crime will be described by an "understatement." Choices B, C, D, and E all call a crime a crime, but "peccadillo" suggests that stealing 4 million dollars is insignificant, a minor fault, a petty crime. This is "understatement."

8. E. The second adjective modifies "countries that have no savings at all," so it cannot be any of the words meaning rich (A, B, C, and D). The correct choice is "indigent," that is, poor. Although A, C, or E might have fit the first blank, choice E makes the most sense overall.

9. A. The sentence tells us that Pierce refused to read about positions different from his own. First, you need a noun to describe a quality of a man like this, and all of the answers except E are possibilities. The second blank calls for a word to go with "to travel" that will also fit this parochial, insular, bigoted, or narrow-minded man. The right answer must mean something like "failure" or refusal. Either A or E will do, but only A has the first word right.

Short Reading Passages

10. C. See lines 15–17. A is irrelevant to this passage, as is E. B is an overstatement, and the executions of Luddites were based on "machine breaking," not peaceful protesting, D.

11. A. See lines 4–7. There is no information within the paragraph to support the other answers, even if they might be historically accurate.

12. B. Pauli proposed the idea of an invisible particle to explain why energy seemed to be missing when atoms lost electrons and changed into other kinds of atoms. There is no information in the passage to support the connection between neutrinos and radiation (choices A and E). D is vague, and C is simply incorrect.

13. D. Pauli said he had done a "terrible thing" by suggesting the existence of a particle that couldn't be detected, and Fermi's paper was rejected because an invisible particle was too speculative. A is too general, nor is there any evidence that Pauli and Fermi either did or did not attempt to find a neutrino, C. The hunt for neutrinos was made possible by the nuclear reactors, rather than the other way around, E. B is not indicated anywhere in the paragraph.

14. C. The author faults the government's power of eminent domain in urban renewal. Lines 4–8 make it clear that the author favors relying on market forces, that is, having developers acquire property only when there is demand for it. B is most likely contrary to the author's beliefs (lines 10–12), and A and E are not suggested by the passage. Although the author might agree with D, nothing in the passage indicates it.

15. B. "Gentrified," from "gentry," which means the upper or ruling class, is a word that has been created to describe the rebuilding of deteriorating areas accompanied by the influx of affluent residents who displace the poor. Because lines 10–11 refer to the poorer residents being "priced out" and therefore forced to move, C and E are not good choices. A and D are also not suggested by the context.

16. D. In Passage 1, the author cites the extensive and unchecked demolition of properties (lines 10–12) as a major problem. In Passage 2, the author mentions that urban renewal has improved and now focuses on, among other things, "selective" demolition (line 23). The author of Passage 2 does not indicate that government involvement has been a major problem, A, or that most projects have failed, C. Neither author refers to B, and neither author makes or implies a judgment on E.

Long Reading Passages

17. E. The first paragraph cites our using the words "shrinks playfully" and, in the second sentence, as a means of suggesting a criticism of modern psychotherapy. The third sentence asks (and suggests an affirmative answer) whether "witchdoctoring" might have "at least marginal value."

18. A. The allusion to Sahlin's "stone-age economics" is intended to suggest the possibility of a stone-age psychiatry that may have some relevance to the modern world. The idea is advanced tentatively, in the form of a question that concludes the paragraph.

19. D. The passage never makes outrageous claims for tribal therapy, but it does assert that it "may be more effective in the treatment of their own people," with the added qualification "especially when it comes to mental and emotional disorders."

20. B. The second paragraph concludes with a reference to the "condition of expectant faith," Freud's words of praise for tribal healers who create this feeling that can have a "great therapeutic effect." That is, a patient who expects to be healed is more likely to recover.

21. B. The third paragraph describes the much greater range of ills that traditional shamans would treat, including a frozen foot. Modern psychotherapists can be expected to deal with the mental afflictions of choices A, C, D, and E, but not with the broken arm.

22. D. The word "marked" is an adjective here, meaning conspicuous or obvious.

23. A. The phrase is best paraphrased by between body and mind. Although "psychic" as a noun can mean a person sensitive to forces beyond the physical world, here it means that which is of the mind.

24. C. As it is used in this context, "psychosomatic" means originating in the mind and carries no suggestion of imaginary or unreal.

25. A. Freud, the second paragraph says, believed in the importance of the "condition of expectant faith" based on the patient's trust in the therapist's skill. Torrey, in the fourth paragraph, insists upon the importance of the "cultural bond" uniting the therapist and the client. The best answer here is choice A.

26. C. "To take issue with" is to argue, disagree, contest with. Torrey is disagreeing with assumed superiority of the Western scientist.

27. **E.** The author deliberately uses the words "mumbo-jumbo, charlatans, psychotics," and "eye of newt" not because he agrees with them but because he realizes that many of his readers approach this subject with these prejudices. The phrase "shaman's method" does not have the pejorative denotation or connotations of the four other choices.

28. **C.** The passage is suggesting that we study tribal lore before we dismiss it because it may have uses even in modern Western society. The passage is not so unrealistic as to assert that tribal medicine is superior to Western, and its chief purpose is not to criticize the West.

Section 6: Mathematics

1. **E.** First add the number in the parentheses, then square the total.

$$(3 + 5)^2 = (8)^2 = 64$$

2. **D.** Each term in the sequence must be divisible by 4, and 438 is not divisible by 4.

3. **C.** If $y + 2$ is positive, it means that $y + 2$ must be greater than zero. That is,

$$y + 2 > 0$$
$$y > -2$$

4. **C.** If the plumber works for 6 consecutive hours, the charge is $45 for the first hour plus $20 for each of the five additional hours:

$$\$45 + 5(\$20) = \$45 + \$100 = \$145$$

5. **C.** Notice how drawing some line segments can assist you in finding the necessary lengths.

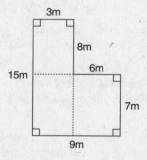

The perimeter is the sum of the lengths of the sides.

$$P = 15 + 3 + 8 + 6 + 7 + 9 = 48m$$

6. **B.** Since $a = p + prt,$

$$a - p = p + prt - p$$
$$a - p = prt$$
$$\frac{a - p}{pt} = \frac{prt}{pt}$$
$$\frac{a - p}{pt} = r$$

Therefore,
$$r = \frac{a - p}{pt}$$

7. **A.** Since Rajiv will be y years old x years from now, he is $y - x$ years old now. Therefore, z years from now he will be $y - x + z$ years old.

8. C. An exponent of $\frac{5}{2}$ means to take the square root of the number raised to a power of 5.

So,
$$z^{\frac{5}{2}} = \sqrt{z^5}$$

9. C. Let x = first number, $2x + 1$ = second number, and $3x - 4$ = third number. Since the average of the three numbers is 55,

$$\frac{x + (2x + 1) + (3x - 4)}{3} = 55$$

Multiplying both sides of the equation by 3,

$$x + (2x + 1) + (3x - 4) = 165$$
$$6x - 3 = 165$$
$$6x - 3 + 3 = 165 + 3$$
$$6x = 168$$
$$\frac{6x}{6} = \frac{168}{6}$$
$$x = \frac{168}{6}$$
$$x = 28 = \text{first number}$$
$$2x + 1 = 57 = \text{second number}$$
$$3x - 4 = 80 = \text{third number}$$

Therefore, the largest number is 80.

10. C. Triangle DBC is a 30-60-90 triangle, which means that the sides DB, CD, and CB are in the ratio $1 : 2 : \sqrt{3}$, respectively.

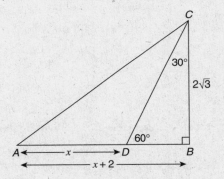

You're given that BC is $2\sqrt{3}$, which means that the common factor for all three sides is 2. Then side BD is $2 \times 1 = 2$. If $BD = 2$, then $AB = x + 2$. The area of $\triangle ABC$ is given as $6\sqrt{3}$. So you can solve as follows:

$$\text{Area} = \frac{1}{2} \times \text{base} \times \text{height}$$
$$6\sqrt{3} = \frac{1}{2}(AB)(BC)$$
$$6\sqrt{3} = \frac{1}{2}(x + 2)(2\sqrt{3})$$
$$6\sqrt{3} = (x + 2)\sqrt{3}$$
$$6 = x + 2$$
$$6 - 2 = x$$
$$4 = x$$

Grid-In Questions

11. Answer: $\frac{5}{8}$. Multiplying both sides of the equation by the LCD of 5,

$$5\left(x + \frac{3}{5}x\right) = 5(1)$$
$$5x + 3x = 5$$
$$8x = 5$$
$$x = \frac{5}{8}$$

12. Answer: 14. Since 60% of the students are girls, 40% of the students are boys. Hence,

$$40\% \text{ of } 35 = (.40)(35)$$
$$= 14 \text{ boys}$$

13. Answer: $\frac{1}{6}$. The average of any three numbers is equal to the sum of the numbers divided by 3.

$$\frac{1}{4} + \frac{1}{6} + \frac{1}{12} = \frac{3}{12} + \frac{2}{12} + \frac{1}{12}$$
$$\text{The sum} = \frac{6}{12}.$$
$$= \frac{1}{2}$$

The average of the numbers is

$$\frac{1}{2} \div 3 = \frac{1}{2} \cdot \frac{1}{3} = \frac{1}{6}$$

14. Answer: 93.5.

$$\frac{317.9 \text{ miles}}{17 \text{ gallons}} = \frac{x \text{ miles}}{5 \text{ gallons}}$$
$$17x = (317.9)(5)$$
$$17x = 1589.5$$
$$x = 1589.5 \div 17$$
$$x = 93.5 \text{ miles}$$

15. Answer: 527. The total of the five verbal SAT scores is 2,635. Dividing that total by 5 (the number of scores) gives 527 as the average.

16. Answer: 45. Since the sum of the measures of the angles of a quadrilateral is 360 and the ratio of the angle measures is 3:5:7:9,

$$3x + 5x + 7x + 9x = 360$$
$$24x = 360$$
$$x = 360 \div 24$$
$$x = 15$$

The smallest angle is $3x = (3)(15) = 45$.

17. Answer: $\frac{7}{12}$. If Jim works for 2 days, he will complete $\frac{2}{6}$, or $\frac{1}{3}$, of the job. If Mike works for 2 days, he will complete $\frac{2}{8}$, or $\frac{1}{4}$, of the job. Together they will complete

$$\frac{1}{3} + \frac{1}{4} = \frac{4}{12} + \frac{3}{12} = \frac{7}{12} \text{ of the job.}$$

18. Answer: 50. Since *BD* is a diagonal of square *ABCD*,

$$BD = 5\sqrt{2}$$

The area of square *BDMN*

$$=(BD)^2$$
$$=(5\sqrt{2})^2$$
$$=25 \times 2$$
$$=50$$

19. Answer: 100. The greatest increase is indicated by the steepest rise in the graph lines, between 1991 and 1992. But you are looking for the greatest *percentage* increase, which means the increase as compared to the starting point. To find percentage increase:

$$\frac{\text{amount of increase}}{\text{starting point}} = \text{percentage increase}$$

1989–1990	20 to 25	$\frac{5}{20} = 25\%$ increase
1990–1991	25 to 50	$\frac{25}{25} = 100\%$ increase
1991–1992	50 to 90	$\frac{40}{50} = 80\%$ increase
1992–1993	decrease	

20. Answer: 264. In △*MNP*, *PM* = *PN* and ∠*PMN* = ∠*PNM* = 42°. Also, in △*MNP*,

$$\angle PMN + \angle PNM + \angle MPN = 180°$$

$$42° + 42° + \angle MPN = 180°$$

$$84° + \angle MPN = 180°$$

$$\angle MPN = 96°$$

Since ∠*MPN* is a central angle,

$$\text{arc } MN = 96°$$

Also, arc *MN* + arc *MQN* = 360°

$$96° + \text{arc } MQN = 360°$$

$$\text{arc } MQN = 264°$$

Section 7: Critical Reading

Long Reading Passages

1. C. The passage makes no comment on the skills of the players in the earlier period as opposed to today. The first paragraph tells us that orchestra conducting is "less than 150 years old" and that it became necessary because orchestras began to increase in size in the late 1700s.

2. E. The sentence structure suggests that "Apollonian" and "Dionysian" are parallel to "Mendelssohn" and "Wagner," to "elegant" and "passionate," and to *clear* and *emotional*. Although Apollo is the sun god, the best choice here is "clear" and "elegant."

3. C. The third paragraph discusses the difficulties of conducting, citing the conductor's having to "play" upon an instrument of one hundred musicians, while the singer or orchestral player must deal with only one.

4. E. The author of Passage 1 presents the "ideal modern conductor" as a synthesis of the "elegant" and the "passionate" schools (lines 35, 26–27).

5. B. The snide parenthesis manages to suggest that music critics are society ladies who are less interested in and less able to judge musical abilities than are musicians. Like the society women, the critics are more important to a conductor's success than are a conductor's real musical abilities. The sentence does not imply that critics are more interested in the players than in the conductor.

6. B. The author compares conductors and politicians, suggesting that both are careerists. They are, like conductors, conspicuously *not* original, disciplined, modest, or indifferent to power.

7. D. The phrase is in fact saying that conductors are self-centered, are egoists.

8. C. The passage suggests that in the "musical community"—that is, the community of musicians and music lovers—music is paramount. In the "music-business community," however, with its cult of personality, music is not the main concern. Although choices D and E may well be true, the passage does not deal with these issues.

9. D. What the sentence in its roundabout way is really saying is that television, unfortunately, makes it possible for viewers to see the front of the conductor. In the concert hall, the conductor's back is to the audience, but television has made it possible for viewers to see every grimace of the conductor. To circumvent is to go around or to avoid, and "dorsal" means back.

10. A. The phrase refers to "listen to the music." The author implies that it will be so bad you had much better have stayed at home.

11. E. At one time or another, the passage mocks or directly attacks conductors, politicians, the public, and the critics, but it spares the instrumentalists who play in the orchestras.

12. A. Unlike the author of Passage 1, the author of Passage 2 wants no part of the conductor's personality or feelings to interfere with what the composer has written. The ideal performance would be "an exact realization of the score." Since the second author is a composer, whereas the first is a conductor, these preferences are understandable.

13. D. Both passages use the word "great," but Passage 2 always puts quotation marks around the word. The author is quoting the word from people like the author of the first passage (and may, in fact, have the first passage specifically in mind), but "great" in the second passage is said with a sneer. It refers to so-called "great" conductors whose qualifications have too little to do with music.

14. B. Both passages assume that a conductor will be male. Since that time, an increasing number of female conductors have appeared before the public. In addition, a gender-neutral style of writing has become more common.

Section 8: Mathematics

1. A.

$$\frac{\text{percent}}{100} = \frac{\text{is number}}{\text{of number}}$$

$$\frac{.25}{100} = \frac{x}{12}$$

Cross multiplying,

$$100x = 3.00$$

$$\frac{100x}{100} = \frac{3.00}{100}$$

$$x = .03 \text{ or } \frac{3}{100}$$

2. C. The maximum number of squares 1 inch by 1 inch will be 16.

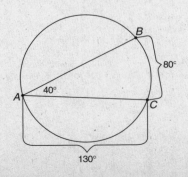

3. E. Let x = original price. Then

$$x - .40x = 5.70$$
$$.60x = 5.70$$
$$x = 9.50$$

Hence, the book originally cost $9.50.

4. A. Multiply the numerator and denominator by 12 (LCD).

$$\frac{12\left(\frac{2}{3} - \frac{1}{2}\right)}{12\left(\frac{1}{6} + \frac{1}{4} + \frac{2}{3}\right)} = \frac{8 - 6}{2 + 3 + 8} = \frac{2}{13}$$

5. D. According to the graph, the tallest "B" (before) bar is county 4.

6. B. Solve this problem by plugging in simple numbers. Start with 1, an odd integer.

$$(1 + 1) \text{ times } (2 \cdot 1 + 1)$$
$$= (2) \text{ times } (2 + 1)$$
$$= 2 \cdot 3$$
$$= 6 \text{ (not odd)}$$

Now, try 2, an even integer.

$$(2 + 1) \text{ times } (2 \cdot 2 + 1)$$
$$= (3) \text{ times } (4 + 1)$$
$$= 3 \cdot 5$$
$$= 15 \text{ (an odd integer)}$$

7. C. Since $\angle A = 40°$, $\overset{\frown}{BC} = 80°$

Since the measure of a circle is $360°$, then

$$\overset{\frown}{AB} = 360° - \left(\overset{\frown}{AC} + \overset{\frown}{BC}\right)$$
$$= 360° - \left(130° + 80°\right) = 360° + 210° = 150°$$

8. **C.** Since two-thirds of the students are boys, $\frac{2}{3}(36) = 24$ boys in the class. Out of the 24 boys in the class, three-fourths of them are under six feet tall, or $\frac{3}{4}(24) = 18$ boys under six feet tall.

9. **D.** Absolute value equations require solving two distinct equations:

$$|3x + 6| = 15$$

$$3x + 6 = 15 \qquad \text{or} \qquad 3x + 6 = -15$$
$$3x + 6 - 6 = 15 - 6 \qquad \text{or} \qquad 3x + 6 - 6 = -15 - 6$$
$$3x = 9 \qquad\qquad\qquad\qquad 3x = -21$$
$$\frac{3x}{3} = \frac{9}{3} \qquad\qquad\qquad\qquad \frac{3x}{3} = \frac{-21}{3}$$
$$x = 3 \qquad \text{or} \qquad\qquad x = -7$$

10. **D.** Since the area of a trapezoid $= \frac{1}{2} \cdot h \cdot (b_1 + b_2)$, we need to find the altitude, h. Draw altitudes in the figure as follows:

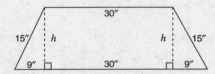

Since the triangles formed are right triangles, use the Pythagorean theorem, which says

$$c^2 = a^2 + b^2$$
$$15^2 = 9^2 + h^2$$
$$225 = 81 + h^2$$
$$h^2 = 225 - 81$$
$$h^2 = 144$$
$$h = \sqrt{144} = 12 \text{ inches}$$

Hence, the area of the trapezoid will be

$$\frac{1}{2} \cdot h \cdot (b_1 + b_2) = \frac{1}{2} \cdot 12 \cdot (30 + 48)$$
$$= (6)(78)$$
$$= 468 \text{ square inches}$$

11. **C.** Since x is an integer, then x could be a negative, zero, or positive whole number. If you plug in some integers for x you can see that 3^x cannot be a negative number or zero so $f(x)$ could not be 3 or 4. Eliminate choices A and B. If x is -2, then $f(x)$ could be $4\frac{1}{9}$ as follows:

$$f(x) = 3^x + 4$$
$$= 3^{-2} + 4$$
$$= \frac{1}{3^2} + 4$$
$$= \frac{1}{9} + 4$$
$$= 4\frac{1}{9}$$

At this point, select choice C and go on to the next problem. If you try some other integers you'll notice that $5\frac{1}{3}$ and 9 are not possible values for $f(x)$.

12. A.

$$y = \frac{1-x}{x}$$

$$y = \frac{1}{x} - \frac{x}{x}$$

$$y = \frac{1}{x} - 1$$

$$y + 1 = \frac{1}{x} - 1 + 1$$

$$y + 1 = \frac{1}{x}$$

Taking the reciprical of both sides of the equation,

$$\frac{1}{y+1} = x$$

13. D. First, calculate the rates of production per day. Two of the factories each make $100,000/15 = 6,667$ hubcaps per day. The third plant makes $1.3 \times 6,667 = 8,667$ hubcaps per day. The total production rate is $8,667 + 2(6,667) = 22,001$ hubcaps per day. At that rate, it would take 45.5 days to produce a million hubcaps.

14. B. Solve as follows:

$$4\sqrt{y+3} + 14 = 50$$

$$4\sqrt{y+3} = 36$$

$$\frac{4\sqrt{y+3}}{4} = \frac{36}{4}$$

$$\sqrt{y+3} = 9$$

$$\left(\sqrt{y+3}\right)^2 = (9)^2$$

$$y + 3 = 81$$

$$y + 3 - 3 = 81 - 3$$

$$y = 78$$

Anytime you square both sides of an equation you must check for extraneous roots. So check: $y = 78$

$$4\sqrt{y+3} + 14 = 4\sqrt{78+3} + 14$$

$$= 4\sqrt{81} + 14$$

$$= 4 \cdot 9 + 14$$

$$= 36 + 14$$

$$= 50$$

15. B. Area $= \frac{1}{2} \times$ base $\times$ height

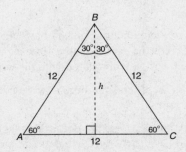

Since $\triangle BCD$ is a 30-60-90 triangle,

$$h = \frac{\sqrt{3}}{2}(BC)$$
$$= \frac{\sqrt{3}}{2}(12)$$
$$= 6\sqrt{3}$$

Hence, area of $\triangle ABC$

$$= \frac{1}{2}(AC)(BD)$$
$$= \frac{1}{2}(12)\left(6\sqrt{3}\right)$$
$$= (6)\left(6\sqrt{3}\right)$$
$$= 36\sqrt{3} \text{ square yards}$$

Section 9: Critical Reading

Sentence Completion

1. **E.** If trucks are the "only" means of transport, then there can be no public transportation, and a word that denotes this is needed. The best choice is "nonexistent," that is, not in existence.

2. **D.** The clue in the second part of the sentence describes the stories as often "less than three pages long." Although any one of the answers could make sense, only "economy" is specifically related to the short length of the stories.

3. **B.** For the first blank, each of the first four choices would be suitable, but the second blank requires a verb that follows from the paternal sympathy with the program. Either B or E is appropriate, but "obligatory" is a better adjective choice than "habitual."

4. **B.** The missing word must describe someone who acts in opposition to the "best economic advisors." Choices A, D, and E all denote a conservative, and choice C is neutral. A "maverick" is a person who acts independently, deriving from the term for an unbranded, lost calf that any rancher could claim.

5. **B.** The "but" signals a word that is very different from "conservative" in meaning. Although "liberal" in some contexts is the opposite of "conservative," that use refers to politics, not clothing, and the best choice here is B "flamboyant," which means ornate or showy.

6. **D.** If the protests put the warden at risk, they were probably "vigorous" or "outspoken" and not "tactful," "realistic," or "unregarded," although "realistic" might work. "Poaching" is "illegal" but also very "something" that makes people risk breaking the law. The possibilities here are "profitable" or its synonym "lucrative." The best choice, then, is D, which has "outspoken protests" and "lucrative pursuit."

7. **C.** The "Although" signals the possibility of smaller particles being found, so B and C are the best first words. With the phrase "or are very close to" in the sentence, "have approached" is redundant, whereas "have reached" makes good sense.

8. **C.** The blanks must be the opposites or contradictions of "affable" and "articulate," given the "neither" and "nor." Of the choices, not "morose" and not "reticent" would be the closest to "affable" and "articulate." The adjectives "sullen," "quiet," or "aggressive" could work but not paired with the words given here.

9. **A.** If there is a "problem" for Spanish composers, the missing word must be "refused." With B, D, or E, there would be no problem, and C makes no sense.

10. **A.** The two missing adjectives modify "reason" and are defined by "not a change in thinking" and "but a shortage of money." The choices that most clearly refer to belief and money are "ideological" and "economic."

Short Reading Passages

11. **A.** The Daniel Boone legend is well-known, which suggests that it is cited here as a familiar example. Also, the sentence is in parentheses—an aside, something that isn't critical to the main idea. It precedes the comments about Trickster, ruling out C, and it concerns legends, not "coup" stories, D. The paragraph does not address the idea in E at all, and it is not humorous, B.

12. **B.** It is the only statement based directly on information in the passage. See lines 6–10. The other answers here may or may not be true, but no information in the passage attests to their accuracy.

13. **D.** A and B are not suggested by the paragraph, and C is incorrect because the tone of the paragraph is objective, not critical. The paragraph also does not imply that the South should have won the war, even with its military advantages, E.

14. **E.** The Northern advantages are all long-term, especially food production. Each of the other choices draws a conclusion beyond any implications in the passage.

15. **C.** All the sentences predict a too-rosy future for television, and the similarity between the sentence structure in lines 5–7 ("If...[then] surely") underscores the idea that these statements are going to turn out to be untrue. The tone indicates that the passage will be critical of the optimism, given events that followed, and will not simply be a "recounting of the early days," B, or of television's growing popularity, A. D and E are completely irrelevant to the passage.

16. **C.** They assumed that the images projected by television would be much more powerful than voices on the radio, which led them to predict that television would profoundly affect people's actions. See lines 5–10. A is incorrect because they believed that people could change. Line 14 also suggests that they believed happiness was measurable in some way. Therefore, D is also incorrect. B and E are irrelevant. The pundits of line 2 emphasize the power of the image, not television's democratic nature or its popularity.

Long Reading Passages

17. **A.** Since all rain is naturally acidic, the passage suggests that the name is inadequate. Although the paragraph says that the name may sound "sinister," it does not suggest that acid rain is not a serious problem. Acid rain with a low pH is a serious problem.

18. **E.** Areas downwind of industrial polluters are likely to be affected by acid rain.

19. **A.** It can be inferred that an acidic reading of less than pH 2, which is "six to eight times more acidic than vinegar," is less than one point lower than the pH of vinegar, since "each integer is 10 times more acidic" than the one before it. So the vinegar pH would be approximately 2.

20. **E.** The record itself is not in doubt. What is questionable is if this record for intense pollution is a record anyone would want to set.

21. **E.** The pH scale is neutral at 7, more acidic below, and more alkaline above. So pH 11 would be the most alkaline.

22. **C.** In the fifth paragraph, the passage points to "natural alkaline rock, like limestone," that "helps to neutralize acid rain."

23. **C.** The word "eerily" means strangely or weirdly.

24. **B.** Irony is a set of circumstances or result that is just the opposite of what might be expected. Here the expected result was the solution to a pollution problem (the smokestacks), and the result was increased pollution somewhere else.

25. **A.** The "silver lining" here was the beneficial effect of the sulfur emissions in fertilizing the soil. The reference to "cloud" is especially apt in this case.

26. **B.** The seventh paragraph suggests that the chief opponents in the acid rain debate are the environmentalists who want the pollution reduced and the industrialists who would probably have to pay the cost of reducing emissions.

27. D. The passage implies that choices A, B, C, and E would reduce acid rain but does not present reduction of the use of sulfur fertilizer as an opportunity to stem pollution.

28. D. The rain falls on places far from the source of the pollutants, even crossing international boundaries at times.

Section 10: Writing—Multiple Choice

Improving Sentences

1. A. The original is the right version. The two complete sentences are separated by a semicolon, avoiding the run-on, to be found in B and E. D will not work because "while" introduces a dependent clause, but the semicolon should introduce a complete sentence. C is not wrong in its punctuation, but it alters the meaning of the original sentence.

2. D. The original version of this sentence has no errors of grammar, but D is also correct and four words shorter. The second clause in B is a sentence fragment; it has no main verb. C is wordy, repeating the word "construction." To avoid the illogical comparison of "construction" and "*King Lear,*" E should read "*King Lear*'s."

3. C. The issue in this sentence is clarity, rather than grammar. All five versions are grammatical, but C makes the point most clearly. The point is that though the capability has long been known, no one has made use of this knowledge until very recently ("just"). C correctly subordinates half of the sentence, using "although."

4. B. This sentence has a pronoun ("which") without a specific antecedent. B corrects this by adding the noun "schedule." Both D and E lack a specific antecedent. What is it that will be "decreased" or "altered"?

5. A. Though the original version is longer than the other choices, it is the only one that keeps the comparison logical. The unchangeable part of the sentence has "as important as enjoying" so the first part must have an action parallel to "enjoying." The nouns of B, C, D, and E are not a similar activity.

6. D. The problem of the original sentence is its verbosity. The phrase "of a . . . nature" is always verbose; the adjective by itself will say the same. The trouble with B is that "trusting" and "trustworthy" have very different meanings. A trusting person may be trustworthy or devious, and a trustworthy person may be trusting or skeptical.

7. A. The original is the best version. Since the sentence begins with the phrase "A very old plant," the first words after this introductory phrase should refer to a plant, singular, not to plants such as cornflowers, B. C, D, and E misplace the modifier by following the initial phrase with "painting" not a "plant."

8. B. Though the original sentence is not wrong, it treats the two clauses as equal. Choice B, by subordinating the past to the present, establishes a more meaningful relationship between the parts. C shifts from passive to active, while E uses the present tense to describe action in the past.

9. B. This is a dangling modifier. The sentence seems to say that the essay did the struggling! B eliminates this problem, clearly associating *John* with the opening phrase about struggling.

10. D. This sentence is testing for verbosity. All of the first four choices are grammatical, but D alone avoids the unnecessary repetition of the word "mountains."

11. D. In the original sentence, and in C, the "they" has no antecedent. Who is "they"? D is more concise than B (a passive) and E.

12. E. To be sure the reader does not think the mayor spent so much money on cosmetic surgery, E places the modifier "after a multi-million dollar face-lift" next to what it modifies, the Champs Elysees. The four other versions of the sentence place the modifier nearer to Chirac.

13. A. The sentence is saying "completing...was as satisfying as." The original version is the most concise and the most clearly parallel of the five choices.

14. D. Both B and C can be eliminated, since the phrase that begins the sentence must modify the Canadians, not the city in Florida. The problem with A and E is the idiom "descend into." One can descend into a coal mine or into hell, but the correct idiom in this context is "descend on."

15. C. The series here uses two main verbs in the past tense ("stopped," "ran"); the third verb in the series should also use the past tense.

Answer Sheets for Practice Test 3

(Remove These Sheets and Use Them to Write Your Essay and Mark Your Answers)

Section 1

Begin your essay on this page and continue on the next page if necessary. Do not write outside the essay boxes provided.

CUT HERE

CUT HERE

Section 2

1 (A) (B) (C) (D) (E)
2 (A) (B) (C) (D) (E)
3 (A) (B) (C) (D) (E)
4 (A) (B) (C) (D) (E)
5 (A) (B) (C) (D) (E)
6 (A) (B) (C) (D) (E)
7 (A) (B) (C) (D) (E)
8 (A) (B) (C) (D) (E)
9 (A) (B) (C) (D) (E)
10 (A) (B) (C) (D) (E)
11 (A) (B) (C) (D) (E)
12 (A) (B) (C) (D) (E)
13 (A) (B) (C) (D) (E)
14 (A) (B) (C) (D) (E)
15 (A) (B) (C) (D) (E)
16 (A) (B) (C) (D) (E)
17 (A) (B) (C) (D) (E)
18 (A) (B) (C) (D) (E)
19 (A) (B) (C) (D) (E)
20 (A) (B) (C) (D) (E)

Section 3

1 (A) (B) (C) (D) (E)
2 (A) (B) (C) (D) (E)
3 (A) (B) (C) (D) (E)
4 (A) (B) (C) (D) (E)
5 (A) (B) (C) (D) (E)
6 (A) (B) (C) (D) (E)
7 (A) (B) (C) (D) (E)
8 (A) (B) (C) (D) (E)
9 (A) (B) (C) (D) (E)
10 (A) (B) (C) (D) (E)
11 (A) (B) (C) (D) (E)
12 (A) (B) (C) (D) (E)
13 (A) (B) (C) (D) (E)
14 (A) (B) (C) (D) (E)
15 (A) (B) (C) (D) (E)
16 (A) (B) (C) (D) (E)
17 (A) (B) (C) (D) (E)
18 (A) (B) (C) (D) (E)
19 (A) (B) (C) (D) (E)
20 (A) (B) (C) (D) (E)
21 (A) (B) (C) (D) (E)
22 (A) (B) (C) (D) (E)
23 (A) (B) (C) (D) (E)
24 (A) (B) (C) (D) (E)
25 (A) (B) (C) (D) (E)
26 (A) (B) (C) (D) (E)
27 (A) (B) (C) (D) (E)
28 (A) (B) (C) (D) (E)
29 (A) (B) (C) (D) (E)
30 (A) (B) (C) (D) (E)
31 (A) (B) (C) (D) (E)
32 (A) (B) (C) (D) (E)
33 (A) (B) (C) (D) (E)
34 (A) (B) (C) (D) (E)
35 (A) (B) (C) (D) (E)
36 (A) (B) (C) (D) (E)

Section 4

1 (A) (B) (C) (D) (E)
2 (A) (B) (C) (D) (E)
3 (A) (B) (C) (D) (E)
4 (A) (B) (C) (D) (E)
5 (A) (B) (C) (D) (E)
6 (A) (B) (C) (D) (E)
7 (A) (B) (C) (D) (E)
8 (A) (B) (C) (D) (E)
9 (A) (B) (C) (D) (E)
10 (A) (B) (C) (D) (E)
11 (A) (B) (C) (D) (E)
12 (A) (B) (C) (D) (E)
13 (A) (B) (C) (D) (E)
14 (A) (B) (C) (D) (E)
15 (A) (B) (C) (D) (E)
16 (A) (B) (C) (D) (E)
17 (A) (B) (C) (D) (E)
18 (A) (B) (C) (D) (E)
19 (A) (B) (C) (D) (E)
20 (A) (B) (C) (D) (E)
21 (A) (B) (C) (D) (E)
22 (A) (B) (C) (D) (E)
23 (A) (B) (C) (D) (E)
24 (A) (B) (C) (D) (E)
25 (A) (B) (C) (D) (E)
26 (A) (B) (C) (D) (E)
27 (A) (B) (C) (D) (E)
28 (A) (B) (C) (D) (E)

Section 5

1 (A) (B) (C) (D) (E)
2 (A) (B) (C) (D) (E)
3 (A) (B) (C) (D) (E)
4 (A) (B) (C) (D) (E)
5 (A) (B) (C) (D) (E)
6 (A) (B) (C) (D) (E)
7 (A) (B) (C) (D) (E)
8 (A) (B) (C) (D) (E)
9 (A) (B) (C) (D) (E)
10 (A) (B) (C) (D) (E)

Section 5 (continued)

11. 12. 13. 14.

Section 5 (continued)

15.

16.

17.

18.

19.

20.

Section 6

1. A B C D E
2. A B C D E
3. A B C D E
4. A B C D E
5. A B C D E
6. A B C D E
7. A B C D E
8. A B C D E
9. A B C D E
10. A B C D E
11. A B C D E
12. A B C D E
13. A B C D E
14. A B C D E
15. A B C D E
16. A B C D E
17. A B C D E
18. A B C D E
19. A B C D E
20. A B C D E
21. A B C D E
22. A B C D E
23. A B C D E
24. A B C D E
25. A B C D E
26. A B C D E
27. A B C D E
28. A B C D E

Section 7

1. A B C D E
2. A B C D E
3. A B C D E
4. A B C D E
5. A B C D E
6. A B C D E
7. A B C D E
8. A B C D E
9. A B C D E
10. A B C D E
11. A B C D E
12. A B C D E
13. A B C D E
14. A B C D E
15. A B C D E

CUT HERE

Section 9 *(continued)*

11.

12.

13.

14.

15.

16.

17.

18.

19.

20.

Section 10

1 Ⓐ Ⓑ Ⓒ Ⓓ Ⓔ
2 Ⓐ Ⓑ Ⓒ Ⓓ Ⓔ
3 Ⓐ Ⓑ Ⓒ Ⓓ Ⓔ
4 Ⓐ Ⓑ Ⓒ Ⓓ Ⓔ
5 Ⓐ Ⓑ Ⓒ Ⓓ Ⓔ
6 Ⓐ Ⓑ Ⓒ Ⓓ Ⓔ
7 Ⓐ Ⓑ Ⓒ Ⓓ Ⓔ
8 Ⓐ Ⓑ Ⓒ Ⓓ Ⓔ
9 Ⓐ Ⓑ Ⓒ Ⓓ Ⓔ
10 Ⓐ Ⓑ Ⓒ Ⓓ Ⓔ
11 Ⓐ Ⓑ Ⓒ Ⓓ Ⓔ
12 Ⓐ Ⓑ Ⓒ Ⓓ Ⓔ
13 Ⓐ Ⓑ Ⓒ Ⓓ Ⓔ
14 Ⓐ Ⓑ Ⓒ Ⓓ Ⓔ
15 Ⓐ Ⓑ Ⓒ Ⓓ Ⓔ

CUT HERE

Practice Test 3

Section 1: Writing—Essay

Time: 25 Minutes

1 Essay Question

You have 25 minutes to plan and write an essay on the topic below. DO NOT WRITE ON ANOTHER TOPIC. AN ESSAY ON ANOTHER TOPIC WILL NOT BE SCORED.

The essay is intended to give you the chance to show your writing skills. Be sure to express your ideas on the topic clearly and effectively. The quality of your writing is much more important than the quantity, but to cover the topic adequately, you may want to write more than one paragraph. Be specific.

Your essay must be written on the two lined pages provided. You will not be given any additional paper. If you keep your handwriting to a reasonable size, write on every line, and avoid wide margins, you should have enough space to complete your essay.

Directions: Read the following paragraph and assignment carefully. Then prepare and write a persuasive essay. Be sure to support your reasons with specific examples that will make your essay more effective.

"We learn, as we say, by 'trial and error.' Why do we always say that? Why not 'trial and rightness' or 'trial and triumph'? The old phrase puts it that way because that is, in real life, the way it is done."

—Lewis Thomas

Assignment: Thomas suggests that learning is a result of making mistakes rather than doing things correctly. Do you agree or disagree with Thomas? Using an example or examples from your reading or your personal observation, write an essay to support your position.

THE PROCTOR WILL ANNOUNCE WHEN 25 MINUTES HAVE PASSED. AT THAT TIME, YOU MUST STOP WRITING. IF YOU FINISH YOUR ESSAY BEFORE 25 MINUTES HAVE PASSED, YOU MAY NOT GO ON TO ANY OTHER SECTION OF THE EXAM. THE PROCTOR WILL ANNOUNCE WHEN TO START THE NEXT SECTION.

Section 2: Mathematics

Time: 25 Minutes

20 Questions

Directions: Solve each problem in this section by using the information given and your own mathematical calculations, insights, and problem-solving skills. Then select the one correct answer of the five choices given and mark the corresponding circle on your answer sheet. Use the available space on the page for your scratch work.

Notes

1. All numbers used are real numbers.

2. Calculators can be used.

3. Some problems may be accompanied by figures or diagrams. These figures are drawn as accurately as possible EXCEPT when it is stated in a specific problem that a figure is not drawn to scale. The figures and diagrams are meant to provide information useful in solving the problem or problems. Unless otherwise stated, all figures and diagrams lie in a plane.

Data That Can Be Used for Reference

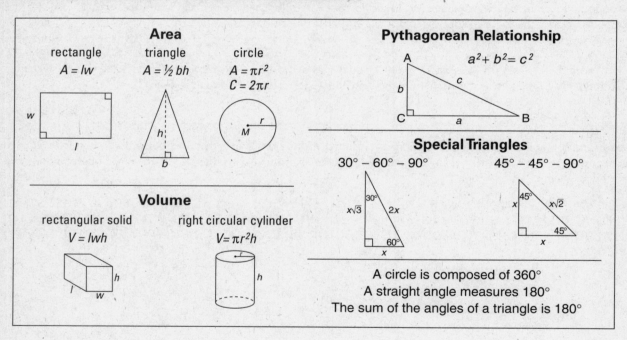

Area

rectangle
$A = lw$

triangle
$A = \frac{1}{2}bh$

circle
$A = \pi r^2$
$C = 2\pi r$

Volume

rectangular solid
$V = lwh$

right circular cylinder
$V = \pi r^2 h$

Pythagorean Relationship

$a^2 + b^2 = c^2$

Special Triangles

$30° - 60° - 90°$

$45° - 45° - 90°$

A circle is composed of 360°
A straight angle measures 180°
The sum of the angles of a triangle is 180°

1. If $3m + n = 7$, then $9m + 3n =$

    A. $\dfrac{7}{9}$

    B. $\dfrac{7}{3}$

    C.   10

    D.   21

    E.   63

2. If it takes 18 minutes to fill $\frac{2}{3}$ of a container, how long will it take to fill the rest of the container at the same rate?

    A.   6 minutes

    B.   9 minutes

    C.   12 minutes

    D.   27 minutes

    E.   36 minutes

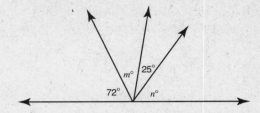

3. In the figure above, what is the number of degrees in the sum of $m + n$?

    A.   103

    B.   97

    C.   93

    D.   83

    E.   72

4. If x is between 0 and 1, which of the following statements must be true?

    I. $x^2 > 1$

    II. $x^2 > 0$

    III. $x^2 > x$

    A.   I only

    B.   II only

    C.   III only

    D.   I and II only

    E.   II and III only

GO ON TO THE NEXT PAGE

5. Tom is just 4 years older than Fran. The total of their ages is 24. What is the equation for finding Fran's age?

- **A.** $x + 4x = 24$
- **B.** $x + 4 = 24$
- **C.** $4x + 2x = 24$
- **D.** $x + (x + 4) = 24$
- **E.** $4x + 1 = 24$

6. If a plane travels 840 miles in $1\frac{1}{2}$ hours, how many hours will it take for the plane to travel 3,500 miles at the same speed?

- **A.** $2\frac{7}{9}$
- **B.** $4\frac{1}{16}$
- **C.** $5\frac{5}{6}$
- **D.** $6\frac{1}{4}$
- **E.** $6\frac{1}{2}$

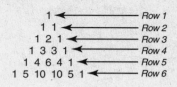

7. If the seventh row was shown in the diagram above, it could not have any

- **A.** even numbers.
- **B.** odd numbers.
- **C.** perfect numbers.
- **D.** prime numbers.
- **E.** perfect cube numbers.

8. If $x = \frac{3}{4}$ and $y = \frac{4}{7}$, then $\frac{y - x}{y + x} =$

- **A.** -1
- **B.** $-\frac{5}{7}$
- **C.** $-\frac{5}{37}$
- **D.** $\frac{1}{7}$
- **E.** $\frac{11}{21}$

9. In a class of 40 students, there are 24 girls. What percent of the class are boys?

   A. 16%
   B. 24%
   C. 40%
   D. 50%
   E. 60%

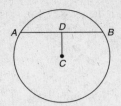

Note: Figure not drawn to scale.

11. On the circle above with center C, $CD \perp AB$, $AB = 24$, and $CD = 5$. What is the radius of the circle?

   A. 19
   B. 17
   C. 13
   D. 12
   E. 7

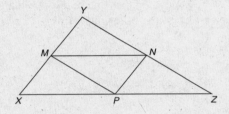

10. In $\triangle XYZ$ above, points M, N, and P are midpoints. If $XY = 10$, $YZ = 15$, and $XZ = 17$, what is the perimeter of $\triangle MNP$?

   A. $10\frac{2}{3}$
   B. 14
   C. 16
   D. 21
   E. 42

12. George scored an average of 80% on three tests. What score must he get on the fourth test to bring his average to 85%?

   A. 85%
   B. 88%
   C. 90%
   D. 95%
   E. 100%

GO ON TO THE NEXT PAGE

13. If $x(y - z) = t$, then $y =$

A. $\left(\dfrac{t}{x}\right) + z$

B. $\dfrac{tz}{x}$

C. $t + x - z$

D. $\dfrac{(t + z)}{x}$

E. $t - x + z$

15. If $m * n = \dfrac{m + n - 1}{n^2}$, then $2 * 3 =$

A. $\dfrac{4}{9}$

B. $\dfrac{2}{3}$

C. 1

D. $1\dfrac{1}{3}$

E. 2

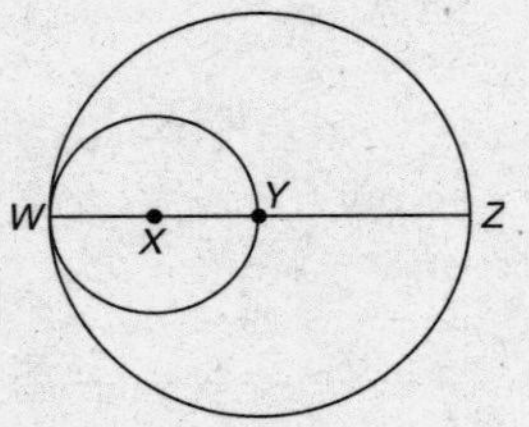

14. In the figure above, X and Y are the centers of the two circles. If the area of the larger circle is 144π, what is the area of the smaller circle?

A. 72π

B. 36π

C. 24π

D. 12π

E. It cannot be determined from the information given.

16. If $\dfrac{a}{b} = \dfrac{c}{d}$ and a, b, c, and d are positive integers, then which of the following is true?

A. $\dfrac{a}{b} = \dfrac{d}{c}$

B. $ac = bd$

C. $a + d = b + c$

D. $\dfrac{d}{b} = \dfrac{c}{a}$

E. $\dfrac{a}{d} = \dfrac{c}{b}$

$$6x - 12 = -6y$$
$$5y + 5x = 15$$

17. Which of the following is the number of solutions in the system of equations shown above?

   A. More than three
   B. Exactly three
   C. Exactly two
   D. Exactly one
   E. None

19. If the diameter of circle R is 30% of the diameter of circle S, the area of circle R is what percent of the area of circle S?

   A. 9%
   B. 15%
   C. 30%
   D. 60%
   E. 90%

18. If y varies directly as x and if $x = 18$ when $y = 12$, what is y when $x = 20$?

   A. $11\frac{4}{5}$
   B. $13\frac{1}{3}$
   C. 14
   D. 16
   E. 30

20. The midpoint of XY is B. The coordinates of X are $(-4, 3)$, and the coordinates of B are $(5, -2)$. What are the coordinates of Y?

   A. $\left(\frac{1}{2}, \frac{1}{2}\right)$
   B. $(1, 1)$
   C. $(6, -7)$
   D. $(14, -3)$
   E. $(14, -7)$

IF YOU FINISH BEFORE TIME IS CALLED, CHECK YOUR WORK ON THIS SECTION ONLY. DO NOT WORK ON ANY OTHER SECTION IN THE TEST.

Section 3: Writing—Multiple Choice

Time: 25 Minutes

36 Questions

In this section, choose the best answer for each question and blacken the corresponding space on the answer sheet.

Directions: The following questions test correctness and effective expression. In selecting the answer, pay attention to grammar, diction, sentence structure, and punctuation. In the following questions, part or all of each sentence is underlined. The A answer repeats the underlined portion of the original sentence, while the next four offer alternatives. Choose the answer that best expresses the meaning of the original sentence, and at the same time is grammatically correct and stylistically superior. The correct choice should be clear, unambiguous, and concise.

EXAMPLE:

The forecaster predicted <u>rain and the sky was clear.</u>

A. rain and the sky was clear.
B. rain but the sky was clear.
C. rain the sky was clear.
D. rain, but the sky was clear.
E. rain being as the sky was clear.

The correct answer is D.

---

1. The melting of Antarctic ice affects ocean <u>currents, and the sunlight's penetration of the water and the growth of microorganisms are also affected.</u>

    A. currents, and the sunlight's penetration of the water and the growth of microorganisms are also affected.
    B. currents; also affected are the sunlight's penetration of the water and the growth of microorganisms.
    C. currents, and it also affects the sunlight's penetration of the water and the growth of microorganisms.
    D. currents, the sunlight's penetration of the water and the growth of microorganisms.
    E. currents, with the sunlight's penetration of the water and the growth of microorganisms also being affected.

2. Coffee drinking may protect against cancer of the colon, <u>which is surprising since coffee drinking increases</u> the risk of heart attack.

    A. which is surprising since coffee drinking increases
    B. and this is surprising since coffee drinking increases
    C. surprising, since coffee drinking increases
    D. and this surprises us because coffee drinking increases
    E. which surprises since coffee drinking increases

3. The excavations at Ceren reveal <u>the prosperity of the rural Mayans, the staples of their diet, and</u> the architecture of their homes.

   A. the prosperity of the rural Mayans, the staples of their diet, and

   B. the prosperity of the rural Mayan; the staples of their diets; and

   C. the prosperity of the rural Mayans, and the staples of their diet, and

   D. the rural Mayans, the prosperity and the diet they ate, as well as

   E. how prosperous the rural Mayans were, what their diet was, and

4. Human cells grown in a test tube can reproduce as many as sixty <u>times then they die</u> from old age.

   A. times then they die

   B. times but then they die

   C. times and then they die

   D. times; then they die

   E. times; before dying

5. <u>In the official portrait of Richard III, it shows an attractive and healthy man, and does not present</u> the deformed demon of Shakespeare's play.

   A. In the official portrait of Richard III, it shows an attractive and healthy man, and does not present

   B. In the official portrait of Richard III, an attractive, healthy man is shown; it does not present

   C. The official portrait of Richard III shows an attractive and healthy man, not

   D. The official portrait of Richard III shows a man who is attractive and healthy, and does not present

   E. Richard III, in the official portrait, is a man who is attractive and healthy, and he is not

6. <u>George Eliot was an ardent and knowledgeable lover of music, and she had</u> little skill in composing melodious verse.

   A. George Eliot was an ardent and knowledgeable lover of music, and she had

   B. George Eliot loved music ardently and knowledgeably, and she

   C. George Eliot was ardent and knowledgeable in her love of music, and she had

   D. George Eliot was an ardent, knowledgeable music lover, having

   E. Although George Eliot was an ardent, knowledgeable lover of music, she had

7. Nestled in the mountains of southwestern Colorado, <u>the extinction of the town of Silverton is imminent</u> with the closing of its silver mine.

   A. the extinction of the town of Silverton is imminent

   B. the extinction of Silverton as a town is imminent

   C. the imminent extinction of the town of Silverton is likely

   D. the town of Silverton faces imminent extinction

   E. the town of Silverton will become extinct imminently

GO ON TO THE NEXT PAGE

Directions: The following sentences may contain one error of grammar, usage, diction, or idiom. No sentence will contain more than one error, and some have no error. If there is an error, it will be underlined with a letter. Sections of the sentence that are not underlined cannot be changed. In selecting your answer, observe the requirements of standard written English. If there is an error, choose the one underlined part that must be changed to correct the sentence. If there is no error, choose E.

EXAMPLE:

The film <u>tell the story</u> of a cavalry captain and <u>his wife</u> who <u>try to</u> <u>rebuild their lives</u> after the Civil War.
　　　A　　　　　　　　　　　　　　　　　B　　　　　C　　　D

<u>No Error.</u>
E

The correct answer is A.

---

8. <u>Strange as it now seems,</u> Japan and Italy once
　　　　A

　<u>agreed to limit</u> car imports because Japan
　　　B

　<u>fears competition</u> <u>from Italian cars.</u> <u>No Error.</u>
　　　C　　　　　　　D　　　　　　E

9. In July, 1991, <u>there were</u> darkness at noon
　　　　　　　A

　<u>in Mexico City,</u> as the moon <u>passed between</u>
　　　B　　　　　　　　　　C

　the sun <u>and the Earth.</u> <u>No Error.</u>
　　　　D　　　　　E

10. The advertisement for Neil Simon's play *Rumors*

　<u>features</u> three <u>sets of mechanical false teeth</u>
　　A　　　　　　B

　<u>who appear</u> <u>to be talking</u> to each other. <u>No Error.</u>
　　C　　　D　　　　　　　　E

11. You can grow a number of spring-flowering

　bulbs <u>indoors, but</u> if the plants <u>are to blossom,</u>
　　　　A　　　　　　　　　B

　<u>one must</u> carefully <u>control the light.</u> <u>No Error.</u>
　　C　　　　　　D　　　　　E

12. <u>Despite lagging productivity</u> by <u>its work force,</u>
　　　　　A　　　　　　　　B

　the Cuban government <u>has continued</u> to <u>provide</u>
　　　　　　　　　C　　　　　D

　a first-rate health-care program. <u>No Error.</u>
　　　　　　　　　　　　　E

13. <u>Nowadays most medical authorities agree</u> that
　　　　　　A

　<u>huge doses</u> of <u>just about any substance</u> is
　　　B　　　　　C

　<u>likely to be dangerous.</u> <u>No Error.</u>
　　　D　　　　　　E

14. <u>As a resulting of overgrazing,</u> firewood cutting,
　　　A

　and <u>increased cultivation,</u> the Sahara Desert has
　　　B

　<u>steadily grown</u> <u>larger</u> in this decade. <u>No Error.</u>
　　C　　　　D　　　　　　　　E

15. <u>To safeguard wildlife,</u> the state of Florida will
　　　A

　<u>line its highways</u> with high fencing, <u>forcing</u>
　　B　　　　　　　　　　　C

　panthers <u>to scoot</u> beneath the roads through
　　　D

　specially designed animal underpasses. <u>No Error.</u>
　　　　　　　　　　　　　　　E

16. Hypnotism, chewing-gum, and

　<u>nicotine-releasing skin patches</u> are <u>probably</u> the
　　A　　　　　　　B

　<u>most used method</u> to break the
　　C

　cigarette smoking habit. <u>No Error.</u>
　　　D　　　　　　E

17. The <u>decline in</u> the industrial average was much

      A

smaller <u>compared</u> <u>to the 1929 decline</u> because

      B   C

the Dow index <u>stands with</u> a much higher level

           D

today. <u>No Error.</u>

     E

18. <u>Missing the forehand volley,</u> a <u>relative easy shot,</u>

    A   B

Morea fell behind <u>early in the match,</u> and

                C

<u>he never recovered.</u> <u>No Error.</u>

    D   E

19. <u>In an area</u> of <u>the Pacific Ring of Fire</u> of

    A   B

<u>special interest to</u> volcanologists <u>lie</u> the western

    C   D

Siberian Kamchatka Peninsula. <u>No Error.</u>

                       E

20. Bears, mountain lions, beavers, <u>deer,</u> squirrels,

                      A

and coyotes <u>inhabit</u> Sequoia Park, and <u>they</u> may

         B   C

be <u>dangerous to campers.</u> <u>No Error.</u>

    D   E

21. <u>No Latin American matador</u> <u>can become</u> famous

    A   B

<u>without he succeeds</u> in Spain where bullfighting

        C

<u>was invented.</u> <u>No Error.</u>

    D   E

22. The discovery of the existence of a fifth force

<u>could have</u> enormous <u>impact on</u> theoretical

    A   B

physicists who <u>are trying to develop</u> a unified

               C

theory <u>to explain the interactions of matter.</u>

          D

<u>No Error.</u>

 E

23. When it is five o'clock in New York, <u>it is</u>

                      A

<u>only three in</u> Texas, and <u>it will be</u> two o'clock

    B   C

in California <u>or Oregon.</u> <u>No Error.</u>

        D   E

24. New Englanders seem to believe that <u>us Texans</u>

                      A

talk <u>oddly,</u> but we think <u>they are the ones</u> who

    B   C

<u>have strange ways of speaking.</u> <u>No Error.</u>

    D   E

25. <u>To encourage better reading skills,</u> teachers in the

    A

public schools <u>now requisite</u> students to submit

         B

weekly diaries <u>listing the books,</u> magazines, and

        C

newspapers <u>they have read.</u> <u>No Error.</u>

    D   E

26. The best <u>examples of plays</u> that can <u>be produced</u>

        A   B

with a minimum of <u>expense for</u> settings and

           C

costumes <u>must be</u> Wilder's *Our Town.* <u>No Error.</u>

    D   E

GO ON TO THE NEXT PAGE

Directions: The following passages are early drafts of student essays. Some parts of them need to be revised.

Read the selections carefully and answer the questions that follow. There will be questions about sentence structure, diction, and usage in individual sentences or parts of sentences. Other questions will deal with the whole essay or paragraphs, and ask you to decide about organization, development, and appropriate language. Choose the answer that follows the requirements of standard written English, and most effectively expresses the intended meanings.

Questions 27–32 are based on the following passage.

(1) I'm sure that many people wish that this statement would work for them. (2) I'm sure that they would like to have all the best things handed them on a silver plate. (3) But this is not how life works. (4) My father was not handed all of his possessions that he has now. (5) He worked hard to get them. (6) We didn't have them handed to us free of charge, and I am glad it went this way.

(7) People will respect others who work hard for a living versus people who get all of their success handed or given to them. (8) Hard work builds self-esteem. (9) Who are you if you do not even appreciate yourself? (10) People who never work lose the opportunity of learning about themselves, and do not know what self esteem is. (11) And they are not as happy as people who do know.

(12) So even if the money in this world could be yours free, it would be better to not take it. (13) In the long run you would be happier without it. (14) You might not be rich but you would have your self-respect and the respect of others. (15) And without self respect you will not be happy.

27. Which of the following is the best version of sentence 3 (reproduced below)?

But this is not how life works.

A. Leave it as it is.
B. But life does not work this way.
C. And this is not how life works.
D. Life doesn't work like that.
E. Since life is not like this.

28. Which of the following is the best combined version of sentences 4 and 5 (reproduced below)?

My father was not handed all of the possessions that he has now. He worked hard to get them.

A. My father was not handed all of the possessions he has now, but he worked hard for them.
B. My father was not handed, but worked hard for all of the possessions that he now has.
C. My father was not handed, but worked hard for all his possessions.
D. My father worked hard to obtain all his possessions.
E. My father worked hard for all the possessions that he has now.

29. Which of the following best describes the function of paragraphs one and two of this passage?

A. The first paragraph makes an assertion which the second paragraph explains.
B. Paragraph one makes an assertion which paragraph two contradicts.
C. Paragraph one raises a question which is answered in paragraph two.
D. Paragraph one offers an abstract idea which is supported by concrete examples in paragraph two.
E. Paragraph one presents generalizations which are supported by references to personal experience in the second paragraph.

30. Which of the following is the best version of sentence 7 (reproduced below)?

> *People will respect others who work hard for a living versus people who get all of their success handed or given to them.*

A. Leave it as it is.
B. People will respect others that work hard for a living more than those who succeed because it was handed to them.
C. People respect others working hard for a living more than those who get success handed or given to them.
D. People will respect hard work versus those who get success handed to them.
E. People respect those who work hard for a living more than those whose success is unearned.

31. The final paragraph of the passage differs from the first and second because it

A. argues that unearned riches are not to be desired.
B. asks rhetorical questions.
C. is entirely directly addressed to the reader.
D. introduces a new topic for discussion.
E. uses examples from personal experience.

32. The writer's purpose in the last paragraph is

A. to summarize his position.
B. to summarize objections to his point of view.
C. to propose a solution to the question raised in the first two paragraphs
D. to introduce a final example.
E. to allow his reader to make up his own mind.

Questions 33–36 are based on the following passage.

(1) I had not looked forward to going to my cousin's wedding in Idaho. (2) I did not want to go because it was on the last weekend of the summer, and I would rather have spent it with my friends at home. (3) I never had wanted to visit Idaho, even though my cousins lived there. (4) My family and I only had stand-by airline tickets, and we missed two flights, so we ended up waiting at the airport for three hours before we even left. (5) Finally having arrived there after nine at night, the weather was cold and rainy. (6) It made me feel like this would be the worst weekend of my life.

(7) When we woke up the next morning at the motel, I looked out the window, and it looked dismal, the sky was gray, and you could see small patches of rain falling. (8) My family and I ate a light breakfast and left for the wedding. (9) It was a half hour drive to the wedding. (10) My cousin was getting married in a park. (11) By the time we got there it was starting to clear up. (12) The wedding was outdoors in the woods, and just when the bride came in, the sun came out. (13) You could feel everybody's spirits lift.

(14) After that everything seemed to go right. (15) The food at the wedding party was great. (16) There was a good band. (17) The friends of my cousin who were my age were fun. (18) When the time came to go home the next day, I was sorry to leave. (19) Next year I may go to college in Idaho.

33. Which of the following is the best version of the underlined part of sentence 5 (reproduced below)?

> *Finally having arrived there after nine at night, the weather* was cold and rainy.

A. Leave it as it is.
B. Having finally arrived there after nine at night, the weather
C. Arrived there finally, after nine at night, the weather
D. Not getting there until after nine at night, the weather
E. When we finally got there, after nine at night, the weather

34. Which of the following is the best version of sentence 6 (reproduced below)?

> *It made me feel like this would be the worst weekend of my life.*

A. Leave it as it is.
B. I felt like this would be the worst weekend of my life.
C. I thought that this would be the worst weekend of my life.
D. It felt like this would be the worst weekend of my life.
E. It seemed like this would be the worst weekend of my life.

GO ON TO THE NEXT PAGE

35. Which of the following is the best version of the underlined portion of sentence 7 (reproduced below)?

> *When we woke up the next morning at the motel, I looked out the window, and <u>it looked dismal, the sky was gray, and you could see</u> small patches of rain falling.*

A. Leave it as it is.

B. looked dismal; the sky was gray, and you could see

C. looked dismal, the sky was gray; and you could see

D. looked dismal, and the sky was gray, and you could see

E. looked dismal. The sky was gray, you could see

36. All of the following strategies are used by the writer of the passage EXCEPT

A. frequent reliance on figurative language.

B. chronological arrangement of events.

C. relating the first and last sentence of the passage.

D. use of a first person speaker.

E. use of details of weather to convey mood.

IF YOU FINISH BEFORE TIME IS CALLED, CHECK YOUR WORK ON THIS SECTION ONLY. DO NOT WORK ON ANY OTHER SECTION IN THE TEST.

Section 4: Critical Reading

Time: 25 Minutes

28 Questions

In this section, choose the best answer for each question and blacken the corresponding space on the answer sheet.

Directions: Each blank in the following sentences indicates that something has been omitted. Consider the lettered words beneath the sentence and choose the word or set of words that best fits the whole sentence.

EXAMPLE:

With a million more people than any other African nation, Nigeria is the most _____ country on the continent.

- A. impoverished
- B. successful
- C. populous
- D. developed
- E. militant

The correct answer is C.

---

1. As the boat drifted closer and closer to the rocks, the people on the beach became increasingly _____ about its safety.

   - A. cowardly
   - B. intrepid
   - C. apprehensive
   - D. eager
   - E. receptive

2. If only a native can understand the dialect of this region, even the best foreign linguist will be _____ by the indigenous speakers.

   - A. mistaken
   - B. baffled
   - C. misrepresented
   - D. addressed
   - E. translated

3. Carlson described the changes he had made in the story as merely _____, not censorship, because the alterations were made with the writer's prior knowledge and _____.

   - A. editing . . . permission
   - B. revising . . . prohibition
   - C. expurgation . . . warrant
   - D. corrections . . . disapproval
   - E. decimation . . . connivance

4. The thousand-mile trek across the wilderness was a severe test of the children's _____ and their capacity to adapt.

   - A. proportion
   - B. immaturity
   - C. openness
   - D. weakness
   - E. resilience

GO ON TO THE NEXT PAGE

5. A change in fashion to a very thin look is not just an innocent _____ or trend; it is a serious _____ for many women who may suffer from dangerous eating disorders.

   A. victim . . . peril
   B. prank . . . challenge
   C. whim . . . undertaking
   D. fad . . . hazard
   E. idea . . . response

6. The public was _____ by the use of human bones and teeth in the jewelry and made their disapproval clear by refusing to buy any of the _____ items.

   A. enthralled . . . unusual
   B. fascinated . . . remarkable
   C. horrified . . . ghoulish
   D. repulsed . . . amiable
   E. hypnotized . . . grisly

7. In the unsuccessful conference, none of the speakers _____ much response from the audience, but Dr. Schultz's address reached the _____ in tediousness.

   A. aggrandized . . . pinnacle
   B. elicited . . . nadir
   C. attributed . . . record
   D. raised . . . ebb
   E. induced . . . medley

8. In a landscape so calm and beautiful, it was hard to believe that anything _____ could occur.

   A. untoward
   B. temperate
   C. halcyon
   D. seemly
   E. refined

Directions: Questions follow each of the passages below. Using only the stated or implied information in each passage and in its introduction, if any, answer the questions.

Questions 9–10 are based on the following passage.

As a child in Victorian England, Florence Nightingale used to sew up the wounds her sister had inflicted upon her dolls and put splints on her dog's injured paws. Nightingale was a member of a
(5) wealthy and socially prominent family and, as a female, barred from the formal study of the sciences. Nevertheless, as she grew up she pored over the reports of medical commissions and hospitals. She visited hospitals in England and throughout
(10) Europe. In the end, she convinced her conservative family to allow her to become the superintendent of a charitable nursing home in London. Then, in 1854, during the Crimean War, she took a team of nurses to Scutari in Turkey. The hospital death rate
(15) fell from 42 to two percent.

9. The passage suggests that Florence Nightingale became a nurse because

   A.   nursing was a highly respected profession in the early 19th century.

   B.   her parents were wealthy enough to sponsor her studies and recognized her strong interest in medicine.

   C.   her religious feelings could find no other appropriate outlet.

   D.   she was dissatisfied with the usual role of a woman in upper middle-class Victorian society.

   E.   the conventions of the time would not allow her to become a veterinarian.

10. The primary function of the last sentence of the paragraph is to

   A.   act as a transition to a new idea that will be presented in the next paragraph.

   B.   suggest the importance of Florence Nightingale's nurses in the Crimean War.

   C.   refute the 19th century idea that women were incapable of becoming physicians.

   D.   dramatize the terrible conditions in military hospitals during the 19th century.

   E.   provide a factual detail to support the main idea of the paragraph.

Questions 11–12 are based on the following passage.

Early 19th century American steam engines were inferior to late 18th century British steam engines. An example of American technology lagging behind? Not according to historian George Basalla.
(5) Rather, the American engines—more dangerous and less fuel-efficient—were the result of specific choices made by American engineers. At the time, America was rich in resources but poor in skills, so high fuel consumption didn't matter as much as
(10) the ease of construction and maintenance of high-pressure operation. (High-pressure engines could also go faster, an important consideration for a larger landmass.) According to Basalla, what appear today to be design flaws in the American engine should be
(15) seen instead as the result of a designer working within the boundaries of a given time and place.

11. The main topic of the paragraph is the

   A.   superiority of British steam engines.

   B.   reasons American technology was poor compared to British technology.

   C.   great importance of fuel efficiency in England.

   D.   reasons for the choices of American steam engine designers.

   E.   importance of high-pressure operation in American steam engines.

12. The function of the question in lines 3–4 is to

   A.   suggest an explanation that proves to be the wrong one.

   B.   show that there are no easy answers to technological problems.

   C.   show the absurdity of the statement in the first sentence.

   D.   question the debt that American technology owed to British technology.

   E.   introduce the idea that natural resources are a key factor.

GO ON TO THE NEXT PAGE

Questions 13–14 are based on the following passage.

Even oil industry leaders have been forced to pay attention to global warming in Alaska since their exploration season on the North Slope has dropped from 200 to 100 days in only three (5) decades. The reason for this is what scientists call the "feedback processes." When the region's abundant snow and ice melt away, more areas of water and earth are exposed to the sun. Those darker surfaces absorb much higher amounts of solar radia- (10) tion, and, as they expand in size, they take in more heat. Basically, this means that the warming builds upon itself; the more surfaces that are exposed to the sun, the faster global warming occurs.

13. The effect of the phrase "Even oil industry leaders" in the first sentence is to show that

   A. global warming has economic consequences that are not fully understood by the layperson.

   B. people in states other than Alaska have reasons to be concerned about the pace of global warming.

   C. productivity decreases in warmer climates.

   D. the problem in Alaska must be serious if those not usually sensitive to environmental problems are taking notice.

   E. the price of gasoline may be directly related to global warming.

14. Which of the following best describes "feedback processes" (line 6)?

   A. recurring cycles of solar radiation

   B. a vicious circle of warming causing more warming

   C. melting snow and ice absorbing solar radiation

   D. exposure to the sun causing increased heat absorption

   E. lighter surfaces becoming darker surfaces

Questions 15–21 are based on the following passage.

The rabies virus, which can cause disease in any mammal, is spread by the bite of an infected animal. It is lethal once symptoms develop but can be blocked by timely administration of a series of vac- (5) cine injections soon after an attack. The vaccine, which today may be given in an arm rather than the abdomen, is derived from a killed rabies virus. The inactivated virus prods the immune system to destroy active virus, especially when the injections

(10) are combined with application of rabies-specific antibodies to the wound area [see "Rabies" by Martin M. Kaplan and Hilary Koprowski; *Scientific American,* January 1980].

Unfortunately, in any year thousands of people (15) who are probably uninfected undergo treatment because they do not know whether the animal that bit them had rabies. These high numbers are disturbing because therapy is costly and because vaccination of any kind carries a risk of side effects. (The expense (20) is a major reason veterinarians and others who are very likely to encounter rabid animals are generally the only people immunized prophylactically.)

Even more distressing, most people who die of rabies are lost simply because they live in impover- (25) ished nations. Those who are attacked by infected animals often lack access to therapy or cannot pay for it.

Routine immunization of the animal species most likely to transmit the virus to humans would (30) be a more efficient, health-conscious way to save human lives and, not incidentally, to spare animals from suffering. To an extent, such inoculation is already a reality. In many wealthy nations, including the U.S., periodic injection of pet dogs with (35) vaccine has all but stopped canine transmission to humans. Disease caused by cats can be limited in the same way.

In developing countries, however, obtaining veterinary care can be extremely difficult, which is (40) one reason why dogs continue to account for at least 90 percent of all human deaths from rabies. Another problem is that even where pet rabies is under good control, wild animals—not being very amenable to collection and carting to the local (45) veterinarian—pose a threat.

For these unattended groups, distribution of vaccine-laced baits for animals to eat in the field is showing particular promise. This approach is already halting the spread of rabies by foxes in (50) many parts of western Europe and Canada. More preliminary work suggests rabies in other species can be controlled as well.

Indeed, a vaccine-filled bait for raccoons is now being tested in the U.S. If the results are good, the (55) bait method might finally check an epidemic of raccoon rabies that has been spreading up the East Coast from Florida since the 1950s. If baiting can be perfected for distribution to dogs in developing countries, then the goal of sharply curtailing human (60) cases worldwide would finally seem feasible.

This encouraging state of affairs stands in marked contrast to the situation in the 1960s, when research into vaccinating wild animals started in earnest. By then immunization had already reduced

(65) the incidence of dog rabies in the U.S. But infection by foxes, skunks, raccoons, and bats—the other significant rabies reservoirs in this country—was a continuing concern. Compared with dogs, those groups have less direct contact with humans,
(70) but collectively they are more abundant.

To control rabies in free-ranging animals, health officials in the 1950s had depended on thinning populations that harbored the offending virus. They tried gassing of dens, poisoning, trapping, and
(75) shooting, among other tactics. The workers reasoned that destruction of enough animals would so reduce a population that any infected individuals would die without tangling with another animal. When diseased creatures disappeared, only healthy
(80) ones would remain. Yet the strategy halted the spread of the malady in target groups only some of the time.

15. All of the following could be infected with rabies EXCEPT

A. raccoons.

B. cats.

C. humans.

D. skunks.

E. carrion birds.

16. The passage suggests that a human infected with rabies by a dog bite who did nothing for a long period of time would

A. be unable to spread the disease to another human.

B. probably never be aware of having been infected.

C. die.

D. be cured by a vaccine injection.

E. be cured by applying rabies-specific antibodies in the area of the bite.

17. The passage suggests that throughout the world the largest cause of human exposure to the rabies virus is from

A. dogs that have not been immunized.

B. dogs that have been immunized.

C. cats that have not been immunized.

D. cats that have been immunized.

E. wild animals such as raccoons, foxes, or skunks.

18. It can be inferred that the number of fatalities from rabies in the United States is small because

I. most dogs have been immunized by injections.

II. people exposed to the virus have access to immediate treatment.

III. the rabies virus is rare in the wild-animal populations of the United States.

A. I only

B. I and II only

C. I and III only

D. II and III only

E. I, II, and III

19. As it is used in line 60, the word "feasible" means

A. unpredictable.

B. inexpensive.

C. hygienic.

D. practicable.

E. endurable.

20. At present, humans infected with rabies virus can be treated by

I. a vaccine injection in the abdomen.

II. a vaccine injection in the arm.

III. an oral recombinant vaccine.

A. I only

B. II only

C. I and II only

D. II and III only

E. I, II, and III

21. Vaccine-laced baits would be most effective in preventing rabies among

I. wild-animal populations susceptible to rabies.

II. domestic animals in areas where injections are impossible.

III. wild or domestic animals already infected with disease.

A. III only

B. I and II only

C. I and III only

D. II and III only

E. I, II, and III

GO ON TO THE NEXT PAGE

Questions 22–28 are based on the following passage.

The following passage is from the autobiography of a young black woman who was among the first women to attend the New England prep school, St. Paul's.

Outside my personal circle, the school that term seemed to buzz, buzz. Class officers, it seemed, were often called upon to talk. We talked day and evening, in club activities and rehearsals, in the
(5) houses, in the hallways, in our rooms, in the bathrooms, and in meetings after meetings. We gossiped. We criticized. We whined. We analyzed. We talked trash. We talked race relations, spiritual life, male-female relations, teacher-student trust. We
(10) talked confidentially. We broke confidences and talked about the results. We talked discipline and community. We talked Watergate and social-fabric stuff.

I did not follow the Watergate hearings. I did not
(15) rush to the third floor of the Schoolhouse for the ten-thirty *New York Times* delivery to read about it; nor did I crowd around the common-room TV to watch the proceedings. I could not bother to worry about which rich and powerful white people had
(20) hoodwinked which other rich and powerful white people. It seemed of a piece with their obsession with fairness.

I was unprepared, therefore, to dine at the Rectory with Mr. Archibald Cox, the St. Paul's
(25) alumnus whom President Nixon had fired when, as U.S. Special Prosecutor, Mr. Cox began to reveal the Watergate break-in and cover-up. Seated around him were the Rector and a handful of faculty members and student leaders. I said as little as
(30) possible in order to conceal my ignorance. Mr. Cox was acute. He referred to the Watergate players and the major events in witty shorthand. I couldn't quite follow, so I ate and smiled and made periodic conversation noises.

(35) Then he wanted to hear about St. Paul's School. There had been so many changes since his time. I found myself saying, in answer to his question, or the Rector's signal, that I was more aware of being black at St. Paul's than I was of being a girl. I used
(40) a clever phrase that I stole from somewhere and hoped he hadn't already heard: "Actually, we're still more like . . . a boys' school with girls in it. But black people's concerns—diversifying the curriculum and that sort of thing—the truth is that that's
(45) more important to me than whether the boys have the better locker room."

Pompous it was, and I knew it, but better to be pompous in the company of educated and well-off white folk, better even to be stone wrong, than to
(50) have no opinion at all.

Mr. Cox thought a moment. God forbid he should go for the cross-examination. I added more. "Black concerns here at school may look different, but are not really, from the concerns that my par-
(55) ents have taught me all my life at home." I put that one in just so he'd know that I had a family. "And believe me, Sir, my mama and daddy did not put President Nixon into the White House. *We* didn't do that!"

(60) Mr. Cox wrinkled his lean, Yankee face into a mischievous smile. His voice whispered mock conspiracy. He leaned toward me. "Do you know who Nixon hates worst of all?"

I shook my head no. I had no idea.

(65) "Our kind of people."

My ears felt hot. I wanted to jump on the table. I wanted go back home and forget that I'd ever come. I wanted to take him to West Philly, and drop him off at the corner of Fifty-second and Locust,
(70) outside Foo-Foo's steak emporium, right by the drug dealers, and leave him there without a map or a bow tie. Then tell me about our kind of people.

The Rector gave me a look that urged caution. I fixed my face. "What kind of people are those?" I
(75) asked.

"Why, the educated Northeastern establishment," he said. The Rector smiled as if relieved.

22. The speaker's lack of interest in the Watergate hearings is chiefly due to her

   A. feeling alienated from the others at her school.

   B. concern with issues of gender rather than politics.

   C. belief that it was just another rich white person's problem.

   D. eagerness to be accepted by her peers at school.

   E. fear that it would separate her from her family's values.

23. In line 21, the phrase "of a piece" means

   A. consistent with.

   B. a small part of.

   C. indifferent to.

   D. partly to blame for.

   E. inconsistent with.

24. The word "acute" in line 31 means

    A. sharp-pointed.

    B. shrewd.

    C. critical.

    D. angular.

    E. severe.

25. The speaker in line 52 uses the phrase "cross-examination" because

    A. she wishes to amuse the others in the discussion.

    B. she feels she has committed a serious crime.

    C. she prefers to be wrong than to have no opinion at all.

    D. Archibald Cox is a lawyer.

    E. she has misunderstood Cox's questions.

26. When the speaker responds with the thoughts expressed in lines 66–72 ("My ears felt hot . . . people"), she is responding especially to what single word in the dialogue before?

    A. "Nixon" (line 63)

    B. "hates" (line 63)

    C. "worst" (line 63)

    D. "Our" (line 65)

    E. "people" (line 65)

27. It can be inferred from the passage that the "Rector smiled as if relieved" (line 77) because he

    A. has been afraid the speaker would say something shocking.

    B. disapproves of political arguments.

    C. has not understood what the speaker has been thinking.

    D. is too conventional to imagine a violent difference in opinion or in background.

    E. is amused by Archibald Cox's witty remark.

28. The passage as a whole is characterized by the speaker's

    A. lack of feeling and self-discipline.

    B. candor and self-awareness.

    C. bitterness and sense of unfairness.

    D. hypocrisy and self-deception.

    E. naiveté and charm.

IF YOU FINISH BEFORE TIME IS CALLED, CHECK YOUR WORK ON THIS SECTION ONLY. DO NOT WORK ON ANY OTHER SECTION IN THE TEST.

Practice Test 3

Section 5: Mathematics

Time: 25 Minutes

20 Questions

Directions: This section is composed of two types of questions. Use the 25 minutes allotted to answer both question types. For questions 1–10, select the one correct answer of the five choices given and mark the corresponding circle on your answer sheet. Your scratch work should be done on any available space in the section.

Notes

1. All numbers used are real numbers.

2. Calculators can be used.

3. Some problems may be accompanied by figures or diagrams. These figures are drawn as accurately as possible EXCEPT when it is stated in a specific problem that a figure is not drawn to scale. The figures and diagrams are meant to provide information useful in solving the problem or problems. Unless otherwise stated, all figures and diagrams lie in a plane.

Data That Can Be Used for Reference

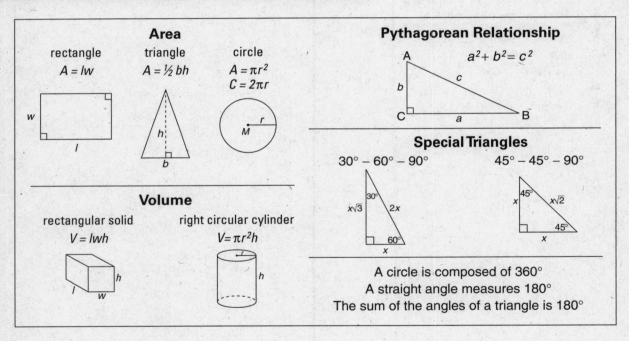

1. What is the sales tax on $132.95 if the tax rate is 7%?

    A. $ 0.93

    B. $ 6.30

    C. $ 9.31

    D. $63.06

    E. $93.07

3. If D is the set of odd integers and E is the set of even integers, then what is the intersection of sets D and E?

    A.   {0}

    B.   {1, 2, 3, 4, 5,...}

    C.   {0, 1, 2, 3, 4, 5,...}

    D.   { }

    E.   The set of all integers

2. What is the value of $1^{12} + 1^{-15} + 1^{0}$?

    A.   3

    B.   2

    C.   0

    D.   −2

    E.   −3

4. What is 30% of $\frac{25}{18}$?

    A. $\frac{5}{108}$

    B. $\frac{5}{12}$

    C. $\frac{25}{54}$

    D. $\frac{25}{6}$

    E. $\frac{125}{3}$

GO ON TO THE NEXT PAGE

5. Bob is older than Jane, but he is younger than Jim. If Bob's age is b, Jane's age is c, and Jim's age is d, then which of the following is true?

A. $c < b < d$

B. $b < c < d$

C. $b < d < c$

D. $c < d < b$

E. $d < c < b$

7. The angles of a quadrilateral are in the ratio of 2: 3: 4: 6. What is the degree measure of its largest angle?

A. 72°

B. 120°

C. 144°

D. 150°

E. 180°

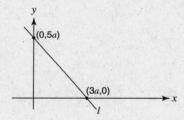

6. What is the slope of line l in the figure?

A. $\dfrac{5}{3}$

B. $\dfrac{3}{5}$

C. 0

D. $-\dfrac{5}{3}$

E. $-\dfrac{3}{5}$

8. Today is Lucy's fourteenth birthday. Last year she was three years older than twice Charlie's age at that time. Using C for Charlie's age now, which of the following can be used to determine Charlie's age now?

A. $13 - 3 = 2(C - 1)$

B. $14 - 3 = 2C$

C. $13 - 3 = 2C$

D. $13 + 3 = 2C$

E. $13 + 3 = 2(C - 1)$

9. What are the x-intercepts for the parabola $y = x^2 + 4x - 12$?

   A. $(6, 0)$ and $(-2, 0)$

   B. $(-6, 0)$ and $(2, 0)$

   C. $(0, 6)$ and $(0, -2)$

   D. $(0, -6)$ and $(0, 2)$

   E. The parabola does not have any x-intercepts.

10. If the average of two numbers is y and one of the numbers is equal to z, then the other number is equal to

   A. $2z - y$

   B. $\dfrac{(y + z)}{2}$

   C. $z - y$

   D. $2y - z$

   E. $y - 2z$

GO ON TO THE NEXT PAGE

Directions for Student-Produced Response Questions (Grid-ins): Questions 11–20 require you to solve the problem and enter your answer by carefully marking the circles on the special grid. Examples of the appropriate way to mark the grid follow.

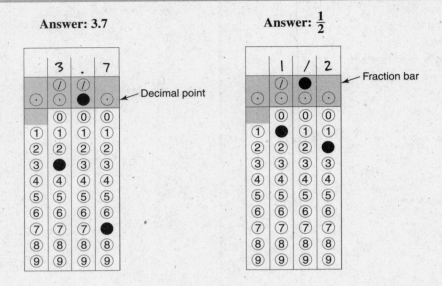

Answer: 3.7

Answer: $\frac{1}{2}$

Decimal point

Fraction bar

Answer: $1\frac{1}{2}$

Do not grid in mixed numbers in the form of mixed numbers. Always change mixed numbers to improper fractions or decimals.

Change to 1.5   or   Change to $\frac{3}{2}$

Answer: 123

Space permitting, answers can start in any column. Each grid-in answer that follows is correct.

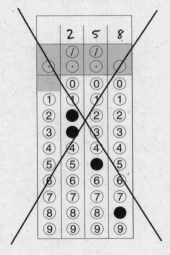

Note: Circles must be filled in correctly to receive credit. Mark only one circle in each column. No credit will be given if more than one circle in a column is marked. Example:

Answer: 258 (no credit)

GO ON TO THE NEXT PAGE

Answer: $\frac{8}{9}$

Accuracy of decimals: Always enter the most accurate decimal value that the grid will accommodate. For example: An answer such as .8888 . . . can be gridded as .888 or .889. Gridding this value as .8, .88, or .89 is considered inaccurate and therefore not acceptable. The acceptable grid-ins of $\frac{8}{9}$ are:

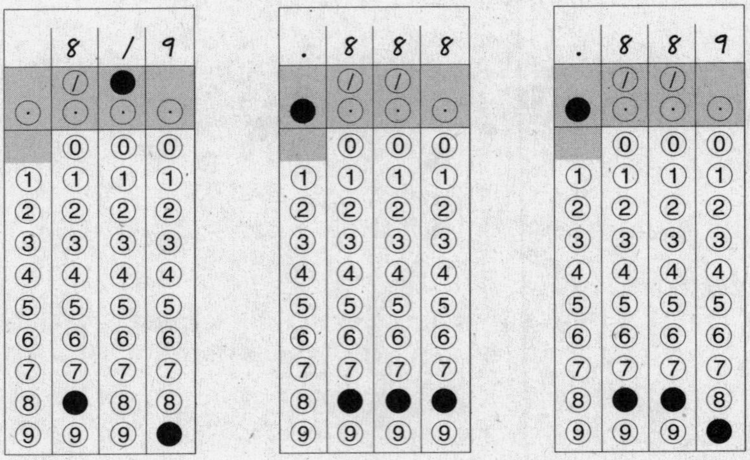

Be sure to write your answers in the boxes at the top of the circles before doing your gridding. Although writing out the answers above the columns is not required, it is very important to ensure accuracy. Even though some problems may have more than one correct answer, grid only one answer. Grid-in questions contain no negative answers.

11. If $12a = 5b$, then $\frac{a}{b} =$

13. How many different outfits can be obtained from 5 shirts, 3 pairs of slacks, and 3 sports jackets?

12. At a particular university, the ratio of males to females is 5 to 3. What percent of the students are female? (Disregard the % sign when gridding your answer.)

14. If $\sqrt{m - 3} = 6$, then $m =$

Friendly Fruit Stand Price List

apples	60¢ each
bananas	20¢ each
cantaloupes	59¢ each or 2 for $1
oranges	39¢ each or 3 for $1

15. Mr. and Mrs. Adams are planning to attend a company picnic and need to make a fruit salad for the occasion. Their recipe calls for 5 apples, 10 bananas, 4 cantaloupes, and 5 oranges. Based on the prices given above, what is the least amount they could spend at the fruit stand to buy all the fruit they need for their salad? (Disregard the $ sign when gridding your answer.)

16. Ben's average for seven math exams is 89%. What percent must he score on the next exam to raise his average to 90%? (Disregard the % sign when gridding your answer.)

17. What is the area of a square whose diagonal has a length of 12?

Products	1980	1982	1984	1986	1988	1990
A	$4.20	$4.60	$5.00	$5.40	$5.80	$6.20
B	$6.30	$6.45	$6.60	$6.75	$6.90	$7.05

18. The chart above shows the prices of products A and B from 1980 to 1990. Using the chart, in what year will product A cost 40¢ more than product B?

GO ON TO THE NEXT PAGE

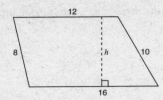

19. What is the height (*h*) of the trapezoid if its area is 98?

20. What is the length in centimeters of a chord that is 12 centimeters from the center of a circle whose radius is 20 centimeters?

IF YOU FINISH BEFORE TIME IS CALLED, CHECK YOUR WORK ON THIS SECTION ONLY. DO NOT WORK ON ANY OTHER SECTION IN THE TEST.

Section 6: Critical Reading

Time: 25 Minutes

28 Questions

In this section, choose the best answer for each question and blacken the corresponding space on the answer sheet.

Directions: Each blank in the following sentences indicates that something has been omitted. Consider the lettered words beneath the sentence and choose the word or set of words that best fits the whole sentence.

EXAMPLE:

With a million more people than any other African nation, Nigeria is the most _____ country on the continent.

- A. impoverished
- B. successful
- C. populous
- D. developed
- E. militant

The correct answer is C.

---

1. By banning cameras from the courtroom, the judge has _____ the public access to the most important civil-rights trial.

- A. belied
- B. denied
- C. defied
- D. afforded
- E. disowned

2. The grocer reluctantly admitted that, despite his care, shoplifting was still _____.

- A. exceptional
- B. sporadic
- C. commonplace
- D. redundant
- E. hackneyed

3. The work that once takes two men one week might well, one year later, take the same two men three weeks, since as Parkinson's law _____, "Work _____ so as to fill the time for its completion."

- A. urges . . . grows easier
- B. explains . . . becomes familiar
- C. states . . . decreases
- D. forbids . . . increases
- E. asserts . . . expands

4. Although they loudly cheered the news of the renewed contract, the _____ of many workers was _____ by a fear that this would be the last year of government support.

- A. sorrow . . . tempered
- B. happiness . . . augmented
- C. gladness . . . enervated
- D. euphoria . . . moderated
- E. buoyancy . . . debilitated

GO ON TO THE NEXT PAGE

5. The local conversation was nothing if not _____ for no sentence was ever more than four words long.

    A. ambiguous

    B. timely

    C. vague

    D. terse

    E. cordial

6. If both political parties can abandon _____ positions in the face of economic realities, a _____ may be achieved that will permit the government to function.

    A. sensible . . . compromise

    B. dogmatic . . . consensus

    C. incisive . . . schism

    D. irrational . . . dichotomy

    E. reasoned . . . division

7. The universal Victorian preference of the more conventional morality of Charlotte Brontë to that of her sister is indicative of the nineteenth century reader's _____ conformity.

    A. impolitic

    B. genteel

    C. discordant

    D. iconoclastic

    E. individualistic

8. Though the first thirty pages are interesting and lively, chapter after chapter about obscure musicians grows _____, and the book never recovers the _____ of its opening chapter.

    A. unmanageable . . . pace

    B. tedious . . . verve

    C. repetitive . . . torpor

    D. dull . . . lethargy

    E. boring . . . challenge

9. Some of the dangerous dishes on the menu are _____, but most are made without peppers or other spices and are as mild as most American restaurant food.

    A. bland

    B. palatable

    C. torrid

    D. insipid

    E. piquant

10. As a young man, he regarded France as _____, but in his malcontent maturity, he considered visiting any place outside of Ireland to be _____.

    A. hostile . . . irritating

    B. perfect . . . jocund

    C. irksome . . . drab

    D. Edenic . . . perplexing

    E. ideal . . . painful

Directions: Questions follow each of the passages below. Using only the stated or implied information in each passage and in its introduction, if any, answer the questions.

Questions 11–12 are based on the following passage.

At many times in our planet's history, north has become south and south has become north. Paleogeologists have discovered this phenomenon by investigating rocks. When rocks are being
(5) formed from magmas, atoms within their crystals respond to the earth's magnetic field by "pointing" toward the magnetic north pole. By age dating the rocks and noting their magnetic alignment, scientists can determine where on earth the north pole
(10) was located at that time because as the rocks solidified, they trapped that information within them. The study of ancient lava flows has revealed that at certain periods in history magnetic north was directly opposite its present location. In fact, it has been
(15) determined that magnetic reversal has occurred on average every 500,000 years.

11. "Magnetic reversal" refers to

   A. the atoms in rock crystals pointed toward the magnetic north pole.

   B. north becoming south and south becoming north.

   C. the reversal of direction in ancient lava flows.

   D. a reversal of the direction of convection currents in the earth's outer core.

   E. a disturbance in the regular 500,000-year cycle of the magnetic field.

12. According to the paragraph, which of the following was crucial to the discovery of magnetic reversal?

   A. change in direction of lava flows

   B. extinction of certain species 500,000 years ago

   C. the rapid change from "normal" to "reversed" polarity

   D. solidification of rocks formed from magma

   E. reversal in the direction of convection currents 500,000 years ago

Questions 13–16 are based on the following passages.

Passage 1

The poet Emily Dickinson was an eccentric, almost reclusive woman who never married. In the town of Amherst, Massachusetts, where she lived, people knew she could write verse, but of what real
(5) use was that, except for writing a condolence note or a compliment to accompany a gift. During her lifetime, her writing was treated as not very significant. Of course, there wasn't much of it, at least that people knew about. Only a few of her many
(10) poems were published while she was alive. Now, in our own time, she is one of America's most celebrated poets. In some ways, Emily Dickinson's life is a variation on the Cinderella story. She was transformed from a rather drab spinster to a fasci-
(15) nating woman—not by a fairy godmother but by the poetry she wrote.

Passage 2

The ideas in Emily Dickinson's poems are provocative, and she is skillful with metaphors, rhythm, and euphony. But it is Dickinson's atten-
(20) tion to the individual word that distinguishes her style. From extant manuscripts it is obvious that she weighed each word of her poems and was meticulous in choosing the right one. In some manuscripts she would write down nine or ten different
(25) words for the same idea so that she could study which one would best suit her purpose in a poem. One reason her poems are so economical is that she respected the importance of every word she chose.

13. The author of Passage 1 emphasizes which of the following about Emily Dickinson?

   A. the contrast between her quiet life and her talent

   B. her inability to be taken seriously as a writer during her lifetime

   C. the isolated life she led

   D. her reputation as a poet today

   E. the psychological motivations for her poetry

GO ON TO THE NEXT PAGE

14. In Passage 1, line 2, the word "reclusive" most nearly means

    A. snobbish.

    B. ill-natured.

    C. uninteresting.

    D. solitary.

    E. unconventional.

15. The author of Passage 2 is most impressed by Emily Dickinson's

    A. provocative ideas.

    B. ability to choose vivid imagery.

    C. precision with language.

    D. diligence in revising her work.

    E. skill with poetic meters.

16. Which of the following best describes the attitudes of the authors towards Emily Dickinson?

    A. The author of Passage 1 feels her life is more interesting than her poetry, while the opposite is true for the author of Passage 2.

    B. Both authors consider her an important poet.

    C. Both authors express surprise that a sheltered woman could write such great poetry.

    D. The author of Passage 1 feels Dickinson's life was pathetic, while the author of Passage 2 does not.

    E. The author of Passage 1 is more interested in the ideas in Dickinson's poems than is the author of Passage 2.

Questions 17–28 are based on the following passage.

Bilingual ballots have never enjoyed much public support because the public has never known much about their origin and rationale. For instance, it is often assumed that any non-English speaker is entitled
(5) to vote in his or her native tongue. The reality is that this right applies only to linguistic minorities who have historically faced discrimination at the polls—Hispanics, Asians, and Native Americans—and only in areas where they meet strict requirements. A lan-
(10) guage group must represent more than 5 percent of the local population and have below-average rates of voter turnout and English literacy. Moreover, the cost of assisting non-English-speaking voters is quite modest. San Francisco officials have estimated
(15) that the annual expense of trilingual English–Spanish–Chinese ballots comes to less than three cents per household. In 1984, a federal survey of eighty-three "covered" jurisdictions found that it cost them a grand total of $388,000, or 7.6 percent of

(20) election expenses, to provide bilingual ballots. Hardly an exorbitant price to safeguard what the Supreme Court has called a "fundamental right because it is preservative of all rights."

The trend toward bilingual ballots originated in
(25) the Voting Rights Act of 1965. This law suspended literacy requirements for voting in southern states where they had been systematically used to disfranchise African-Americans. A related provision, sponsored by Senator Robert F. Kennedy, prohib-
(30) ited such tests elsewhere for voters who had completed the sixth grade on U.S. soil in a school whose "predominant classroom language was other than English." In other words, native-born U.S. citizens could no longer be prevented from voting
(35) simply because they had grown up in a non-English-speaking environment. Puerto Ricans were the main beneficiaries of this section, particularly in New York, where a 1921 amendment to the state constitution (aimed principally at Yiddish-speaking
(40) Jews) had denied the franchise to anyone unable to read English.

Federal courts soon went further. Banning English literacy tests was a hollow gesture, they reasoned, if formerly excluded voters still faced a
(45) language barrier at the polls. Accordingly, they mandated bilingual election materials for Puerto Rican voters in Philadelphia, Chicago, and New York. "It is simply fundamental," wrote one judge, "that voting instructions and ballots, in addition to
(50) any other material which forms part of the official communication to registered voters prior to an election, must be in Spanish as well as in English, if the vote of Spanish-speaking citizens is not to be seriously impaired."
(55) Bilingual voting, like bilingual education, was designed to compensate for decades of inequality, a goal that could not be achieved through strictly "equal" treatment. Simply prohibiting the English literacy test, or ending the segregation of Mexican
(60) and Chinese American students, was insufficient to restore rights that linguistic minorities had lost through no fault of their own. For such groups, affirmative measures were needed to guarantee equal opportunity. Clearly, this approach can lead to
(65) anomalies, as when naturalized citizens of "Spanish origin" are entitled to bilingual ballots but their Portuguese- or French-speaking neighbors are not. Congressional critics of the expanded Voting Rights Act have argued that its effect is "to mandate an
(70) 'unequal protection of the laws,'" privileging some minority voters over others from non-English-speaking backgrounds—namely, that it favors non-white immigrants and indigenous minorities over white Euro-ethnics.

(75)   Under current law an individual's need for a bilingual ballot does not enter into the equation. Perhaps it should. Why encourage immigrants to become U.S. citizens and then limit their ability to participate in our political system? Why not make
(80) every effort to eliminate language barriers to voting? It is true that most applicants for naturalization must pass an English literacy test (except for those aged fifty or older who have been legal U.S. residents for at least twenty years). But the level of pro-
(85) ficiency required is quite low. In 1982, an average year, the Immigration and Naturalization Service turned down only twenty-nine out of 201,507 petitions for citizenship because of inability to speak, read, or write the English language. The literacy
(90) skills required to decipher voter registration notices or complex ballot propositions are normally the last to be acquired in a second language.

17. It can be inferred from the passage that objections have been made to the use of bilingual ballots on the grounds that

  I.   they cost too much taxpayer money.
  II. any non-English speaker can demand a bilingual ballot.
  III. any Spanish-speaking voter can demand a bilingual ballot.

  A. I only
  B. I and II only
  C. I and III only
  D. II and III only
  E. I, II, and III

18. Which of the following non-English-speaking groups could qualify for a bilingual ballot in an American election at the present time?

  A. an Italian-speaking group making up 6 percent of the local population
  B. a Samoan-speaking group making up 2 percent of the local population
  C. a Portuguese-speaking group with above-average rates of English literacy
  D. a Korean-speaking group making up 12 percent of the local population
  E. a Spanish-speaking group with above-average rates of voter turnout

19. In the first paragraph, the concluding phrase, "fundamental right because it is preservative of all rights," refers to the fact that

  A. laws are necessary to preserve order and justice in any society.
  B. the courts must be the final arbiter of what is and what is not permitted.
  C. by voting, citizens can guarantee that all their other rights are not lost.
  D. the rights of one class or group must be preserved for all classes or groups.
  E. the freedom of the citizenry is more important than the expenditure of a small sum of money.

20. Under the Voting Rights Act of 1965, a native-born, Spanish-speaking American citizen who did not read English would

  A. not be permitted to vote under any circumstances.
  B. not be permitted to vote if he or she had completed six grades in any school.
  C. be permitted to vote under any circumstances.
  D. be permitted to vote if he or she had completed six grades in a Spanish-speaking school in the United States.
  E. be permitted to vote if he or she passed a literacy test.

21. The second paragraph suggests that, before 1965, there were laws designed to keep all of the following from voting EXCEPT

  A. native-born Hispanics.
  B. Irish Catholics.
  C. African-Americans.
  D. Yiddish-speaking Jews.
  E. foreign-language speakers unable to speak English.

22. The word "franchise" in line 40 means

  A. ownership.
  B. marketing privilege.
  C. the right to vote.
  D. corporate rights.
  E. a team that represents a city.

GO ON TO THE NEXT PAGE

23. In line 43, the phrase "a hollow gesture" can be best interpreted to mean

    A. a useless action.
    B. a resounding success.
    C. an empty boast.
    D. a sacred motion.
    E. a foolish joke.

24. Which of the following statements could reasonably be used to argue against the belief that all the laws supporting bilingual voting should be repealed because they discriminate against white immigrants from Europe?

    I.   Since many native English speakers have trouble understanding the complex language of ballots, non-English speakers are not at a serious disadvantage.
    II. Though the laws may be imperfect, it is better to spare a large number of other voters from discrimination.
    III. Elimination of bilingual voting would decrease the incidence of election fraud.

    A. I only
    B. II only
    C. III only
    D. I and II only
    E. I, II, and III

25. Bilingual voting equality could not be achieved by strictly equal treatment of all foreign-language speakers because

    A. some minorities had been subject to unequal treatment for many years.
    B. the complexity of Asian languages is greater than that of European languages.
    C. the costs of printing languages such as Korean or Chinese are higher than those for printing Spanish.
    D. some minorities control more of the wealth than others.
    E. under any circumstances, equal treatment is impossible because all minorities are different.

26. Which of the following citizens would probably have the most difficulty in obtaining a bilingual ballot in his or her native language?

    A. a Hispanic immigrant from Argentina
    B. a white immigrant from Spain
    C. a white immigrant from Greece
    D. a non-white immigrant from Taiwan
    E. a Hispanic immigrant from El Salvador

27. The effect of the final paragraph of the passage is to suggest that

    I.   the literacy test required of naturalized citizens is an inadequate test of the literacy required of a voter.
    II. the Voting Rights Act of 1965 is inadequate and additional laws should be enacted to enable all voters to vote.
    III. the availability of a bilingual ballot should be determined chiefly by the voters' need for language assistance.

    A. III only
    B. I and II only
    C. I and III only
    D. II and III only
    E. I, II, and III

28. From this passage, the reader can infer that the author's attitude toward the "English Only" movement, a group urging the elimination of bilingual schools and ballots, is one of

    A. enthusiastic approval.
    B. guarded approval.
    C. approval in theory, but not in practice.
    D. guarded disapproval.
    E. strong disapproval.

IF YOU FINISH BEFORE TIME IS CALLED, CHECK YOUR WORK ON THIS SECTION ONLY. DO NOT WORK ON ANY OTHER SECTION IN THE TEST.

Section 7: Mathematics

Time: 20 Minutes

15 Questions

Directions: Solve each problem in this section by using the information given and your own mathematical calculations, insights, and problem-solving skills. Then select the one correct answer of the five choices given and mark the corresponding circle on your answer sheet. Use the available space on the page for your scratch work.

Notes

1. All numbers used are real numbers.

2. Calculators can be used.

3. Some problems may be accompanied by figures or diagrams. These figures are drawn as accurately as possible EXCEPT when it is stated in a specific problem that a figure is not drawn to scale. The figures and diagrams are meant to provide information useful in solving the problem or problems. Unless otherwise stated, all figures and diagrams lie in a plane.

Data That Can Be Used for Reference

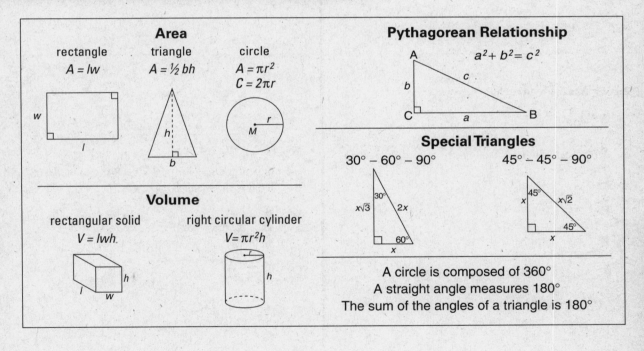

GO ON TO THE NEXT PAGE

1. If $\frac{3}{x} = 6$, then $x - 1 =$

A. 1

B. $\frac{1}{2}$

C. $-\frac{1}{2}$

D. $-\frac{2}{3}$

E. $-1\frac{1}{2}$

2. What is the reciprocal of $\dfrac{.25 \times \frac{2}{3}}{.06 \times 15}$?

A. $\frac{3}{20}$

B. $\frac{5}{27}$

C. $\frac{2}{3}$

D. $\frac{27}{5}$

E. $\frac{20}{3}$

3. Harmon's new sports car averages 35 miles per each gallon of gasoline. Assuming that Harmon is able to maintain his average miles per gallon, how far can he drive on 12 gallons of gas?

A. $2\frac{11}{12}$ miles

B. 42 miles

C. 350 miles

D. 420 miles

E. 700 miles

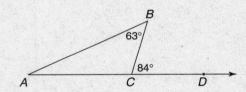

4. Given $\triangle ABC$ with $\angle BCD = 84°$ and $\angle B = 63°$, what is the measure of $\angle A$?

A. 21°

B. 27°

C. 84°

D. 96°

E. 116°

5. Teachers will be assigned special camp duty one day of the week during a seven-day camping trip. If all the days of the week (Monday through Sunday) are tossed into a cap and each teacher chooses one day of the week, what is the probability that the first teacher will randomly select a weekday (Monday through Friday)?

A. $\frac{1}{7}$

B. $\frac{2}{7}$

C. $\frac{1}{5}$

D. $\frac{5}{7}$

E. $\frac{5}{2}$

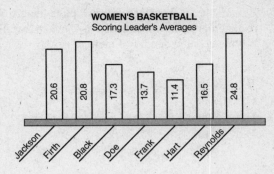

WOMEN'S BASKETBALL
Scoring Leader's Averages

6. According to the bar graph above, Reynolds's average score exceeds Doe's average score by how many points?

A. 13.4
B. 11.1
C. 8.3
D. 7.4
E. 2.3

7. Given a positive even integer y, which of the following cannot be evenly divisible by y?

A. $y - 2$
B. $y + 2$
C. $2y + 2$
D. $3y$
E. $y + 1$

GO ON TO THE NEXT PAGE

8. What is the total surface area in square meters of a rectangular solid whose length is 7 meters, width is 6 meters, and depth is 3 meters?

   A. 32m^2
   B. 81m^2
   C. 126m^2
   D. 162m^2
   E. 252m^2

9. The first five numbers in a sequence are 3, 7, 15, 31, and 63. What is the next number in the sequence?

   A. 94
   B. 125
   C. 126
   D. 127
   E. 189

10. Maria plans to make sandwiches for a picnic. She has three types of bread from which to choose (rye, sourdough, and white), four types of meat from which to choose (salami, bologna, ham, and pastrami), and three types of cheese from which to choose (Swiss, cheddar, and jack). If Maria will use only one type of bread, one type of meat, and one type of cheese on each sandwich, how many different kinds of sandwiches can Maria make?

   A. 3
   B. 4
   C. 10
   D. 17
   E. 36

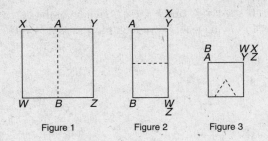

Figure 1   Figure 2   Figure 3

11. In Figure 1, a square piece of paper is folded along dotted line *AB* so that *X* is on top of *Y* and *W* is on top of *Z* (Figure 2). The paper is then folded again so that *B* is on top of *A* and *WZ* is on top of *XY* (Figure 3). A small triangle is cut out of the folded paper as shown in Figure 3. If the paper is unfolded, which of the following could be the result?

A.

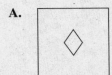

B.

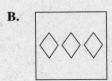

C.

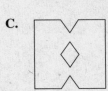

D.

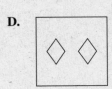

E.

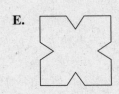

12. A girl runs *k* miles in *n* hours. How many miles will she run in *x* hours at the same rate?

A.   *knx*

B. $\frac{k}{n}$

C. $\frac{kx}{n}$

D.   *kx*

E. $\frac{kn}{x}$

13. A circle whose center is the origin passes through the point *P* (−3, 4). What is the length of the radius of the circle?

A.   1
B.   5
C.   7
D.   10
E.   25

GO ON TO THE NEXT PAGE

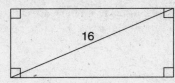

Note: Figure not drawn to scale.

14. If the diagonal of a rectangle is 16, then what is its area in square units?

A. 32
B. 64
C. 160
D. 256
E. It cannot be determined from the information given.

15. If $a = 1 + 5^{-x}$ and $b = 1 + 5^{x}$, which of the following is an expression for a in terms of b?

A. $\dfrac{1}{b}$

B. $b - 1$

C. $\dfrac{1}{b - 1}$

D. $\dfrac{b}{b - 1}$

E. $1 - b$

IF YOU FINISH BEFORE TIME IS CALLED, CHECK YOUR WORK ON THIS SECTION ONLY. DO NOT WORK ON ANY OTHER SECTION IN THE TEST.

STOP

Section 8: Critical Reading

Time: 20 Minutes

15 Questions

In this section, choose the best answer for each question and blacken the corresponding space on the answer sheet.

Directions: Questions follow the passages below. Using only the stated or implied information in each passage and in the introduction, if any, answer the questions.

Questions 1–13 are based on the following two passages.

The following are critical commentaries by two well-known American film reviewers on the 1960s film The Graduate.

Passage 1

The Graduate is a director's picture because even its mistakes are the proofs of a personal style. Style is more an attitude toward things than the things themselves. It can be a raised eyebrow or a

(5)   nervous smile or a pair of shrugged shoulders. It can even be an averted glance. By playing down some of the more offensive qualities of the book, Nichols expresses his own attitude toward the material. The main trouble with the book is its

(10)   reduction of the world to the ridiculous scale of an overgrown and outdated Holden Caulfield. Charles Webb's Benjamin Braddock expresses himself with a monosyllabic smugness that becomes maddeningly self indulgent as the book unravels into

(15)   slapstick passion. He is superior to his pathetic parents and adults generally. He is kind to the wife of his father's law partner even though she seduces him with cold-bloodedly calculating carnality. Ben then falls in love with Elaine, his mistress's daugh-

(20)   ter, and makes her marry him through the sheer persistence of his pursuit.

The screenplay has been improved by a series of little changes and omissions constituting a pattern of discretion and abstraction. The hero is made less

(25)   bumptious, the predatory wife less calculating, the sensitive daughter less passive, and the recurring parental admonitions are reduced in number and intensity. The very end of the movie is apparently the result of an anti-cliché improvisation. In the book,

(30)   Ben interrupts Elaine's wedding (to another) before the troths have been plighted. In the movie, the bride kisses the groom before Ben can disrupt the proceeding, but the bride runs off just the same. And

this little change makes all the difference in drama-

(35)   tizing the triumph of people over proceedings. An entire genre of Hollywood movies had been constructed upon the suspenseful chase-to-the-altar proposition that what God hath joined together no studio scriptwriter can put asunder. *The Graduate*

(40)   not only shatters this monogamous mythology; it does so in the name of a truer love. . . . I was with *The Graduate* all the way because I responded fully to its romantic feelings. Some people have complained that the Bancroft-Hoffman relationship is

(45)   more compelling than the subsequent Ross-Hoffman relationship. I don't agree. It is easier to be interesting with an unconventional sexual relationship than with a conventional love pairing. *The Graduate* is moving precisely because its hero passes from a

(50)   premature maturity to an innocence regained, an idealism reconfirmed. That he is so much out of his time and place makes him more of an individual and less of a type. Even the overdone caricatures that surround the three principals cannot diminish

(55)   the cruel beauty of this love story.

Passage 2

Part of the fun of movies is in seeing "what everybody's talking about," and if people are flocking to a movie, or if the press can con us into thinking that they are, then ironically, there is a sense in

(60)   which we want to see it, even if we suspect we won't enjoy it, because we want to know what's going on. Even if it's the worst inflated pompous trash that is the most talked about (and it usually is) and even if that talk is manufactured, we want to

(65)   see the movies because so many people fall for whatever is talked about that they make the advertisers' lies true.

An analyst tells me that when his patients are not talking about their personal hang-ups and their im-

(70)   mediate problems they talk about the situations and characters in movies like *The Graduate,* and they talk about them with as much personal involvement

GO ON TO THE NEXT PAGE

345

as about their immediate problems. The high-
school and college students identifying with Dustin
(75) Hoffman's Benjamin are not that different from the
stenographer who used to live and breathe with the
Joan Crawford-working girl and worry about
whether that rich boy would really make her
happy—and considered her pictures "great." They
(80) don't see the movie as a movie but as part of the
soap opera of their lives. The person who responds
this way does not respond more freely but less
freely and less fully than the person who is aware of
what is well done and what is badly done in a
(85) movie, who can accept some things in it and reject
others, who uses all his senses in reacting, not just
his emotional vulnerabilities. The small triumph of
The Graduate was to have domesticated alienation
and the difficulty of communication, by making
(90) what Benjamin is alienated from a middle-class
comic strip and making it absurdly evident that he
has nothing to communicate—which is just what
makes him an acceptable hero for the large movie
audience. *The Graduate* isn't a bad movie, it's en-
(95) tertaining, though in a fairly slick way. What's surprising is that so many people take it so seriously.

What's funny about the movie are the laughs on
that dumb sincere boy who wants to talk about art
in bed. But then the movie begins to pander to
(100) youthful narcissism, glorifying his innocence, and
making the predatory (and now crazy) woman the
villainess. Commercially this works: the inarticu-
late dull boy becomes a romantic hero for the audience to project into with all those squishy and now
(105) conventional feelings of look, his parents don't
communicate with him; look, he wants truth not
sham, and so on. But the movie betrays itself and
its own expertise, sells out its comic moments that
click along with the rhythm of a hit Broadway
(110) show, to make the oldest movie pitch of them all—
asking the audience to identify with the simpleton
who is the latest version of the misunderstood
teenager and the pure-in-heart boy next door. It's
almost painful to tell kids who have gone to see
(115) *The Graduate* eight times that once was enough for
you because you've already seen it [in other ver-
sions]. How could you convince them that a movie
that sells innocence is a very commercial piece of
work when they're so clearly in the market to buy
(120) innocence? *The Graduate* only wants to succeed
and that's fundamentally what's the matter with it.
This kind of moviemaking shifts values, shifts
focus, shifts emphasis, shifts everything for a surefire response. Mike Nichols's "gift" is that he lets the
(125) audience direct him; this is demagoguery in the arts.

The success of *The Graduate* is sociological: the
revelation of how emotionally accessible modern
youth is to the same old manipulation. The recur-
rence of certain themes in movies suggests that
(130) each generation wants romance restated in slightly
new terms, mooning away in fixation on themselves and thinking this fixation meant movies had
suddenly become an art, and their art.

1. It can be inferred from the first paragraph of
Passage 1 that Charles Webb is

   A. the director of the film *The Graduate*.
   B. the author of the novel on which the film
   The Graduate is based.
   C. the author of the screenplay of *The Graduate*.
   D. the actor playing Benjamin Braddock in the
   film *The Graduate*.
   E. a character in *The Catcher in the Rye*.

2. In Passage 1, line 6, the phrase "playing down"
means

   A. concluding.
   B. minimizing.
   C. making unscrupulous use of.
   D. excluding.
   E. participating in.

3. By referring to the novel *The Graduate*'s
"reduction of the world to the ridiculous scale of
an overgrown and outdated Holden Caulfield" (the
hero of Salinger's *The Catcher in the Rye*), the
author of Passage 1 suggests that

   I.   the characterization of Benjamin Braddock
   in the novel is inferior to that in the film.
   II. the Salinger novel is overgrown and
   outdated.
   III. the film is superior to the novel *The
   Graduate*.

   A. III only
   B. I and II only
   C. I and III only
   D. II and III only
   E. I, II, and III

4. As it is used in Passage 1, the word "bumptious" (line 25) means

    A. passive.

    B. slovenly.

    C. yokel-like.

    D. arrogant.

    E. jolting.

5. According to the critic of Passage 1, the most original event in the plot of the film is having

    A. Benjamin fall in love with Elaine, the daughter of his mistress.

    B. the older woman the seducer of the younger man.

    C. Benjamin pursue Elaine despite her engagement to another man.

    D. Benjamin interrupt Elaine's wedding after vows are exchanged.

    E. the young lovers united at the end.

6. According to Passage 1, the theme of the film *The Graduate* is the

    A. recovery of idealism through love.

    B. self-indulgent narcissism of youth.

    C. older generation's failure to nurture the younger.

    D. myth of the monogamous marriage.

    E. superiority of institutions to people.

7. The argument of the first paragraph of Passage 2 (lines 56–67) is that

    A. the advertising for films is often false.

    B. too many people believe advertisers and go to bad movies as a result.

    C. people go to movies partly to discover what has made a film popular or talked about.

    D. people waste time and money at trashy movies because they cannot see the falsity of advertising.

    E. more people would go to better films if advertising were more honest.

8. According to the critic of Passage 2, the popular success of *The Graduate* is due to the fact that Benjamin

    A. is empty-headed.

    B. is alienated.

    C. is unable to communicate with his parents.

    D. matures in the course of the film.

    E. is sincere.

9. In Passage 2, the meaning of the word "gift" in line 124 is

    A. present.

    B. talent.

    C. secret.

    D. idea.

    E. blessing.

10. When Passage 2 says that Mike Nichols "lets the audience direct him" (lines 124–125), it is saying that

    A. a good director has a firm hold on all the details of a film.

    B. Nichols's films are badly directed because they are too difficult for many audiences to follow.

    C. Nichols does not pay enough attention to the needs of his actors.

    D. Nichols gives the audience what he knows it likes.

    E. Nichols is indifferent to commercial success.

11. According to Passage 2, *The Graduate* is sociologically valuable because it

    A. exposes the sentimentality of a generation.

    B. expresses the universality of alienation in the modern world.

    C. teaches mutual respect between the sexes.

    D. expresses the nature of the difficulties generations that cannot communicate must face.

    E. reveals how different the generation of the late 1960s is from older generations.

12. Of the following phrases from Passage 2, all might be applied by their author to the author of the first passage EXCEPT

    A. a critic who is "not that different from the stenographer who used to live and breathe with the Joan Crawford-working girl" (lines 75–77)

    B. a critic who sees a movie as "part of the soap opera of" his life (lines 80–81)

    C. a critic who "uses all his senses in reacting, not just his emotional vulnerabilities" (lines 86–87)

    D. a critic "clearly in the market to buy innocence" (lines 119–120)

    E. a critic "emotionally accessible . . . to the same old manipulation" (lines 127–128)

GO ON TO THE NEXT PAGE

13. With which of the following comments on the film would the authors of both Passage 1 and Passage 2 agree?

   I. The presentation of Ben's parents is a caricature.
   II. The older woman who seduces Ben is presented as predatory.
   III. The latter part of the movie attempts to present Ben as an exemplar of innocence.

   A. II only
   B. I and II only
   C. I and III only
   D. II and III only
   E. I, II, and III

Questions 14–15 are based on the following passage.

A person experiencing synesthesia may "see" green when hearing a particular musical note, or taste sweetness when touching a circular object. Rather than remaining separate, the senses get
(5) mixed up. Francis Galton, Charles Darwin's cousin, published a paper on synesthesia in 1880, but many people dismissed the phenomenon, attributing it to the effects of drug use or perhaps childhood memories. In recent years, however, research suggests that
(10) synesthesia results from a kind of cross-wiring in the brain—that is, two normally separate areas of the brain elicit activity in each other. In studying synesthesia, scientists are learning how the brain processes sensory information and uses it to make
(15) connections between seemingly unrelated inputs. An interesting finding, according to one study, is that synesthesia is much more common in creative people than in the general population.

14. The author of the passage cites the article by Francis Galton primarily to

   A. show the importance of synesthesia to the scientific community.
   B. explain how the phenomenon received its name.
   C. suggest that Charles Darwin was interested in the phenomenon.
   D. dismiss the idea that synesthesia is merely the result of childhood memories.
   E. indicate that the phenomenon of synesthesia was recognized in the 19th century.

15. Which of the following statements is suggested by the last sentence of the paragraph?

   A. The brain processes of creative people are identical to the brain processes of people who experience synesthesia.
   B. People unable to experience synesthesia will be inclined to prefer professions requiring logical thinking.
   C. Creativity may be related to the ability to make connections between seemingly unrelated inputs.
   D. Because of cross-wiring in the brain, creative people are often unstable and erratic.
   E. The frequent occurrence of synesthesia among creative people is probably related to drug use.

IF YOU FINISH BEFORE TIME IS CALLED, CHECK YOUR WORK ON THIS SECTION ONLY. DO NOT WORK ON ANY OTHER SECTION IN THE TEST.

Section 9: Mathematics

Time: 25 Minutes

20 Questions

Directions: This section is composed of two types of questions. Use the 25 minutes allotted to answer both question types. For questions 1–10, select the one correct answer of the five choices given and mark the corresponding circle on your answer sheet. Your scratch work should be done on any available space in the section.

Notes

1. All numbers used are real numbers.

2. Calculators can be used.

3. Some problems may be accompanied by figures or diagrams. These figures are drawn as accurately as possible EXCEPT when it is stated in a specific problem that a figure is not drawn to scale. The figures and diagrams are meant to provide information useful in solving the problem or problems. Unless otherwise stated, all figures and diagrams lie in a plane.

Data That Can Be Used for Reference

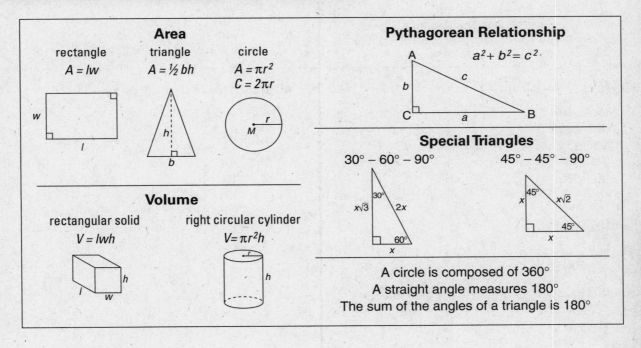

GO ON TO THE NEXT PAGE

1. The length of a rectangle is $6l$, and the width is $4w$. What is the perimeter?

    A. $24lw$
    B. $20lw$
    C. $10lw$
    D. $12l + 8w$
    E. $6l + 4w$

3. What is the average of $\frac{2}{3}, \frac{3}{4}$, and $\frac{5}{6}$?

    A. $\frac{10}{13}$
    B. $\frac{10}{39}$
    C. $\frac{27}{4}$
    D. $\frac{3}{4}$
    E. $\frac{9}{4}$

2. $4 \times 5^2 - |6 - 8 \times 7| =$

    A. 50
    B. 86
    C. 150
    D. 350
    E. 386

4. What is the value of y if $y\sqrt{.04} = 8$?

    A. .04
    B. .4
    C. 4.0
    D. 40
    E. 400

5. How many inches are in m yards and n feet?

   A. $m + n$

   B. $36m + 12n$

   C. $36(m + n)$

   D. $3m + n$

   E. $12(m + n)$

7. The endpoints of the diameter of a circle have coordinates $(-5, 8)$ and $(-3, 5)$. What are the coordinates of the center of the circle?

   A. $\left(-4, \dfrac{13}{2}\right)$

   B. $\left(-1, \dfrac{3}{2}\right)$

   C. $\left(1, \dfrac{-3}{2}\right)$

   D. $(-8, 13)$

   E. $(-2, 3)$

6. If $\dfrac{3x^2 - 7x + 16}{x^2 + 4} = 3$, then $x =$

   A. -4

   B. $-\dfrac{4}{7}$

   C. 0

   D. $\dfrac{4}{7}$

   E. 4

8. What is the value of $\dfrac{10^{20} + 10^{21}}{10^{20}}$?

   A. 10

   B. 11

   C. 20

   D. 2^{21}

   E. 10^{21}

GO ON TO THE NEXT PAGE

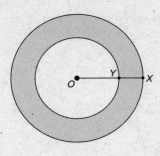

9. In the circles above, $OX = 10$ and $XY = 2$. What is the ratio of the area of the shaded region to the area of the larger circle?

A. $\dfrac{1}{5}$

B. $\dfrac{4}{5}$

C. $\dfrac{16}{25}$

D. $\dfrac{9}{25}$

E. $\dfrac{1}{25}$

10. How many four-digit numbers are possible if the first digit cannot be zero and the number is divisible by 5?

A.   900

B.   1,458

C.   1,800

D.   2,000

E.   4,500

Directions for Student-Produced Response Questions (Grid-ins): Questions 11–20 require you to solve the problems and enter your answers by carefully marking the circles on the special grid. Examples of the appropriate way to mark the grid follow.

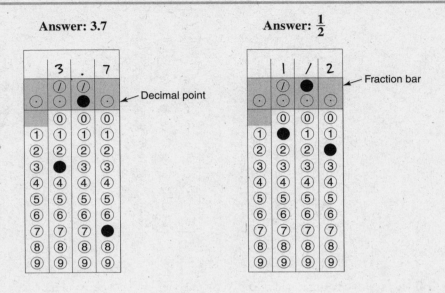

Answer: 3.7   Answer: $\frac{1}{2}$

Answer: $1\frac{1}{2}$

Do not grid in mixed numbers in the form of mixed numbers. Always change mixed numbers to improper fractions or decimals.

Change to 1.5   or   Change to $\frac{3}{2}$

GO ON TO THE NEXT PAGE

Answer: 123

Space permitting, answers can start in any column. Each grid-in answer that follows is correct.

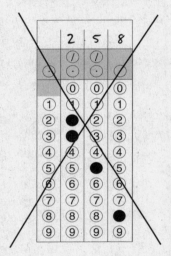

Note: Circles must be filled in correctly to receive credit. Mark only one circle in each column. No credit will be given if more than one circle in a column is marked. Example:

Answer: 258 (no credit)

Answer: $\frac{8}{9}$

Accuracy of decimals: Always enter the most accurate decimal value that the grid will accommodate. For example: An answer such as .8888 . . . can be gridded as .888 or .889. Gridding this value as .8, .88, or .89 is considered inaccurate and therefore not acceptable. The acceptable grid-ins of $\frac{8}{9}$ are:

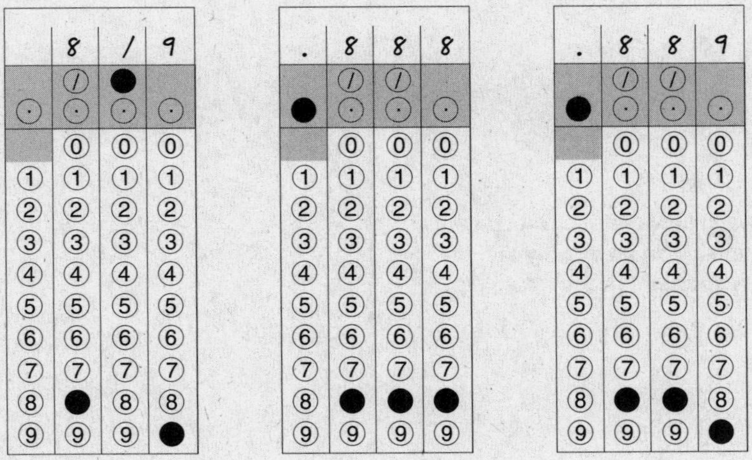

Be sure to write your answers in the boxes at the top of the circles before doing your gridding. Although writing out the answers above the columns is not required, it is very important to ensure accuracy. Even though some problems may have more than one correct answer, grid only one answer. Grid-in questions contain no negative answers.

11. If $F = \frac{9}{5}C + 32$, what is F when $C = 19$?

12. Red, green, and white jellybeans are combined in a ratio of 5:4:3, respectively. What is the ratio of green jelly beans to the total number of jelly beans?

13. A picture 8 inches by 10 inches is bordered by a frame that is $1\frac{1}{2}$ inches wide. What is the total area of the picture and the frame in square inches?

GO ON TO THE NEXT PAGE

Review Test Areas

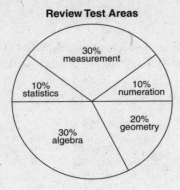

14. According to the graph above, if the test contains 5 numeration problems, then how many algebra problems would be expected?

Note: Figure not drawn to scale.

15. If, in the figure above, $y = 3x$, then $x =$

16. If 150% of y is equal to 60% of z, and y and z are not zero, then $y/z =$

17. Three-fourths of a circle is divided into six equal parts. What fractional part of the whole circle does each piece represent?

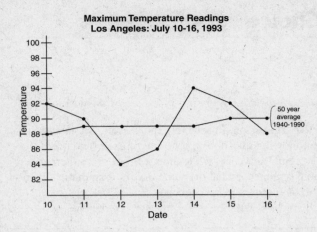

**Maximum Temperature Readings
Los Angeles: July 10-16, 1993**

50 year
average
1940-1990

18. Of the seven days shown in the graph above, what percent of the days did the maximum temperature exceed the average temperature? (Disregard the % sign when gridding your answer.)

19. How many days would it take for two people working together to complete a job if it takes one person 6 days working alone and it takes the other person 10 days working alone to complete the same job?

20. A fraction is equivalent to $\frac{2}{3}$. If its numerator is decreased by 2 and its denominator is increased by 3, the new fraction is equivalent to $\frac{1}{3}$. What is the original fraction?

IF YOU FINISH BEFORE TIME IS CALLED, CHECK YOUR WORK ON THIS SECTION ONLY. DO NOT WORK ON ANY OTHER SECTION IN THE TEST.

Section 10: Writing—Multiple Choice

Time: 10 Minutes

15 Questions

In this section, choose the best answer for each question and blacken the corresponding space on the answer sheet.

Directions: The following questions test correctness and effective expression. In selecting the answer, pay attention to grammar, diction, sentence structure, and punctuation. In the following questions, part or all of each sentence is underlined. The A answer repeats the underlined portion of the original sentence, while the next four offer alternatives. Choose the answer that best expresses the meaning of the original sentence, and at the same time is grammatically correct and stylistically superior. The correct choice should be clear, unambiguous, and concise.

EXAMPLE:

The forecaster predicted <u>rain and the sky was clear.</u>

- **A.** rain and the sky was clear.
- **B.** rain but the sky was clear.
- **C.** rain the sky was clear.
- **D.** rain, but the sky was clear.
- **E.** rain being as the sky was clear.

The correct answer is D.

---

1. Alexander Frater was educated in Australia, <u>when he emigrated to England,</u> and eventually became a correspondent for a London newspaper.

   - **A.** when he emigrated to England,
   - **B.** emigrated to England,
   - **C.** while he emigrated to England,
   - **D.** emigrating to England,
   - **E.** from whence he emigrated to England,

2. In Hawaii, <u>they are emphasizing the Hawaiian language as a part of</u> a renaissance in the native culture, including music and dance.

   - **A.** they are emphasizing the Hawaiian language as a part of
   - **B.** the emphasis on the Hawaiian language is part of
   - **C.** they are putting emphasis on Hawaiian as a language as part of
   - **D.** by emphasizing the Hawaiian language, they are creating a part of
   - **E.** the emphasis on the Hawaiian language is to them a part of

3. Women are starting small businesses <u>twice as fast as men; one of</u> twenty working women is now self-employed.

   - **A.** twice as fast as men; one of
   - **B.** twice as fast as men one of
   - **C.** twice as fast as men, one of
   - **D.** two times as fast as men, one of
   - **E.** two times as fast as men one of

4. <u>Illiteracy costs more than five billion dollars in unemployment and welfare benefits yearly, affecting one-fifth of the adult population.</u>

   A.   Illiteracy costs more than five billion dollars in unemployment and welfare benefits yearly, affecting one-fifth of the adult population.

   B.   Yearly, illiteracy costs more than five billion dollars in unemployment and welfare benefits, affecting one-fifth of the adult population.

   C.   Affecting one-fifth of the adult population, illiteracy costs more than five billion dollars in unemployment and welfare benefits yearly.

   D.   Yearly affecting one-fifth of the adult population, illiteracy costs more than five billion dollars in unemployment and welfare benefits.

   E.   Costing more than five billion dollars in unemployment and welfare benefits, illiteracy affects one-fifth of the adult population yearly.

5. Luis Jimenez's fiberglass sculpture *Fiesta Jarabe* <u>depicting a traditional hat dance, and placed</u> just north of the Mexican border.

   A.   depicting a traditional hat dance, and placed

   B.   depicting a traditional hat dance, and is placed

   C.   depicting a traditional hat dance

   D.   depicts a traditional hat dance, placed

   E.   depicts a traditional hat dance and is placed

6. At one time, nearly all of Kuwait's 700 oil wells were on <u>fire the crippled</u> refineries were closed.

   A.   fire the crippled

   B.   fire but the crippled

   C.   fire, crippled, the

   D.   fire; the crippled

   E.   fire, crippled

7. The sky-diver compared his feelings of elation <u>to winning a lottery, scoring a touchdown, or beating</u> the odds in Las Vegas.

   A.   to winning a lottery, scoring a touchdown, or beating

   B.   to when one wins a lottery, scores a touchdown, or beats

   C.   to winning a lottery, to scoring a touchdown, or beating

   D.   to winning a lottery, to scoring a touchdown, or to beating

   E.   to a win in a lottery, scoring a touchdown, or beating

8. <u>In 1982, Arun Shourie exposed a multi-million dollar scandal that involved the Prime Minister's son, and he</u> lost his job as a newspaper editor.

   A.   In 1982, Arun Shourie exposed a multi-million dollar scandal that involved the Prime Minister's son, and he

   B.   Arun Shourie, exposing in 1982 a multi-million dollar scandal that involved the Prime Minister's son, lost

   C.   In 1982, having exposed a multi-million dollar scandal that involved the Prime Minister's son, Arun Shourie

   D.   It was 1982 when Arun Shourie exposed a multi-million dollar scandal involving the Prime Minister's son, and he

   E.   In 1982, Arun Shourie exposed a multi-million dollar scandal that involved the Prime Minister's son, and consequently he

9. The population of beluga whales in the Gulf of St. Lawrence has failed to <u>increase, and this</u> worries many marine biologists.

   A.   increase, and this

   B.   increase; and this

   C.   increase; this

   D.   increase, which

   E.   increase, a fact that

GO ON TO THE NEXT PAGE

10. The developer plans to dismantle and move a fourteenth-century English church to Nevada <u>which will give it</u> the oldest church in the western hemisphere.

    A. which will give it
    B. and this will give it
    C. which will give the state
    D. and this will give the state
    E. to give the state

11. Banking regulators have seized a Georgia savings bank and charged that the institution <u>both used deceptive lending and business practices and it misled</u> its stockholders.

    A. both used deceptive lending and business practices and it misled
    B. both used deceptive business lending practices and it misled
    C. used deceptive lending and business practices and misled
    D. both used lending and business practices that were deceptive, misleading
    E. used both deceptive and misleading business and lending practices, and it misled

12. For three years, the group called White Flag <u>has virtually ignored Chicago, the city where they started in.</u>

    A. has virtually ignored Chicago, the city where they started in.
    B. have virtually ignored Chicago, the city where they started in.
    C. has virtually ignored Chicago, the city where it started.
    D. has virtually ignored Chicago, where they started.
    E. have virtually ignored the city where they started, Chicago.

13. Readers admire Margaret Fuller's <u>eagerness to succeed, that she is willing to work hard, and her refusal to give up.</u>

    A. eagerness to succeed, that she is willing to work hard, and her refusal to give up.
    B. eagerness for success, willingness to work hard, and that she refuses to give up.
    C. being eager to succeed, willing to work hard, and her refusal to give up.
    D. eagerness to succeed, willingness to work hard, and refusal to give up.
    E. being eager to succeed, being willing to work hard, and refusing to give up.

14. Understanding why a sentence or a paragraph is awkward is essentially no different <u>from when you see</u> why a mathematical proof is unconvincing.

    A. from when you see
    B. from if you see
    C. from seeing
    D. than when you see
    E. than if you see

15. <u>Where the main purpose of the greenhouse is</u> to raise half-hardy plants for planting out in the garden or to grow flowering plants in pots for cut flowers and for bringing into the house.

    A. Where the main purpose of the greenhouse is
    B. When the main purpose of the greenhouse is
    C. The main purpose of the greenhouse is
    D. If the main purpose of the greenhouse were
    E. While the main purpose of the greenhouse is

IF YOU FINISH BEFORE TIME IS CALLED, CHECK YOUR WORK ON THIS SECTION ONLY. DO NOT WORK ON ANY OTHER SECTION IN THE TEST.

Scoring Practice Test 3

Answer Key for Practice Test 3

Section 2: Mathematics

1. D	6. D	11. C	16. D
2. B	7. D	12. E	17. E
3. D	8. C	13. A	18. B
4. B	9. C	14. B	19. A
5. D	10. D	15. A	20. E

Section 3: Writing—Multiple Choice

1. D	10. C	19. D	28. D
2. C	11. C	20. C	29. A
3. A	12. E	21. C	30. E
4. D	13. B	22. E	31. C
5. C	14. A	23. C	32. A
6. E	15. E	24. A	33. E
7. D	16. C	25. B	34. C
8. C	17. D	26. A	35. B
9. A	18. B	27. B	36. A

Section 4: Critical Reading

1. C	8. A	15. E	22. C
2. B	9. D	16. C	23. A
3. A	10. B	17. A	24. B
4. E	11. D	18. B	25. D
5. D	12. A	19. D	26. D
6. C	13. D	20. C	27. A
7. B	14. B	21. B	28. B

Section 5: Mathematics

1. C	6. D	11. 5/12	16. 97
2. A	7. C	12. 37.5	17. 72
3. D	8. A	13. 45	18. 2000
4. B	9. B	14. 39	19. 7
5. A	10. D	15. 8.78	20. 32

Section 6: Critical Reading

1. B	**8.** B	**15.** C	**22.** C
2. C	**9.** C	**16.** B	**23.** A
3. E	**10.** E	**17.** E	**24.** B
4. D	**11.** B	**18.** D	**25.** A
5. D	**12.** D	**19.** C	**26.** C
6. B	**13.** A	**20.** D	**27.** E
7. B	**14.** D	**21.** B	**28.** E

Section 7: Mathematics

1. C	**5.** D	**9.** D	**13.** B
2. D	**6.** B	**10.** E	**14.** E
3. D	**7.** E	**11.** D	**15.** D
4. A	**8.** D	**12.** C	

Section 8: Critical Reading

1. B	**5.** D	**9.** B	**13.** E
2. B	**6.** A	**10.** D	**14.** E
3. C	**7.** C	**11.** A	**15.** C
4. D	**8.** A	**12.** C	

Section 9: Mathematics

1. D	**6.** D	**11.** 66.2	**16.** 2/5
2. A	**7.** A	**12.** 1/3	**17.** 1/8
3. D	**8.** B	**13.** 143	**18.** 57,1
4. D	**9.** D	**14.** 15	**19.** 3.75
5. B	**10.** C	**15.** 45	**20.** 6/9

Section 10: Writing—Multiple Choice

1. B	**5.** E	**9.** E	**13.** D
2. B	**6.** D	**10.** E	**14.** C
3. A	**7.** A	**11.** C	**15.** C
4. C	**8.** C	**12.** C	

Analyzing Your Test Results

The charts on the following pages should be used to carefully analyze your results and spot your strengths and weaknesses. The complete process of analyzing each subject area and each individual problem should be completed for each practice test. These results should then be reexamined for trends in types of errors (repeated errors) or poor results in specific subject areas. *This reexamination and analysis is of tremendous importance to you in assuring maximum test preparation benefit.*

Reviewing the Essay

Have an English teacher, tutor, or someone else with good writing skills read and evaluate your essay using the Essay Checklist given below. Have your reader evaluate the complete essay as good, average, or marginal. Note that your paper would actually be scored from 1 to 6 by two trained readers (actual total score 2–12). But since we are trying only for a rough approximation, the simple good, average, or marginal overall evaluation will give you a general feeling for your score range.

Use the following checklist to evaluate your essay:

- Does the essay focus on the topic and complete the assigned task?
  (Circle one: Excellent   Average   Poor)

- Is the essay well organized, well developed, and consistent in argument?
  (Circle one: Excellent   Average   Poor)

- Does the essay use specific supporting details?
  (Circle one: Excellent   Average   Poor)

- Does the writing use correct grammar, usage, punctuation, and spelling?
  (Circle one: Excellent   Average   Poor)

- Is the handwriting legible?
  (Circle one: Excellent   Average   Poor)

Critical Reading Analysis Sheet

Section 4	Possible	Completed	Right	Wrong
Sentence Completion	8			
Short Reading Passages	6			
Long Reading Passages	14			
Subtotal	28			
Section 6	**Possible**	**Completed**	**Right**	**Wrong**
Sentence Completion	10			
Short Reading Passages	6			
Long Reading Passages	12			
Subtotal	28			
Section 8	**Possible**	**Completed**	**Right**	**Wrong**
Long Reading Passages	13			
Short Reading Passages	2			
Subtotal	15			
Overall Critical Reading Totals	71			

Mathematics Analysis Sheet

Section 2	Possible	Completed	Right	Wrong
Multiple Choice	20			
Subtotal	20			
Section 5	Possible	Completed	Right	Wrong
Multiple Choice	10			
Grid-Ins	10			
Subtotal	20			
Section 7	Possible	Completed	Right	Wrong
Multiple Choice	15			
Subtotal	15			
Section 9	Possible	Completed	Right	Wrong
Multiple Choice	10			
Grid-Ins	10			
Subtotal	20			
Overall Math Totals	75			

Note: Only 3 math sections (about 55 questions) count on your actual exam on the new SAT.

Writing—Multiple-Choice Analysis Sheet

Section 3	Possible	Completed	Right	Wrong
Improving Sentences	7			
Identifying Sentence Errors	19			
Improving Paragraphs	10			
Subtotal	36			
Section 10	Possible	Completed	Right	Wrong
Improving Sentences	15			
Subtotal	15			
Overall Writing—Multiple-Choice Totals	51			

Analysis/Tally Sheet for Problems Missed

One of the most important parts of test preparation is analyzing why you missed a problem so that you can reduce the number of mistakes. Now that you have taken the practice test and checked your answers, carefully tally your mistakes by marking them in the proper column.

	Reason for Mistakes				
	Total Missed	Simple Mistake	Misread Problem	Lack of Knowledge	Lack of Time
Section 4: Critical Reading					
Section 6: Critical Reading					
Section 8: Critical Reading					
Subtotal					
Section 2: Mathematics					
Section 5: Mathematics					
Section 7: Mathematics					
Section 9: Mathematics					
Subtotal					
Section 3: Writing—Multiple Choice					
Section 10: Writing—Multiple Choice					
Subtotal					
Total Reading, Math, and Writing					

Reviewing the preceding data should help you determine *why* you are missing certain problems. Now that you've pinpointed the type of error, compare it to other practice tests to spot other common mistakes.

Complete Answers and Explanations for Practice Test 3

Section 2: Mathematics

1. **D.** Multiplying each side by 3

$$3m + n = 7$$
$$3(3m + n) = 3(7)$$

Therefore, $9m + 3n = 21$

2. **B.** If $\frac{2}{3}$ of the container is full, there remains $\frac{1}{3}$ of the container to fill. The time to fill $\frac{1}{3}$ of the container will be half as long as the time needed to fill $\frac{2}{3}$ of the container. Hence, $\frac{1}{2}$ (18 minutes) = 9 minutes.

3. D. Since the sum of the angles is 180°,

$$m + n + 72 + 25 = 180$$

$$m + n + 97 = 180$$

$$m + n = 180 - 97$$

$$m + n = 83$$

Hence, the sum of $m + n$ is 83°.

4. B. Since the square of a positive number is a positive number, choice B is the correct answer.

5. D. If Tom is 4 years older than Fran, if we call Fran's age x, Tom's age must be 4 years more, or $x + 4$. Therefore, since the total of their ages is 24, Fran's age + Tom's age = 24.

$$x + (x + 4) = 24$$

6. D.

$$\frac{840 \text{ miles}}{1\frac{1}{2} \text{ hours}} = \frac{3500 \text{ miles}}{x \text{ hours}}$$

Cross multiplying yields

$$840x = 3500 \cdot 1\frac{1}{2}$$
$$840x = 5250$$

$$x = 5250 \div 840$$

$$x = 6\frac{1}{4} \text{ hours}$$

7. D. The seventh row will be 1-6-15-20-15-6-1, which contains no prime numbers.

8. C.

$$\frac{y - x}{y + x} = \frac{\frac{4}{7} - \frac{3}{4}}{\frac{4}{7} + \frac{3}{4}}$$

Multiplying by the lowest common denominator, which is 28,

$$= \frac{28\left(\frac{4}{7} - \frac{3}{4}\right)}{28\left(\frac{4}{7} + \frac{3}{4}\right)}$$

$$= \frac{16 - 21}{16 + 21}$$

$$= -\frac{5}{37}$$

9. C. There are $40 - 24 = 16$ boys in the class.

$$\frac{\text{is number}}{\text{of number}} = \frac{\text{percent}}{100}$$

$$\frac{16}{40} = \frac{x}{100}$$

$$40x = 1600$$

$$x = 40$$

Hence, 40% of the class are boys.

10. D. Perimeter of $\triangle MNP = \frac{1}{2}$(perimeter of $\triangle XYZ$)

$$= \frac{1}{2}(XY + YZ + XZ)$$

$$= \frac{1}{2}(10 + 15 + 17)$$

$$= \frac{1}{2}(42)$$

$$= 21$$

11. C. Using the Pythagorean theorem, $a^2 + b^2 = c^2$

$$(BC)^2 = (CD)^2 + (DB)^2$$
$$= 5^2 + 12^2$$
$$= 25 + 144$$
$$= 169$$
$$(BC) = \sqrt{169} = 13$$

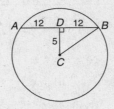

Hence, the radius of the circle is 13.

12. E. So far, George has averaged 80% on each of three tests. Therefore, his *total* points scored equals three times 80, or 240 points. In order to average 85% of four tests, George needs a total point score of four times 85, or 340 points. Since George presently is 100 points short of 340, he needs to get 100 points, or 100%, on the fourth test.

13. A.

$$\text{If } x(y - z) = t$$
$$\frac{\overset{1}{\cancel{x}}(y - z)}{\cancel{x}_1} = \frac{t}{x}$$
$$y - z = \frac{t}{x}$$
$$y - z + z = \left(\frac{t}{x}\right) + z$$
$$y = \left(\frac{t}{x}\right) + z$$

14. B. Area of larger circle = 144π. Since area = πr^2, then

$$\pi r^2 = 144\pi$$
$$r^2 = 144$$
$$r = 12$$

$$\text{radius of a larger circle} = 12$$
$$\text{diameter of a smaller circle} = 12$$
$$\text{radius of a smaller circle} = 6$$
$$\text{area of a smaller circle} = \pi r^2$$
$$= \pi(6)^2$$
$$= 36\pi$$

15. A. Substituting 2 for *m* and 3 for *n* gives

$$2 * 3 = \frac{2 + 3 - 1}{3^2}$$
$$= \frac{5 - 1}{9}$$
$$= \frac{4}{9}$$

16. D. If $\frac{a}{b} = \frac{c}{d}$, then, by cross multiplying, $ad = bc$.

If $\frac{d}{b} = \frac{c}{a}$, then cross multiplying gives the same result, $ad = bc$.

Hence, if $\frac{a}{b} = \frac{c}{d}$, then $\frac{d}{b} = \frac{c}{a}$.

17. E. First, rearrange and simplify the first equation as follows. Add $+12$ and $+6y$ to both sides of the equation $6x - 12 = -6y$, and you get

$$
\begin{aligned}
6x - 12 \quad\quad &= -6y \\
+12 + 6y &= +6y + 12 \\
\hline
6x \quad\quad + 6y &= \quad\quad 12
\end{aligned}
$$

Now, dividing through by 6 leaves

$$x + y = 2$$

Next, rearrange and simplify the second equation as follows.

$$5y + 5x = 15 \text{ is the same as } 5x + 5y = 15$$

Now, dividing through by 5 leaves

$$x + y = 3$$

The equations $x + y = 2$ *and* $x + y = 3$ have no solutions in common because you can't add the same two numbers and get two different answers.

18. B. Since y varies directly as x, $y = kx$ for some constant k. Since $x = 18$ when $y = 12$,

$$12 = k \cdot 18$$
$$k = \frac{12}{18} = \frac{2}{3}$$
$$\text{and } y = \left(\frac{2}{3}\right)x$$

Hence, when $x = 20$,

$$y = \left(\frac{2}{3}\right)(20)$$
$$= \frac{40}{3}$$
$$= 13\frac{1}{3}$$

19. A. Ratio of diameters = ratio of radii.

$$\frac{d_1}{d_2} = \frac{r_1}{r_2} = \frac{30}{100} = \frac{3}{10}$$

Ratio of area = (ratio of radii)^2.

$$\frac{A_1}{A_2} = \left(\frac{r_1}{r_2}\right)^2$$
$$\frac{A_1}{A_2} = \frac{9}{100}$$

Hence the area of circle R is $\frac{9}{100}$, or 9%, of the area of circle S.

20. E. If the coordinates of two points X and Y are (x_1, y_1) and (x_2, y_2), respectively, then the coordinates of the midpoint B (m_1, m_2) of xy are

$$\left(\frac{x_1 + x_2}{2}, \frac{y_1 + y_2}{2}\right) = (m_1, m_2)$$

Hence

$$m_1 = \frac{x_1 + x_2}{2} \qquad \text{and} \qquad m_2 = \frac{y_1 + y_2}{2}$$

$$5 = \frac{(-4 + x_2)}{2} \qquad \text{and} \qquad -2 = \frac{(3 + y_2)}{2}$$

$$(2)(5) = (2)\left(\frac{-4 + x_2}{2}\right) \qquad \text{and} \qquad (2)(-2) = 2\left(\frac{3 + y_2}{2}\right)$$

$$10 = -4 + x_2 \qquad\qquad\qquad -4 = 3 + y_2$$

$$10 + 4 = -4 + x_2 + 4 \qquad\qquad -4 - 3 = 3 + y_2 - 3$$

$$14 = x_2 \qquad\qquad\qquad\qquad -7 = y_2$$

Therefore, the coordinates of Y are $(x_2, y_2) = (14, -7)$.

Section 3: Writing—Multiple Choice

Improving Sentences

1. D. The original version has faulty parallelism and is verbose. B is not so wordy, but it shifts from the active verb ("affects") to "affected are." The "also being affected" of E is no better. The best choice is D, which is the most concise of the five and a parallel construction of the series.

2. C. This is another of those sentences in which the pronouns have no specific antecedents, but refer to a general idea or the entire first clause. Changing pronouns (from "which" to "this") does no good. To repair a sentence like this, you must either supply a specific antecedent (you might say "a fact which is surprising"), or get rid of the pronoun. Choice C eliminates the pronoun.

3. A. This sentence is a series; the original version here is the best of the five—parallel, correctly punctuated with commas, and concise. The semicolons of B are incorrect; C has an extra "and." D and E break up the parallel construction.

4. D. This sentence runs on two sentences without any punctuation or connective between them. Here the semicolon is the best choice with the two independent clauses. It won't work in E because the second clause is no longer independent; it is now a sentence fragment.

5. C. Set sentence C against A, and you see that four words ("In," "it," "and," and "does") can be cut with no change of meaning. None of the four other versions of the sentence is as economical as C, though they are all grammatical, except A which has the vague pronoun "it."

6. E. The original sentence here is not really wrong, but it is less effective because it treats all the elements as equal, while the superior version, E, subordinates the first clause, making the meaning of the relation between parts of the sentence clearer. Here choice D is a shorter sentence than E, but the gain in clarity is worth more than the gain in economy.

7. D. The phrase that begins this sentence begins with the past participle "Nestled," and, predictably, that opening participial phrase dangles. The town, not its extinction, nestles, so we can eliminate A, B, and C. Choice D is more concise than E.

Identifying Sentence Errors

8. C. The verb "agreed" and the opening phrase "strange as it now seems" place the action of this sentence in the past. The verb "fears" ought to be "feared," since the point of the sentence is that though Japan once feared Italian competition, it no longer does.

9. A. The singular subject "darkness" does not agree with the plural verb "were"; the verb should be "was."

10. C. It is the pronoun "who" not the verb "appear" that is in error here. The pronoun refers to the sets of teeth, mechanisms not human beings, so the correct pronoun is "which" or "that."

11. **C.** The sentence changes from a second person subject ("you") to a third person ("one"). It should be either "you can . . . you must" or "one can . . . one must."

12. **E.** There is no error in this sentence.

13. **B.** A subject and verb in this sentence are separated and do not agree. Since the singular verb "is" is not underlined and cannot be changed, "huge doses" must be changed to "a huge dose" to correct the grammar.

14. **A.** The opening phrase is not idiomatic. We say "as a result of" or "resulting from."

15. **E.** There is no error in the sentence.

16. **C.** Since the first part of the sentence lists three, the singular "method" should be the plural "methods."

17. **D.** The error in this sentence is the unidiomatic use of the preposition "with." The usual expression to denote the index level is "stands at."

18. **B.** The error is the confusion of an adjective and an adverb. The right word to modify the adjective "easy" here is the adverb "easily."

19. **D.** The subject of the sentence, the singular "Peninsula," follows the verb, the plural "lie." It should be "lies."

20. **C.** The "they" in this sentence is an ambiguous pronoun. It could refer to any of the animals including the deer, beavers, and squirrels which are not, as a rule, dangerous.

21. **C.** The problem is the phrase "without he succeeds." A better one would be "without success" or "without succeeding."

22. **E.** The sentence is grammatical and idiomatic.

23. **C.** The sequence of tenses here is inconsistent. The first and second verbs use the present tense ("is," "is") but the third uses the future instead of another present.

24. **A.** If you ignore the "Texans" the error is easy to find: "that us talk oddly." It is an error of pronoun case, using the objective "us" rather than the subjective "we" as the subject of a clause.

25. **B.** This is a diction error. The word "requisite" is a noun or an adjective, but not the verb the context calls for. The right word is the verb "require."

26. **A.** There is an agreement problem here. The sentence gives only one example, Wilder's *Our Town*. To be consistent, the sentence has to begin with "The best example . . . "

Improving Paragraphs

27. **B.** The problem in this sentence is the pronoun "this" which has no specific antecedent. Choices A, C, and E all keep the vague "this," while in D the vague pronoun is "that." Only B avoids the difficulty; "this" modifies "way."

28. **D.** These sentences are verbose, especially since "was not handed" in 4 is followed in 6 with the repetitive "He didn't have them handed to him." This part of 4 should be eliminated in the revision. Another redundancy is following "possessions" with "that he has," since possessions are what "he has." Here D, the shortest, is also the best revision.

29. **A.** In the first paragraph, the writer asserts that life does not hand us things for free, and that he is glad this is so. The second paragraph gives reasons to explain this view. Choice E is inaccurate since the personal references are in the first paragraph, while the second is more general.

30. **E.** The phrase "get all of their success handed or given to them" is awkward and verbose. There is no need for both "given" and "handed." B has usage errors ("that" for "who," the vague "it"). The comparison in C is not parallel, and in D it is illogical, comparing work with people who work. E maintains a clear parallel and is not wordy.

31. **C.** The final paragraph uses the pronoun "you." Though "you" is used once in the second paragraph, all the other sentences use the third person.

32. **A.** The last paragraph summarizes the writer's position—that unearned wealth will not bring happiness.

33. **E.** The only version here that avoids a dangling participle is E, which supplies a subject and verb ("we . . . got"). In A, B, C, and D, it is the weather that arrives after nine, not the wedding guests.

34. **C.** The trouble here is the use of "like" as a conjunction in the phrase "feel like this would be . . ." The error is minor, but given a chance to revise the sentence, you are better off with C, which eliminates "like." All the other choices use "like" as a conjunction, though the verbs are different.

35. **B.** The issue here is the comma splice. Since "the sky was gray" is a complete sentence, it should be separated from "dismal" by either a semicolon or a period. E corrects the original error, but introduces another comma splice after "gray."

36. **A.** The passage does not rely on figurative language (metaphor and simile). It does arrange events chronologically, connect the first and last sentence (by repeating "Idaho"), use a first person speaker ("I"), and use details of the weather to convey mood (sentences 5–7 and 12–13).

Section 4: Critical Reading

Sentence Completion

1. **C.** The adjective needed here will describe the growing fear of the watchers of the endangered boat. Choice B "intrepid" means fearless, and "cowardly" A, although it describes a fearful person, is for those who fear for themselves, not others. The best choice is "apprehensive," meaning uneasy, anxious, or troubled by fears.

2. **B.** "Native" and "indigenous" here mean the same thing. Since even the best language students who are foreign will not understand the native speaker, the missing word must mean something like puzzled or bewildered. The best choice, then, is "baffled."

3. **A.** With the use of "merely" and "not censorship," the sentence implies that the missing first word describes some minor changes in a test, something like "editing," or "revising," or "corrections" but not so serious as "expurgation" or "decimation." The phrase "with the writer's prior knowledge and" suggests that the last word must mean something like approval. In B the use of "prohibition" and in C the use of "disapproval" won't work, so the correct choice must be A "permission."

4. **E.** The missing noun probably describes a strength, since it is being tested and is parallel to the phrase "capacity to adapt." The best choice is "resilience," that is, the capacity to bounce back, to recover strength or good spirits.

5. **D.** The first noun is probably a synonym for "trend," but although D "fad" looks like the best choice, "prank" or "whim" might work. The second noun describes a serious threat (*not* an "innocent" or harmless "trend"). Either "peril" A (danger) or "hazard" D (risk) will do, but since D has the better first answer, it is the better choice.

6. **C.** Since the second half of the sentence tells us of the public's "disapproval," the missing participle must reflect this attitude. Either "horrified" C or "repulsed" D will fit. Only "ghoulish" continues the expression of condemnation. A "repulsed" public would not find the jewelry "amiable."

7. **B.** The first term, a verb, has "response" as its object; choices A and C do not fit this context. The second term, a noun, describes a point that can be reached. Only choices A, B, and C might fit here. Thus, the correct choice is B. "Elicited" means evoked or drew, while "nadir" means the lowest point.

8. **A.** Since the missing word must be surprising in an atmosphere of "calm" and beauty, choices B, C, D, and E are all unsuitable. But "untoward," that is, perverse, unseemly, unexpected, fits well.

Short Reading Passages

9. **D.** "Nevertheless" (in line 7) indicates that Nightingale pursued her interest despite social attitudes, suggesting that she was dissatisfied with a woman's usual role. She convinced her family to allow her to do something that was considered off-limits for a woman of her class; they did not sponsor her studies (choice B). Nothing in the passage supports A, and Nightingale's religious feelings are not addressed at all, C. In spite of her putting splints on her dog's paws, there is no indication in the rest of the paragraph that she wanted to be a veterinarian, E.

10. B. The author cites the reduction in the hospital death rate immediately after stating that Nightingale took a team of nurses to Turkey. D might seem correct, but the emphasis is on the reduction in the death rate, not on the horrible conditions in hospitals. E might also seem possible, but this detail is used specifically to dramatize the effect of the nurses, which is not the main idea of the paragraph. C is irrelevant because the passage deals with Nightingale's becoming a nurse, not a physician. Finally, the reader has no way of determining whether A is true.

11. D. This is the main idea of the paragraph, whereas E, A, and C are minor points. The passage does not describe American technology as "poor," B. See lines 4–7.

12. A. The author presents the idea of a lagging American technology merely to argue against it in the rest of the paragraph. B and C make no sense in context, and the "debt" owed by American technology to British technology is not addressed at all. E is irrelevant to the question in lines 3–4.

13. D. By using the phrase "Even oil industry leaders," the author of the paragraph is suggesting that global warming is of concern not only to confirmed environmentalists but also to people whose primary interest is in making a profit, not in preserving the environment. A and B are perhaps true, but the phrase doesn't pertain to them. C and E are points not even considered in the paragraph.

14. B. When warming causes snow and ice to melt, more areas are exposed to the sun. These areas then take in more solar radiation and heat, thus increasing the speed of warming.

Long Reading Passages

15. E. The passage mentions raccoons, cats, humans, and skunks as rabies victims. Since the first paragraph explicitly limits the disease to any "mammal," carrion birds are not susceptible to the virus.

16. C. Unless rabies is treated by "timely" injections of vaccine, it is a fatal disease (lines 3–5).

17. A. Although dogs are no longer the major carriers in countries with good veterinary services and laws requiring inoculation, they still account for "90 percent of all human deaths from rabies," chiefly in developing nations.

18. B. The number of fatalities from the disease is small in the United States because most dogs have been immunized, people are aware of the danger of the disease, and those at risk of having been infected are treated before the symptoms of the disease can develop. The virus is not rare in wild-animal populations. In lines 55–56, the passage refers to an epidemic among raccoons in America.

19. D. The word "feasible" means practicable or possible.

20. C. The treatment of humans can now include vaccine injections (in the abdomen or arm) and application of rabies-specific antibodies in the wound area. The passage makes no mention of an oral recombinant vaccine.

21. B. The vaccine-laced bait should be useful in dealing with wild populations and with dogs in countries where large-scale inoculation is impossible. The vaccine would not be useful in animals already infected, since once the symptoms of the disease develop, it is too late to save the victim.

22. C. In lines 18–21, the speaker says she did not follow the Watergate proceedings because it was just a case of one set of rich white people hoodwinking another set.

23. A. "Of a piece" means part of, consistent with, or in keeping with.

24. B. In this context, the word "acute" means shrewd or clever. Although some of the other meanings can apply in other contexts, the word here is opposed to "ignorance" and associated with wit.

25. D. The words here are the thoughts of the speaker, not what she says. Throughout the passage, the reader knows both what she says and also what she thinks but does not say. Aware here of the "pompous" remarks she had just made, she is not eager to elaborate on these second-hand ideas, and remembering that Cox is a lawyer, she hopes to herself that he will not cross-examine her further.

26. D. The comic scene she imagines—Cox left in West Philly "without a map or a bow tie"—is her response to his inclusive "Our." The speaker does not feel of a piece with the white New England establishment, and it is the pronoun which inspires her thoughts.

27. A. The Rector, a shrewd observer throughout the passage, has some idea of what is going on in the speaker's mind. For a moment, he is afraid she will blurt out something that will embarrass the school. He is relieved that the moment has passed without incident.

28. B. Because the passage was written some time after the events and allows the reader to know the thoughts of the speaker, the selection as a whole is very frank, even self-critical. The author understands herself and reveals this understanding very candidly. None of the other choices is appropriate.

Section 5: Mathematics

1. C. To find the tax at 7% on $132.95, simply round off and multiply (the rule for rounding off is "5 or above rounds up"): 7% times $133.

$$.07 \times \$133 = \$9.31$$

Use a calculator without rounding off,

$$.07 \times \$132.95 = \$9.306 \text{ or } \$9.31$$

2. A. Since 1 raised to any power = 1,

$$1^{12} + 1^{-15} + 1^0 = 1 + 1 + 1 = 3$$

3. D. The intersection of two sets is the set of elements that the two sets have in common. Since the sets have no elements in common, their intersection is the empty set = { }.

4. B. $\dfrac{\text{percent}}{100} = \dfrac{\text{is number}}{\text{of number}}$

Cross multiplying

$$\frac{30}{100} = \frac{x}{\frac{25}{18}}$$

$$100x = \frac{\overset{5}{\cancel{30}}}{1} \times \frac{25}{\underset{3}{\cancel{18}}}$$

$$100x = \frac{125}{3}$$

$$x = \frac{\overset{5}{\cancel{125}}}{3} \times \frac{1}{\underset{4}{\cancel{100}}}$$

$$x = \frac{5}{12}$$

5. A. b = Bob's age, c = Jane's age, d = Jim's age.

Since Bob is older than Jane, $c < b$.

Since Bob is younger than Jim, $b < d$.

Hence, $c < b$, and $b < d$, or $c < b < d$.

6. D. You could quickly eliminate choices A, B, and C, since the line goes down to the right the slope must be negative. Using the following formula would give you the slope.

$$m = \frac{y_1 - y_2}{x_1 - x_2}$$
$$= \frac{5a - 0}{0 - 3a}$$
$$= \frac{5a}{-3a}$$
$$= -\frac{5}{3}$$

7. C. Let $2x$ = first angle, $3x$ = second angle, $4x$ = third angle, and $6x$ = fourth angle. Since the sum of the measures of the angles in a quadrilateral must be $360°$,

$$2x + 3x + 4x + 6x = 360°$$

$$15x = 360$$

$$\frac{15x}{15} = \frac{360}{15}$$

$$x = 24°$$

$$2x = 48° = \text{first angle}$$

$$3x = 72° = \text{second angle}$$

$$4x = 96° = \text{third angle}$$

$$6x = 144° = \text{fourth angle}$$

Hence, the largest angle of the quadrilateral has a measure of $144°$.

8. A. If today Lucy is 14, then last year she was 13. Likewise, if Charlie's age now is C, then last year he was $C - 1$. Now, put these into an equation:

$$\underbrace{\text{Lucy's age last year}}_{13} \underset{=}{\downarrow} \underbrace{\text{is three years older than twice Charlie's age last year.}}_{2(C-1) + 3}$$

Transposing, $13 - 3 = 2(C - 1)$.

9. B. To find x-intercepts, set $y = 0$ and solve for x.

$$x^2 + 4x - 12 = 0$$

$$(x + 6)(x - 2) = 0$$

$$x + 6 = 0 \text{ or } x - 2 = 0$$

$$x = -6 \text{ or } x = 2$$

10. D. Let x = the missing number. Since the average of x and z is y,

$$\frac{1}{2}(x + z) = y$$

$$2 \times \frac{1}{2}(x + z) = 2y$$

$$x + z = 2y$$

$$x + z - z = 2y - z$$

$$x = 2y - z$$

Grid-In Questions

11. Answer: $\frac{5}{12}$. Dividing both sides of the equation $12a = 5b$ by $12b$,

$$\frac{12a}{12b} = \frac{5b}{12b}$$

$$\frac{a}{b} = \frac{5}{12}$$

12. Answer: 37.5. Since the female students make up 3 parts out of the total 8 parts, the percent of students that are female is

$$\frac{3}{8} = \frac{x}{100}$$
$$8x = 300$$
$$x = \frac{300}{8}$$
$$x = 37\frac{4}{8}$$
$$x = 37\frac{1}{2} = 37.5$$

13. Answer: 45. Since each of the 5 shirts may be matched with each of the 3 pairs of slacks, and these combinations may in turn be matched with each of the 3 sports jackets, the total number of combinations possible is

$$5 \cdot 3 \cdot 3 = 45$$

14. Answer: 39. Squaring both sides of the original equation yields

$$\left(\sqrt{m-3}\right)^2 = 6^2$$
$$m - 3 = 36$$
$$m = 39$$

Checking the answer in the original equation for extraneous solutions,

$$\sqrt{m-3} = \sqrt{39-3}$$
$$= \sqrt{36}$$
$$= 6$$

Hence, $m = 6$ is the solution for the given equation.

15. Answer: 8.78.

5 apples:	$5 \times .60 = \$3.00$
10 bananas:	$10 \times .20 = \$2.00$
4 cantaloupes:	$2 \times 1.00 = \$2.00$ ($4 = 2 \times 2$ for \$1)
5 oranges:	$\$1.00 + 2 \times .39 = \$1.78$ (3 for \$1 and 39 cents each for the other two)

To find the total, add

$$\$3.00 + \$2.00 + \$2.00 + \$1.78 = \$8.78$$

16. Answer: 97. To average 89% for seven exams, Ben must have a total of (89)(7), or 623 points. To average 90% for eight exams, Ben must have a total of (90)(8), or 720 points. Therefore, his score on the eighth exam must be

$$720 - 623 = 97\%$$

17. Answer: 72. The length of the side of a square with diagonal 12 is

$$12 \div \sqrt{2} = \frac{12}{\sqrt{2}}$$

The area of a square with side length x is

$$A = x^2$$
$$= \left(\frac{12}{\sqrt{2}}\right)$$
$$= \frac{144}{2}$$
$$= 72$$

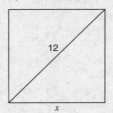

18. Answer: 2000. Simply continue the chart as follows, adding 40 cents for each two years to Product A and 15 cents for each two years to Product B.

Products	1992	1994	1996	1998	2000
A	$6.60	$7.00	$7.40	$7.80	$8.20
B	$7.20	$7.35	$7.50	$7.65	$7.80

It is evident that the correct answer is 2000.

19. Answer: 7. The area of a trapezoid is

$$A = \frac{1}{2} h \left(b_1 + b_2\right)$$
$$98 = \frac{1}{2} h \left(12 + 16\right)$$
$$98 = \frac{1}{2} h \left(28\right)$$
$$98 = 14h$$
$$7 = h$$

20. Answer: 32. By the Pythagorean theorem,

$$x^2 + 12^2 = 20^2$$
$$x^2 + 144 = 400$$
$$x^2 = 256$$
$$x = 16$$

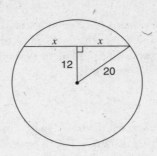

Therefore, the length of the chord is

$$2x = 32 \text{ centimeters}$$

Section 6: Critical Reading

Sentence Completion

1. **B.** The clue in the sentence is "banning." If cameras have been banned, the public will not see the whole story, so their "access," right to approach, has been curtailed. The best word here is "denied," B. "Belied" means lied about.

2. **C.** The adverb "reluctantly" and the phrase "despite his care" suggest that the adjective that modifies "shoplifting" here is one that distresses the grocer and, so you can infer, one that means frequent. The only word that is close is "commonplace"; that is, common or ordinary.

3. **E.** The sentence presents the example of the same number of workers taking more time for the same job as an example of Parkinson's law. The missing word in the law must explain this phenomenon. If work does something to fill the time for its completion, and the time for its completion has increased, then work must grow larger to fill the longer time. The missing word cannot be "decreases" or "grows easier." The right answer must be D or E, and "expands," E, goes better with "fill." The missing verb must be a synonym for "states" or "says." Choices B, C, and E would work, but E also has the best second answer.

4. **D.** The noun must reflect the mood of loud cheering or something happy, such as "happiness" B, "gladness" C, "euphoria" D, or "buoyancy" E. The second word must qualify this mood, however, because the first clause begins with "although." A proper word here could be "tempered" A or "moderated" D. The words "enervated" and "debilitated," although they can mean weaken, cannot be used in this context. They refer to physical weakness. Only D has two good choices; "euphoria" is a feeling of well-being.

5. **D.** The clues in the sentence tell you that the missing word must describe a conversation with no sentence longer than four words. The correct answer is "terse"; that is, brief or to the point. None of the other choices is plausible.

6. **B.** The second term, a noun, must be a word that accords with a functioning government, so you can eliminate "schism," "dichotomy," and "division." Either "compromise" or "consensus" (agreement) will fit. The first term, an adjective, describes a position that should be abandoned. Therefore, "dogmatic" is a much better choice than "sensible."

7. **B.** The words "conventional," "morality," and "conformity" suggest that the missing adjective to modify "conformity" will express the correctness of the Victorian reader. Choice B "genteel" means polite, refined, well bred—just what would be expected. The incorrect answers are all adjectives describing the opposite of what is suggested by "conventional morality."

8. **B.** The opening clause with its "though" at the beginning suggests that the missing adjective will be the opposite of "lively" and "interesting." The second missing word refers to the "lively" first chapter, so it must be a noun synonym for liveliness. The choice of "tedious" B, "repetitive" C, "dull" D, or "boring" E would do for the first blank, but only "pace" A or "verve" B are possible for the second. The right response must be B. Words like "torpor" and "lethargy" are the opposite of what is needed for the second noun, and "verve" means vigor or energy.

9. **C.** The useful clues here are "dangerous," "without peppers or other spices," and "mild," with the latter two set in opposition to the missing adjective by the word "but." Choices A, B, and D are just what you don't want. Both C, "torrid" (that is, fiery or very hot), or E, "piquant," are possible, but because "piquant" suggests an agreeable tartness and these dishes are dangerous, "torrid" is better.

10. E. The second adjective, expressing the response of a malcontent (a dissatisfied or rebellious person), must be disparaging, and the first adjective, coming before the "but," must be opposite in effect. The favorable first adjectives are B "perfect," D "Edenic," and E "ideal," and the pejorative second words are A "irritating," C "drab," and E "painful." The correct choice must be E.

Short Reading Passages

11. B. See lines 12–16. A might seem tempting, but the pointing of atoms in rock crystals was only the means by which magnetic reversal was shown to have occurred. The passage does not consider a change in the direction of lava flows, C, or convection currents, D. The paragraph does state that it appears that magnetic reversal occurs on average ever 500,000 years; however, magnetic reversal is not a disturbance in some other undefined 500,000-year cycle of the magnetic field, E.

12. D. The solidified rocks can be age dated, and the alignment of atoms in the rocks reveals magnetic reversal. The speed with which the reversal takes place is not indicated in the paragraph, C, nor is species extinction, B, mentioned. The study of lava flows is important, E, but only because the lava flows produce magma, not because their direction shifts.

13. A. The final sentence of the paragraph clearly makes a contrast between the "drab spinster" and the poet. B, C, and D are secondary points, and E is an issue not addressed in the passage.

14. D. The sense of Dickinson in the paragraph is that she was a solitary person. None of the other definitions makes sense in context. Nowhere is Dickinson described as snobbish or ill-natured, choices A and B, and the word "eccentric," which precedes "reclusive," means E and is the opposite of C, making these poor choices for "reclusive."

15. C. The details in Passage 2 emphasize Dickinson's insistence on choosing the right word. See lines 19–21. The author mentions A, and refers to her metaphors and rhythm, B and E, but it is her precision with language that is emphasized. D is indicated in the passage, but it is not what impresses the author; rather, it is "the means to an end," that is, Dickinson's precision.

16. B. See lines 10–12 in Passage 1 and lines 17–19 in Passage 2. The author of Passage 1 focuses on her life, but doesn't indicate he finds her life more "interesting" than her work, A. He also doesn't describe her as "pathetic," even though she lived a secluded life, D. The author of Passage 2 doesn't address Dickinson's life at all, C, and the author of Passage 1 doesn't address the ideas in her poems, E.

Long Reading Passages

17. E. Most of the first paragraph deals with what has been "often assumed" about bilingual ballots but which is untrue. The author attempts to respond to objections about the high costs and bilingual ballots on demand by pointing out what the costs are and what rules govern the qualifications for bilingual ballots.

18. D. Because the rules specify that a language group must make up "more than 5 percent of the local population," choice B would not qualify. The minorities who might qualify are Hispanic, Asian, and Native Americans, so choices A and C will not qualify. Choice E is disqualified because the group does not have a "below average" rate of "voter turnout." An Asian minority of 12 percent would qualify if it had a below-average voter turnout and English literacy.

19. C. The phrase refers to voting, a "fundamental right" of all citizens, which is the means the people have to preserve all their other rights. A watchful public seeing that a candidate or a law may limit its rights can vote against that candidate or law. Some of the other answers may be true, but they are not the point of the phrase in the passage.

20. D. In lines 25–33, the passage explains that a condition of the Voting Rights Act was the suspension of literacy tests for foreign-language speakers whose "predominant classroom language was other than English" who had completed six grades in an American school.

21. B. The second paragraph refers to laws intended to exclude voters who were Hispanic (line 36), African American (line 28), Yiddish speakers (line 39), and nonspeakers of English (lines 33–36) but makes no reference to Irish Catholics, who would presumably be English-speaking whites.

22. C. As it is used in line 40, the word "franchise" means the right to vote, the central issue in the passage.

23. A. The phrase "a hollow gesture" means an action with no consequence, a useless motion, an empty gesture. Choice A is the best of the five definitions.

24. B. The second statement is a responsible reply to the argument that all bilingual voting materials should be abolished. Granting that some discrimination may now exist, it argues that by repeal of the laws, those who are injured now would not be helped and those who are now enfranchised would lose their votes. The first statement, even if true, is not an argument against bilingual voting. The third statement, if true, would support the argument against bilingual voting.

25. A. If everyone starts from the same position, equal treatment should be the fairest way. If some groups start with a serious disadvantage, however, equal treatment will simply preserve the disadvantage. Therefore, to achieve equality, those groups who have not had a head start need to be helped more to catch up.

26. C. The fourth paragraph deals with the disadvantage of non-English-speaking white Europeans (save Hispanics). The only example of the white non-Hispanic European on this list is C, the Greek.

27. E. The final paragraph suggests all three. If only one in nearly seven thousand fails the literacy-in-English test, the test must be seriously flawed. Questions like "Why not make every effort to eliminate language barriers to voting?" call for the reader's assent, and "Perhaps it should" suggests that "need" should be taken into account in determining who should have a bilingual ballot.

28. E. As the last paragraph makes clear, the author of this passage favors liberalizing the laws to make bilingual ballots more available. The author would, you can be sure, strongly disapprove of a movement that attempted to restrict or abolish the use of bilingual ballots in American elections.

Section 7: Mathematics

1. C. Because $\frac{3}{x} = \frac{6}{1}$, cross multiplying gives

$$6 \cdot x = 3$$
$$x = \frac{1}{2}$$

Therefore, $x - 1 = \left(\frac{1}{2}\right) - 1 = -\frac{1}{2}$

2. D.

$$\frac{.25 \times \frac{2}{3}}{.06 \times 15} = \frac{\frac{25}{100} \times \frac{2}{3}}{\frac{6}{100} \times \frac{15}{1}}$$

$$= \frac{\frac{1}{4} \times \frac{2}{3}}{\frac{3}{50} \times \frac{15}{1}} = \frac{\frac{1}{6}}{\frac{9}{10}} = \frac{1}{6} \times \frac{10}{9} = \frac{5}{27}$$

Therefore, the reciprocal of $\frac{.25 \times \frac{2}{3}}{.06 \times 15}$ is the reciprocal of $\frac{5}{27}$, or $\frac{27}{5}$.

3. D. Since Harmon's sports car averages 35 miles for each gallon of gas, on 12 gallons, he'll be able to drive 12×35, or 420 miles.

4. A. $\angle BCD = \angle A + \angle B$ (exterior angle of a triangle equals the sum of the opposite two).

Then $84° = \angle A + 63°$

and $\angle A = 21°$

5. D. Using the probability formula

$$\text{probability} = \frac{\text{number of lucky chances}}{\text{total number of chances}}$$

The chance of choosing a weekday $= \frac{5 \text{ weekdays}}{7 \text{ total days}} = \frac{5}{7}$.

6. B. Reynold's average score was 24.8, and Doe's average score was 13.7. Therefore, $24.8 - 13.7 = 11.1$.

7. E. If y is a positive even integer, y could be 2. Choices A, B, C, and D are all evenly divisible by 2. Only choice E, $y + 1$, which is 3, is not evenly divisible by 2. Since E will always be an odd number, if y is even, it would never be divisible by an even number.

8. D. A rectangular solid consists of six rectangular faces. This one in particular has two 7 × 6, two 6 × 3, and two 7 × 3 rectangles with areas of 42, 18, and 21, respectively. Therefore, the total surface area will be

$$2(42) + 2(18) + 2(21) = 84 + 36 + 42 = 162 \text{ square meters}$$

9. D. Since each term of the sequence is one more than twice the preceding term, the sixth term of the sequence is $2 \cdot 63 + 1 = 126 + 1 = 127$.

Or you might have noticed the difference between each number and solved it as follows:

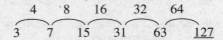

10. E. Total number of different combinations ("how many different kinds") is found by multiplying the number of ways for each item. Therefore, three different breads times four different meats times three different cheeses = $3 \times 4 \times 3 = 36$.

11. D. Try it yourself with scissors and a square piece of paper.

12. C. Distance = rate × time.

$$d = rt$$
$$k = rn$$
$$r = \left(\frac{k}{n}\right) \text{ miles per hour}$$

Therefore, $d = rt$

$$d = \left(\frac{k}{n}\right)(x) = \frac{kx}{n}$$

13. B. Using the distance formula,

$$d = \sqrt{(x_1 - x_2)^2 + (y_1 - y_2)^2}$$

The endpoints of the radius are (–3, 4) and (0, 0),

$$r = \sqrt{(-3 - 0)^2 + (4 - 0)^2}$$
$$= \sqrt{(-3)^2 + (4)^2}$$
$$= \sqrt{9 + 16}$$
$$= \sqrt{25}$$
$$r = 5$$

14. E. Because there are many different rectangles with a diagonal of 16, the lengths of the sides cannot be determined, and therefore the area of the rectangle cannot be determined.

15. D. First change the expression by removing the negative exponent.

$$a = 1 + 5^{-x} = 1 + \frac{1}{5^x}$$

Since $b = 1 + 5^x$, $5^x = b - 1$

and $a = 1 + \frac{1}{5^x}$

$$= 1 + \frac{1}{b - 1}$$
$$= \frac{b - 1}{b - 1} + \frac{1}{b - 1}$$
$$= \frac{b - 1 + 1}{b - 1}$$
$$= \frac{b}{b - 1}$$

Section 8: Critical Reading

Long Reading Passages

1. B. Mike Nichols is the director of the film based on the novel *The Graduate,* by Charles Webb. The critic prefers Nichols's film to Webb's novel.

2. B. To "play down" is to minimize, to reduce the importance of. To exclude goes one step further.

3. C. The critic suggests that there are several limitations in the characterization of Ben Braddock in the novel; it is, in fact, its "main trouble." Since Nichols's film avoids or mitigates these faults, the film is better than the book. Though the phrase criticizes Webb's hero, it does not accuse Salinger's novel of being overgrown and outdated.

4. D. The word "bumptious" means arrogant, offensively conceited. It is not related to the word "bumpkin," which means yokel.

5. D. The critic says Ben's arriving at the wedding too late to prevent the final vows and then running away with the bride "shatters . . . a monogamous mythology" of an "entire genre of Hollywood movies."

6. A. *The Graduate,* according to Passage 1, is the story of a passage from a premature maturity to an innocence regained, an idealism reconfirmed, a passage made possible by love.

7. C. Although the author of the passage would probably agree with A, B, and D, the first paragraph is about why people go to movies that are talked about, even though they may expect them to be bad. They go not to see a good movie but to find out what everyone is talking about.

8. A. The critic in an unflattering remark about the taste of the mass audience says (lines 91–94) that Benjamin "has nothing to communicate, which is just what makes him an acceptable hero for the large movie audience." Brains, the passage implies, are not box-office.

9. B. Nichols's "gift" (which the critic puts in ironic quotation marks) is his talent, his singular ability.

10. D. The line is a denigration of the director. Nichols has no point of view of his own, the passage suggests; he anticipates just what an audience wants and gives that to them. His object is the "surefire response" and nothing more.

11. A. The last paragraph of Passage 2 finds sociological interest in the success of the film because it reveals that an educated generation is just as sentimental and self-satisfied as older generations who doted on romance in film.

12. C. Choices A, B, D, and E are essentially the same; they are complaining of moviegoers who identify too intensely with the heroes or heroines of film and see films only as emotional reflections of their own lives, not as works of art, or craft, or fiction. Choice C describes a critic who sees a film objectively, who does not became so emotionally involved that he cannot separate reality from cinema.

13. E. Both critics imply that Ben's parents are caricatures. The first refers to the "overdone caricatures that surround the three principals" (lines 53–54) and the second to the "middle-class comic strip" (lines 90–91). Both critics use the word "predatory" to describe the older woman (lines 25 and 101). Both see Ben as an exemplar of innocence (lines 50, 100, 118–120), although the first praises this aspect of the film, and the second regards it as trite.

Short Reading Passages

14. E. By referring to an article written in 1880, the author of the passage suggests that recognition of synesthesia is not recent. However, the article cited doesn't "show the importance" of the concept, A. Also, nothing indicates that Galton's article deals with the origin of the word synesthesia, B. Although the passage identifies Galton as Darwin's cousin, nothing suggests that Darwin himself was interested in the phenomenon, C.

15. C. A is an overstatement. (Beware of words like "identical" in multiple-choice questions.) Similarly, B and D are unwarranted generalizations and E is a hypothesis not touched upon in the passage.

Section 9: Mathematics

1. **D.** The perimeter of a rectangle is equal to the sum of the dimensions of its sides. For this rectangle,

    $$\text{perimeter} = 6l + 4w + 6l + 4w$$
    $$= 6l + 6l + 4w + 4w$$
    $$= 12l + 8w$$

2. **A.** Remember the order of operations.

    $$4 \cdot 5^2 - |6 - 8 \cdot 7| = 4 \cdot 25 - |6 - 56|$$
    $$= 100 - |-50|$$
    $$= 100 - 50$$
    $$= 50$$

3. **D.** The average is the sum of the numbers divided by 3. First, get a common denominator, then divide by 3.

    $$\left(\frac{2}{3} + \frac{3}{4} + \frac{5}{6}\right) \div 3 = \left(\frac{8}{12} + \frac{9}{12} + \frac{10}{12}\right) \div 3$$
    $$= \frac{27}{12} \div 3$$
    $$= \frac{9}{4} \cdot \frac{1}{3}$$
    $$= \frac{3}{4}$$

4. **D.** First, take the square root of .04, which is .2.

    $$y\sqrt{.04} = 8$$
    $$.2y = 8$$
    $$\frac{.2y}{.2} = \frac{8}{.2}$$
    $$y = 40$$

5. **B.** Since m yards $= 36m$ inches and n feet $= 12n$ inches, m yards and n feet $=$

    $(36m + 12n)$ inches.

6. **D.** First multiply each side by $x^2 + 4$.

    $$\frac{3x^2 - 7x + 16}{x^2 + 4} = 3$$
    $$\frac{3x^2 - 7x + 16}{x^2 + 4}(x^2 + 4) = 3(x^2 + 4)$$
    $$3x^2 - 7x + 16 = 3(x^2 + 4)$$
    $$3x^2 - 7x + 16 = 3x^2 + 12$$
    $$3x^2 - 7x + 16 - 3x^2 = 3x^2 + 12 - 3x^2$$
    $$-7x + 16 = 12$$
    $$-7x + 16 - 16 = 12 - 16$$
    $$-7x = -4$$
    $$\frac{-7x}{-7} = \frac{-4}{-7}$$
    $$x = \frac{4}{7}$$

7. A. The center of the circle is the midpoint of its diameter.

The coordinates of the center of the circle are:

$$\left(\frac{-5+-3}{2}, \frac{8+5}{2}\right) = \left(\frac{-8}{2}, \frac{13}{2}\right) = \left(-4, \frac{13}{2}\right)$$

8. B.

$$\frac{10^{20} + 10^{21}}{10^{20}} = \frac{10^{20}(1+10)}{10^{20}}$$
$$= 1 + 10$$
$$= 11$$

Or

$$\frac{10^{20} + 10^{21}}{10^{20}} = \frac{10^{20}}{10^{20}} + \frac{10^{21}}{10^{20}}$$
$$= 1 + 10$$
$$= 11$$

9. D. The area of the larger circle is $\pi r^2 = \pi(10^2) = 100\pi$

The area of the smaller circle is $\pi(8^2) = 64\pi$

The area of the shaded region is $100\pi - 64\pi = 36\pi$.

The ratio of the shaded region area to the area of the larger circle is $\frac{36\pi}{100\pi} = \frac{9}{25}$

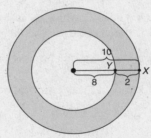

10. C. Since the first digit cannot be 0, there are 9 possibilities for the first digit (1–9).

For the second and third digits there are 10 possibilities (0–9).

Since the number must be divisible by 5, the last digit must be 0 or 5, and there are only two possibilities for the last digit.

Therefore, the total number of possible four-digit numbers is $9 \times 10 \times 10 \times 2 = 1800$.

Grid-In Questions

11. Answer: 66.2. Because $F = \frac{9}{5}C + 32$ and $C = 19$,

$$F = \left(\frac{9}{5}\right) \times \left(\frac{19}{1}\right) + 32$$
$$= \left(\frac{171}{5}\right) + 32$$
$$= 34.2 + 32$$
$$= 66.2$$

12. Answer: $\frac{1}{3}$. The total combination of red, green, and white jelly beans is made up of $5 + 4 + 3 = 12$ parts. Since the green jelly beans make up 4 parts of the total 12 parts, the portion of green jelly beans in the combination is $\frac{4}{12} = \frac{1}{3}$.

13. Answer: 143. Since the width of the frame is $1\frac{1}{2}$ inches, the dimensions of the rectangle containing both the frame and the picture are

$$\text{width} = 8 + 1\frac{1}{2} + 1\frac{1}{2} = 11 \text{ inches}$$

$$\text{length} = 10 + 1\frac{1}{2} + 1\frac{1}{2} = 13 \text{ inches}$$

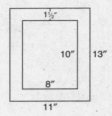

The area of this rectangle is the product of its base times its height. So

$$\text{area} = bh = (11)(13) = 143 \text{ square inches}$$

14. Answer: 15. Numeration is 10%, and algebra is 30%, which means that there should be three times as many algebra problems. If there are 5 numeration problems, there should be

$$5 \times 3 = 15 \text{ algebra problems}$$

15. Answer: 45. $x + y = 180°$ (x plus y forms a straight line, or straight angle). Since $y = 3x$, substituting gives

$$3x + x = 180°$$

$$4x = 180°$$

$$x = 45°$$

16. Answer: $\frac{2}{5}$. Since 150% of y is equal to 60% of z,

$$\frac{150}{100}y = \frac{60}{100}z$$

Multiplying both sides of the equation by the LCD of 100 yields

$$100\left(\frac{150}{100}y\right) = 100\left(\frac{60}{100}z\right)$$

$$150y = 60z$$

$$\frac{150y}{150z} = \frac{60z}{150z}$$

$$\frac{y}{z} = \frac{60}{150}$$

$$\frac{y}{z} = \frac{2}{5}$$

17. Answer: $\frac{1}{8}$. Let n = whole circle. Three-fourths of the circle divided by 6 is

$$\frac{3}{4}n \div 6 = \frac{3}{4}n \cdot \frac{1}{6}$$
$$= \frac{3}{24}n$$
$$= \frac{1}{8}n$$

Therefore, each piece will be $\frac{1}{8}$ of the whole circle.

18. Answer: 57.1. There were 4 days (July 10, 11, 14, and 15) on which the maximum temperature exceeded the average. Therefore, $\frac{4}{7}$ is 57.1%.

19. Answer: 3.75. Let x = number of days to complete the job working together. The first person will complete $x/6$ part of the job in x days, and the other person will complete $x/10$ part of the job in x days. Since they complete the job in x days working together,

$$\frac{x}{6} + \frac{x}{10} = 1$$

Multiplying both sides of the equation by 30 yields

$$30\left(\frac{x}{6} + \frac{x}{10}\right) = (30)(1)$$
$$5x + 3x = 30$$
$$8x = 30$$
$$x = \frac{30}{8}$$
$$x = 3\frac{3}{4} = 3.75$$

Therefore, it will take the two people 3.75 days to complete the job working together.

20. Answer: $\frac{6}{9}$. Let x = numerator of original fraction and y = denominator of original fraction.

Therefore, $\frac{x}{y} = \frac{2}{3}$ and $x = \frac{2}{3}y$.

The new fraction is

$$\frac{x-2}{y+3} = \frac{1}{3}$$

Since $x = \frac{2}{3}y$

$$3(x-2) = 1(y+3)$$
$$3x - 6 = y + 3$$
$$3\left(\frac{2}{3}y\right) - 6 = y + 3$$
$$2y - 6 = y + 3$$
$$y - 6 = 3$$
$$y = 9$$

Therefore, $x = \frac{2}{3}y = \left(\frac{2}{3}\right)(9) = 6$

and the original fraction is $\frac{x}{y} = \frac{6}{9}$

Section 10: Writing—Multiple Choice

Improving Sentences

1. **B.** The sentence presents a series of three parts in chronological order. The first and third parts of the series use indicative verbs in the past tense, but the second element is subordinated in A, C, D, and E. To keep the three parts parallel, there should be no "when," "while," or "whence," and the verb should be in the past tense to maintain the parallel ("was educated," "emigrated," "became").

2. **B.** All four of the erring versions of this sentence have a vague pronoun ("they" or "them" in E). They who? B is the clearest and the briefest sentence.

3. **A.** The original sentence is correct. The two independent clauses are separated by the semicolon. A period would also work here, but a comma or no punctuation at all will produce a comma splice or a run-on sentence.

4. **C.** In this section of the exam, when all of a long sentence is underlined, there is a good chance that the problem being tested is the placement of a modifier. Here the phrase "affecting one-fifth of the adult population" modifies "illiteracy." The good answer will find a way to keep the two together. D keeps the two together, but misplaces "yearly" so that it appears to modify "affecting" rather than "costs." E also misplaces "yearly."

5. **E.** This is a sentence fragment, with two participles but no main verb. A, B, and C retain the participle "depicting" but do not supply a main verb. D adds a verb but the participle "placed" now modifies "dance." E has the two required main verbs.

6. **D.** There are two complete sentences here, run together with no punctuation between them. They should be punctuated as two sentences with a period after fire, or with a semicolon, as in choice D.

7. **A.** The three elements of the series here should be kept parallel. Choice A uses three gerunds. B, C, and E are not parallel; D is wordier than A.

8. **C.** In choices A, D, and E, the pronoun "he" could refer to either Arun Shourie or the Prime Minister's son. B and C avoid this ambiguity. The sequence of verb tenses is clearer in C; by placing the exposure before the job loss, B suggests that the first action was the cause of the second.

9. **E.** The pronouns ("this" and "which") in A, B, C, and D have no specific antecedent; E avoids this vagueness by adding the noun "fact."

10. **E.** This sentence uses a pronoun with no specific antecedent, and tries to correct the error by changing the pronoun; neither "which" nor "this" will work, but eliminating the pronoun eliminates the error.

11. **C.** With the correlatives "both . . . and," the same structure should follow each conjunction. Since A and B begin with "both used," the "and" should be followed by a verb, not the pronoun "it." D never completes the "both" with an "and." E uses "both . . . and" correctly (to introduce adjectives that are parallel), but it is a very wordy sentence, four words longer than C. C avoids a lot of trouble simply by not using "both . . . and."

12. **C.** The issues in this sentence are the agreement of the verb and pronoun with the subject "group" and the phrase "where . . . in." Since "group" refers to a single unit, we should take it to be singular and use the singular "has ignored" and "it." In the phrase "the city where in" the "in" is unnecessary.

13. **D.** The sentence is testing parallel elements in a series. The series could use three nouns or three clauses beginning with "that" or three gerunds to keep the parallelism, though the "that" clauses would be wordy. None of the wrong answers uses all three consistently, but D uses three nouns ("eagerness," "willingness," and "refusal").

14. **C.** The phrase "is no different from" is another way of saying "is like." Comparisons, whether negative ("not different") or not, should be kept as parallel as possible. Here we need a parallel to the gerund "understanding." The addition of subject ("you") and verbs in A, B, D, or E is unnecessary. The parallel is the most concise choice, the gerund "seeing."

15. **C.** This is a sentence fragment. Introduced by "where," it is a dependent clause. The change to "when," or "if," or "while" does not make the clause independent. C rightly drops the subordinating conjunction, and the sentence is now complete.

SAT Score Range Approximator

The following charts are designed to give you only a very approximate score range, not an exact score. When you take the actual new SAT, you will see questions similar to those in this book; however, some questions may be slightly easier or more difficult. Needless to say, this may affect your scoring range.

Because one section of the new SAT is experimental (it doesn't count toward your score), *for the purposes of this approximation, do not count Section 9.* Remember: On the actual test, the experimental section could appear *anywhere* on your test.

How to Approximate Your Score in Critical Reading

1. Add the total number of correct responses for the three Critical Reading sections. **Remember,** *for the purposes of this approximation, do not count Section 9.*
2. Add the total number of incorrect responses (only those attempted or marked in) for those sections.
3. The total number of incorrect responses for the Critical Reading sections should be divided by 4, giving you an adjustment factor (round off to the nearest whole number, if necessary).
4. Subtract this adjustment factor from the total number of correct responses to obtain a raw score.
5. This raw score is then scaled to a range from 200 to 800.

   Example:

   If the total number of correct answers is 40 out of a possible 70

   and 20 problems were attempted but missed,

   dividing 20 by 4 gives an adjustment factor of 5.

   Subtracting this adjustment factor of 5 from the original 40 correct gives a raw score of 35.

   This raw score is then scaled to a range from 200 to 800.

6. Using your scores:

   _____ – _____ = _____
     correct answers   wrong answers ÷ 4   raw score

7. Use the following table to match your raw score for Critical Reading and the corresponding approximate score range:

Raw Score	Approximate Score Range
62–71	720–800
51–61	630–710
36–50	530–620
25–35	460–520
12–24	360–450
6–11	300–350
1–5	250–290
–4–0	200–240

Keep in mind that this is only an *approximate* score range.

How to Approximate Your Score in Mathematics

1. Add the total number of correct responses for the three Mathematics sections. **Remember,** *for the purposes of this approximation, do not count Section 9.*

2. Add the total number of incorrect responses for the multiple-choice questions only.

3. The total number of incorrect responses for the multiple-choice questions should be divided by 4, giving you an adjustment factor (round off to the nearest whole number).

4. Subtract this adjustment factor from the total number of correct responses to obtain a raw score.

5. This raw score is then scaled to a range from 200 to 800.

   Example:

   If the total number of correct answers is 30 out of a possible 55

   and 16 multiple-choice problems were attempted but missed,

   dividing 16 by 4 gives an adjustment factor of 4.

   Subtracting this adjustment factor of 4 from the original 30 correct gives a raw score of 26.

   This raw score is then scaled to a range from 200 to 800.

   Note: No deduction is made for incorrect grid-in responses.

6. Using your scores:

   _____ – _____ = _____

   Total correct answers   wrong answers on multiple choice ÷ 4   raw score

7. Use the following table to match your raw score for Mathematics and the corresponding approximate score range:

Raw Score	Approximate Score Range
49–55	710–800
41–48	640–700
26–40	500–630
11–25	380–490
5–10	310–370
1–4	240–300
–4–0	200–230

Keep in mind that this is only an *approximate* score range.

How to Approximate Your Score in Writing

Although the scoring techniques for the actual new SAT Writing sections are very precise, this rough method should give you a very general indication of your scoring range.

Let's start with the Writing Multiple-Choice sections.

1. Add the total number of correct responses for the two Writing Multiple-Choice sections.

2. Add the total number of incorrect responses for the multiple-choice questions.

3. The total number of incorrect responses for the multiple-choice questions should be divided by 4, giving you an adjustment factor (round off to the nearest whole number).

4. Subtract this adjustment factor from the total number of correct responses to obtain the Writing Multiple-Choice raw score.

5. This raw score is then scaled as a writing multiple-choice sub-score from 20 to 80.

Example:

If your essay is scored a 4, then multiply that number by 4 to give you an approximate essay score of 16.

If the total number of correct multiple-choice answers is 30 out of a possible 50

and 12 multiple-choice problems were attempted but missed,

dividing 12 by 4 gives an adjustment factor of 3.

Subtracting this adjustment factor of 3 from the original 30 correct gives a multiple-choice raw score of 27.

This raw score of 27 would then be scaled as a writing multiple-choice sub-score from 20 to 80.

6. Using your multiple-choice score:

$$\underbrace{\qquad\qquad}_{\text{correct answers}} - \underbrace{\qquad\qquad}_{\text{wrong answers} \div 4} = \underbrace{\qquad\qquad}_{\text{raw score}}$$

7. Use the following table to match your score for the multiple choice and the corresponding approximate sub-score range:

Raw Score	Approximate Sub-Score Range
41–51	71–80
26–40	54–70
11–25	40–53
0–10	20–39

Now let's look at the Writing Essay.

1. Have an English teacher, tutor, or someone else with good writing skills read and evaluate your essay using the Essay Checklist given after the practice exam.

2. Have your reader evaluate the complete essay as generally good, fair, or poor and give the essay a score of 5, 3, or 1.

3. Remember this is only a very general approximation. On the actual test, your essay will be graded by two readers who are trained to score the essay from 1 (lowest) to 6 (highest). Totaling the two readers' scores will give a sub-score of 2–12.

Now let's look at the composite Writing score from 200 to 800.

Use the chart below with your approximate essay score and your multiple-choice raw score to approximate your score range.

Multiple-choice	Approximate Essay Score		
	1	3	5
46–51	680–720	730–760	780–800
36–45	570–670	610–720	680–770
26–35	470–560	520–600	590–670
16–25	390–460	440–510	510–580
6–15	320–380	370–430	430–500
0–5	250–310	300–360	380–420
−10 – −1	200–240	210–290	270–370

Keep in mind that this is only an *approximate* score range.

PART III

ABOUT THE PSAT/NMSQT

Introduction to the PSAT/NMSQT

General Format of PSAT/NMSQT		
Section 1	**Critical Reading**	**23 Questions**
25 Minutes	Sentence Completion	6 Questions
	Short Reading Passages	4 Questions
	Long Reading Passages	13 Questions
Section 2	**Mathematics**	**20 Questions**
25 Minutes	Multiple Choice	20 Questions
Section 3	**Critical Reading**	**25 Questions**
25 Minutes	Sentence Completion	7 Questions
	Short Reading Passages	8 Questions
	Long Reading Passages	10 Questions
Section 4	**Mathematics**	**18 Questions**
25 Minutes	Multiple Choice	8 Questions
	Grid-ins	10 Questions
Section 5	**Writing Skills**	**39 Questions**
30 Minutes	Improving Sentences	20 Questions
	Identifying Sentence Errors	14 Questions
	Improving Paragraphs	5 Questions
Total Time 2 hours and 10 minutes		**Approximately 125 Questions**

Note: The order of the sections and the number of questions per section may vary.

General Description

The Preliminary Scholastic Assessment Test/National Merit Scholarship Qualifying Test (PSAT/NMSQT) is outstanding practice for taking the SAT. By taking the PSAT/NMSQT, students also compete for national scholarships, get a good sense of their strengths and weaknesses in preparing for the SAT, and get mail from colleges. The PSAT/NMSQT is given in October and is usually taken by high school juniors. To get information about registering for this exam, contact your high school counselor.

The test lasts 2 hours and 10 minutes and consists of two Critical Reading sections (containing sentence completions, questions from short reading passages, and questions from long reading passages), two Math sections (containing multiple-choice and grid-in questions), and one Writing Skills section (containing sentence error identification, sentence improvement, and paragraph improvement questions).

The Critical Reading sections test your ability to read and comprehend and to understand words in context.

The Math sections test your mathematical reasoning ability by asking you to solve problems and word problems in arithmetic, algebra, and geometry.

The Writing Skills section tests your ability to use standard written English to find errors in usage and structure and to choose effective revisions in sentences and paragraphs.

The Critical Reading, math, and writing questions each generate scores of 20 through 80. When you receive your score reports, you will get the three separate scores and two estimates of what your scores might be on the SAT.

The problems are slightly graduated in difficulty within each question type, except for critical reading, which is not in order of difficulty. You receive a penalty for incorrect answers, so don't guess unless you can eliminate at least one choice. On math grid-ins, you receive no penalty for guessing.

Additional information and sample problems are available on the Internet, at www.psat.org.

Critical Reading, Math, and Writing Skills Sections

The SAT strategies, techniques, and sample problems given in the introductory sections of this guide also apply to the PSAT/NMSQT. The sentence completion, and critical reading approaches should be reviewed carefully as the basis for your verbal review (review pages 11–38). In the math sections, reviewing the approaches for SAT multiple-choice math and grid-ins will be very helpful (review pages 42–81). In the writing skills section, reviewing the multiple choice writing skills introduction (review pages 101–126) should give you a good understanding of what to expect and how to approach different problem types.

Answer Sheets for PSAT/NMSQT Practice Test

(Remove These Sheets and Use Them to Mark Your Answers)

Section 1

1 (A) (B) (C) (D) (E)
2 (A) (B) (C) (D) (E)
3 (A) (B) (C) (D) (E)
4 (A) (B) (C) (D) (E)
5 (A) (B) (C) (D) (E)
6 (A) (B) (C) (D) (E)
7 (A) (B) (C) (D) (E)
8 (A) (B) (C) (D) (E)
9 (A) (B) (C) (D) (E)
10 (A) (B) (C) (D) (E)
11 (A) (B) (C) (D) (E)
12 (A) (B) (C) (D) (E)
13 (A) (B) (C) (D) (E)
14 (A) (B) (C) (D) (E)
15 (A) (B) (C) (D) (E)
16 (A) (B) (C) (D) (E)
17 (A) (B) (C) (D) (E)
18 (A) (B) (C) (D) (E)
19 (A) (B) (C) (D) (E)
20 (A) (B) (C) (D) (E)
21 (A) (B) (C) (D) (E)
22 (A) (B) (C) (D) (E)
23 (A) (B) (C) (D) (E)

Section 2

1 (A) (B) (C) (D) (E)
2 (A) (B) (C) (D) (E)
3 (A) (B) (C) (D) (E)
4 (A) (B) (C) (D) (E)
5 (A) (B) (C) (D) (E)
6 (A) (B) (C) (D) (E)
7 (A) (B) (C) (D) (E)
8 (A) (B) (C) (D) (E)
9 (A) (B) (C) (D) (E)
10 (A) (B) (C) (D) (E)
11 (A) (B) (C) (D) (E)
12 (A) (B) (C) (D) (E)
13 (A) (B) (C) (D) (E)
14 (A) (B) (C) (D) (E)
15 (A) (B) (C) (D) (E)
16 (A) (B) (C) (D) (E)
17 (A) (B) (C) (D) (E)
18 (A) (B) (C) (D) (E)
19 (A) (B) (C) (D) (E)
20 (A) (B) (C) (D) (E)

Section 3

24 (A) (B) (C) (D) (E)
25 (A) (B) (C) (D) (E)
26 (A) (B) (C) (D) (E)
27 (A) (B) (C) (D) (E)
28 (A) (B) (C) (D) (E)
29 (A) (B) (C) (D) (E)
30 (A) (B) (C) (D) (E)
31 (A) (B) (C) (D) (E)
32 (A) (B) (C) (D) (E)
33 (A) (B) (C) (D) (E)
34 (A) (B) (C) (D) (E)
35 (A) (B) (C) (D) (E)
36 (A) (B) (C) (D) (E)
37 (A) (B) (C) (D) (E)
38 (A) (B) (C) (D) (E)
39 (A) (B) (C) (D) (E)
40 (A) (B) (C) (D) (E)
41 (A) (B) (C) (D) (E)
42 (A) (B) (C) (D) (E)
43 (A) (B) (C) (D) (E)
44 (A) (B) (C) (D) (E)
45 (A) (B) (C) (D) (E)
46 (A) (B) (C) (D) (E)
47 (A) (B) (C) (D) (E)
48 (A) (B) (C) (D) (E)

Section 4

21 (A) (B) (C) (D) (E)
22 (A) (B) (C) (D) (E)
23 (A) (B) (C) (D) (E)
24 (A) (B) (C) (D) (E)
25 (A) (B) (C) (D) (E)
26 (A) (B) (C) (D) (E)
27 (A) (B) (C) (D) (E)
28 (A) (B) (C) (D) (E)

CUT HERE

Section 4 (continued)

29.
30.
31.
32.

Section 4 (continued)

33. [grid-in answer bubbles]

34. [grid-in answer bubbles]

35. [grid-in answer bubbles]

36. [grid-in answer bubbles]

37. [grid-in answer bubbles]

38. [grid-in answer bubbles]

Section 5

1 Ⓐ Ⓑ Ⓒ Ⓓ Ⓔ
2 Ⓐ Ⓑ Ⓒ Ⓓ Ⓔ
3 Ⓐ Ⓑ Ⓒ Ⓓ Ⓔ
4 Ⓐ Ⓑ Ⓒ Ⓓ Ⓔ
5 Ⓐ Ⓑ Ⓒ Ⓓ Ⓔ

6 Ⓐ Ⓑ Ⓒ Ⓓ Ⓔ
7 Ⓐ Ⓑ Ⓒ Ⓓ Ⓔ
8 Ⓐ Ⓑ Ⓒ Ⓓ Ⓔ
9 Ⓐ Ⓑ Ⓒ Ⓓ Ⓔ
10 Ⓐ Ⓑ Ⓒ Ⓓ Ⓔ

11 Ⓐ Ⓑ Ⓒ Ⓓ Ⓔ
12 Ⓐ Ⓑ Ⓒ Ⓓ Ⓔ
13 Ⓐ Ⓑ Ⓒ Ⓓ Ⓔ
14 Ⓐ Ⓑ Ⓒ Ⓓ Ⓔ
15 Ⓐ Ⓑ Ⓒ Ⓓ Ⓔ

16 Ⓐ Ⓑ Ⓒ Ⓓ Ⓔ
17 Ⓐ Ⓑ Ⓒ Ⓓ Ⓔ
18 Ⓐ Ⓑ Ⓒ Ⓓ Ⓔ
19 Ⓐ Ⓑ Ⓒ Ⓓ Ⓔ
20 Ⓐ Ⓑ Ⓒ Ⓓ Ⓔ

21 Ⓐ Ⓑ Ⓒ Ⓓ Ⓔ
22 Ⓐ Ⓑ Ⓒ Ⓓ Ⓔ
23 Ⓐ Ⓑ Ⓒ Ⓓ Ⓔ
24 Ⓐ Ⓑ Ⓒ Ⓓ Ⓔ
25 Ⓐ Ⓑ Ⓒ Ⓓ Ⓔ

26 Ⓐ Ⓑ Ⓒ Ⓓ Ⓔ
27 Ⓐ Ⓑ Ⓒ Ⓓ Ⓔ
28 Ⓐ Ⓑ Ⓒ Ⓓ Ⓔ
29 Ⓐ Ⓑ Ⓒ Ⓓ Ⓔ
30 Ⓐ Ⓑ Ⓒ Ⓓ Ⓔ

31 Ⓐ Ⓑ Ⓒ Ⓓ Ⓔ
32 Ⓐ Ⓑ Ⓒ Ⓓ Ⓔ
33 Ⓐ Ⓑ Ⓒ Ⓓ Ⓔ
34 Ⓐ Ⓑ Ⓒ Ⓓ Ⓔ
35 Ⓐ Ⓑ Ⓒ Ⓓ Ⓔ

36 Ⓐ Ⓑ Ⓒ Ⓓ Ⓔ
37 Ⓐ Ⓑ Ⓒ Ⓓ Ⓔ
38 Ⓐ Ⓑ Ⓒ Ⓓ Ⓔ
39 Ⓐ Ⓑ Ⓒ Ⓓ Ⓔ

CUT HERE

PSAT/NMSQT Practice Test

Section 1: Critical Reading

Time: 25 Minutes

23 Questions

(1–23)

In this section, choose the best answer for each question and blacken the corresponding space on the answer sheet.

Directions: Each blank in the following sentences indicates that something has been omitted. Consider the lettered words beneath the sentence and choose the word or set of words that best fits the whole sentence.

EXAMPLE:

With a million more people than any other African nation, Nigeria is the most _____ country on the continent.

    A. impoverished
    B. successful
    C. populous
    D. developed
    E. militant

The correct answer is C.

---

1. She preferred _____ objects to people, a bed or a chair to a man or a woman.

    A. sacred
    B. expensive
    C. inanimate
    D. impractical
    E. effete

2. By equating dog owners who violate leash laws with smokers, the city hopes to persuade dog owners that it is inconsiderate, unhealthy, and even _____ to let dogs run free.

    A. salubrious
    B. shameful
    C. ambiguous
    D. edifying
    E. mordant

3. For their patients who could not sleep, Victorian doctors commonly prescribed drugs made chiefly from opium with little or no concern for the _____ nature of these _____.

    A. tonic . . . opiates
    B. addictive . . . narcotics
    C. perilous . . . placebos
    D. soporific . . . remedies
    E. somnolent . . . prescriptions

4. Though Europe has merged its currencies, there is no sign of _____ unity, since 11 different official languages are now used to operate the European Union.

    A. linguistic
    B. financial
    C. commercial
    D. political
    E. religious

GO ON TO THE NEXT PAGE

5. The _____ amounts of rain this winter
have caused a record number of floods, and the
losses are _____ by the increased
number of homes built too close to the rivers.

A. minimal . . . increased
B. scant . . . maximized
C. massive . . . diminished
D. average . . . intensified
E. unprecedented . . . augmented

6. The designer's most _____ idea, one
that shocked the visitors to the museum, was to
_____ in a single small room famous
Renaissance paintings and abstract 20th-century
sculpture.

A. conventional . . . confine
B. unusual . . . exclude
C. conservative . . . combine
D. audacious . . . juxtapose
E. gauche . . . conceal

Directions: Questions follow the passages below. Using only the stated or implied information in the passage and in its introduction, if any, answer the questions.

Questions 7–8 are based on the following passage.

In the 18th and 19th centuries, patent-medicine men traveled across the United States selling magical tonics and miracle cures without any interference from government regulations. In fact, in 1793,
(5) Congress passed laws that permitted patent-medicine manufacturers to protect their formulas, regardless of whether they worked or were demonstrably safe. Then, in 1906, the Pure Food and Drug Act was passed, which allowed a government agency—the
(10) precursor of the Food and Drug Administration—to ensure that medicine labels contained no false or misleading claims. Although this ended the glory days of snake-oil salesmen, since then new regulations of patent medicines have come about only as a
(15) result of disasters that outrage the public.

7. According to the paragraph, before the 20th century, which of the following was most helpful to patent-medicine manufacturers?

   A.   an illiterate public

   B.   a weak Congress

   C.   no government regulation

   D.   highly trained salesmen

   E.   lack of scientific knowledge

8. The last sentence of the paragraph suggests that

   A.   more regulation of patent medicines may occur in the future.

   B.   more patent medicines are sold today than in the past.

   C.   people are confused by the claims of patent-medicine manufacturers.

   D.   no regulation of patent medicine has occurred since 1906.

   E.   Congress has become the watchdog of patent medicines.

Questions 9–10 are based on the following passage.

In 1833 Charles Babbage, a British mathematician, designed an "analytical engine" a steam-driven machine as big as a train. It contained all the main elements of the modern computer: input devices,
(5) memory ("store"), a computing unit ("mill"), a control unit, and output devices. Unfortunately, Babbage never built his engine. Under the best circumstances, the limitations of Newtonian physics might have prevented him, but one of his greatest
(10) obstacles was not considering that information cannot be moved between "mill" and "store" without leaking, like faulty sacks of flour. An even greater obstacle may have been his impatience and lack of diplomacy, which partly accounted for his inability
(15) to get sufficient government funding. But his design does prefigure the logical structure of the modern computer, and he has been called the "father of computing."

9. The terms "store" and "mill" indicate that Babbage

   A.   had a unique imagination.

   B.   used language familiar to the period in which he worked.

   C.   lacked a complete knowledge of Newtonian physics.

   D.   had an imperfect understanding of computer logic.

   E.   chose terminology to appeal to the working class.

10. According to the passage, which of the following was most responsible for Babbage's inability to build his "analytical engine"?

   A.   insufficient funding

   B.   criticism from other mathematicians

   C.   a limited education

   D.   impatience

   E.   the engine's massive size

GO ON TO THE NEXT PAGE

Directions: Questions follow each of the passages below. Using only the stated or implied information in each passage and in its introduction, if any, answer the questions.

Questions 11–16 are based on the following passage.

In the early 1980s, as scientists were perfecting techniques for splicing foreign genes into bacteria, some investigators began suggesting ways to use the technology to benefit the environment. For in-
(5) stance, they proposed that genetically engineered bacteria might be deployed for such tasks as clean-ing oil spills or protecting crops from predation and disease. But the enterprise, known as *environmen-tal biotechnology,* soon came under fire.

(10) Then, as now, the proposals elicited concern that the altered microbes might run amok or that their genes would hop unpredictably to other organisms—a phenomenon termed "horizontal" gene transfer (to distinguish it from the "vertical" transfer occurring
(15) between a parent and its offspring). Such activities, it was feared, might somehow irreparably harm the en-vironment, animals, or people. Some observers even issued dire warnings that the unnatural organisms would destroy the earth. No longer were tabloids
(20) worried about attacks by "killer tomatoes" from outer space; now the danger was homegrown—genetically altered microorganisms that would eat the environment.

Unfortunately, at the time, biologists had little
(25) solid information on which to base responses. They knew almost nothing about the fate of genetically engineered microbes in nature and about the propensity of innate or introduced bacterial genes to migrate to new hosts. That paucity of data is now
(30) being remedied, thanks to unprecedented coopera-tion between genetic researchers and microbial ecologists, who study microorganisms in their nor-mal habitats.

Today at least two strains of genetically engi-
(35) neered bacteria have gained approval (for agricul-tural use) by the U.S. Environmental Protection Agency, and dozens of field trials have been con-ducted. Those trials and more general investiga-tions of gene transfer between bacteria in their
(40) natural habitats indicate that genetically manipu-lated bacteria themselves are unlikely to proliferate out of control. They tend to be fragile and to die out relatively quickly instead of persisting indefinitely; for that reason, their genes probably do not have
(45) much opportunity to spread.

Yet under certain circumstances, the genes can potentially find their way into other bacteria or even into other types of organisms. A key to the safe release of the microbes, then, is to identify the
(50) conditions that will encourage or deter specific bacteria from transferring their genes to other or-ganisms. With such information in hand, biologists can select bacteria that will be least likely to ex-change genes with organisms in the particular site being "treated." As an example, for release into a
(55) lake, biotechnologists might be able to choose a bacterial species that does not readily exchange its genes in water.

11. The author's purpose in this passage is to

A. advise a moratorium on research in the field of environmental biotechnology.

B. show that fears of gene swapping are groundless and that critics have reacted hysterically.

C. explain the difference between "horizontal" and "vertical" gene swapping.

D. show that research indicates that genetically altered bacteria may be safely used in nature under certain conditions.

E. describe the types of research being conducted in the field of environmental technology.

12. According to the passage, critics of environmental biotechnology have been most concerned that introducing altered microbes into the environment will

A. lead to uncontrolled gene transfer.

B. interfere with normal vertical transfer.

C. create new species.

D. eliminate endangered species.

E. transfer human disease to other animals.

13. In line 28, "propensity" most nearly means

A. propriety.

B. inclination.

C. desire.

D. ability.

E. reliability.

14. Which of the following is the most promising safeguard against proliferation of altered bacteria in the environment?

    A. the reluctance of the U.S. Environmental Protection Agency to approve their use

    B. the tendency of altered bacteria to be short-lived

    C. the ability of normal micro-organisms to resist gene transfer

    D. the exclusive use of bacterial species that don't exchange genes in water

    E. the greater strength of "vertical" gene transfer

15. According to the passage, genetically manipulated bacteria might be useful in preserving the environment by

    A. attacking plant diseases.

    B. altering unstable ecosystems.

    C. preventing oil spills.

    D. eliminating the weakest members of a species.

    E. producing larger fruits and vegetables.

16. The author of the passage implies all of the following EXCEPT

    A. people often react fearfully to new technologies.

    B. the possible benefits of using manipulated bacteria for ecological purposes are not worth the risks.

    C. research is needed to identify conditions that will discourage gene transfer in various environments.

    D. genetic researchers have been willing to participate in finding safe applications for their research.

    E. the fragility of genetically manipulated bacteria reduces the possibility of their spreading unpredictably to other organisms.

Questions 17–23 are based on the following paired passages.

The following passages concern women in science, the first in the 19th century, the second in the latter half of the 20th century.

The first passage follows a description of the lack of opportunities for African Americans in science during the 19th century.

Passage 1

Less oppressive, but in some ways analogous, was the lot of American women. As in the case of whites over blacks, men rationalized the denial of opportunity by stereotyping the victims as inher-
(5) ently unfit for it. God and nature made women to raise families and adorn society (or "man" the factories), most men liked to believe. Intellectual pursuits were manifestly outside women's sphere. For a woman to aspire to serious scientific work was
(10) deemed especially grotesque, unseemly, hopeless, and impermissible.

Yet there were rents in the crinoline[1] curtain. Mothers, after all, raised sons, who might benefit from a home atmosphere of polite learning and in-
(15) formed reverence for God's work in nature. So no outcry arose when, in the second quarter of the nineteenth century, genteel girls and women took up science as a polite study rather than as preparation for a career. Female academies and seminaries,
(20) like their male counterparts in those years, added a variety of science courses and even invested in expensive telescopes, physical and chemical apparatus, and natural history collections. Many sought to equal the quality of courses at men's schools,
(25) though no women's school achieved a full range of college-level science courses until 1865. A few such schools could draw on nearby male professional scientists of some eminence for occasional lectures.

(30) Science reached women outside the classroom also. Many women attended the public lectures on science that were especially popular in the 1830s and 1840s. Both men and women wrote popular books and magazine articles on science for the
(35) growing women's market. Women wrote ten such books on botany alone from 1819–1859. From the late 1820s to the early 1870s, Mrs. Almira Phelps sold more than a quarter-million copies of her *Familiar Lectures on Botany,* the most popular of
(40) her books on science for children, drawing mostly on a few serious books by others. Several women, notwithstanding stereotypes, liked insects well enough to write popular yet knowledgeable articles on entomology.

[1] A woman's petticoat made from a stiff fabric.

GO ON TO THE NEXT PAGE

Passage 2

(45)   Science has a vested interest in the idea of the intellectual meritocracy. It is important to scientists to believe that they act rationally, that they do not distort or ignore evidence, that neither their work nor their profession is seriously influenced by poli-
(50) tics, ambition, or prejudice.

    Such, clearly, cannot be the case. Scientists, like all other people, make decisions on the basis of a shared social reality, are pulled about by convictions rooted in emotional prejudice, act on inherited
(55) ideas of what is natural, and are certainly influenced by politics, ambition, and issues of class, sex, and race. But, as they have a strong need to believe they are guided by intellectual objectivity, they have a more difficult time than other kinds of workers do
(60) in perceiving themselves as discriminatory.

    Thus, the atmosphere in which women in science have been held back, put off, discouraged and demoralized, and frozen in position is particularly disturbing because of its defensive denial that what
(65) is happening is happening. In business, a woman looks into the eyes of a corporation executive who says openly to her, "We know what you're all about, we've held you off as long as we could, and now you'll have to take us to court to get what you
(70) want." In science, a woman looks into the eyes of a man who thinks of himself as decent, fair-minded, above all reasonable, and who says to her, "I really don't know what you're talking about. Surely you're not saying we've discriminated against you."

(75)   Although one knows that life for women in science will not be the same in the next 40 years as it has been in the last, right now the statistics on women in science bears out the claim that they are half in, half out. Yes, there is change and growth
(80) recorded in the statistics, but that growth in real numbers is small and painfully disproportionate. Between 1978 and 1980, employment of women in science and engineering increased over five times faster than employment of men. Despite this growth,
(85) women represented about 13 percent of all employed scientists and engineers, and in real numbers the total employment for men in scientific and engineering fields was computed at 2,245,300 while for women it was 314,800. The statistical picture for
(90) women in science is graphic and sobering.

17. In line 12, "rents" most nearly means

    A. holes.
    B. payments.
    C. disputes.
    D. exceptions.
    E. fissures.

18. According to the author of Passage 1, women became involved in science initially because

    A. their husbands and fathers wanted them to improve their minds.
    B. they wanted to give deeper meaning to their lives.
    C. they wanted to help provide an atmosphere of learning at home.
    D. they sensed future career possibilities in an increasingly important field.
    E. the prejudice against their participation in scientific research was rapidly decreasing.

19. In Passage 2, line 46, "intellectual meritocracy" most nearly means

    A. government managed by intellectuals.
    B. a system without discrimination.
    C. a system based on intellectual achievement and ability.
    D. government by the best people available.
    E. a system that is open to change and improvement.

20. According to the author of Passage 2, science is

    A. a good field for women because of opportunities to advance.
    B. dominated by men who stereotype women as too emotional to be objective.
    C. less rewarding than business because of the attitudes toward women.
    D. influenced by the society's prejudices and convictions.
    E. guided by men whose primary concern is maintaining the status quo.

21. What would be the likely response by the author of Passage 2 to the information presented in Passage 1?

  A. Prejudice against women in science has in fact grown stronger in the past 100 years.

  B. Because of their achievements, women have overcome most of the prejudice against them.

  C. Attitudes similar to those in the 19th century continue to influence behavior, even in a field that is supposed to be immune from prejudices.

  D. Women have made progress in science, but only because of changes in discrimination laws.

  E. The negative attitude toward women scientists today is very different from the negative attitude described in Passage 1.

22. Which of the following best describes the difference between Passage 1 and Passage 2?

  A. In Passage 1, women are described as enjoying their social roles, whereas in Passage 2 they are shown to be angry and rebellious.

  B. The women described in Passage 1 are anti-intellectual, whereas the women described in Passage 2 are serious and determined.

  C. The author of Passage 1 presents facts with no opinions, and the author of Passage 2 presents opinions with no facts.

  D. Passage 1 presents an optimistic view of the future, and Passage 2 presents a pessimistic view.

  E. The author of Passage 1 presents his subject historically, whereas the author of Passage 2 is arguing a position.

23. Passage 2 is more concerned than Passage 1 with

  A. the social stereotyping of women.

  B. male scientists' denial that female scientists are the objects of discrimination.

  C. salary differences between men and women scientists.

  D. the types of scientific work that women must perform because of discrimination.

  E. the difficulties of women scientists torn between their profession and their families.

IF YOU FINISH BEFORE TIME IS CALLED, CHECK YOUR WORK ON THIS SECTION ONLY. DO NOT WORK ON ANY OTHER SECTION IN THE TEST.

Section 2: Mathematics

Time: 25 Minutes

20 Questions

(1–20)

Directions: Solve each problem in this section by using the information given and your own mathematical calculations, insights, and problem-solving skills. Then select the one correct answer of the five choices given and mark the corresponding circle on your answer sheet. Use the available space on the page for your scratch work.

Notes

1. All numbers used are real numbers.

2. Calculators may be used.

3. Some problems may be accompanied by figures or diagrams. These figures are drawn as accurately as possible EXCEPT when it is stated in a specific problem that a figure is not drawn to scale. The figures and diagrams are meant to provide information useful in solving the problem or problems. Unless otherwise stated, all figures and diagrams lie in a plane.

Data That Can Be Used for Reference

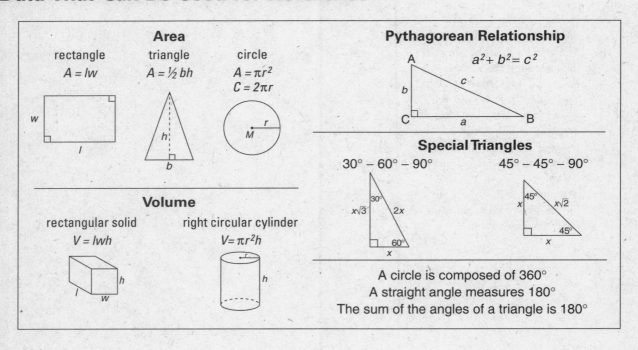

Area

rectangle $A = lw$

triangle $A = \frac{1}{2}bh$

circle $A = \pi r^2$ $C = 2\pi r$

Volume

rectangular solid $V = lwh$

right circular cylinder $V = \pi r^2 h$

Pythagorean Relationship

$a^2 + b^2 = c^2$

Special Triangles

$30° - 60° - 90°$

$45° - 45° - 90°$

A circle is composed of 360°

A straight angle measures 180°

The sum of the angles of a triangle is 180°

1. What is 864,925 rounded to the nearest thousand?

   A.   865,925
   B.   860,000
   C.   865,000
   D.   864,900
   E.   864,000

3. If $(a + b) = -3$, then $(a + b)^3 =$

   A.   −27
   B.   −9
   C.   −6
   D.   9
   E.   27

2. If $x = 2$, then $3x^2 + (3x)^2 =$

   A.   24
   B.   30
   C.   36
   D.   48
   E.   72

4. If the product of six integers is negative, then at most how many of the six integers could be negative?

   A.   six
   B.   five
   C.   four
   D.   three
   E.   two

GO ON TO THE NEXT PAGE

5. If the sum of three consecutive integers is 141, what is the largest of the three integers?

    A.   45

    B.   46

    C.   47

    D.   48

    E.   49

6. If $\frac{z}{3} = 25$, then $5z =$

    A.   375

    B.   360

    C.   125

    D.   80

    E.   75

7. If $m^4 + n^4 = 0$, what is the value of $9m - 5n$?

    A.   9

    B.   5

    C.   4

    D.   0

    E.   −1

8. If Marcos travels at an average speed of 55 miles per hour, how many hours would it take for him to travel d miles?

    A. $55d$

    B. $\frac{d}{55}$

    C. $\frac{55}{d}$

    D. $d + 55$

    E. $d - 55$

9. If $a + 5 = 3b$ and $a = 4b - 11$, what is the value of b?

   A.   13

   B.   6

   C.   –2

   D.   –6

   E.   –13

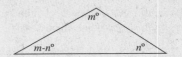

Note: Figure not drawn to scale.

11. In the figure above, if $n = 50$, what is the value of m?

   A.   40

   B.   50

   C.   90

   D.   100

   E.   140

10. If the volume of a cube is 64, what is the area of one face of the cube?

   A.   96

   B.   64

   C.   32

   D.   16

   E.   8

12. If x is an integer and $3x + 11$ is even, which of the following must be even?

   A. x

   B. $x + 1$

   C. x^2

   D. $2x + 1$

   E. x^3

GO ON TO THE NEXT PAGE

13. If a rectangular box with dimensions z, $2/z$, and y has a volume of 12, what must y equal?

    A.   12
    B.   6
    C.   4
    D.   3
    E.   2

14. What is the value of the ratio of x to y if $xy = 21$?

    A.   21 to 1
    B.   7 to 3
    C.   3 to 7
    D.   1 to 21
    E.   It cannot be determined from the information given.

15. If the diameter of a circle P is 40 percent of the diameter of circle Q, then the area of circle P is what percentage of the area of circle Q?

    A.   16
    B.   20
    C.   40
    D.   80
    E.   It cannot be determined from the information given.

16. If $x^5 = 9$ and $x^6 = y/11$, which of the following is an expression for x in terms of y?

    A. $\dfrac{9y}{11}$
    B. $\dfrac{11y}{9}$
    C. $\dfrac{y}{99}$
    D. $\dfrac{99}{y}$
    E. $99y$

17. For how many integer values of x will the value of the expression $3x - 4$ be an integer greater than 4 and less than 250?

    A. 86

    B. 85

    C. 84

    D. 83

    E. 82

19. Tickets numbered from 1 through 50 are placed in a container, and one ticket will be selected at random. What is the probability that the ticket selected will have a number on it divisible by 3?

    A. $\dfrac{3}{50}$

    B. $\dfrac{1}{5}$

    C. $\dfrac{3}{10}$

    D. $\dfrac{8}{25}$

    E. $\dfrac{1}{3}$

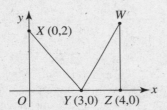

Note: Figure not drawn to scale.

18. In the figure above, if the area of $\triangle OXY$ equals the area of $\triangle WYZ$, which of the following are the coordinates of W?

    A. $(4, 4)$

    B. $(4, 5)$

    C. $(4, 6)$

    D. $(4, 8)$

    E. $(4, 10)$

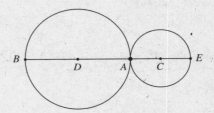

20. In the figure above, C and D are the centers of the two circles, and $AD = AE$. If the area of the smaller circle is 100π, what is the area of the larger circle?

    A. 1600π

    B. 800π

    C. 400π

    D. 200π

    E. 100π

IF YOU FINISH BEFORE TIME IS CALLED, CHECK YOUR WORK ON THIS SECTION ONLY. DO NOT WORK ON ANY OTHER SECTION IN THE TEST.

Section 3: Critical Reading

Time: 25 Minutes

25 Questions

(24–48)

In this section, choose the best answer for each question and blacken the corresponding space on the answer sheet.

Directions: Each blank in the following sentences indicates that something has been omitted. Consider the lettered words beneath the sentence and choose the word or set of words that best fits the whole sentence.

EXAMPLE:

With a million more people than any other African nation, Nigeria is the most _____ country on the continent.

    A. impoverished

    B. successful

    C. populous

    D. developed

    E. militant

The correct answer is C.

---

24. A kind and very modest philanthropist, Merrill donates money generously and _____ to many worthy causes.

    A. cynically

    B. commercially

    C. blatantly

    D. parsimoniously

    E. unobtrusively

25. The farmers believed that their crop failures were caused by the influx of Easterners, so they steadfastly _____ the sale of land to the newcomers.

    A. infringed

    B. commuted

    C. intensified

    D. discouraged

    E. exacted

26. Although most of the avalanches in Colorado occur in _____ mountain regions and pose no threat to human lives or property, the population _____ in some mountain counties has greatly increased the danger.

    A. obscure . . . decline

    B. populated . . . increase

    C. remote . . . explosion

    D. uninhabited . . . vacuum

    E. steep . . . deficiency

27. For almost a century, Maryland and Pennsylvania quarreled about their border, and even fought several small _____ about it.

    A. skirmishes

    B. dissents

    C. protests

    D. contractions

    E. invasions

28. The retiring judge's office shelves were filled with _____ of his years on the bench, including a _____ of the famous espionage trial over which he presided.

    A. exigencies . . . disclosure
    B. verdicts . . . daguerreotype
    C. legacies . . . archetype
    D. memorabilia . . . memento
    E. souvenirs . . . commentary

29. Edgar Lee Masters used to walk through cemeteries reading the _____ on the gravestones to find ideas for his poems.

    A. epithets
    B. illuminations
    C. epigrams
    D. illustrations
    E. epitaphs

30. Advances in the film industry depend on _____ developments in such fields as photography, projection, processing, recording, and sound reproduction.

    A. pictorial
    B. technological
    C. cinematic
    D. artistic
    E. financial

GO ON TO THE NEXT PAGE

Directions: Questions follow the passages below. Using only the stated or implied information in each passage and in its introduction, if any, answer the questions.

Questions 31–32 are based on the following passage.

In 1860, a historian wrote that during the Middle Ages consciousness "lay dreaming or half awake." A 19th century writer condemned the period as "a thousand years without a bath." This idea that the
(5) Middle Ages were dominated by gloom, ignorance, superstition and a lack of progress (and that Europe was reborn during the Renaissance) has been largely discredited, though it persists in terms we still use pejoratively. "Medieval," for example, can
(10) describe everything from cumbersome, antiquated regulations to barbarous practices of governments we don't like. And "the Dark Ages," once designating the Middle Ages, is still around to mean any primitive stage of development.

31. Which of the following best describes the main idea of this paragraph?

   A. A comparison of the Middle Ages to the Renaissance

   B. A mocking criticism of the view of 19th century scholars and writers

   C. An illustration of the persistence of an outmoded idea

   D. A celebration of the creativity of the Middle Ages

   E. An example of careless use of language

32. Which of the following best defines the word "pejoratively" as it is used in this paragraph (line 9)?

   A. negatively

   B. humorously

   C. redundantly

   D. ironically

   E. skeptically

Questions 33–34 are based on the following passage.

The design of a typewriter (and computer) keyboard is named for the first six letters on the left side in the top row: QWERTY. Designed in 1873, the QWERTY keyboard was intended to slow typ-
(5) ists down by scattering the most common letters all over the rows and putting them mostly on the left side, where a right-handed typist would have to use his or her left hand. Were the designers merely being perverse? In 1873 typewriters jammed if adja-
(10) cent keys were struck in quick succession, and QWERTY was a solution. Later, when the problem of jamming had been eliminated and a more efficient keyboard was designed, it was too late. Vested interests—such as typists and typing teachers—
(15) have successfully quashed any keyboard redesign for over 60 years.

33. The best definition of "perverse" (line 9) as it is used in this passage is

   A. contrary.

   B. immoral.

   C. improper.

   D. imaginative.

   E. short-sighted.

34. Which of the following implications is NOT supported by the paragraph?

   A. Redesign of the QWERTY keyboard would involve huge costs beyond simply the manufacture of new keyboards.

   B. More people are right-handed than left-handed.

   C. Although the arrangement of the QWERTY keyboard is not optimal for fast typing, it has survived for over 60 years.

   D. Among other vested interests, the manufacturers of keyboards would be opposed to changing keyboard design.

   E. The QWERTY keyboard will never be replaced.

Questions 35–36 are based on the following passage.

In the novel *The Mysterious Island,* written in the 1870s, one of Jules Verne's characters predicts that "water will one day be employed as fuel, that hydrogen and oxygen . . . used singly or together (5) will furnish an inexhaustible source of heat and light." That science-fiction idea may become reality. Fuel cells—in which hydrogen can be used to produce electricity—are already in place on the space shuttle and in some large buildings, for ex-(10) ample, and engineers are working on a variety of other applications. One use of the fuel cell receiving great attention is in powering automobiles. While the Verne character's concern was the dwindling supply of coal, today's is dependence on for-(15) eign oil and concerns about the environment.

35. The quotation from *The Mysterious Island* (lines 3–6) serves to

    A. introduce the idea of the fuel cell.

    B. demonstrate Verne's prophetic writings.

    C. explain the impact of fuel shortages.

    D. emphasize the value of science fiction.

    E. put into perspective environmental concerns.

36. Based on the paragraph, it is likely that the writer

    A. advocates the replacement of the internal combustion engine.

    B. opposes battery-powered or hybrid automobiles.

    C. expects automobile makers to reject hydrogen-powered automobiles.

    D. believes fuel cell technology will advance.

    E. is primarily concerned with automobile emissions.

Questions 37–38 are based on the following passage.

In the 19th century, wool was England's most valuable export, and the General Enclosure Act of 1801 standardized landlords' existing practice of fencing in open land to graze large herds of sheep. (5) For example, in 1820 the Duchess of Sutherland dispossessed 15,000 tenants and replaced them with 131,000 sheep. One of the far-reaching effects of enclosure was that peasants, who could no longer use the open lands for their own farming, were dri-(10) ven into towns and cities. They became paupers with nothing to sell but their own labor, and that at whatever price the market offered. Essentially, enclosure "freed" peasants to become an army of cheap labor for the Industrial Revolution's grim (15) new factories.

37. The example in lines 5–7 is used for all of the following EXCEPT to

    A. show the callous nature of the aristocracy.

    B. dramatize the effect of enclosure on the peasants.

    C. draw an ironic parallel between the sheep and the tenants.

    D. explain why the General Enclosure Act was adopted.

    E. provide a specific illustration.

38. The word "freed" in line 13 is in quotation marks because it

    A. is used in an informal way.

    B. refers to the slave-like position of rural workers.

    C. indicates the irony of the peasants' situation after enclosure.

    D. contrasts the plight of the workers with the condition of the landlords.

    E. is a direct quotation from the General Enclosure Act of 1801.

GO ON TO THE NEXT PAGE

Directions: Questions follow the passage below. Using only the stated or implied information in the passage and in its introduction, if any, answer the questions.

Questions 39–48 are based on the following passage.

Between 1840 and 1924, when the laws restricting Asian immigration were enacted, thousands of Chinese, Japanese, and Koreans migrated to the United States and Hawaii. In each case, immigra-
(5) tion was prompted by active recruitment of labor for plantation, railroad, mining, or field work. And in each case, anti-Asian sentiment resulted ultimately in the passage of exclusion laws. Filipinos were permitted to immigrate until 1934, when they
(10) too were barred by law from further entry.

The relatively small Asian population consisted largely of laborers without the means or, in some cases, the inclination to return to their homelands. Partly because their time was consumed in struggles
(15) for a livelihood, the Asian point of view on the immigrant experience is rarely presented in writings in English or even in Asian languages. Some unknown immigrants carved poems in Chinese into the walls of the barracks on Angel Island, where they were
(20) held before being allowed to enter the United States between 1910 and 1940. Autobiographical information about a Japanese house servant and a Chinatown merchant was collected by Hamilton Holt, editor of *The Life Stories of Undistinguished Americans*
(25) (1906). And Carlos Bulosan, a self-taught Filipino farm worker, was able only because of the mandatory rest required by his tuberculosis to write his account of the life of the Filipino migrants in the American West immediately prior to the
(30) Depression. But with these exceptions, Asian immigrant workers vanished without leaving behind much written account of their individual lives in America. Although some letters and diaries written in Asian languages have survived earthquake, fire,
(35) and Japanese relocation, the general privation and loneliness of Asian immigrant life, sequestered as it was in field labor camps or urban ethnic enclaves, must have dampened the desire to communicate. In the face of pervasive American ignorance and an-
(40) tipathy toward Asians, an Asian writer could hardly know where to begin and what audience to address. Moreover, since they were segregated from the mainstream of American social and economic life and prevented by law from becoming naturalized
(45) American citizens with voting and civil rights, many early immigrants did not learn English and did not consider the culture it represented as something that belonged to them or to which they could contribute.

(50) Then, too, autobiographical writing and popular fiction were not in the tradition of the Asian cultures that produced the first immigrants. Even in the Philippines, where the American curricula and educational system had been instituted after the
(55) Spanish-American War, the majority of peasants had not the privilege of schooling, and most of the Filipino immigrants were illiterate. In fact, labor recruiters, in search of a docile labor force, preferred those who had little formal education. In
(60) China and Korea, writing and literature were the domain of the literati, who traditionally confined themselves to poetry and the classical essay. Autobiography as such was virtually unknown, since for a scholar to write a book about himself
(65) would have been deemed egotistical in the extreme. Fiction was considered frivolous. Farmers and peasants performed as storytellers, dramatic dancers, and singers, but rarely expressed themselves through the written word. And certainly they
(70) did not write autobiographies.

Quite understandably, then, the earliest Asian-American writers were not representative of the general population of Asian Americans. Foreign students, scholars, and diplomats, who were, to-
(75) gether with merchants, exempted from the Asian exclusion laws and who generally received better treatment in America than did Asian laboring people, comprise a disproportionately large part of the early Asian-American literary voice. Their writing
(80) is characterized by efforts to bridge the gap between East and West and plead for tolerance by making usually highly euphemistic observations about the West on one hand while explaining Asia in idealized terms on the other. Since many of these
(85) early Asian writers in English felt that they themselves understood two points of view and, in some cases, two epochs—to them the West stood for modernity and the East for tradition—they viewed themselves as straddling two worlds. Since they
(90) found that elements from two vastly different cultures could be combined within themselves, they concluded that there could be points of compatibility between other people of the two cultures. They saw themselves as ambassadors of goodwill to the
(95) West. Most of them, however, did not believe that social class distinctions could be bridged. Their writing is marked by dissociation from the Asian common people, whether in Asia or in the West, and even their pleas for racial tolerance are made

(100) primarily on behalf of members of their own privi-
leged class. They tended to accept discrimination
against the poor and uneducated members of their
own race as reasonable, questioning instead the
logic of discrimination against the educated elite.

39. This passage is primarily concerned with

    A. anti-Asian sentiments in the United States in
the late 19th and early 20th centuries.

    B. the poor living conditions of early Asian
immigrant laborers.

    C. illiteracy among early Asian immigrants.

    D. the reasons that early Asian immigrants left
little record of their experiences.

    E. the relationship between Asian laborers and
educated Asian Americans.

40. The Asian exclusion laws mentioned in the first
paragraph

    A. barred the immigration of all Asians except
Filipinos.

    B. prohibited Asian immigrants from voting.

    C. allowed only certain Asians to immigrate to
the United States.

    D. were enacted because Asian immigrants were
taking jobs from U.S. citizens.

    E. were responsible for discouraging Asian-
American workers from writing about their
experiences.

41. "Privation" in line 35 most nearly means

    A. lack of comforts and necessities.

    B. lack of educational opportunity.

    C. inhumane treatment.

    D. lack of privacy.

    E. sterility.

42. All the following inferences can be drawn from
the passage EXCEPT

    A. many immigrant laborers were not taught
English.

    B. most Americans were not interested in
reading about the immigrant laborers'
experiences.

    C. Asian laborers did not mix freely with
American citizens.

    D. Asian culture did not encourage the writing
of novels and short stories.

    E. Asian laborers were hostile to the United
States and longed to return to their
homelands.

43. The author cites *The Life Stories of
Undistinguished Americans* because it

    A. shows Asian laborers' low self-esteem.

    B. includes information about two Asian-
American workers.

    C. includes the only existing writing by early
Asian immigrants.

    D. was edited by an American rather than an
Asian.

    E. sympathetically portrays the plight of the
Asian immigrants.

44. According to the passage, one of the reasons so
many of the early Asian immigrant laborers were
uneducated was that

    A. educated Asians disdained American culture
and traditions and weren't interested in
coming to America.

    B. labor recruiters found it easy to dupe
uneducated Asians with false promises.

    C. formal education was considered
unnecessary in most Asian countries.

    D. labor recruiters thought uneducated workers
would be less likely to cause trouble.

    E. illiterate Asians agreed to come to the United
States because they knew they would have
more opportunities for an education than in
their own countries.

45. "Enclaves" as it is used in line 37 most nearly
means

    A. slums.

    B. ghettos.

    C. restricted areas.

    D. labor camps.

    E. tenements.

46. From the last paragraph of the passage, the reader
can infer that early Asian-American writers who
were educated

    A. were eager to be accepted in their new
country.

    B. wrote works of no literary value.

    C. wrote works that were accepted readily by
the American audience.

    D. portrayed their native countries more
realistically than they portrayed America.

    E. wrote only autobiographies and other
nonfictional works.

GO ON TO THE NEXT PAGE

47. According to the author, educated Asian immigrants

    A. preferred the customs of America to the traditions of their homelands.

    B. urged American readers to be tolerant and understanding of the plight of immigrants.

    C. believed that in America, social class distinctions should disappear.

    D. felt that their education should exempt them from discrimination by Americans.

    E. adopted English as their written language as a sign of their commitment to America.

48. "Highly euphemistic observations" in line 82 most nearly means

    A. untruthful comments.

    B. observations in language designed to be inoffensive.

    C. seemingly profound statements that in fact contain little meaning.

    D. flowery, redundant compliments.

    E. observations designed to provoke intelligent discussions about the blending of two cultures.

IF YOU FINISH BEFORE TIME IS CALLED, CHECK YOUR WORK ON THIS SECTION ONLY. DO NOT WORK ON ANY OTHER SECTION IN THE TEST.

Section 4: Mathematics

Time: 25 Minutes

18 Questions

(21–38)

Directions: This section is composed of two types of questions. Use the 25 minutes allotted to answer both question types. For questions 21–28, select the one correct answer of the five choices given and mark the corresponding circle on your answer sheet. Your scratch work should be done on any available space in the section.

Notes

1. All numbers used are real numbers.

2. Calculators may be used.

3. Some problems may be accompanied by figures or diagrams. These figures are drawn as accurately as possible EXCEPT when it is stated in a specific problem that a figure is not drawn to scale. The figures and diagrams are meant to provide information useful in solving the problem or problems. Unless otherwise stated, all figures and diagrams lie in a plane.

Data That Can Be Used for Reference

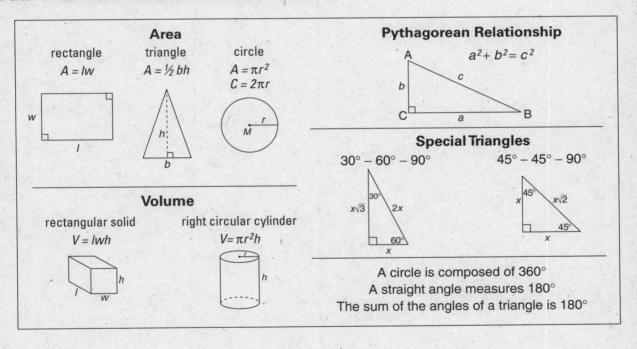

Area

rectangle
$A = lw$

triangle
$A = \frac{1}{2}bh$

circle
$A = \pi r^2$
$C = 2\pi r$

Pythagorean Relationship

$a^2 + b^2 = c^2$

Special Triangles

$30° - 60° - 90°$

$45° - 45° - 90°$

Volume

rectangular solid
$V = lwh$

right circular cylinder
$V = \pi r^2 h$

A circle is composed of 360°
A straight angle measures 180°
The sum of the angles of a triangle is 180°

GO ON TO THE NEXT PAGE

21. A shirt that regularly sells for $40 is on sale for $28. What is the percent decrease?

    A. $8\frac{1}{3}$

    B.   12

    C.   30

    D. $42\frac{6}{7}$

    E.   70

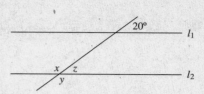

Note: Figure not drawn to scale.

23. In the figure above line$_1$ is parallel to line$_2$. What is the value of $x + y$?

    A.   40°

    B.   120°

    C.   160°

    D.   180°

    E.   320°

22. If $x + y < 50$ and $xy > 50$, then which of the following is *not* a possible value of x?

    A.   15

    B.   40

    C.   44

    D.   46

    E.   52

24. If $m = (n + 5)^4$, then $-(3n + 15)^4$ equals which of the following?

    A. $-81m$

    B. $-27m$

    C. $-9m$

    D. $27m$

    E. $81m$

25. Which of the following is equal to
$(5x + 2)(3x - 4) - (2x - 3)(x + 2)$?

   A. $13x^2 - 14$

   B. $13x^2 + 2$

   C. $13x^2 - 13x - 14$

   D. $13x^2 - 13x - 2$

   E. $13x^2 - 15x - 2$

27. What is the length of $\overline{PQ}$ if P has coordinates
$(-8, 1)$ and Q has coordinates $(-4, -5)$?

   A. $2\sqrt{13}$

   B.   10

   C. $4\sqrt{10}$

   D.   16

   E.   52

26. The perimeter of a rectangle is 42, and its length is
8 more than its width. What is the length of the
rectangle?

   A.   25

   B.   17

   C. $16\frac{1}{2}$

   D. $14\frac{1}{2}$

   E. $6\frac{1}{2}$

28. A fruit drink made from orange juice and water is
diluted with more water so that the final solution is
$\frac{1}{4}$ water. If the original solution was 90% orange
juice and two liters of water were added, how
many liters are in the final solution of the fruit
drink?

   A.   6

   B.   8

   C.   10

   D.   12

   E.   14

GO ON TO THE NEXT PAGE

Directions for Student-Produced Response Questions (Grid-ins): Questions 29–38 require you to solve the problem and enter your answer by carefully marking the circles on the special grid. Examples of the appropriate way to mark the grid follow.

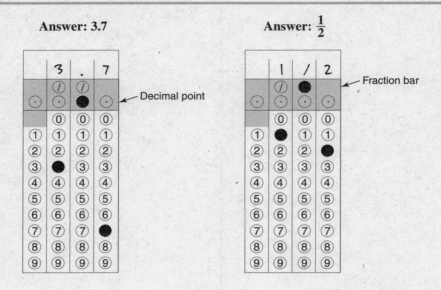

Answer: 3.7   **Answer:** $\frac{1}{2}$

Answer: $1\frac{1}{2}$

Do not grid in mixed numbers in the form of mixed numbers. Always change mixed numbers to improper fractions or decimals.

Change to 1.5   or   **Change to** $\frac{3}{2}$

Answer: 123

Space permitting, answers can start in any column. Each grid-in answer that follows is correct.

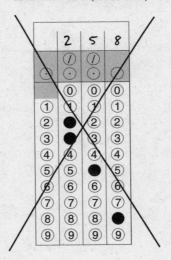

Note: Circles must be filled in correctly to receive credit. Mark only one circle in each column. No credit will be given if more than one circle in a column is marked. Example:

Answer: 258 (no credit)

GO ON TO THE NEXT PAGE

Answer: $\frac{8}{9}$

Accuracy of decimals: Always enter the most accurate decimal value that the grid will accommodate. For example: An answer such as .8888 . . . can be gridded as .888 or .889. Gridding this value as .8, .88, or .89 is considered inaccurate and therefore not acceptable. The acceptable grid-ins of $\frac{8}{9}$ are:

Be sure to write your answers in the boxes at the top of the circles before doing your gridding. Although writing out the answers above the columns is not required, it is very important to ensure accuracy. Even though some problems may have more than one correct answer, grid only one answer. Grid-in questions contain no negative answers.

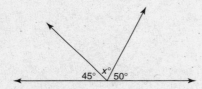

45° $x°$ 50°

29. In the figure above, $x =$

The product of the digits is 8.

The sum of the digits is 7.

30. What is the smallest 3-digit number that has the two characteristics listed above?

31. If $\frac{m+n}{m} = \frac{10}{9}$, then $\frac{n}{m} =$

32. Set A consists of all multiples of 4 between 50 and 65. Set B consists of all multiples of 3 between 50 and 65. What is one possible number that is in Set A but NOT in Set B?

33. In a certain species of fish, 0.3 percent of a school are born with physical defects. If a school of fish contains 21 individuals with such defects, how many fish are in the school?

34. If $(2z + 5)(3z + 4) = az^2 + bz + c$ for all values of z, what is the value of b?

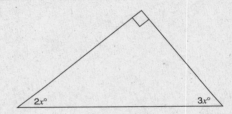

35. In the figure above, what is the value of x?

GO ON TO THE NEXT PAGE

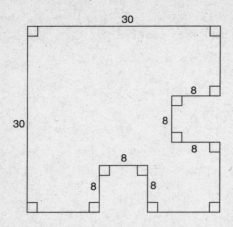

36. What is the perimeter of the 12-sided figure above?

37. If $5x + 9y = 28$ and x and y are positive integers, what is the value of x?

38. If the ratio of the side of cube X to the side of cube Z is $\frac{1}{3}$, then what is the ratio of the volume of cube X to the volume of cube Z?

IF YOU FINISH BEFORE TIME IS CALLED, CHECK YOUR WORK ON THIS SECTION ONLY. DO NOT WORK ON ANY OTHER SECTION IN THE TEST.

Section 5: Writing Skills

Time: 30 Minutes

39 Questions

(1–39)

In this section, choose the best answer for each question and blacken the corresponding space on the answer sheet.

Directions: The following questions test correctness and effective expression. In selecting the answer, pay attention to grammar, diction, sentence structure, and punctuation. In the following questions, part or all of each sentence is underlined. The A answer repeats the underline of the original sentence, while the next four offer alternatives. Choose the answer that best expresses the meaning of the original sentence, and at the same time is grammatically correct and stylistically superior. The correct choice should be clear, unambiguous, and concise.

EXAMPLE:

In her performance, Eartha Kitt sang songs <u>in English, in French, and she sang in Arabic.</u>

    A.   in English, in French, and she sang in Arabic.
    B.   in English and French, and she also sang in Arabic.
    C.   in English and French, singing also in Arabic.
    D.   in English, French, and Arabic.
    E.   in English, in French, and Arabic.

The correct answer is D.

---

1. The beginnings of van Dyke's short stories are <u>as good as, if not better,</u> his endings.

    A.   as good as, if not better
    B.   good as, if not better
    C.   as good as, if not better than
    D.   as good and better than
    E.   as good and better as

2. To germinate properly, the seeds of the sweet pea must be planted <u>in either spring or fall.</u>

    A.   in either spring or fall.
    B.   in either the spring or in the fall.
    C.   either in the spring or the fall.
    D.   either the spring or in the fall.
    E.   either in spring or the fall.

3. Bryant Park and Washington Square, Manhattan's finest squares, <u>lined with buildings whose architects</u> were aware that they were creating walls to enclose space.

    A.   lined with buildings whose architects
    B.   are lined by buildings whose architects
    C.   are lined by architects with buildings that
    D.   with buildings by architects who
    E.   surrounded by buildings whose architects

4. <u>It is feared by many real estate agents</u> that the Internet will soon replace them.

    A.   It is feared by many real estate agents
    B.   It is the fear of many real estate agents
    C.   By many real estate agents, it is feared
    D.   Many real estate agents have the fear
    E.   Many real estate agents fear

GO ON TO THE NEXT PAGE

5. The anthropologist Scoditti set out to record the islanders' songs, to understand their ritual dances, <u>and he wanted to explain the symbolism</u> of their carvings.

   A.   and he wanted to explain the symbolism
   B.   also wanting to explain the symbolism
   C.   explaining the symbolism
   D.   and to explain the symbolism
   E.   and explaining the symbolism

6. If the repairs of the rockets are completed by June, <u>the launch taking place in July.</u>

   A.   the launch taking place in July.
   B.   the launch having taken place in July.
   C.   the launch will take place in July.
   D.   the launch has taken place in July.
   E.   the launch will have taken place in July.

7. A notorious speakeasy during Prohibition, <u>Ernest Hemingway made this saloon his favorite haunt,</u> and it is still a popular tourist attraction.

   A.   Ernest Hemingway made this saloon his favorite haunt
   B.   Ernest Hemingway's favorite was to haunt this saloon
   C.   this saloon was Ernest Hemingway's favorite haunt
   D.   the favorite haunt of Ernest Hemingway was this saloon
   E.   this saloon became the favorite haunt of Ernest Hemingway

8. The Secretary of State's visit to China, it is hoped, will lay the groundwork for the Premier's visit to Washington, <u>and this is when</u> the disarmament treaty will be signed.

   A.   and this is when
   B.   at which time
   C.   which is when
   D.   and that is when
   E.   and this the time when

9. If one digs beneath the snow in the garden, <u>you may find</u> the scarlet flowers of the hardy cyclamen.

   A.   you may find
   B.   you may come upon
   C.   you come across
   D.   one may find
   E.   one finds

10. Like New York City, the Internet has long traffic delays, easy access to pornography, and <u>there are far too many self-centered babblers.</u>

    A.   there are far too many self-centered babblers.
    B.   it also has far too many self-centered babblers.
    C.   and far too many self-centered babblers.
    D.   and there are too many self-centered babblers by far.
    E.   and it has far too many self-centered babblers.

11. The knot garden, a blend of geometry and plants, <u>creates patterns to please the eye.</u>

    A.   creates patterns to please the eye.
    B.   creates patterns which pleases the eyes.
    C.   create eye-pleasing patterns.
    D.   create a pattern that pleases the eye.
    E.   please the eye by creating a pattern.

12. John Adams and Thomas Jefferson were often bitter political adversaries, <u>and they maintained a personal relationship</u> that outlasted their rivalry.

    A.   and they maintained a personal relationship
    B.   but they maintained a personal relationship
    C.   but a personal relationship was maintained by them
    D.   so a personal relationship was maintained
    E.   thus maintaining a personal relationship

13. <u>Audubon recorded in watercolors not only</u> the birds of America but also the plants and the animals.

    A.   Audubon recorded in watercolors not only
    B.   Audubon's watercolors not only recorded
    C.   Audubon's watercolors recording not only
    D.   Audubon recorded not only in watercolors
    E.   Audubon not only recorded in watercolors

14. Many large corporations support the literacy project, <u>they donate</u> materials developed by literacy experts to reading centers throughout the country.

    A.   they donate
    B.   they make donations of
    C.   and they donate
    D.   and donating
    E.   to donate

15. In the legend, the evil Ravana abducts the virtuous Sita, carries her off to Ceylon, and <u>he is defeated there by Rama in a final battle.</u>

    A. he is defeated there by Rama in a final battle.

    B. there, in a final battle, he is defeated by Rama.

    C. falls to Rama there in a final battle.

    D. is defeated there, in a final battle, by Rama.

    E. it is there that he is defeated by Rama in a final battle.

16. Yielding to the public demand for a happy ending, <u>the end of the film will be edited to reunite the lovers.</u>

    A. the end of the film will be edited to reunite the lovers.

    B. the lovers will be reunited at the end of the film.

    C. the end of the film will reunite the lovers after being edited.

    D. after editing the film will reunite the lovers.

    E. the director will edit the end of the film to reunite the lovers.

17. Some kind of expansion of the permanent five-member Security Council <u>is inevitable, it may come</u> in the very near future.

    A. is inevitable, it may come

    B. is inevitable, and it may come

    C. is inevitable it may come

    D. is inevitable, coming

    E. is inevitable, maybe it will come

18. Late night talk-radio programs that give the Chinese listener a chance to speak openly <u>have surprised and delighted a huge audience.</u>

    A. have surprised and delighted a huge audience.

    B. have been a surprise and a delight to a huge audience.

    C. surprised a huge audience, also delighting it.

    D. surprised as well as delighting a huge audience.

    E. were surprising and a delight to a huge audience.

19. The notion that human beings will usually act to benefit themselves is an idea that for even the most idealistic <u>is with easy comprehension.</u>

    A. is with easy comprehension.

    B. is to comprehend easily.

    C. is easy to comprehend.

    D. is easy for comprehending.

    E. is with ease in comprehending.

20. The increases in tourism and resort building <u>reflecting the health of the Chilean economy,</u> which has expanded by 12% this year.

    A. reflecting the health of the Chilean economy,

    B. reflect the health of the Chilean economy,

    C. reflecting signs of the health of the Chilean economy,

    D. clear indications of the health of the Chilean economy,

    E. and the increasing health of the Chilean,

GO ON TO THE NEXT PAGE

Directions: The following sentences may contain one error of grammar, usage, diction, or idiom. No sentence will contain more than one error, and some have no error. If there is an error, it will be underlined and have a letter beneath it. Sections of the sentence that are not underlined cannot be changed. In selecting your answer, observe the requirements of standard written English. If there is an error, choose the one underlined part that must be changed to correct the sentence. If there is no error, choose E.

EXAMPLE:

The violinist and her will audition for the conductor as soon as they have completed their studies. No error.
          A   B   C   D   E

The correct answer is A.

---

21. The report written by experts on Asia
               A
recommend a large loan from the World Bank
   B   C
to repair the roads battered by floods. No error.
  D   E

22. Everywhere you look in New York City, one sees
                                A
the white-brick apartment buildings that sprang up
                              B
after the war like mushrooms. No error.
     C   D   E

23. In virtual every year, the young men set sail for
    A   B
other islands to participate in a series of gift
             C   D
exchanges. No error.
        E

24. Last year, Americans spent millions on
               A   B
tobacco products, and despite the warnings
against smoking, they spend even more this year
    C   D
and next. No error.
        E

25. Neither Henry James nor James Whistler, both
                                A
great lovers of France, were able to earn a living
                B   C
in Paris, and moved to London. No error.
         D   E

26. Walking on coral from their earliest years, the
    A
Kitawans develop soles as tough as leather and
        B   C
they find the tender feet of Westerners very odd.
    D
No error.
  E

27. Edwards is a lazy journalist who will not do
      A   B   C
hardly any work until a deadline approaches.
                     D
No error.
  E

28. The city punishes the self-employed in not being
      A   B   C
a corporation with the unincorporated business
          D
tax. No error.
    E

29. Like <u>London's</u> subway system, <u>that of Boston</u> is
         A   B

    easy <u>to learn</u> and expensive <u>to use.</u> <u>No error.</u>
         C   D   E

30. The <u>older</u> houses of the Florida Keys <u>mirrors</u> a
          A   B

    <u>multicultural legacy</u> of Bahamian, New England,
            C

    African, <u>and Creole influences.</u> <u>No error.</u>
                D   E

31. Investment strategists <u>in</u> the New York offices of
                         A

    Morgan Stanley <u>continue to</u> <u>believe</u> that stocks
                   B   C

    are <u>the best possible</u> investment. <u>No error.</u>
         D   E

32. <u>Like Shakespeare,</u> Whitman's writings <u>continue</u>
         A   B

    <u>to be</u> relevant <u>to</u> our culture. <u>No error.</u>
     C   D   E

33. The large gilt mirror <u>above the fireplace</u> <u>giving</u>
                        A   B

    the room <u>the atmosphere</u> of a Viennese apartment
             C

    <u>of the nineteenth century.</u> <u>No error.</u>
         D   E

34. New York City is <u>more populous</u> than <u>any one</u> of
                 A   B

    30 states and <u>has</u> a budget larger than <u>that of</u> 45.
             C   D

    <u>No error.</u>
     E

GO ON TO THE NEXT PAGE

Directions: The following passage is an early draft of an essay. Some parts need to be revised.

Read the selection carefully and answer the questions that follow. There will be questions about sentence structure, diction, and usage in individual sentences or parts of sentences. Other questions will deal with the whole essay or paragraphs and ask you to decide about organization, development, and appropriate language. Choose the answer that follows the requirements of standard written English and most effectively expresses the intended meanings.

Questions 35–39 are based on the following passage.

(1) I was born in California and my mother and father were born in Thailand. (2) Thailand used to be called Siam. (3) A few years ago they went to Thailand to visit my grandparents at the time when a new king was being crowned.

(4) My grandparents lived in a small town not far from the capital city, which is called Bangkok. (5) The coronation ceremony of a Thai king is very ancient. (6) It has a long history and has been passed down from very olden times. (7) On coronation day, a Brahmin poured holy water on the king's hands. (8) Then, after the ceremony the king could issue royal commands with the help of the Hindu gods Siva, Vishnu, and Brahma. (9) Later, Buddhist monks also participate in the coronation. (10) In modern times, the Representatives and Senators will also offer holy water to the king. (11) Thus, combining the religious and the political.

(12) Unlike the musical *The King and I,* Thailand today is a democracy, but it still has a king. (13) The coronation of the king combined the new democratic people plus religion and ancient ceremony. (14) Thus, Thailand honors the past and marches into the future.

35. Which of the following is the best version of sentences 1 and 2 (reproduced below)?

> *I was born in California and my mother and father were born in Thailand. Thailand used to be called Siam.*

A. Leave it as it is.
B. I was born in California, and my mother and father were born in Thailand, which used to be called Siam.
C. I was born in California, but my parents were born in Thailand, which used to be called Siam.
D. Born in California, my parents are from Siam, which is now called Thailand.
E. I was born in California. My parents were born in Thailand. Thailand was formerly called Siam.

36. Which of the following is the best way to revise and combine sentences 5 and 6 (reproduced below)?

> *The coronation ceremony of a Thai king is very ancient. It has a long history and has been passed down from very olden times.*

A. The coronation ceremony of a Thai king has a long ancient history and has been passed down from very old times.
B. The long ancient history of the coronation ceremony of a Thai king has been passed down from olden times.
C. A Thai king's coronation ceremony, passed down from ancient times.
D. The coronation ceremony of a Thai king has been passed down from ancient times.
E. Passed down from olden times, the ancient coronation ceremony of a Thai king has a long history.

37. Which of the following is the most effective version of the underlined portions of sentences 10 and 11 (reproduced below)?

> *In modern times, the Representatives and Senators <u>will also offer holy water to the king. Thus combining the religious and the political.</u>*

A. Leave it as it is.
B. also offer holy water to the king. Thus combining the religious and the political.
C. also will offer holy water to the king. Thus, they combine religion and politics.
D. also offer holy water to the king, adding a political element to the religious.
E. combined religion and politics when offering holy water to the king.

38. Which of the following sentences in the second paragraph can best be omitted or moved to a different paragraph in the essay?

    A. the fourth
    B. the seventh
    C. the eighth
    D. the ninth
    E. the tenth

39. In the context of the third paragraph, which of the following is the best version of the underlined portion of sentence 12 (reproduced below)?

> _Unlike the musical_ The King and I, _Thailand today is a democracy_ but it still has a king.

    A. Leave it as it is.
    B. Unlike the musical _The King and I_, Thailand today is democratic
    C. Unlike the musical _The King and I_, modern Thailand is democratic
    D. Unlike the country in the musical _The King and I_, Thailand today is democratic
    E. Thailand today, unlike the musical _The King and I_, is a democracy

IF YOU FINISH BEFORE TIME IS CALLED, CHECK YOUR WORK ON THIS SECTION ONLY. DO NOT WORK ON ANY OTHER SECTION IN THE TEST.

Scoring PSAT/NMSQT Practice Test

Answer Key

Section 1: Critical Reading

1. C	7. C	13. B	19. C
2. B	8. A	14. B	20. D
3. B	9. B	15. A	21. C
4. A	10. A	16. B	22. E
5. E	11. D	17. A	23. B
6. D	12. A	18. C	

Section 2: Mathematics

1. C	6. A	11. C	16. C
2. D	7. D	12. B	17. E
3. A	8. B	13. B	18. C
4. B	9. B	14. E	19. D
5. D	10. D	15. A	20. C

Section 3: Critical Reading

24. E	31. C	38. C	45. B
25. D	32. A	39. D	46. A
26. C	33. A	40. C	47. D
27. A	34. E	41. A	48. B
28. D	35. A	42. E	
29. E	36. D	43. B	
30. B	37. D	44. D	

Section 4: Mathematics

21. C	26. D	31. 1/9 or .111	36. 152
22. E	27. A	32. 52, 56, or 64	37. 2
23. E	28. D	33. 7,000	38. 1/27
24. A	29. 85	34. 23	
25. E	30. 124	35. 18	

Section 5: Writing Skills

1. C	12. B	23. A	34. E
2. A	13. A	24. D	35. C
3. B	14. C	25. B	36. D
4. E	15. C	26. E	37. D
5. D	16. E	27. C	38. A
6. C	17. B	28. B	39. D
7. C	18. A	29. E	
8. B	19. C	30. B	
9. D	20. B	31. E	
10. C	21. B	32. A	
11. A	22. A	33. B	

Analyzing Your Test Results

The charts on the following pages should be used to carefully analyze your results and spot your strengths and weaknesses. The complete process of analyzing each subject area and each individual problem should be completed for the practice test. These results should then be reexamined for trends in types of errors (repeated errors) or poor results in specific subject areas. *This reexamination and analysis is of tremendous importance to you in ensuring maximum test-preparation benefit.*

Critical Reading Analysis Sheet

Section 1	Possible	Completed	Right	Wrong
Sentence Completion	6			
Short Reading Passages	4			
Long Reading Passages	13			
Subtotal	23			
Section 3	**Possible**	**Completed**	**Right**	**Wrong**
Sentence Completion	7			
Short Reading Passages	8			
Long Reading Passages	10			
Subtotal	25			
Overall Critical Reading Totals	48			

Mathematics Analysis Sheet

Section 2	Possible	Completed	Right	Wrong
Multiple Choice	20			
Subtotal	20			

Section 4	Possible	Completed	Right	Wrong
Multiple Choice	8			
Grid-Ins	10			
Subtotal	18			
Overall Math Totals	38			

Writing Skills Analysis Sheet

Section 5	Possible	Completed	Right	Wrong
Improving Sentences	20			
Identifying Sentence Errors	14			
Improving Paragraphs	5			
Overall Writing Skills Totals	39			

Analysis/Tally Sheet for Problems Missed

One of the most important parts of test preparation is analyzing *why* you missed a problem so that you can reduce the number of mistakes. Now that you have taken the practice test and checked your answers, carefully tally your mistakes by marking them in the proper column.

Reason for Mistakes					
	Total Missed	Simple Mistake	Misread Problem	Lack of Knowledge	Lack of Time
Section 1: Critical Reading					
Section 3: Critical Reading					
Subtotal					
Section 2: Mathematics					
Section 4: Mathematics					
Subtotal					
Section 5: Writing					
Total Reading, Math, and Writing					

Reviewing the preceding data should help you determine *why* you are missing certain problems. Now that you've pinpointed the types of errors, focus on eliminating them.

Complete Answers and Explanations for PSAT/NMSQT Practice Test

Section 1: Critical Reading

Sentence Completion

1. **C.** The missing word should describe an object like a bed or chair. Only "inanimate" (without life) makes sense in this context.

2. **B.** The word needed here must accord with the words "inconsiderate" and "unhealthy" and refer to a man or woman. "Mordant," which means "caustic," does not quite fit this context, so the best choice is "shameful."

3. **B.** Any of the nouns except "placebos" might fit here, though D and E are less good than A or B. Neither "soporific" nor "somnolent" can work here, since a doctor would have some concern about the sleep-inducing properties. "Tonic" (invigorating) is clearly a bad choice, but "addictive" and "narcotics" make good sense of the sentence.

4. **A.** Since the second half of the sentence refers to the eleven different languages, the right answer must be "linguistic."

5. **E.** Since the rains have caused so many floods, the first adjective must be either C "massive" or E "unprecedented." The second word must mean something like "increased," but with only C and E to choose from, the answer must be "augmented."

6. **D.** The first adjective should mean something like "shocking"; of the five choices, either B "unusual" or D "audacious" is a possibility. The verb must mean something like "put together." Words like "confine" A and "combine" C would work, but these letters have already been eliminated. The best choice is "juxtapose" D.

Short Reading Passages

7. **C.** See lines 3–4. Although illiteracy may have been more widespread in the 18th and 19th centuries, nothing in the passage indicates this or suggests that illiteracy, A, or lack of scientific knowledge, E, benefited the manufacturers of patent medicines. Also, there is no evidence of a "weak" Congress, B, only one that hadn't yet addressed the problem. Finally, the "snake-oil" salesmen may have been fast-talking, but nothing suggests they were "highly trained," D. Be careful not to choose answers merely because they are plausible. Instead, rely on information provided or implied by the text.

8. **A.** The sentence states that new regulations occur only when the public is outraged. This suggests that future problems with patent medicines could lead to public pressure, which in turn could lead to more regulation. B and C may be accurate but are not indicated by the last sentence, and D and E are simply untrue.

9. **B.** "Store" and "mill" would be familiar terms because of their association with the processing of grain. Computer and electronic terminology didn't yet exist. Note that the author of the passage also uses a metaphor suitable for Babbage's time to describe information leakage: " . . . like faulty sacks of flour" (line 12). A may be true but is not related to the choice of the terms. C and D are irrelevant, and E supposes that Babbage was concerned about appealing to the working class, which is not supported anywhere in the paragraph.

10. **A.** See lines 14–15. His impatience, D, may have been a factor in his inability to get funding, but only one factor. There is no suggestion that a lack of education stopped Babbage, C, and although the design called for a machine as big as a train, nothing implies that this kept Babbage from building it, E. Nowhere in the paragraph are other mathematicians mentioned.

Long Reading Passages

11. D. The passage doesn't suggest a moratorium is needed, A; in fact, it calls for further research. Nor does it suggest fears are "groundless," B; see lines 44–45. C is a minor point in the passage, and although the passage mentions research, it does not describe it, E.

12. A. Uncontrolled gene transfer is the possibility that most concerns critics. Nothing indicates that B will occur, and C, D, and E are not specifically mentioned in the passage.

13. B. This is the best definition considering the context. The word can also mean C, but that definition is appropriate to conscious beings, not bacterial genes. D may seem to fit context, but it—like A and E—is not a correct definition of the word.

14. B. In lines 40–43, the passage specifically mentions the fragility of the altered bacteria. C and E are not mentioned. D is correct in only one instance; it is cited as an example. While the EPA is mentioned in the passage, nothing suggests it is reluctant, A.

15. A. See lines 4–8. C is incorrect; altered bacteria may help clean up oil spills but they don't prevent them. E might be possible but is not mentioned as a benefit. The meaning of B is unclear, and D is simply incorrect.

16. B. Nowhere in the passage is it implied that the benefits are not worth the risks. In fact, the author clearly indicates that with further research, altered bacteria can be safely used. All of the other points are either implied or stated in the passage.

17. A. This is the best definition considering the context. Although B is also a correct definition, it clearly doesn't fit here. E is also a correct definition of the word but is not as appropriate as A for cloth (crinoline). C and D are simply incorrect definitions.

18. C. See lines 12–15. Although B might be true, it is not implied in the passage. Neither is A; in fact, the passage suggests that men felt women were unsuited for intellectual pursuits. D and E are simply inaccurate.

19. C. Note the root word "merit." In the context of the passage, "government" (A and D) is not appropriate; "system" is a better choice. Although a meritocracy excludes sex or race discrimination, it does discriminate on the basis of ability. Therefore, B is incorrect. E is irrelevant.

20. D. See lines 51–57. Although a contrast is drawn with business, it is not related to the rewards of a career in either field, C. B is not specifically supported in the passage, while E is not addressed. A is incorrect; science may be a good field for women, but the passage indicates that it still does not offer them abundant opportunities.

21. C. The attitudes described in Passage 1 are behind the convictions and inherited ideas that, according to the passage, influence 20th century scientists (lines 48–57). Passage 2 suggests that although B *should* be true, it is not as of yet (lines 82–89). A is not accurate, according to Passage 2, and D is not addressed in the passage. The attitudes described in Passage 2 are not significantly different from those described in Passage 1, E.

22. E. The purposes of the passages are very different: Passage 1 is a historical account, while Passage 2 is arguing a point. Women's feelings aren't described in Passage 1 and are barely touched upon in Passage 2, A. The women referred to in Passage 1, while not encouraged by men to engage in intellectual pursuits, are not themselves described as anti-intellectual, B. At first C may sound like a good answer, but Passage 2, for example, does include facts in the form of statistics. The future is not discussed in Passage 1, D.

23. B. Passage 1 doesn't address the attitudes of scientists apart from the attitudes of men in general, whereas Passage 2 specifically targets scientists. Both passages are concerned with social stereotypes A, C, and E are not covered in either passage, and D is touched on in Passage 1 but not in Passage 2.

Section 2: Mathematics

Multiple Choice

1. C. In 864,925, the number in the thousands place is 4. Because the number immediately to the right of 4 is 5 or larger (9), round the thousands digit up to a 5, which yields 865,000.

2. D. If $x = 2$, then $3x^2 + (3x)^2 = 3(2^2) + (3 \cdot 2)^2$

$$= 3 \cdot 4 + (6)^2$$
$$= 12 + 36$$
$$= 48$$

3. A. If $a + b = -3$, then $(a + b)^3 = (-3)^3 = -27$.

4. B. Because the product of an odd number of negative integers is a negative integer, the maximum number of the six integers that could be negative is five.

5. D. Let $x =$ first integer

$x + 1 =$ second integer

$x + 2 =$ third integer

Since the sum of the three integers is 141,

$$x + x + 1 + x + 2 = 141$$
$$3x + 3 = 141$$
$$3x + 3 - 3 = 141 - 3$$
$$3x = 138$$
$$\frac{3x}{3} = \frac{138}{3}$$
$$x = 46$$

The largest integer is $x + 2 = 48$.

6. A. If $\frac{z}{3} = 25$, then multiplying both sides of the equation by 3 yields

$$3 \cdot \frac{z}{3} = 3 \cdot 25$$
$$z = 75$$

Hence $5z = 5 \cdot 75 = 375$

7. D. For any numbers m and n, $m^4 \geq 0$ and $n^4 \geq 0$.

Since $m^4 + n^4 = 0$, then both $m = 0$ and $n = 0$. Therefore $9m - 5n = (9)(0) - 5(0) = 0$.

8. B. Since Distance = Rate × Time,

$$\text{Time} = \frac{\text{Distance}}{\text{Rate}}$$

The distance that Marcos travels is d miles at a rate of 55 miles per hour. Hence the time it takes is $\frac{d}{55}$ hours.

9. B. Substituting $a = 4b - 11$ for a in the equation $a + 5 = 3b$, yields

$$4b - 11 + 5 = 3b$$
$$4b - 6 = 3b$$
$$4b - 6 - 3b = 3b - 3b$$
$$b - 6 = 0$$
$$b - 6 + 6 = 0 + 6$$
$$b = 6$$

10. D. The volume of a cube with side length x is x^3. If $x^3 = 64$, then $x = 4$.

The area of any face of the cube is $x^2 = 4^2 = 16$.

11. C. Since the sum of the angles in any triangle must equal $180°$,

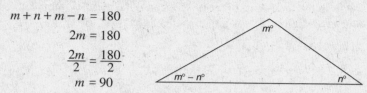

$$m + n + m - n = 180$$
$$2m = 180$$
$$\frac{2m}{2} = \frac{180}{2}$$
$$m = 90$$

Note: The given value of $n = 50$ is not needed to solve for m.

12. B. Since the sum of two odd integers is an even integer, and $3x + 11$ is even, then $3x$ must be odd. Since the product of two odd integers is an odd integer, then x must be an odd integer. Hence $x + 1$ must be an even integer.

13. B. The volume of a rectangular box is lwh. With the given dimensions and volume $V = lwh$

$$12 = (z)\left(\frac{2}{z}\right)(y)$$
$$12 = 2y$$
$$\frac{12}{2} = \frac{2y}{2}$$
$$6 = y$$

14. E. There are many different values for x and y such that $xy = 21$. Therefore, there are many different values for the ratio of x to y, and thus the ratio cannot be determined from the information given.

15. A. The radius of circle P will also be 40% of the radius of circle Q. Because the area of any circle is πr^2, the radius will be used to compare the areas of the two circles. Since

$$40\% = .40 = .4$$

and

$$(.4)^2 = (.16) = 16\%$$

the area of circle P will be 16% of the area of circle Q.

16. C. Since

$$x^6 = x^5 \cdot x = \frac{y}{11} \text{ and } x^5 = 9,$$
$$9x = \frac{y}{11}$$
$$\frac{1}{9}(9x) = \frac{1}{9}\left(\frac{y}{11}\right)$$
$$x = \frac{y}{99}$$

17. E. For the expression $3x - 4$ to be greater than 4 and less than 250,

$$4 < 3x - 4 < 250$$

Add 4,

$$4 + 4 < 3x - 4 + 4 < 250 + 4$$
$$8 < 3x < 254$$

Divide by 3,

$$\frac{8}{3} < \frac{3x}{3} < \frac{254}{3}$$
$$2\frac{2}{3} < x < 84\frac{2}{3}$$

Since x is an integer, $x = 3, 4, 5 \ldots 82, 83, 84$. Hence there are 82 integer values of x.

18. **C.** In the figure, $OX = 2$ and $OY = 3$, and the area of $\triangle XOY$ is $\frac{1}{2}(OX)(OY) = \frac{1}{2}(2)(3) = 3$.

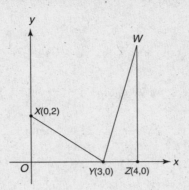

For the area of $\triangle WYZ$ to be the same,

$$\frac{1}{2}(YZ)(WZ) = \frac{1}{2}(1)(WZ) = 3$$

$$\frac{1}{2}(WZ) = 3$$

$$2 \cdot \frac{1}{2}(WZ) = 2 \cdot 3$$

$$WZ = 6$$

Hence the coordinates of W are $(4, 6)$.

19. **D.** In the set of numbers from 1 to 50 inclusive, there are 16 numbers divisible by 3: 3, 6, 9, . . . , 48. Therefore, the probability that a ticket selected will have a number divisible by 3 is $\frac{16}{50} = \frac{8}{25}$.

20. **C.**

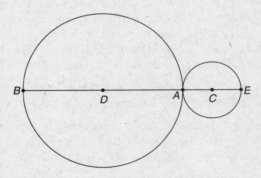

Since the area of the smaller circle is 100π and the area of any circle is πr^2, then

$$\pi r^2 = 100\pi$$

$$\frac{\pi r^2}{\pi} = \frac{100\pi}{\pi}$$

$$r^2 = 100$$

So $r = 10$ is the radius of the smaller circle.

Since $AD = AE$, the diameter of the smaller circle is the same as the radius of the larger circle, so the larger circle's diameter is 20.

Hence the area of the larger circle

$$\pi r^2 = \pi(20)^2$$

$$= 400\pi$$

Section 3: Critical Reading

Sentence Completions

24. E. The missing adverb must describe the giving of a man described as "kind and modest." Of the five choices, only "unobtrusively" (that is, "quietly") fits well.

25. D. Since the farmers dislike the Easterners, the missing verb should denote something like "refusal." The only possibility is "discouraged" D.

26. C. The first adjective could be "obscure" A, "remote" C, or "uninhabited" D, but the noun should denote a large or growing number of people who are threatened. The two possibilities are B and C, but B has been eliminated already.

27. A. The right answer must follow logically from the verb "fought" and also accord with the adjective "small." The best choice is "skirmishes," which is idiomatic and relevant.

28. D. The first missing noun cannot be A, but the four other choices are possible. The best choice for the second noun is "memento" (a keepsake, reminder, or souvenir). B is a remote possibility, but a "daguerreotype" is an early nineteenth-century photograph, surely long predating an espionage trial.

29. E. Choices B and D make little sense. An "epithet" is a characterizing word or phrase, such as rosy-fingered (Dawn) or thunder-bearing (Jove). An epigram is a terse and witty saying. The best choice here is "epitaph," the inscription about the dead on a tomb or monument.

30. B. Only the more generalized "technological" could apply to all of the fields listed in this series. The words "pictorial" and "cinematic" fit several but not all of the terms, such as "sound reproduction."

Short Reading Passages

31. C. See lines 4–9. The point of the passage is to show that although an idea has been discredited, it can live on in certain words. The tone of the passage isn't "mocking," B, and the Renaissance is mentioned only in passing, A. The passage doesn't "celebrate" the Middle Ages, D; the author simply points out that the 19th century view has been discredited. E is the second best answer but is imprecise because the use of terms such as "medieval" and "Dark Ages" is not due to carelessness but rather to the persistence of an old idea.

32. A. From context, it is clear that the term is negative ("cumbersome, antiquated regulations," "barbarous practices," "primitive stage of development"). None of the other answers makes sense.

33. A. In the context of the paragraph, "perverse" suggests contrariness, a conscious decision to act against good sense. Although the word can mean an unwillingness to do what is right or good (B or C), these definitions are too strong here. Both D and E are incorrect definitions of "perverse."

34. E. Although no redesign has been successfully implemented for 60 years, the passage doesn't suggest that it could never happen. Words like "never" and "always" frequently signal an incorrect answer. There is evidence in the paragraph to support all of the other choices.

35. A. The paragraph deals primarily with the reality of the fuel cell, and the Verne quotation is a clever way to introduce the idea behind it. See lines 6–11. Both B and D focus on science fiction, which is not the subject of the passage. The Verne quotation doesn't "explain" anything, C, nor does it put environmental concerns "in perspective," E.

36. D. The writer says that "engineers are working on a variety of other applications," indicating that the technology will advance. He/She is not "advocating" or "opposing" anything (A or B). It is also not accurate to say that the passage is "primarily" concerned with auto emissions, E; it is "primarily" concerned with the fuel cell. C is not addressed at all in the passage.

37. D. This example in lines 5–7 doesn't pertain to the reasons that the General Enclosure Act was adopted. (Notice the word EXCEPT in the question.) All of the other choices are functions of this particular example.

38. **C.** The quotation marks are an indication that the word is used ironically or informally, A, and the ironic use makes more sense. After the Enclosure Act, these peasants were not free but rather paupers forced to work in factories for little money. They were actually freer when they could farm the land for themselves; and therefore B is not accurate. The Enclosure Act had nothing to do with "freeing" peasants, E.

Long Reading Passages

39. **D.** The passage touches on A, B, C, and E, but its main emphasis is on the explanation of why so little writing was produced by the early Asian immigrants.

40. **C.** See lines 71–77. A is incorrect because most Filipinos were also barred by these laws in 1934. D is incorrect; the passage doesn't imply that this was the reason for passage of the laws. B and E are irrelevant, since the exclusion laws barred immigration.

41. **A.** The concept of lack, or absence, is central to the word. Therefore, C is incorrect. B is too limited. D, while it may sound correct, is not; "privacy" is not part of the definition of "privation." Also, in context, "lack of privacy" doesn't make sense. E is an incorrect definition and also doesn't fit the context.

42. **E.** Note (lines 11–13) that some immigrants had no desire to return to their homelands. A (lines 44–45), B (lines 36–40), C (lines 35–36), and D (lines 60–64) are inferences that can be drawn from the passage.

43. **B.** The author cites the book as one of the few sources of autobiographical information about Asian immigrants. D is true but not the reason the author cites the book. C is incorrect because this isn't the only existing writing. The passage doesn't indicate whether the Asian workers are presented sympathetically or unsympathetically, E. A is also incorrect; the title of the book is not related to Asian self-esteem.

44. **D.** See lines 57–59. The docility of the work force, not its gullibility, is cited; therefore B is not correct. A is clearly untrue; see the final paragraph of the passage. Nothing indicates whether either C or E is a true statement.

45. **B.** This is the best choice in this context. One meaning of "ghetto" is a section of a city where many members of a minority live—an "urban ethnic enclave." These enclaves are not necessarily slums, A, nor do they necessarily consist of tenements, E. Neither C nor D fits the context here.

46. **A.** This inference can be drawn from lines 95–101. The passage does not imply that their works were of no value, B, nor that they were accepted by an American audience, C. D is incorrect because the passage states that these writers described Asia in idealized—not realistic—terms. The inference in E is contradicted by the third paragraph of the passage.

47. **D.** See lines 96–101. The passage doesn't state that they "preferred" America, A, but rather that they felt able to combine the two cultures. C is contradicted in lines 95–96. B might seem a good choice, but see lines 101–103. Nothing in the passage suggests E.

48. **B.** At first glance, A may seem a good choice, but "euphemistic" does not mean untrue; it means disguising unpleasant truths by using inoffensive or "polite" terms (for example, "passed away" instead of "died"). C, D, and E are not supported by context nor are they correct definitions of the word.

Section 4: Mathematics

21. **C.** The amount of decrease is 40 – 28 = \$12.

The percent of decrease = $\dfrac{\text{amount of decrease}}{\text{original price}}$

$$= \frac{12}{40}$$
$$= \frac{3}{10}$$
$$= 30\%$$

22. E. Since 52 would have to be added to a negative number to be less than 50, and since 52 times a negative number is less than 50, then 52 could not be a value for x.

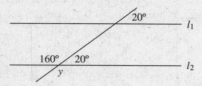

23. E. If l_1 and l_2 are parallel, then $z = 20°$. If $z = 20°$, angle x equals $160°$, because they form a straight line. Since x and y are vertical, angle y is also $160°$. Therefore, $160° + 160° = 320°$.

24. A. Since $(3n + 15)$ can be factored and written as $[3(n + 5)]$, then $-(3n + 15)^4$ can be written as $-[3(n + 5)]^4$. Notice that the negative sign is outside the brackets, so it is not affected. $-[3(n + 5)]^4 = -[3^4(n + 5)^4]$, which can be simplified to $-[81(n + 5)^4]$, since $3^4 = 3 \times 3 \times 3 \times 3 = 81$. Now replace $(n + 5)^4$ with m, and you get $-81m$.

25. E. $(5x + 2)(3x - 4) - (2x - 3)(x + 2)$

$$= (15x^2 + 6x - 20x - 8) - (2x^2 - 3x + 4x - 6)$$
$$= (15x^2 - 14x - 8) - (2x^2 + x - 6)$$
$$= 15x^2 - 14x - 8 - 2x^2 - x + 6$$
$$= 13x^2 - 15x - 2$$

26. D. Let x = width and $x + 8$ = length.

Since the perimeter of the rectangle is 42,

$$2x + 2(x + 8) = 42$$
$$2x + 2x + 16 = 42$$
$$4x + 16 = 42$$
$$4x = 26$$
$$x = \frac{26}{4} = 6\frac{1}{2}$$
$$x + 8 = 14\frac{1}{2}$$

Therefore, the length of the rectangle is $14\frac{1}{2}$.

27. A. The distance between two points (x_1, y_1) and (x_2, y_2) is:

$$d = \sqrt{(x_1 - x_2)^2 + (y_1 - y_2)^2}$$
$$= \sqrt{(-8 + 4)^2 + (1 + 5)^2}$$
$$= \sqrt{16 + 36}$$
$$= \sqrt{52}$$
$$= \sqrt{4 \times 13}$$
$$d = 2\sqrt{13}$$

28. D. You could set up an equation.

Original solution + amount of pure water = new solution

Let x be the unknown amount of original solution. Solutions will be expressed in terms of concentration of water.

$$.10(x) + 2 = .25(x + 2)$$

Now solve for x.

$$.10x + 2 = .25x + .50$$

Subtract .50 from each side.

$$.10x + 1.5 = .25x$$

Next subtract .10x from each side.

$$1.5 = .15x$$

Finally divide each side by .15.

$$10 = x$$

x is the number of liters in the original solution. Since the final solution is two additional liters of water, the final solution will be 12 liters.

Grid-Ins

29. Answer: 85

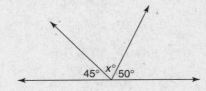

Since the three angles form a straight line

$$45 + x + 50 = 180$$

$$x + 95 = 180$$

$$x + 95 - 95 = 180 - 95$$

$$x = 85$$

30. Answer: 124

Since the sum of the digits is 7, no digit can be greater than 7. Since the product of the digits is 8, the choices of the digits are 1,2,4 or 2,2,2. The smallest 3-digit number would be 124.

31. Answer: $\frac{1}{9}$ or .111

Since

$$\frac{m+n}{m} = \frac{10}{9}$$

$$\frac{m}{m} + \frac{n}{m} = \frac{10}{9}$$

$$1 + \frac{n}{m} = \frac{10}{9}$$

$$1 + \frac{n}{m} - 1 = \frac{10}{9} - 1$$

$$\frac{n}{m} = \frac{10}{9} - \frac{9}{9}$$

$$\frac{n}{m} = \frac{1}{9} \text{ or } .111...$$

Note that answers $\frac{1}{9}$ and .111 are correct, but .1 and .11 are *not* correct in this situation.

32. Answer: 52, 56, or 64

The multiples of 4 between 50 and 65 are

$$A = \{52, 56, 60, 64\}$$

The multiples of 3 between 50 and 65 are

$$B = \{51, 54, 57, 60, 63\}$$

The numbers in Set A but *not* in Set B are 52, 56, and 64. Note that although more than one answer is possible, you need to grid in only one of them for full credit.

33. Answer: 7,000

Let x = number of fish in the school

$$0.3 \text{ percent of } x \text{ is } 21$$
$$0.003x = 21$$
$$\frac{0.003x}{0.003} = \frac{21}{0.003}$$
$$x = 7,000$$

There are 7,000 fish in the school.

34. Answer: 23

Multiplying
$$(2z + 5)(3z + 4) = 6z^2 + 8z + 15z + 20$$
$$= 6z^2 + 23z + 20$$

Since
$$(2z + 5)(3z + 4) = az^2 + bz + c \text{ for all values of } z,$$
$$6z^2 + 23z + 20 = az^2 + bz + c$$

and

$$b = 23$$

35. Answer: 18

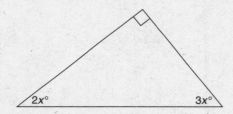

Since the sum of the angles in any triangle must equal 180°,

$$2x + 3x + 90 = 180$$
$$5x + 90 = 180$$
$$5x + 90 - 90 = 180 - 90$$
$$5x = 90$$
$$\frac{5x}{5} = \frac{90}{5}$$
$$x = 18$$

36. Answer: 152

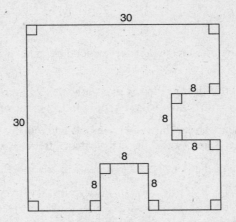

The perimeter of this 12-sided figure is the same as the perimeter of a square with side length 30 plus four additional segments of length 8.

$$\text{Perimeter} = 4 \cdot 30 + 4 \cdot 8$$
$$= 120 + 32$$
$$= 152$$

The perimeter is 152 units.

37. Answer: 2

Since x and y are positive integers and $5x + 9y = 28$, the only possible values for y are 1, 2, and 3. If y were greater than 3, x would have to be a negative integer.

Substituting 1, 2, or 3 for y will show that $y = 2$ is the only value that will yield an integer value for x.

Hence,

$$5x + 9 \cdot 2 = 28$$
$$5x + 18 = 28$$
$$5x + 18 - 18 = 28 - 18$$
$$5x = 10$$
$$\frac{5x}{5} = \frac{10}{5}$$
$$x = 2$$

38. $\frac{1}{27}$

Let S = Length of a side of cube X

$3S$ = Length of a side of cube Z

The volume of cube $X = S^3$ and the volume of cube $Z = (3S)^3 = 27S^3$

The ratio of their volumes is $\frac{S^3}{27S^3} = \frac{1}{27}$

Section 5: Writing Skills

Improving Sentences

1. C. There are two phrases here that must be complete, "as good as" and "if not better than." Of the choices here, only C is complete.

2. A. The original version is correct. With correlatives like "either . . . or," the same structure should follow each of the conjunctions. You could also write "either in spring or in fall," but the original version is more brief.

3. B. The original sentence is a fragment, lacking a main verb. B corrects this error. The choice of preposition ("with" or "by") is not important. Both D and E are also sentence fragments.

4. E. Although the original version of this sentence is grammatical, the more direct active voice is a more vigorous sentence using three fewer words.

5. D. This sentence is testing parallelism. It begins with two infinitives ("to record," "to understand") controlled by the verb "set out." The best version simply repeats the infinitive ("to explain").

6. C. The sentence, as it stands, is a fragment. The main clause needs an indicative verb in the future tense.

7. C. The phrase that begins this sentence dangles, and A and B make it appear that the "speakeasy" and "Hemingway" are the same. Though E is grammatical, the more concise C is the best choice here.

8. B. Three of the choices here use a pronoun ("this," "which," and "that") with no antecedent, that is, no specific noun or pronoun to refer to. Only B avoids this problem.

9. D. Both D and E avoid the shift from the pronoun "one" at the beginning to "you." Since the original sentence presents the finding as only a possibility ("may"), D is the better of the two choices since it does not change the meaning.

10. C. This is another test of parallelism with a series. Here the first two elements are noun phrases ("traffic delays," "access to pornography") that are objects of the verb "has." The parallel is a third object of this verb, "too many self-centered babblers." The introduction of a second verb breaks up the parallelism.

11. A. The original sentence is correct. All of the four other choices have agreement errors ("pleases," "create," "create," and "please").

12. B. To make sense, the sentence needs a conjunction like "but" that suggests a contrast between the first part ("adversaries") and the second ("personal relationship"). B is better than C because it avoids the wordier passive voice.

13. A. The original version is correct. It places the "not only" before "the birds," so that "not only" precedes the parallel phrase "the plants." C places the "not only" properly, but has no main verb.

14. C. As it stands, the sentence is run-on. The addition of "and" corrects the comma splice.

15. C. The first two verbs in this sentence ("abducts" and "carries") are active, but the third verb is passive in A, B, D, and E. C keeps all three verbs in the active voice. C is also the most economical of the five choices.

16. E. Seeing the participle at the beginning of the sentence, the wise test-taker will check to see if the participle dangles. Who yields to public demand? Not the end of a film or the lovers in a film. Only E supplies a human agent that the participial phrase could logically modify.

17. B. Without a conjunction, A and E are comma splices. C is a run-on sentence. D changes the meaning by leaving out the "may." By adding the conjunction "and," B corrects the comma splice.

18. A. The original sentence is better than the four alternatives. It uses two parallel active verbs in the perfect tense. In C, D, and E, the two verbs have different forms. B is a parallel structure but a wordier one than A, using eleven words instead of seven.

19. **C.** If you focus on the phrase "an idea that . . ." you should hear the idiomatic rightness of "is easy to comprehend." The adjective "easy" modifies the noun "idea." D also has the adjective "easy" but the idiom with "easy" is the infinitive rather than the preposition and gerund.

20. **B.** The sentence is a fragment, lacking a main verb. Only B supplies the verb needed to make the sentence complete.

Identifying Sentence Errors

21. **B.** Despite the distraction of the plural "experts," the subject here is the singular "report," so the verb should be the singular "recommends."

22. **A.** Since the sentence uses "you" in the first clause, it should continue to use "you," not "one."

23. **A.** The adverb "virtually," not the adjective "virtual," should modify the adjective "every."

24. **D.** The present tense "spend" makes no sense with the phrase "this year and next"; the verb should be in the future tense, "will spend."

25. **B.** With "neither . . . nor," the subject is singular, either James or Whistler, but not both. The parenthetical phrase using "both" does not change this fact, so the verb should be the singular "was able."

26. **E.** This sentence is correct. Though an opening participle may often dangle, this one does not.

27. **C.** Since "hardly" is a negative, the "not" makes a double negative; it should be omitted.

28. **B.** This is an error in idiom. The sentence should read "punishes for" rather than "punishes in."

29. **E.** The sentence is correct. "London's subway system" and "that of Boston" are properly parallel.

30. **B.** This is another error in agreement. The plural "houses" requires the plural verb "mirror."

31. **E.** There are no errors in this sentence.

32. **A.** This sentence should read either "Like Shakespeare's, Whitman's writing" or "Like Shakespeare, Whitman wrote" to maintain the logic of the comparison: writings to writings, or writer to writer.

33. **B.** As it stands, this is a sentence fragment, lacking a main verb. The participle "giving" should be "gives."

34. **E.** This sentence is correct.

Improving Paragraphs

35. **C.** The best version subordinates the second sentence, avoiding the repetition of the word "Thailand." The "but" that replaces the "and" is a better choice of conjunction, since it emphasizes the difference between the two birthplaces. The participle in D is out of place, and E has too many short sentences.

36. **D.** The original here is wordy since "has a long . . . history," "ancient," and "has been passed down from very olden times" all say virtually the same thing. C is too short, since it is a fragment, lacking a main verb. The best choice here is D.

37. **D.** In both A and B, the second sentence is a fragment. The future tense in C and the past tense in E are awkward; both are inferior to D.

38. **A.** The second paragraph is about the coronation ceremony, but the fourth sentence is about the writer's grandparents. The sentence can be omitted or moved to the first paragraph, where it logically follows the third sentence.

39. **D.** Though it requires more words, only D avoids the illogical comparison of a country (Thailand) and a musical comedy (*The King and I*).

PSAT/NMSQT Score Range Approximator

The following charts are designed to give you only a very general approximate score range, not an exact score. When you take the actual PSAT/NMSQT, you will see questions similar to those in this book; however, some questions may be slightly easier or more difficult. Needless to say, this may affect your scoring range.

How to Approximate Your Score in Critical Reading

1. Add the total number of correct responses for the two Critical Reading sections.
2. Add the total number of incorrect responses (only those attempted or marked in) for those sections.
3. The total number of incorrect responses for the Critical Reading sections should be divided by 4, giving you an adjustment factor (round off to the nearest whole number, if necessary).
4. Subtract this adjustment factor from the total number of correct responses to obtain a raw score.
5. This raw score is then scaled to a range of 20 through 80.

   For example:

   If the total number of correct answers was 30 out of a possible 48

   and 16 problems were attempted but missed,

   dividing 16 by 4 gives an adjustment factor of 4.

   Subtracting this adjustment factor of 4 from the original 30 correct gives a raw score of 26.

   This raw score is then scaled to a range of 20 through 80.

6. Using your scores:

   _____ – _____ = _____

   correct answers   wrong answers ÷ 4   raw score

7. Use the following table to match your raw score for Critical Reading and the corresponding approximate score range:

Raw Score	Approximate Score Range
40–48	60–80
30–39	50–59
20–29	40–49
0–19	20–39

Keep in mind that this is only an *approximate* score range.

How to Approximate Your Score in Mathematics

1. Add the total number of correct responses for the two Mathematics sections.
2. Add the total number of incorrect responses for the multiple-choice questions.
3. The total number of incorrect responses for these multiple-choice questions should be divided by 4, giving you an adjustment factor for multiple choice (round off to the nearest whole number).
4. Subtract this adjustment factor from the total number of correct responses to obtain a raw score.
5. This raw score is then scaled to a range of 20 through 80.

   For example:

   If the total number of correct answers was 20 out of a possible 38,

   and 8 multiple-choice problems were attempted but missed,

   dividing 8 by 4 gives an adjustment factor of 2 for multiple choice.

   Subtracting this adjustment factor of 2 from the original 20 correct gives a raw score of 18.

6. Using your scores:

   _____ − _____ = _____
   correct answers   wrong answers ÷ 4   raw score

   Note: You receive no deduction for incorrect grid-in responses.

7. Use the following table to match your raw score for Mathematics and the corresponding approximate score range:

Raw Score	Approximate Score Range
30–38	60–80
20–29	45–59
10–19	34–44
0–9	20–33

Keep in mind that this is only an *approximate* score range.

How to Approximate Your Score in Writing Skills

1. Add the total number of correct responses for the Writing Skills section.

2. Add the total number of incorrect responses (only those attempted or marked in) for that section.

3. The total number of incorrect responses for the Writing Skills section should be divided by 4, giving you an adjustment factor (round off to the nearest whole number, if necessary).

4. Subtract this adjustment factor from the total number of correct responses to obtain a raw score.

5. This raw score is then scaled to a range of 20 through 80.

   For example:

   If the total number of correct answers was 25 out of a possible 39

   and 12 problems were attempted but missed,

   dividing 12 by 4 gives an adjustment factor of 3.

   Subtracting this adjustment factor of 3 from the original 25 correct gives a raw score of 22.

6. Using your scores:

   _____ − _____ = _____
   correct answers   wrong answers ÷ 4   raw score

7. Use the following table to match your raw score for Writing Skills and the corresponding approximate score range:

Raw Score	Approximate Score Range
30–39	63–80
20–29	50–62
10–19	40–49
0–9	20–39

Keep in mind that this is only an *approximate* score range.

List of Sources

Sincere appreciation is given to the following authors and companies for allowing the use of excerpts from their outstanding works.

"The Graduate," from *Going Steady,* by Pauline Kael, reprinted by permission of Curtis Brown, Ltd. Copyright 1969 by Pauline Kael. Originally published in *Harper's* magazine.

Hold Your Tongue, copyright 1992 by James Crawford (pp. 192–193, 195–196). Reprinted by permission of Addison-Wesley Publishing Company, Inc.

"The Voice of the Earth," by Theodore Roszack, reprinted by permission of Simon & Schuster, Inc. Copyright 1992 by Theodore Roszack.

"The Graduate," by Andrew Sarris, reprinted by permission of the author and *The Village Voice.*

"Control of Rabies in Wildlife," by William G. Winkler and Konrad Bogel, reprinted by permission of *Scientific American.* Copyright June 1992. All Rights Reserved.

"Early Results from the Hubble Space Telescope," by Eric J. Chaison, reprinted by permission of *Scientific American.* Copyright June 1992. All Rights Reserved.

"The Waste Makers," by Vance Packard, reprinted by permission of Vance Packard. Copyright 1960.

"MEDIASPEAK: How Television Makes Up Your Mind," by Donna Woolfolk Cross. Reprinted by permission of The Putnam Publishing Group. Copyright 1983 by Donna Woolfolk Cross.

"The Joy of Music," by Leonard Bernstein, reprinted by permission of The Robert Lantz-Joy Harris Literary Agency. Copyright 1959.

The Conquest of Paradise, by Kirkpatrick Sale, reprinted by permission of Alfred A. Knopf, Inc. Copyright 1990.

Themes and Episodes, by Igor Stravinsky and Robert Craft, reprinted by permission of Alfred A. Knopf, Inc. Copyright 1966.

The Mysterious History of Columbus, by John Noble Wilford, reprinted by permission of Alfred A. Knopf, Inc. Copyright 1991 by Alfred A. Knopf, Inc.

"Global Warming on Trial," from *Natural History,* by Wallace S. Broecker, reprinted by permission of American Museum of Natural History. Copyright 1992.

Gauguin, by Belinda Thompson, reprinted by permission of Thames and Hudson, Inc. Copyright 1987.

Black Ice, by Lorene Cary, reprinted by permission of Random House Publishers. Copyright 1992. Originally published by Alfred A. Knopf, Inc.

Planet Earth, by Jonathan Weiner, reprinted by permission of Bantam Books, Inc. Copyright 1986.

"Gene Swapping," from *Bacterial Gene Swapping in Nature,* by Robert V. Miller. *Scientific American,* Volume 278, No. 1, January 1998 (p. 66).

The Launching of Modern American Science, 1846–1876 by Robert Bruce. Alfred A. Knopf, Inc., New York, 1987 (pp. 78–79).

Women in Science, by Vivian Gornick. Simon & Schuster, New York, 1984 (pp. 70–71).

Asian American Literature: An Introduction to the Writings and Their Social Context, by Elaine H. Kim, Temple University Press, Philadelphia. 1982 (pp. 23–24).

"The Coming Climate," by Thomas R. Karl, Neville Nicholls, and Jonathan Gregory. Copyright 1997. Reprinted by permission of the authors. Includes British Crown copyright.

Additional Resources

Cliffs Math Review for Standardized Tests, by Jerry Bobrow, Ph.D. Wiley Publishing, Inc., Hoboken, New Jersey, 1985.

CliffsQuickReview Basic Math and Pre-Algebra, by Jerry Bobrow, Ph.D. Wiley Publishing, Inc., Hoboken, New Jersey, 2001.

CliffsQuickReview Algebra I, by Jerry Bobrow, Ph.D. Wiley Publishing, Inc., Hoboken, New Jersey, 2001.

Cliffs Verbal Review for Standardized Tests, by William A. Covino, Ph.D., and Peter Z. Orton, M. Ed. Wiley Publishing, Inc., Hoboken, New Jersey, 1986.

The Final Touches

1. Make sure that you are familiar with the testing center location and nearby parking facilities.

2. Spend your last few days of preparation primarily reviewing strategies, techniques, and directions for each area.

3. Don't "cram" the night before the exam. It's a waste of time!

4. Remember to bring the proper materials to the test: identification, admission ticket, three or four sharpened no. 2 pencils, a watch, a good eraser, and an approved calculator.

5. On the new SAT, the first section will be the writing assignment—the essay.

6. Keep in mind the writing process—prewriting, writing, and proofreading.

7. On the multiple-choice questions, start off crisply, first working the questions you know and then coming back and trying the other questions.

8. If you can eliminate one or more of the choices, make an educated guess.

9. Mark in reading passages, underline key words, write out information, and make notations on diagrams. Take advantage of being permitted to write in the test booklet.

10. Make sure that you are answering "what is being asked" and that your answer is reasonable.

11. Remember that within each question type, the math questions generally progress from easier to more difficult.

12. Using the Successful Overall Approaches (see Introduction, pages 6–8) is the key to getting the answers right that you should get right—resulting in a good score on the new SAT and PSAT/NMSQT.